Paper 1.3

MANAGING PEOPLE

For exams in December 2005 and June 2006

Study Text

In this June 2005 new edition

- A new user-friendly format for easy navigation

- Exam-centred topic coverage, directly linked to ACCA's syllabus and study guide

- Exam focus points showing you what the examiner will want you to do

- Regular fast forward summaries emphasising the key points in each chapter

- Questions and quick quizzes to test your understanding

- Exam question bank containing exam standard questions with answers

- A full index

BPP's **i-Learn** and **i-Pass** products also support this paper.

FOR EXAMS IN DECEMBER 2005 AND JUNE 2006

First edition 2001
Fifth edition June 2005

ISBN 0 7517 2315 0 (Previous edition 0 7517 1662 6)

British Library Cataloguing-in-Publication Data
A catalogue record for this book
is available from the British Library

Published by

BPP Professional Education
Aldine House, Aldine Place
London W12 8AW

www.bpp.com

Printed in Great Britain by W M Print Ltd,
Frederick Street, Walsall,
West Midlands,
WS2 9NE.

We are grateful to the Association of Chartered
Certified Accountants for permission to reproduce past
examination questions. The suggested solutions in the
exam answer bank have been prepared by BPP
Professional Education.

Contents

Introduction

The BPP Study Text –The BPP Effective Study Package – Help yourself study for your ACCA exams – Syllabus and Study Guide – The exam paper – Oxford Brookes BSc (Hons) in Applied Accounting – Oxford Institute of International Finance MBA – Continuing Professional Development – Syllabus mindmap

Part A Management and team development

Part B Recruitment and selection

Part C Training and development

Part D Motivation and leadership

Part E: Effective communication practices

Review form and free prize draw
Order form

Computer-based learning products from BPP

If you want to reinforce your studies by **interactive** learning, try BPP's **i-Learn** product, covering major syllabus areas in an interactive format. For **self-testing**, try **i-Pass,** which offers a large number of **objective test questions**, particularly useful where objective test questions form part of the exam.

See the order form at the back of this Text for details of these innovative learning tools.

Learn Online

Learn Online uses BPP's wealth of teaching experience to produce a fully **interactive** e-learning resource **delivered via the Internet**. The site offers comprehensive **tutor support** and features areas such as **study, practice, email service, revision** and **useful resources**.

Visit our website www.bpp.com/acca/learnonline to sample aspects of Learn Online free of charge.

Learning to Learn Accountancy

BPP's ground-breaking **Learning to Learn Accountancy** book is designed to be used both at the outset of your ACCA studies and throughout the process of learning accountancy. It challenges you to consider how you study and gives you helpful hints about how to approach the various types of paper which you will encounter. It can help you **focus your studies on the subject and exam**, enabling you to **acquire knowledge, practise and revise efficiently and effectively**.

The BPP Study Text

Aims of this Study Text

To provide you with the knowledge and understanding, skills and application techniques that you need if you are to be successful in your exams

This Study Text has been written around the **Managing People** syllabus.

- It is **comprehensive**. It covers the syllabus content. No more, no less.

- It is written at the **right level**. Each chapter is written with ACCA's syllabus and study guide in mind

- It is targeted to the **exam**. We have taken account of the pilot paper, guidance the examiner has given and the assessment methodology.

To allow you to study in the way that best suits your learning style and the time you have available, by following your personal Study Plan (see page (viii))

You may be studying at home on your own until the date of the exam, or you may be attending a full-time course. You may like to (and have time to) read every word, or you may prefer to (or only have time to) skim-read and devote the remainder of your time to question practice. Wherever you fall in the spectrum, you will find the BPP Study Text meets your needs in designing and following your personal Study Plan.

To tie in with the other components of the BPP Effective Study Package to ensure you have the best possible chance of passing the exam (see page (vi))

The BPP Effective Study Package

Recommended period of use	The BPP Effective Study Package
From the outset and throughout	**Learning to Learn Accountancy** Read this invaluable book as you begin your studies and refer to it as you work through the various elements of the BPP Effective Study Package. It will help you to acquire knowledge, practise and revise, efficiently and effectively.
Three to twelve months before the exam	**Study Text and i-Learn** Use the Study Text to acquire knowledge, understanding, skills and the ability to apply techniques. Use BPP's **i-Learn** product to reinforce your learning.
Throughout	**Learn Online** Study, practise, revise and take advantage of other useful resources with BPP's fully interactive e-learning site with comprehensive tutor support.
Throughout	**i-Pass** **i-Pass**, our computer-based testing package, provides objective test questions in a variety of formats and is ideal for self-assessment.
One to six months before the exam	**Practice & Revision Kit** Try the numerous examination-format questions, for which there are realistic suggested solutions prepared by BPP's own authors. Then attempt the two mock exams.
From three months before the exam until the last minute	**Passcards** Work through these short, memorable notes which are focused on what is most likely to come up in the exam you will be sitting.
One to six months before the exam	**Success CDs** The CDs cover the vital elements of your syllabus in less than 90 minutes per subject. They also contain exam hints to help you fine tune your strategy.

Help yourself study for your ACCA exams

Exams for professional bodies such as ACCA are very different from those you have taken at college or university. You will be under **greater time pressure before** the exam – as you may be combining your study with work. There are many different ways of learning and so the BPP Study Text offers you a number of different tools to help you through. Here are some hints and tips: they are not plucked out of the air, but **based on research and experience**. (You don't need to know that long-term memory is in the same part of the brain as emotions and feelings – but it's a fact anyway.)

The right approach

1 The right attitude

Believe in yourself	Yes, there is a lot to learn. Yes, it is a challenge. But thousands have succeeded before and you can too.
Remember why you're doing it	Studying might seem a grind at times, but you are doing it for a reason: to advance your career.

2 The right focus

Read through the Syllabus and learning outcomes	These tell you what you are expected to know and are supplemented by Exam focus points in the text.
Study the Exam Paper section	Past papers are likely to be good guides to what you should expect in the exam.

3 The right method

The whole picture	You need to grasp the detail – but keeping in mind how everything fits into the whole picture will help you understand better. <ul><li>The **Introduction** of each chapter puts the material in context.</li><li>The **Syllabus content**, **Study guide** and **Exam focus points** show you what you need to **grasp**.</li></ul>
In your own words	To absorb the information (and to practise your written communication skills), it helps to **put it into your own words**. <ul><li>**Take notes.**</li><li>Answer the **questions** in each chapter. You will practise your written communication skills, which become increasingly important as you progress through your ACCA exams.</li><li>Draw **mindmaps**. We have an example for the whole syllabus.</li><li>Try **'teaching' a subject** to a colleague or friend.</li></ul>
Give yourself cues to jog your memory	The BPP Study Text uses **bold** to **highlight key points**. <ul><li>Try **colour coding** with a highlighter pen.</li><li>Write **key points** on cards.</li></ul>

4   **The right review**

Review, review, review	It is a **fact** that regularly reviewing a topic in summary form can **fix it in your memory**. Because **review** is so important, the BPP Study Text helps you to do so in many ways.
	• **Chapter roundups** summarise the 'Fast forward' key points in each chapter. Use them to recap each study session.
	• The **Quick quiz** is another review technique you can use to ensure that you have grasped the essentials.
	• Go through the **Examples** in each chapter a second or third time.

Developing your personal Study Plan

BPP's **Learning to Learn Accountancy** book emphasises the need to prepare (and use) a study plan. Planning and sticking to the plan are key elements of learning success.
There are four steps you should work through.

Step 1   How do you learn?

First you need to be aware of your style of learning. The BPP **Learning to Learn Accountancy** book commits a chapter to this **self-discovery**. What types of intelligence do you display when learning? You might be advised to brush up on certain study skills before launching into this Study Text.

BPP's **Learning to Learn Accountancy** book helps you to identify what intelligences you show more strongly and then details how you can tailor your study process to your preferences. It also includes handy hints on how to develop intelligences you exhibit less strongly, but which might be needed as you study accountancy.

Are you a **theorist** or are you more **practical**? If you would rather get to grips with a theory before trying to apply it in practice, you should follow the study sequence on page (ix). If the reverse is true (you like to know why you are learning theory before you do so), you might be advised to flick through Study Text chapters and look at examples, case studies and questions (Steps 8, 9 and 10 in the **suggested study sequence**) before reading through the detailed theory.

Step 2   How much time do you have?

Work out the time you have available per week, given the following.

- The standard you have set yourself
- The time you need to set aside later for work on the Practice & Revision Kit and Passcards
- The other exam(s) you are sitting
- Very importantly, practical matters such as work, travel, exercise, sleep and social life

Hours

Note your time available in box A.   A   [   ]

Step 3 **Allocate your time**

- Take the time you have available per week for this Study Text shown in box A, multiply it by the number of weeks available and insert the result in box B.

B [　　　　]

- Divide the figure in box B by the number of chapters in this text and insert the result in box C.

C [　　　　]

Remember that this is only a rough guide. Some of the chapters in this book are longer and more complicated than others, and you will find some subjects easier to understand than others.

Step 4 **Implement**

Set about studying each chapter in the time shown in box C, following the key study steps in the order suggested by your particular learning style.

This is your personal **Study Plan**. You should try and combine it with the study sequence outlined below. You may want to modify the sequence a little (as has been suggested above) to adapt it to your **personal style**.

BPP's **Learning to Learn Accountancy** gives further guidance on developing a study plan, and deciding where and when to study.

Suggested study sequence

It is likely that the best way to approach this Study Text is to tackle the chapters in the order in which you find them. Taking into account your individual learning style, you could follow this sequence.

Key study steps	Activity
Step 1 **Topic list**	Each numbered topic is a numbered section in the chapter.
Step 2 **Introduction**	This gives you the big picture in terms of the context of the chapter. The content is referenced to the Study Guide, and Exam Guidance shows how the topic is likely to be examined. In other words, it sets your objectives for study.
Step 3 **Knowledge brought forward boxes**	In these we highlight information and techniques that it is assumed you have 'brought forward' with you from your earlier studies. If there are topics which have changed recently due to legislation for example, these topics are explained in more detail.
Step 4 **Fast forward**	Fast forward boxes give you a quick summary of the content of each of the main chapter sections. They are listed together in the roundup at the end of each chapter to provide you with an overview of the contents of the whole chapter.
Step 5 **Explanations**	Proceed methodically through the chapter, reading each section thoroughly and making sure you understand.
Step 6 **Key terms and Exam focus points**	• Key terms can often earn you *easy marks* if you state them clearly and correctly in an appropriate exam answer. • Exam focus points state how we think the examiner intends to examine certain topics.
Step 7 **Note taking**	Take brief notes, if you wish. Avoid the temptation to copy out too much. Remember that being able to put something into your own words is a sign of being able to understand it. If you find you cannot explain something you have read, read it again before you make the notes.

Key study steps	Activity
Step 8 **Examples**	Follow each through to its solution very carefully.
Step 9 **Case studies**	Study each one, and try to add flesh to them from your own experience. They are designed to show how the topics you are studying come alive (and often come unstuck) in the real world.
Step 10 **Questions**	Make a very good attempt at each one.
Step 11 **Answers**	Check yours against ours, and make sure you understand any discrepancies.
Step 12 **Chapter roundup**	Work through it carefully, to make sure you have grasped the significance of all the fast forward points.
Step 13 **Quick quiz**	When you are happy that you have covered the chapter, use the Quick quiz to check how much you have remembered of the topics covered and to practise questions in a variety of formats.
Step 14 **Question practice**	Either at this point, or later when you are thinking about revising, make a full attempt at the Question(s) suggested at the very end of the chapter. You can find these in the Exam Question Bank at the end of the Study Text, along with the answers so you can see how you did. We highlight those that are introductory, and those which are of the standard you would expect to find in an exam. If you have bought i-Pass, use this too.

Short of time: Skim study technique?

You may find you simply do not have the time available to follow all the key study steps for each chapter, however you adapt them for your particular learning style. If this is the case, follow the **skim study** technique below.

- Study the chapters in the order you find them in the Study Text.

- For each chapter:

  - Follow the key study steps 1-3

  - Skim-read through step 5, looking out for the points highlighted in the fast forward boxes (step 4)

  - Jump to step 12

  - Go back to step 6

  - Follow through steps 8 and 9

  - Prepare outline answers to questions (steps 10/11)

  - Try the Quick quiz (step 13), following up any items you can't answer

  - Do a plan for the Question (step 14), comparing it against our answers

  - You should probably still follow step 7 (note-taking), although you may decide simply to rely on the BPP Passcards for this.

Moving on...

However you study, when you are ready to embark on the practice and revision phase of the BPP Effective Study Package, you should still refer back to this Study Text, both as a source of **reference** (you should find the index particularly helpful for this) and as a way to **review** (the Fast forwards, Exam focus points, Chapter roundups and Quick quizzes help you here).

And remember to keep careful hold of this Study Text – you will find it invaluable in your work.

> More advice on Study Skills can be found in BPP's **Learning to Learn Accountancy** book.

Syllabus

Aim

To develop knowledge and understanding of the techniques, processes and procedures which are required to ensure the efficient and effective use and deployment of human resources, and consequently to use the human resource to the fullest possible benefit of the organisation.

Objectives

On completion of this paper candidates should be able to:

- identify, understand and explain the complex interpersonal relationships that exist within organisations
- appreciate the relationship between theory and practice
- understand the nature, processes and procedures of people management
- explain the principles of successful team performance and the need to plan, monitor and evaluate team based work activities
- investigate future personnel requirements and describe recruitment and selection procedures
- understand and describe the principles of motivation
- understand and describe the role and process of employee development
- understand the need for clear and precise communication
- explain the principles of effective counselling
- describe the elements of disciplinary and grievance procedures

Position of the paper in the overall syllabus

The paper is concerned with an understanding of people management and the techniques involved. The paper is constructed in such a way that it provides a broad introduction to the problems and opportunities involved in managing people. It is intended to cultivate an understanding of the importance of good practice in human resource management.

The professional accountant is often in a management position and thus fulfils another role, that of the management of the human resource. It is important therefore that the professional accountant understands issues of management and human resources.

Whilst there are no pre-requisites for this paper, candidates will be expected to demonstrate an understanding of the theory and issues involved in human resource management and to display appropriate writing skills in answering the examination paper.

Managing People is a pre-requisite for paper **3.5 Strategic Business Planning and Development,** where many of the ideas introduced are developed further.

It should also be noted that although the course is divided into five topic areas, the nature of the syllabus means that there will often be overlap between the individual topics.

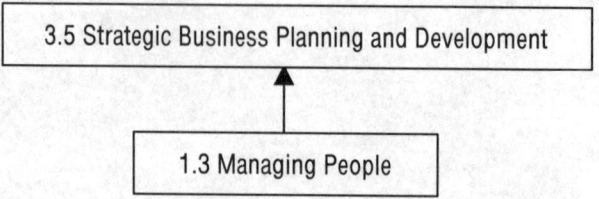

4   **Motivation and leadershoip**

    (a)   Motivation, concepts, models and practices

        (i)   The key theories of motivation
        (ii)   Classical theories
        (iii)   Modern theories
        (iv)   Reward schemes

    (b)   Effective leadership

        (i)   The nature and importance of leadership
        (ii)   Classical theories
        (iii)   Modern theories

5   **Effective communication practices**

    (a)   Working with people – interpersonal skills

        (i)   Interpersonal skills
        (ii)   Effective management practice
        (iii)   Verbal and non verbal communication

    (b)   Communication

        (i)   The need for communication
        (ii)   Communication patterns

    (c)   The role of counselling

        (i)   The role of management
        (ii)   Skills of effective counselling

    (d)   Controlling conflict, grievance and discipline

        (i)   Causes of conflict
        (ii)   Managing conflict
        (iii)   Appropriate procedures
        (iv)   Process understanding
        (v)   The role of management
        (iv)   Appeals

Excluded topics

The syllabus content outlines the area for assessment. No areas of knowledge are specifically excluded from the syllabus.

Key areas of the syllabus

The key topic areas are as follows:

- An understanding of the theory, techniques, processes, procedures and practice of people management and team development

- Differentiation of rules, procedures and processes of people management

- Training and development, the trained workforce, employee assessment

- The theories of motivation and leadership and their application

- Effective communication practices

Paper 1.3

Managing People

Study Guide

MANAGEMENT AND TEAM DEVELOPMENT

1 THE ORGANISATION OF WORK

(a) Explain the need for formal organisations.

(b) Identify organisational types and differences.

2 THE ROLE OF MANAGEMENT

(a) Identify and explain the contribution made by modern writers on management: Drucker, Kanter, Mintzberg, Ouchi, Peters.

(b) Identify and explain the contribution made by classical writers on management: Fayol, Stewart, Taylor, Mayo, Weber.

(c) Identify the difference between classical and modern theories of management.

(d) Identify the differences between individual and group contribution to work performance: Schein.

(e) Outline areas of management authority and responsibility.

(f) List the systems of performance reward for individual and group contribution.

3 THE ROLE OF THE MANAGER

(a) Explain the role of the manager in the organisation of work.

(b) List the management tasks involved in organising the work of others.

(c) Illustrate the role of the manager in achieving tasks.

(d) Identify the responsibilities of the supervisor.

4 INDIVIDUAL AND GROUP BEHAVIOUR

(a) Explain the concept of organisational culture: Anthony, Handy.

(b) Discuss the differences between individual and group behaviour.

(c) Outline the contribution of individuals and teams to organisational success.

(d) Identify individual and team approaches to work.

(e) Understand perception and role theory.

5 TEAM MANAGEMENT

(a) Explain the role of the manager in building the team and developing individuals.

(b) Define the purpose of a team.

(c) Outline the composition of successful teams: Belbin, Peters and Waterman.

(d) Explain the development of a team: Tuckman.

(e) List team building tools.

(f) Examine ways of rewarding a team.

(g) Identify methods to evaluate team performance.

6 OBJECTIVE SETTING

(a) Explain the importance of objective setting.

(b) Compare and contrast profit and other objectives: Drucker, Cyert and March, Marginalist Theories, Simon.

(c) Explain the behavioural theories of objective setting.

(d) Explain the importance of understanding ethics and social responsibility.

(e) Compare and contrast the difference between corporate objectives and personal objectives.

(f) Illustrate the difference between quantitative and qualitative target setting.

(g) Outline the management role in identifying performance standards and accountability.

(h) Identify methods to measure achievement of objectives.

PROFESSIONAL EDUCATION

7 AUTHORITY, RESPONSIBILITY AND DELEGATION

(a) Describe, recognise and understand the importance of organisational structure.

(b) Classical and modern approaches to organisational structure: Burns and Stalker, Contingency Theory, Fayol, Mintzberg, Trist and Bamforth, Urwick, Weber, Woodward.

(c) Define the terms authority, responsibility and delegation.

(d) Explain the term legitimised power: Weber.

(e) Describe the process of determining authority and responsibility.

(f) Examine the case of responsibility without authority.

8 STANDARD SETTING AND PERFORMANCE MANAGEMENT

(a) Define the term performance management.

(b) Identify a process for establishing work standards and performance management.

(c) Outline a method to establish performance indicators.

(d) Illustrate ways of applying performance management.

(e) Describe management contribution to personal development planning.

(f) Explain the term performance related pay.

RECRUITMENT AND SELECTION

9 THE RECRUITMENT AND SELECTION PROCESS

(a) Explain the importance of effective recruitment and selection to the organisation.

(b) Define the recruitment and selection process.

(c) Outline the roles and responsibilities of those involved in the process.

(d) List the most common reasons for ineffective recruitment and selection.

(e) List and describe criteria against which to assess successful recruitment and selection practices.

10 EFFECTIVE RECRUITMENT

(a) Outline a plan for an effective recruitment process.

(b) Identify the stages in the recruitment process.

(c) Compare and contrast the choice of media for job advertising.

(d) Analyse the purpose and effectiveness of the job application form.

(e) Explain the purpose and usefulness of applicant references.

11 THE JOB DESCRIPTION AND PERSONNEL SPECIFICATION

(a) Outline the purpose and use of a job description and person specification.

(b) Explain how to devise a job description and personnel specification: Rodgers, Fraser.

(c) Compare and contrast the purpose of the job description and the person specification.

12 JOB ANALYSIS

(a) Define the purpose of job analysis.

(b) Identify methods of job analysis.

(c) Outline the skills involved in carrying out job analysis.

(d) Justify the use of job analysis.

13 SELECTION METHODS

(a) List alternative methods of selection.

(b) Evaluate the usefulness of selection methods.

(c) Identify those involved in the process of selection.

(d) Establish the skills involved in successful decision making.

(e) Explain the importance to the organisation of good selection decisions.

14 THE SELECTION INTERVIEW

(a) Outline the purpose of the selection interview.

(b) Identify who should be involved in selection interviewing.

(c) Identify the key skills required for selection interviewing.

(d) List the most common reasons for ineffective interviewing.

(e) Explain the importance of the selection interview in the selection process.

15 EQUAL OPPORTUNITIES AND THE MANAGEMENT OF DIVERSITY

(a) Understanding equal opportunities.

(b) Measuring equal value.

(c) Appreciate the legal position.

(d) Explain the appropriateness of managing diversity in the workplace.

(e) Identify individual circumstances and differences.

TRAINING AND DEVELOPMENT

16 THE LEARNING PROCESS

(a) Explain the process of learning in the workplace.

(b) Describe the ways in which individuals learn: Honey and Mumford, Kolb.

(c) Explain the effect on learning of individual differences.

(d) Outline the barriers to learning.

(e) Describe the role of management and the organisation in the learning process.

17 RETENTION, TRAINING AND DEVELOPMENT

(a) Explain the importance of training and development to the organisation and the individual.

(b) Explain the roles and responsibilities of a training manager.

(c) Compare and contrast the various methods used in developing individuals in the workplace.

18 EFFECTIVE TRAINING AND DEVELOPMENT

(a) List the benefits to the organisation and the individual of effective training and development.

(b) Explain the methods used to analyse training needs.

(c) Suggest ways in which training needs can be met.

(d) Describe methods of staff evaluation and follow-up.

(e) Describe the skills involved in developing staff.

(f) Explain the development methods available to management.

(g) Evaluate the effectiveness of in-house and external training courses.

19 COMPETENCE ASSESSMENT

(a) Explain the process of competence assessment.

(b) Outline the purposes and benefits of staff appraisal in the process.

(c) Describe the barriers to effective staff appraisal.

(d) Suggest ways to measure the effectiveness of staff appraisal and the process of assessment.

20 CONDUCTING THE APPRAISAL PROCESS

(a) Identify the benefits of the appraisal process.

(b) Identify the management skills involved in the appraisal process.

(c) Describe the process of preparation of an appraisal interview, including location of interview and pre interview correspondence.

(d) Identify the key communication skills required to conduct an effective appraisal interview.

(e) Explain the importance of feedback from the appraisal interview

21 INDIVIDUAL SKILLS AND DEVELOPMENT

(a) Explain the link between the appraisal process and effective employee development.

(b) Describe the role of the appraisee in the process.

(c) Suggest ways in which self-development can be part of the process.

(d) Describe the role of the manager in work based skills development.

(e) Identify the methods used to develop skills.

(f) Outline how to plan a skills development programme.

(g) Explain the role of mentoring in the process of skills development.

22 THE MANAGEMENT OF HEALTH AND SAFETY

(a) Identify preventative and protective measures.

(b) Describe safety awareness and training.

(c) Outline working conditions and hazards.

(d) Explain the legal context and the obligation of management.

MOTIVATION AND LEADERSHIP

23 MOTIVATION CONCEPTS, MODELS AND PRACTICES

(a) Outline the key theories of motivation.

(b) Outline classical and modern theories of motivation: Argyris, Equity theory, Handy, Herzberg, Maslow, McClelland, McGregor, Vroom

(c) Outline the difference between content and process theories of motivation.

(d) Describe ways in which management can motivate staff.

(e) Explain the importance of the reward system in the process of motivation.

(f) Explain the importance of constructive feedback in motivation.

24 EFFECTIVE LEADERSHIP

(a) Define the term 'leadership'.

(b) Describe the nature and importance of leadership.

(c) Outline classical and modern theories of leadership: Blake and Mouton, Contingency Theory, Fiedler, Handy, Hersey and Blanchard, Likert, Tannenbaum, Trait Theory, White and Lippit.

(d) Compare and contrast the terms 'leadership' and 'management'.

(e) Identify the skills of a leader.

EFFECTIVE COMMUNICATION PRACTICES

25 WORKING WITH PEOPLE – INTERPERSONAL SKILLS

(a) Define the term 'interpersonal skills'.

(b) Explain the importance of developing effective working relationships.

(c) Distinguish between verbal and non-verbal forms of communication.

(d) Compare and contrast the difference between aggressive and assertive behaviour.

(e) Illustrate the link between interpersonal skills and effective management practice.

26 COMMUNICATION

(a) Explain the importance of formal and informal communication in the workplace.

(b) Explain communication models.

(c) List and describe barriers to communication.

(d) Outline the importance to the manager of effective communication.

(e) Describe the effects of poor communication.

(f) List and describe the attributes of effective communication.

(g) List the main methods and patterns of communication.

(h) Explain the importance of the process of consultation.

27 THE ROLE OF COUNSELLING

(a) Define counselling in the management context.

(b) Outline the role of the manager when counselling staff.

(c) Explain the importance of effective counselling.

(d) Identify the skills used in the process of effective counselling.

(e) Suggest reasons why the need to counsel a member of staff may arise.

28 CONTROLLING CONFLICT, GRIEVANCE AND DISCIPLINE

(a) Identify the main causes of conflict within an organisation.

(b) Outline procedures for managing conflict.

(c) Outline a suitable framework (both internal and external to the organisation) for dealing with grievance and disciplinary matters.

(d) Explain the need for effective organisational procedures.

(e) Explain the role of management in respect of disciplinary matters.

(f) Suggest ways in which the outcome of the disciplinary process should be communicated to the individual concerned.

(g) Outline the features of an appeals procedure.

The exam paper

Approach to examining the syllabus

The examination is a **three hour paper** constructed in **two sections**.

Section A consists of a brief scenario with one compulsory question worth 40 marks, comprising a range of 6-7 requirements each carrying between 5-10 marks. The scenario is generally devised to test the application and understanding of a particular topic, although candidates should be aware that more than one topic may form part of the scenario. 'Candidates should *apply* relevant theoretical knowledge from the main areas of the syllabus to the *information contained within the scenario* to achieve the highest marks' (*Student Accountant,* February 2004).

Section B consists of five essay type questions, with one question taken from each of the five topics in the syllabus. Each question carries 15 marks and candidates must attempt four questions.

There are no calculations involved, and candidates should note that the answers in Section B **must be presented in essay form**. Candidates need to show an understanding of the detail of the topic. Candidates should be aware that although the course is made up of a number of discrete topics, examination questions may well require a knowledge of more than one of these topics.

		Number of Marks
Section A:	Compulsory scenario question	40
Section B:	Choice of 4 from 5 essay questions (15 marks each)	60
		100

Additional information

The Study Guide provides more detailed guidance on the syllabus.

Analysis of past papers

The analysis below shows the topics which have been examined so far under the new syllabus and in the Pilot Paper.

June 2005

Section A (compulsory)

1   Case study, based on disciplinary and grievance procedures

Section B (4 questions from 5)

2   Leadership (Blake and Mouton's Managerial Grid)
3   Recruitment (job descriptions and person specifications)
4   Selection (references)
5   Motivation (definition of terms)
6   Good communication

December 2004

Section A (compulsory)

1   Case study, based on groups, team membership and team development

Section B (4 questions from 5)

2   Organisational culture
3   Job analysis
4   Stages in recruitment and selection
5   Job enrichment, job enlargement and job rotation
6   Employee discipline

June 2004

Section A (compulsory)

1   Case study, based on appraisal systems and interviews

Section B (4 questions from 5)

2   Management by Objectives
3   Selection tests
4   Training benefits and methods
5   Leader skills and Action Centred Leadership
6   Discipline

December 2003

Section A (compulsory)

1   Case study, based on improving motivation and morale

Section B (4 questions from 5)

2   Peters & Waterman: excellence
3   Recruitment advertising
4   Training methods and evaluation
5   Content theory of motivation; Theory X and Y
6   Communication directions and patterns

June 2003

Section A (compulsory)

1   Case study, based on communication and committees

Section B (4 questions from 5)

2   Performance management
3   Selection interviews
4   Health and safety hazards and policies
5   Tuckman's stages of team development
6   Counselling in the workplace

December 2002

Section A (compulsory)

1   Case study, based on introduction of equal opportunity policies

Section B (4 questions from 5)

2   Theory Z management approach
3   Internal and external recruitment decisions
4   Learning cycle and learning styles
5   Motivation: process and equity theories
6   Good communication and barriers to communication

June 2002

Section A (compulsory)

1   Case study, based on assertiveness and interpersonal skills

Section B (4 questions from 5)

2   Fayol's managerial functions; role of supervisor/manager
3   Authority, responsibility, effective delegation
4   Stages in recruitment planning
5   Conflict: definition, causes, characteristics
6   Teams and groups; team success-Belbin's roles

December 2001

Section A (compulsory)

1   Case study, based on change from functional to matrix organisation structure

Section B (4 questions from 5)

2   Blake and Mouton managerial grid
3   Person specification and job description
4   Performance appraisal: benefits and methods
5   Motivation: content theory and Maslow
6   Discipline and disciplinary procedures

Pilot paper

Section A (compulsory)

1   Case study based on recruitment of a new member of staff to an accounts department

Section B (4 questions from 5)

2   Teams and informal groups
3   Job analysis
4   Learning styles
5   Rewards and motivation
6   Communication

Oxford Brookes BSc (Hons) in Applied Accounting

The standard required of candidates completing Part 2 is that required in the final year of a UK degree. Students completing Parts 1 and 2 will have satisfied the examination requirement for an honours degree in Applied Accounting, awarded by Oxford Brookes University.

To achieve the degree, you must also submit two pieces of work based on a **Research and Analysis Project.**

- A 5,000 word **Report** on your chosen topic, which demonstrates that you have acquired the necessary research, analytical and IT skills.

- A 1,500 word **Key Skills Statement**, indicating how you have developed your interpersonal and communication skills.

BPP was selected by the ACCA and Oxford Brookes University to produce the official text *Success in your Research and Analysis Project* to support students in this task. The book pays particular attention to key skills not covered in the professional examinations.

BPP also offers courses and mentoring services.

The Oxford Brookes Project Text can be ordered using the form at the end of this Study Text.

Oxford Institute of International Finance MBA

The Oxford Institute of International Finance (OXIIF), a joint venture between the ACCA and Oxford Brookes University, offers an MBA for finance professionals.

For this MBA, credits are awarded for your ACCA studies, and entry to the MBA course is available to those who have completed their ACCA professional stage studies. The MBA was launched in 2002 and has attracted participants from all over the world.

The qualification features an introductory module (*Foundations of Management*). Other modules include *Global Business Strategy, Managing Self Development,* and *Organisational Change & Transformation.*

Research Methods are also taught, as they underpin the **research dissertation**.

The MBA programme is delivered through the use of targeted paper study materials, developed by BPP, and taught over the Internet by OXIIF personnel using BPP's virtual campus software.

For further information, please see the Oxford Institute's website: www.oxfordinstitute.org.

Continuing professional development

ACCA introduced a new continuing professional development requirement for members from 1 January 2005. Members will be required to complete and record 40 units of CPD annually, of which 21 units must be verifiable learning or training activity.

BPP has an established professional development department which offers a range of relevant, professional courses to reflect the needs of professionals working in both industry and practice. To find out more, visit the website: www.bpp.com/pd or call the client care team on 0845 226 2422.

Syllabus mindmap

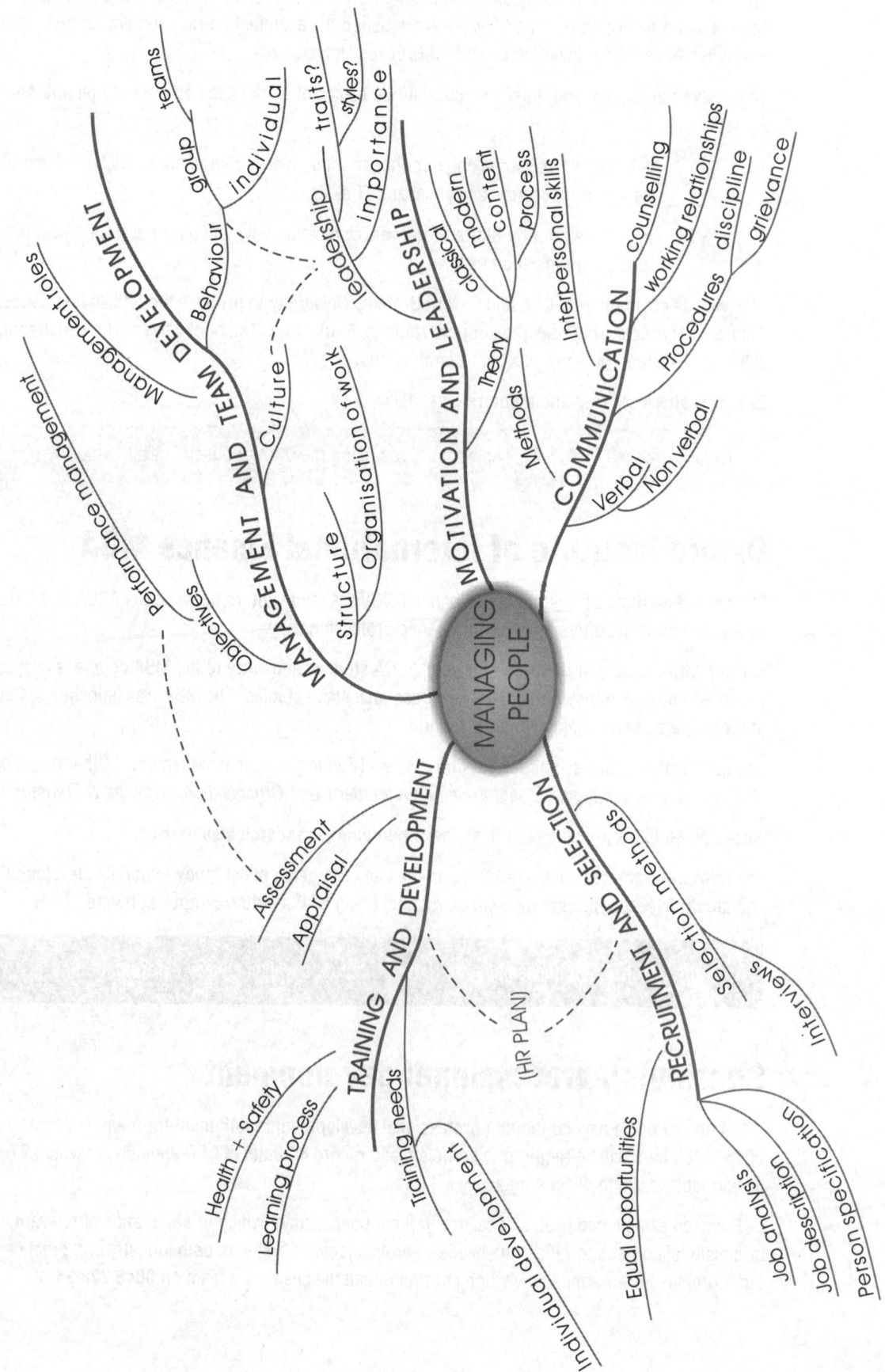

Part A
Management and team development

The organisation of work

Introduction

We begin our study of management by looking at the most common context within which it takes place: an organisation.

The term 'organisation' is commonly used to describe corporate entities (a company, club or charity, for example): we look at some of these in **Section 1**.

However, it is also the managerial task of establishing a framework within which tasks and resources can be allocated and performed: how tasks are grouped together and shared out, who has authority for what, who needs to communicate with whom – and so on.

In **Section 2**, we look at this concept of **organisation structure**, and at some of the classical and modern theories about how to 'do it' best.

In **Sections 3-7**, we look at some of the key decisions that give organisations their distinctive 'shape', including the need for flexibility and the impact of technology.

Apart from getting to grips with the various concepts of organisational structure, the main challenge of this chapter is to appreciate the shift from 'classic' ideas of organisation (stability, efficiency, control) to the **modern** focus on loose, shifting, responsive structures which can survive in faster-changing and more chaotic environments.

Study guide

Section 1 – The organisation of work

- Explain the need for formal organisations
- Identify organisational types and differences

Section 7 – Authority, responsibility and delegation

- Describe, recognise and understand the importance of organisational structure

- Classical and modern approaches to organisational structure: Burns and Stalker, Contingency Theory, Fayol, Mintzberg, Trist and Bamforth, Urwick, Weber, Woodward

Exam guide

The material in this chapter could form the background to questions on most parts of the syllabus, as well as being the subject of a question in its own right, as was the case in December 2001. All the theoretical models are (theoretically) examinable: in any case models such as Burns and Stalker, Fayol and Mintzberg help to give you a vocabulary of technical terms which you can use when discussing organisational issues.

1 Introduction to organisations

Here are some examples of organisations.

- A multinational car manufacturer (eg Ford)
- An accountancy firm (eg Ernst and Young)
- A charity (eg Oxfam)
- A local authority
- A trade union (eg Unison)
- An army

1.1 Why do organisations exist?

> **FAST FORWARD**
>
> **Organisations** achieve results which individuals cannot achieve by themselves.

Organisations:

(a)   **Overcome people's individual limitations**, whether physical or intellectual

(b)   **Enable people to specialise** in what they do best

(c)   **Save time**, because people can work together or do two aspects of a different task at the same time

(d)   **Accumulate** and share **knowledge** (eg about how best to build cars)

(e)   Enable people to **pool their expertise**

(f)   Enable **synergy**: the combined output of two or more individuals working together exceeds their individual output ('None of us is as smart as all of us')

In brief, organisations enable people to be **more productive.**

1.2 What organisations have in common

> **FAST FORWARD**
>
> An organisation is a **social arrangement** which pursues collective goals and controls its own performance.

The definition below states broadly what all organisations have in common.

Key term

> An **organisation** is: 'a *social arrangement* which pursues collective *goals*, which *controls* its own performance and which has a *boundary* separating it from its environment'.

The following table shows how this definition applies to two organisational examples.

Characteristic	Car manufacturer (eg Ford)	Army
Social arrangement: individuals gathered together for a purpose	People work in different divisions, making different cars	Soldiers are in different regiments, and there is a chain of command from the top to the bottom
Collective goals: the organisation has goals over and above the goals of the people within it	Sell cars, make money	Defend the country, defeat the enemy, international peace keeping
Controls performance: performance is monitored against the goals and adjusted if necessary to ensure the goals are accomplished	Costs and quality are reviewed and controlled. Standards are constantly improved	Strict disciplinary procedures, training
Boundary: the organisation is distinct from its environment	*Physical*: factory gates *Social*: employment status	*Physical*: barracks *Social*: different rules than for civilians

1.3 How organisations differ

FAST FORWARD

> Organisations **differ** according to their: ownership, control, activity, orientation, size, legal status, funding and technology.

Organisations differ in many ways. Here are some possible differences.

Factor	Example
Ownership (public vs private)	*Private sector*: owned by private investors/ shareholders. *Public sector*: owned by the government
Control	By the owners themselves, by people working on their behalf, or indirectly by government-sponsored regulators
Activity (ie what they do)	Manufacturing, healthcare, services (and so on)
Profit or non-profit **orientation**	Business exists to make a profit. An army or a charity, on the other hand, are not profit orientated
Size	Sole trader, small business or multinational corporation
Legal status size	Limited company or partnership
Sources of **finance**	Borrowing, government funding, share issues
Technology	High use of technology (eg computer firms) vs low use (eg corner shop)

Two key differences in the list above are *what the organisation does* and whether or not it is *profit orientated*.

1.3.1 What the organisation does

Organisations do many different types of work. Here are some examples.

Industry	Activity
Agriculture	Producing and processing food
Manufacturing	Acquiring raw materials and, by the application of labour and technology, turning them into a product (eg a car)
Extractive/raw materials	Extracting and refining raw materials (eg mining)
Energy	Converting one resource (eg coal) into another (eg electricity)
Retailing/distribution	Delivering goods to the end consumer
Intellectual production	Producing **intellectual property** eg software, publishing, films, music etc
Service industries	These include retailing, distribution, transport, banking, various business services (eg accountancy, advertising) and public services such as education, medicine

1.3.2 Profit vs non-profit orientation

The basic difference in outlook is expressed in the diagram below. Note the distinction between **primary** and **secondary** goals. A primary goal is the most important: the other goals support it.

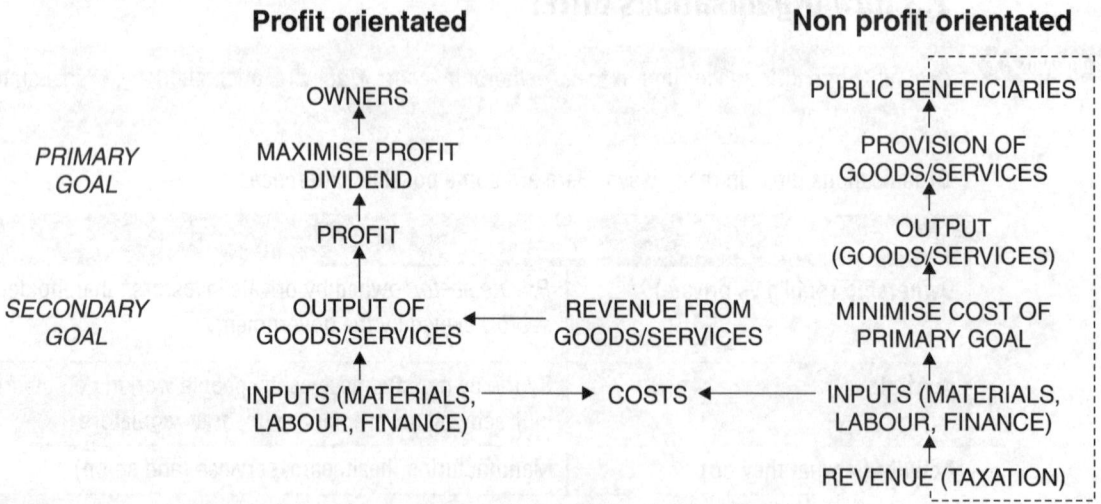

2 Formal organisation structures

2.1 What is organisation structure?

FAST FORWARD

> **Organisation structure** is formed by the grouping of people into departments or sections and the allocation of responsibility and authority.

Key term

> **Organisation structure** is formed by the grouping of people into departments or sections and the allocation of responsibility and authority.

Organisation structure implies a framework intended to:

(a) **Link individuals** in an established network of relationships so that authority, responsibility and communications can be controlled

(b) **Allocate the tasks** required to fulfil the objective of the organisation to suitable individuals or groups

(c) Give each individual or group the **authority** required to perform the allocated tasks, while controlling their behaviour and use of resources in the interests of the organisation as a whole

(d) **Co-ordinate** the objectives and activities of separate units, so that overall aims are achieved without gaps or overlaps in the flow of work

(e) Facilitate the **flow of work**, information and other resources through the organisation.

2.2 Components of organisation structure

FAST FORWARD

> **Mintzberg** suggests that all organisation structures have **five components: strategic apex, middle line** and **operating core**, plus **technostructure** and **support staff**.

Mintzberg suggests that all organisations can be analysed into five components, according to how they relate to the work of the organisation.

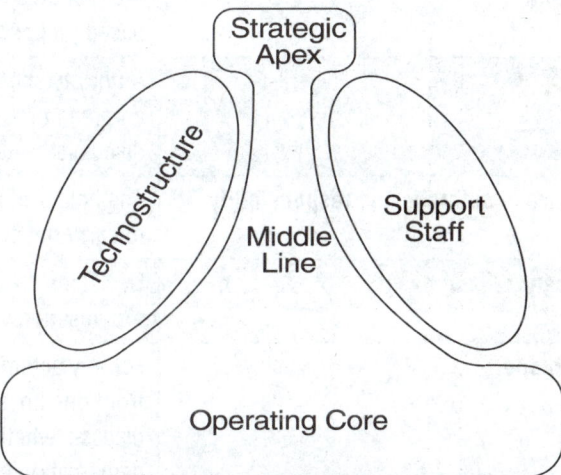

Component	Function
Strategic apex	Ensures the organisation follows its mission. Manages the organisation's relationship with the environment.
Operating core	People *directly* involved in the process of obtaining inputs, and converting them into outputs
Middle line	Conveys the goals set by the strategic apex and controls the work of the operating core in pursuit of those goals: ie middle management.

Component	Function
Technostructure	Analysers determine, and standardise work processes and techniques
Support staff	Ancillary services such as PR, legal counsel, the cafeteria and security staff. Support staff do not plan or standardise production. They function independently of the operating core.

Exam focus point

Mintzberg's components are particularly useful when discussing issues of organisational structure.

2.3 Classical principles of organisation

FAST FORWARD

Classical organisations are based on the principle of **hierarchy**. There is a line of decision making power from the top of the organisation to the bottom. This **scalar chain** is intimately connected to the concept of **span of control**, which is the number of individuals under the direct supervision of any one person.

Henri **Fayol**, an early ('classical') management theorist, suggested that all organisations should follow the 14 guiding principles outlined in the table below, in order to function effectively and efficiently.

Principle	Comment
Division of work	Work should be divided and allocated rationally, based on **specialisation**.
Scalar chain	Authority should flow vertically down a clear chain of command from highest to lowest rank. (This is discussed in Section 3 below.)
Correspondence of **authority** and **responsibility**	The holder of an office should have enough authority to carry out all the responsibilities assigned to him.
Appropriate **centralisation**	Decisions should be taken at the top of the organisation where appropriate.
Unity of **command**	For any action, a subordinate should receive orders from one boss only. Fayol saw dual command as a disease, whether it is caused by imperfect demarcation between departments, or by a superior S2 giving orders to an employee, E, without going via the intermediate superior, S1.
Unity of **direction**	There should be one head and one plan for each activity. Unity of direction relates to the organisation itself, whereas unity of command relates to the personnel in the organisation.
Initiative	Employees should be encouraged to use discretion, within the bounds of their authority.
Subordination of individual interests	The interest of one employee or group of employees should not prevail over that of the general interest of the organisation.

Principle	Comment
Discipline	A fair disciplinary system can be a strength of an organisation.
Order	People and resources should reliably be where they are supposed to be.
Stability of personnel	There should be continuity of employment where possible. Members of the organisation should behave in agreed ways.
Equity	Organisational policies should be just.
Remuneration	Rewards should be 'fair', satisfying both employer and employee alike.
Esprit de corps	Harmony and teamwork are essential to promote discipline and contentment.

Lyndall **Urwick**, the leading British proponent of classical management principles, suggested a similar set of organising principles.

(a) **The scalar chain**

(b) **Specialisation**

(c) **Unity of command**

(d) **Correspondence of authority and responsibility**

(e) **Span of control**: an optimum number of subordinates reporting to each superior

(f) **Reporting by exception**: decisions to be taken as far down the chain as possible, with reference back limited to deviations from plan

(g) **Objective**: structures and processes should only exist if they contribute to the organisation's purposes

(h) **Scientific method**: decisions should be taken rationally on the basis of data

Question
Principles of organisation

Considering each of Fayol's 'classical' principles of organisation, what challenges to these principles can you identify in modern methods of working?

Answer

You may have identified the following important points.

Specialisation is challenged by modern ideas such as 'multi-skilling' and team project management: instead of specialised functions, organisations are trying to encouraged cross-functional working to aid co-ordination in a more flexible way.

Unity of command ('one person, one boss') is challenged by modern ideas such as project/product management and matrix structures (discussed in section 4 of this chapter), where individuals report to different managers according to the task.

Scalar chain is challenged, to an extent, by organisational delayering, empowerment and teamworking. Vertical authority structures (embodied by the idea of the chain) are being replaced by collaborative, 'horizontal' structures which directly link people in multi-functional teams with shared decision-making responsibility.

2.4 Modern approaches to organisation

Modern management theory stresses **flexibility** as a key value, and organisational measures such as matrix and horizontal structures, multi-skilling, empowerment and flexible labour deployment are currently being explored.

Modern management theorists have moved away from 'classical' organisational principles such as those outlined by Fayol. They instead emphasise values such as the following.

(a) **Multi-skilling.** Contrary to the idea of specialisation, multi-skilled teams (where individuals are trained to perform a variety of team tasks, as required) enable tasks to be performed more flexibly, using labour more efficiently.

(b) **Flexibility**. This is perhaps the major value of modern management theory. Arising from the competitive need to respond swiftly (and without organisational trauma) to rapidly-changing customer demands and technological changes, organisations and processes are being re-engineered. This has created the following.

   (i) Smaller, multi-skilled, temporary structures, such as project or task-force teams.

   (ii) Multi-functional units, facilitating communication and co-ordination across departmental boundaries. This is called **matrix organisation**, and it blurs the principle of 'unity of command', since an employee may report both to his department superior *and* to a project or product manager whose job is to manage all areas of activity related to the product or project.

   (iii) Flexible deployment of the labour resource, for example through part-time and temporary working, contracting out tasks, flexitime, annual (rather than daily) hours contracts and so on.

(c) **Empowerment**

   (i) The purpose of empowerment is to free employees from rigorous control by instructions and supervision, and give them freedom to take responsibility for their goals and actions. This may release hidden resources (creativity, initiative, leadership, innovation), which would otherwise remain inaccessible.

   (ii) People are asked to use their own judgement in the interests of the organisation and the customer, within a disciplined context of agreed goals.

2.5 Contingency theory

Contingency theory suggests that there is no one best way to structure (or manage) an organisation. 'It all depends ...' on a number of variables.

Contingency theory holds that there is no universally best organisation structure, but that the best structure for a given organisation will depend on a number of contingent factors, including:

(a) **Age**. The older the organisation, the more formalised its behaviour. Work is repeated, so is more easily formalised.

(b) **Size**. The larger the organisation and the more elaborate and bureaucratic its structure, the larger the average size of the units within it and the more formalised its behaviour.

(c) **Technology**

   (i) The stronger the technical system, the more formalised the work will be, and the more bureaucratic the structure of the operating core.

   (ii) The more sophisticated the technology, the more elaborate and professional the support staff will be.

(d) **Geographical** dispersion. An organisation on one site will be organised differently to one which has geographically separate units, perhaps with different environmental demands (customer groups, infrastructure, legal/economic constraints).

(e) **Personnel** employed. Formalised, standardised structures might be needed for a large, low-skilled work-force.

(f) The **environment**

(g) The type of **activities** the organisation is involved in

(h) The business **strategy**

2.6 The systems approach

An organisation can be viewed as an **open system**, interacting with its environment.

The **systems approach** sees organisations, more dynamically, in terms of a system: 'an entity which consists of interdependent parts'. Rather than focus on administrative structures, this approach views the organisation as an **open system**, which is connected to and interacts with its environment. It takes in inputs from its environment and, through various organisational processes, converts them into outputs.

Inputs	Organisation systems and processes	Outputs
Labour	• Information systems	Products/services
Finance	• Technical systems	Information
Information	• Social systems	Environmental
Materials		impacts

As an open system, an organisation must remain sensitive to changes in its external environment. It must also make **internal adjustments** in order to remain stable.

The systems approach is helpful in:

(a) Drawing attention to the dynamic nature of organisations

(b) Creating an awareness of subsystems which must be integrated (eg the needs of task processes may conflict with the human needs of workers)

(c) Focusing attention on the relationship of the organisation with its environment. (Outward focus is particularly important for customer satisfaction: a shortcoming of the bureaucratic approach)

3 Tall and flat organisations

3.1 Span of control

FAST FORWARD

Span of control or 'span of management' refers to the number of subordinates responsible to a superior.

Key term

> The **span of control** refers to the number of subordinates immediately reporting to a superior official.

In other words, if a manager has five subordinates, the span of control is five.

Classical theorists such as **Urwick** and **Graicunas** suggest the following.

(a) There are physical and mental **limitations** to any given manager's ability to control people, relationships and activities.

(b) There needs to be **tight managerial control** from the top of an organisation downward.

(c) The span of control should therefore be **restricted**, to allow maximum control consistent with the manager's capabilities: usually between three and six. If the span of control is too wide, too much of the manager's time will be taken up with routine problems and supervision, leaving less time for planning. Even so, subordinates may not get the supervision, control and communication that they require.

(d) On the other hand, if the span is too **narrow**, the manager may fail to delegate, keeping too much routine work to himself and depriving subordinates of decision-making authority and responsibility. There may be a tendency to interfere in or over-supervise the work that is delegated to subordinates – and the relative costs of supervision will thus be unnecessarily high. Subordinates tend to be dissatisfied in such situations, having too little challenge and responsibility and perhaps feeling that the superior does not trust them.

A number of factors influence the span of control.

(a) A manager's **capabilities** limit the span of control: there are physical and mental limitations to any single manager's ability to control people and activities.

(b) The **nature of the manager's work load**

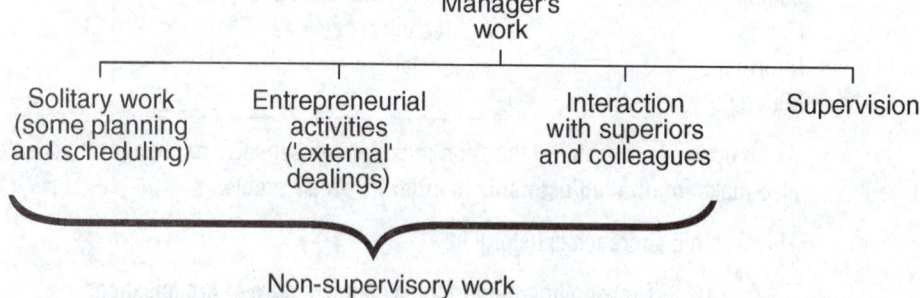

The more non-supervisory work in a manager's workload:

(i) The narrower the span of control
(ii) The greater the delegation of authority to subordinates

(c) The **geographical dispersion** of subordinates

(d) **Subordinates' work:** if all subordinates do similar tasks, a wide span is possible

(e) The **nature of problems** that a supervisor might have to help subordinates with. Time consuming problems suggest a narrow span of control.

(f)   The degree of **interaction between subordinates**. If subordinates can help each other, a wide span is possible.

(g)   If **close group cohesion** is desirable, a narrow span of control might be needed.

(h)   The amount of **support** that supervisors receive from other parts of the organisation.

3.2 Tall and flat organisations

FAST FORWARD

Recent trends have been towards **delayering** organisations of levels of management. In other words, **tall organisations** (with many management levels, and narrow spans of control) are turning into **flat organisations** (with fewer management levels, wider spans of control) as a result of technological changes and the granting of more decision making power to front line employees.

The span of control concept has implications for the length of the **scalar chain**.

Key terms

Scalar chain: the chain of command from the most senior to the most junior.

A **tall organisation** is one which, in relation to its size, has a large number of levels of management hierarchy. This implies a *narrow* span of control.

A **flat organisation** is one which, in relation to its size, has a small number of hierarchical levels. This implies a *wide* span of control.

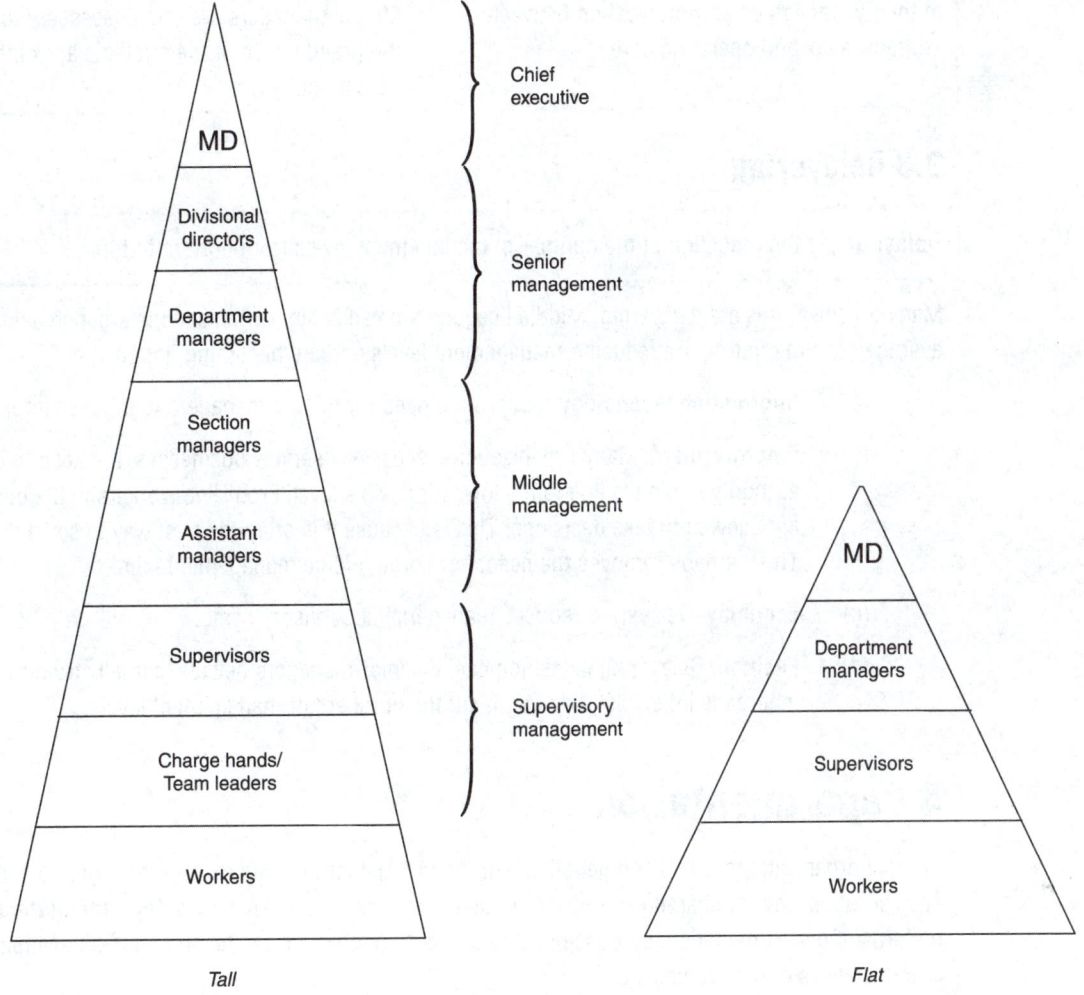

Tall   Flat

The advantages and disadvantages of these organisational forms can be summarised as follows.

Tall organisation

For	Against
Narrow control spans	Inhibits delegation
Small groups enable team members to participate in decisions	Rigid supervision can be imposed, blocking initiative
A large number of steps on the promotional ladders – assists management training	The same work passes through too many hands
	Increases administration and overhead costs
	Extra communication problems, as the strategic apex is further away

Flat organisation

For	Against
More opportunity for delegation	Requires that jobs *can* be delegated. Managers may only get a superficial idea of what goes on. If they are overworked they are more likely to be involved in crisis management
Relatively cheap	Sacrifices control
In theory, speeds up communication between strategic apex and operating core	Middle managers are often necessary to convert the grand vision of the strategic apex into operational terms

3.3 Delayering

Key term

> **Delayering** is the reduction of the number of management levels from bottom to top.

Many organisations are delayering. Middle line jobs are vanishing. Organisations are increasing the average span of control, are reducing management levels and are becoming flatter.

(a)   **Information technology** reduces the need for middle managers to process information.

(b)   **Empowerment**. Many organisations, especially service businesses, are keen to delegate authority down the line to the lowest possible level. Front-line workers in the operating core are allowed to take decisions. This is because it is often the best way to satisfy customers. This perhaps removes the needs for some middle management jobs.

(c)   **Economy**. Delayering reduces managerial/supervisory costs.

(d)   **Fashion**. Delayering is fashionable: if senior managers believe that tall structures are inherently inflexible, they might cut the numbers of management levels.

4 Departmentation   12/01

In most organisations, tasks and people are grouped together in some rational way: on the basis of specialisation, say, or shared technology or customer base. This is known as **departmentation**. Different patterns of departmentation are possible, and the pattern selected will depend on the individual circumstances of the organisation.

Organisations can be **departmentalised** on a **functional** basis (with separate departments for production, marketing, finance etc), a **geographical** basis (by region, or country), a **product** basis (eg world wide divisions for product X, Y etc), a **brand** basis, or a **matrix** basis (eg someone selling product X in country A would report to both a product X manager and a country A manager). Organisation structures often feature a variety of these types, as **hybrid** structures.

4.1 Geographic departmentation

Where the organisation is structured according to geographic area, some authority is retained at Head Office but day-to-day operations are handled on a **territorial** basis (eg Southern region, Western region). Many sales departments are organised territorially.

There are **advantages** of geographic departmentation.

(a)   There is **local decision-making** at the point of contact between the organisation (eg a salesperson) and its customers, suppliers or other stakeholders.

(b)   It may be **cheaper** to establish area factories/offices than to service markets from one location (eg costs of transportation and travelling may be reduced).

But there are **disadvantages** too.

(a)   **Duplication** and possible loss of economies of scale might arise. For example, a national organisation divided into ten regions might have a customer liaison department in each regional office. If the organisation did all customer liaison work from head office it might need fewer managerial staff.

(b)   **Inconsistency** in methods or standards may develop across different areas.

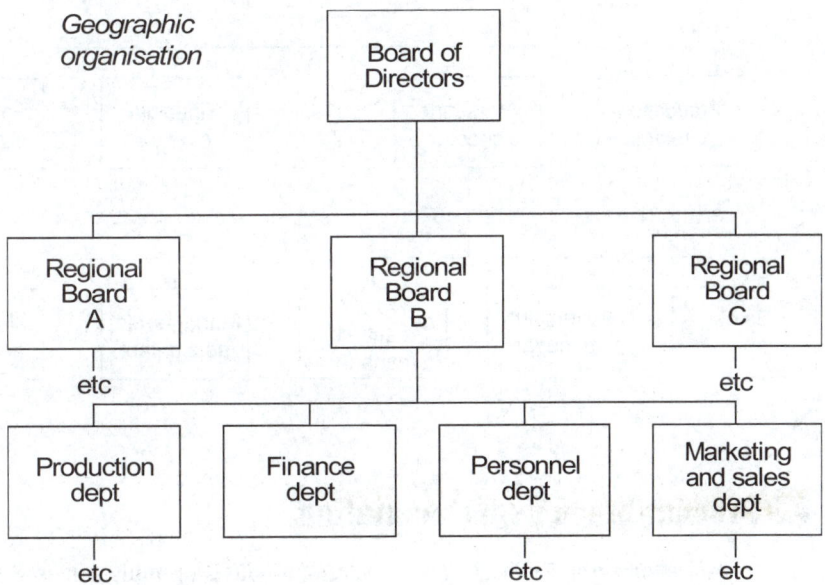

Geographic organisation

4.2 Functional departmentation

Functional organisation involves grouping together people who do similar tasks. Primary functions in a manufacturing company might be production, sales, finance, and general administration. Sub-departments of marketing might be market research, advertising, PR and so on.

Advantages include:

(a) **Expertise is pooled** thanks to the division of work into specialist areas.

(b) It **avoids duplication** (eg one management accounts department rather than several) and enables economies of scale.

(c) It **facilitates** the recruitment, management and development of functional specialists.

(d) It suits **centralised** businesses.

Disadvantages include:

(a) It focuses on internal **processes** and **inputs**, rather than the **customer** and **outputs**, which are what ultimately drive a business. The customer is only interested in the product, and being referred from one functional department to another may not be the most satisfying experience for the customer.

(b) **Communication problems** may arise between different functions, who each have their own jargon.

(c) **Poor co-ordination**, especially if rooted in a tall organisation structure. Decisions by one function/department involving another might have to be referred upwards, and dealt with at a higher level, thereby increasing the burdens on senior management.

(d) Functional structures create **vertical barriers** to information and work flow. Management writer Tom Peters suggests that customer service requires 'horizontal' flow between functions – rather than passing the customer from one functional department to another.

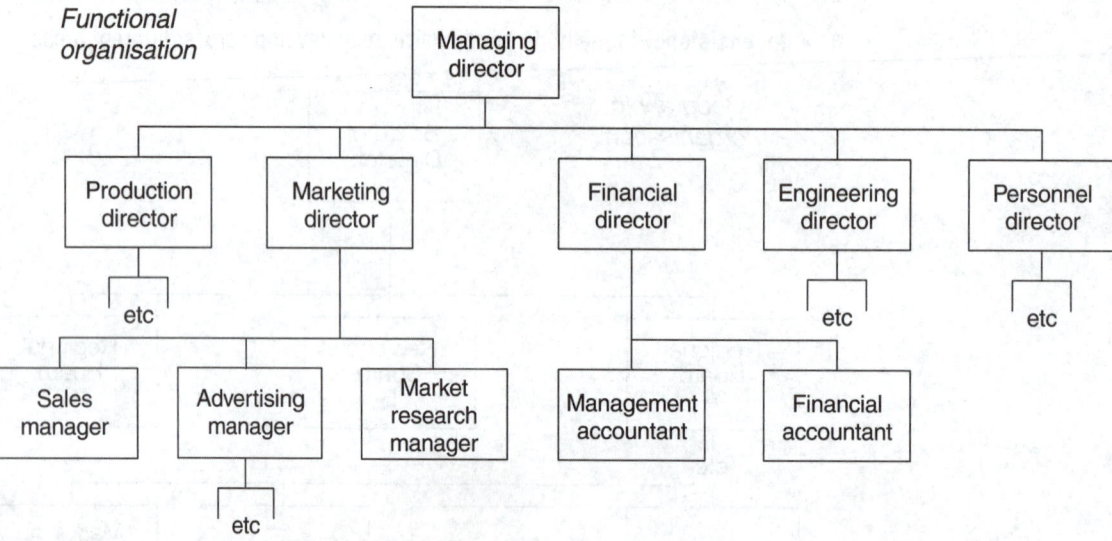

Functional organisation

4.3 Product/brand departmentation

Some organisations group activities on the basis of **products** or product lines. Some functional departmentation remains (eg manufacturing, distribution, marketing and sales) but a divisional manager is given responsibility for the product or product line, with authority over personnel of different functions.

Advantages include:

(a)   **Accountability.** Individual managers can be held accountable for the profitability of individual products.

(b)   **Specialisation.** For example, some salespeople will be trained to sell a specific product in which they may develop technical expertise and thereby offer a better sales service to customers.

(c)   **Co-ordination.** The different functional activities **and efforts** required to make and sell each product can be co-ordinated and integrated by the divisional/product manager.

Disadvantages include:

(a)   It **increases the overhead costs** and managerial complexity of the organisation.

(b)   Different product divisions may **fail to share resources** and customers.

A **brand** is the name (eg 'Persil') or design which identifies the products or services of a manufacturer or provider and distinguishes them from those of competitors. (Large organisations may produce a number of different brands of the same basic product, such as washing powder or toothpaste.) Branding brings the product to the attention of buyers and creates **brand loyalty** – often customers do not realise that two 'rival' brands are in fact produced by the same manufacturer.

(a)   Because each brand is promoted and sold in its own way, the need for specialisation may make brand departmentation effective. As with product departmentation, some functional departmentation remains but brand managers have responsibility for the brand's marketing and this can affect every function.

(b)   Brand departmentation has similar advantages/disadvantages to product departmentation.

Product/brand organisation

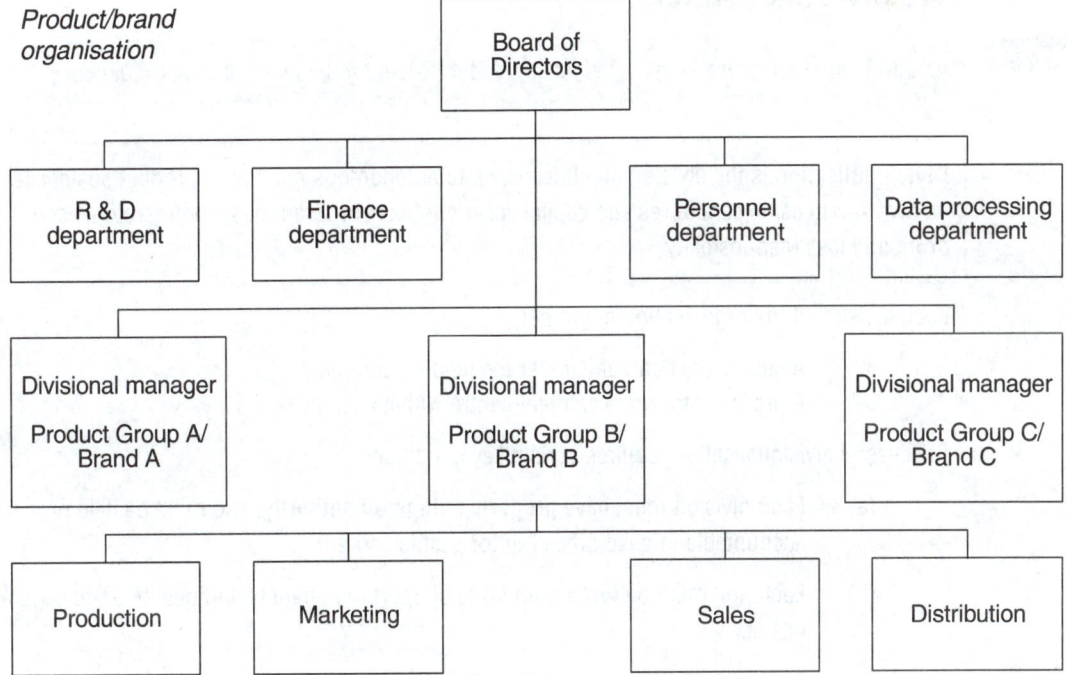

4.4 Customer departmentation

An organisation may organise its activities on the basis of types of customer, or market segment.

(a)   Departmentation by customer is commonly associated with **sales departments** and selling effort, but it might also be used by a jobbing or contracting firm where a team of managers may be given the responsibility of liaising with major customers (eg discussing specifications and completion dates, quality of work, progress chasing etc).

(b)   Many businesses distinguish between **business** customers and **consumers**.

Question

Looking at the 'Product/Brand Organisation' chart following Section 4.3 above, what types of organisation can you identify, and why are these appropriate for their purposes? What *added* type of organisation might this firm use, and in what circumstances?

Answer

- At the head office level, there is functional organisation. This enables standardisation of policy and activity in key 'staff' or support functions shared by the various divisions.

- At divisional level, there is product/brand organisation. This allows the distinctive culture and attributes of each product/brand to be addressed in production processes and marketing approach.

- For each product/brand, there is functional organisation, enabling specialist expertise to be directed at the different activities required to produce, market and distribute a product.

- This firm may further organise its marketing department by customer, if its customer base includes key (high-value, long-term) customer accounts with diverse service needs.

- It may further organise its sales and distribution departments by geographical area, if the customer base is internationally or regionally dispersed: local market conditions and values, and logistical requirements of distribution, can then be taken more specifically into account.

4.5 Divisionalisation

FAST FORWARD

In a **divisional structure** some activities are **decentralised** to business units or regions.

Key term

Divisionalisation is the division of a business into autonomous regions or product businesses, each with its own revenues, expenditures and capital asset purchase programmes, and therefore each with its own profit and loss responsibility.

Each division of the organisation might be:

- A subsidiary company under the holding company
- A profit centre or investment centre within a single company

Successful divisionalisation requires certain key conditions.

(a) Each division must have **properly delegated authority**, and must be held properly accountable to head office (eg for profits earned).

(b) Each unit must be **large enough** to support the quantity and quality of management it needs.

(c) The unit must not rely on head office for excessive **management support**.

(d) Each unit must have a **potential for growth** in its own area of operations.

(e) There should be scope and challenge in the job for the management of each unit.

(f) If units deal with each other, it should be as an 'arm's length' transaction. There should be no insistence on preferential treatment to be given to a 'fellow unit' by another unit of the overall organisation.

The advantages and disadvantages of divisionalisation may be summarised as follows.

Advantages	Disadvantages
• Focuses the attention of management below 'top level' on business performance.	• In some businesses, it is impossible to identify completely independent products or markets for which separate divisions can be set up.
• Reduces the likelihood of unprofitable products and activities being continued.	• Divisionalisation is only possible at a fairly senior management level, because there is a limit to how much discretion can be used in the division of work. For example, every product needs a manufacturing function and a selling function.
• Encourages a greater attention to efficiency, lower costs and higher profits.	
• Knowledge	• There may be more resource problems. Many divisions get their resources from head office in competition with other divisions.
• Gives more authority to junior managers, and so grooms them for more senior positions in the future (planned managerial succession).	
• Reduces the number of levels of management. The top executives in each division should be able to report directly to the chief executive of the holding company.	

4.6 Hybrid structures

As suggested by our question ('Types of organisation'), organisation structures are rarely composed of only one type of organisation, although an all-functional structure is theoretically feasible. 'Hybrid' structures may involve a mix of functional departmentation, ensuring specialised attention to key functions, with elements of (for example):

(a) Product organisation, to suit the requirements of brand marketing or production technologies

(b) Customer organisation, particularly in marketing departments, to service key accounts

(c) Territorial organisation, particularly of sales and distribution departments, to service local requirements for marketing or distribution in dispersed regions or countries

4.7 Matrix and project organisation

Where hybrid organisation 'mixes' organisation types, **matrix** organisation actually *crosses* functional and product/customer/project organisation.

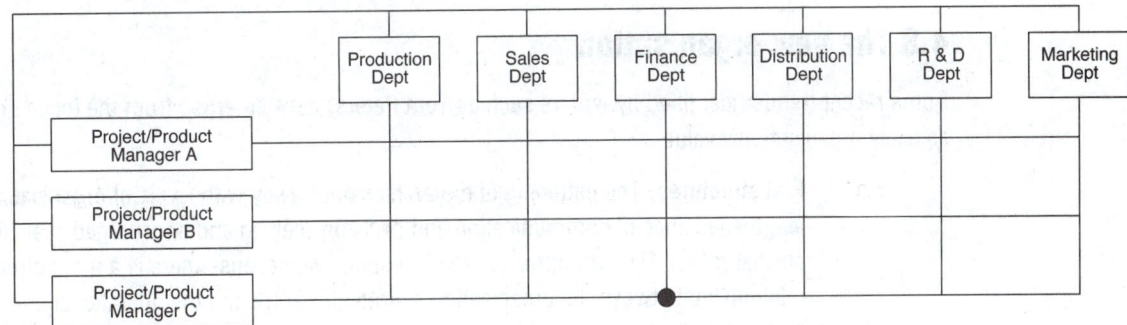

The employees presented by the dot in the above diagram, for example, are responsible to the Finance Manager for their work in accounting and finance for their functional department *and are* responsible to the Project Manager C for their work on the project team: budgeting, management reporting and payroll relevant to the project, say.

Advantages of matrix organisation include:

(a) Greater **flexibility** of:

    (i) **People**. Employees develop an attitude geared to accepting change, and departmental monopolies are broken down.

    (ii) **Workflow and decision-making**. Direct contact between staff encourages problem solving and big picture thinking.

    (iii) **Tasks and structure**. The matrix structure may be readily amended, where projects are completed.

(b) **Inter-disciplinary co-operation** and a mixing of skills and expertise, along with **improved communication** and **co-ordination**.

(c) **Motivation and employee development**: providing employees with greater participation in planning and control decisions.

(d) **Market awareness**: the organisation tends to become more customer/quality focused.

(e) **Horizontal workflow**: Bureaucratic obstacles are removed, and department specialisms become less powerful.

There are **disadvantages**, however.

(a) **Dual authority** threatens a **conflict** between functional managers and product/ project area managers.

(b) An individual with two or more bosses may suffer stress from **conflicting demands** or **ambiguous** roles.

(c) **Cost**: product management posts are added, meetings have to be held, and so on.

(d) **Slower decision making**

Exam focus point

> The December 2001 Section A question explored matrix structure in detail. It also introduced the idea that an organisation may be able to gain the benefits of a matrix organisation without a full restructuring, perhaps by mixing formal and informal structures. Be aware that there are more ways of getting departments talking to each other than full-scale matrix organisation: quality circles, team meetings and hybrid structures, for example.

4.8 The new organisation

Some recent trends (identified by writers such as Tom Peters) have emerged from the focus on **flexibility** as a key organisational value.

(a) **Flat structures.** The flattening of hierarchies does away with levels of organisation which lengthened lines of communication and decision-making and encouraged ever-increasing specialisation. Flat structures are more responsive, because there is a more direct relationship between the organisation's strategic centre and the operational units serving the customer.

(b) **'Horizontal structures'.** What Peters *(Liberation Management)* calls 'going horizontal' is a recognition that functional versatility (through multi-functional project teams and multi-skilling, for example) is the key to flexibility. In the words (quoted by Peters) of a Motorola executive: 'The traditional job descriptions were barriers. We needed an organisation soft enough between the organisational disciplines so that ... people would run freely across functional barriers or organisational barriers with the common goal of getting the job done, rather than just making certain that their specific part of the job was completed.'

(c) **'Chunked' and 'unglued' structures**. So far, this has meant teamworking and decentralisation, or empowerment, creating smaller and more flexible units within the overall structure. Charles Handy's **'shamrock organisation'** (with a three-leafed structured of core, subcontractor and flexible part-time labour) is gaining ground as a workable model for a leaner and more flexible workforce, within a controlled framework.

(d) **Output-focused structures**. The key to all the above trends is the focus on results, and on the customer, instead of internal processes and functions for their own sake. A **project management** orientation and structure, for example, is being applied to the supply of services within the organisation (to internal customers) as well as to the external market, in order to facilitate listening and responding to customer demands.

(e) **'Jobless' structures.** Meanwhile, the employee becomes not a job-holder but the vendor of a portfolio of demonstrated outputs and competencies (Bridges, *Jobshift*). However daunting, this is a concrete expression of the concept of **employability**, which says that a person needs to have a portfolio of skills which are valuable on the open labour market: employees need to be mobile, moving between organisations rather than settling in to a particular job.

5 Centralisation and decentralisation

5.1 What is centralisation?

 A **centralised** organisation is one in which authority is concentrated in one place.

We can look at centralisation in two ways.

(a) **Geography**. some functions may be centralised rather than 'scattered' in different offices, departments or locations.

So, for example, secretarial support, IT support and information storage (filing) may be centralised in specialist departments (whose services are shared by other functions) rather than carried out by staff/equipment duplicated in each departmental office.

(b) **Authority**. Centralisation also refers to the extent to which people have to refer decisions upwards to their superiors. Decentralisation therefore implies increased delegation, empowerment and autonomy at lower levels of the organisation.

5.2 Advantages and disadvantages of centralisation

Centralisation offers greater control and co-ordination; decentralisation offers greater flexibility.

The table below summarises some of the arguments in favour of centralisation and decentralisation.

Pro centralisation	Pro decentralisation/delegation
Decisions are made at one point and so are easier to co-ordinate.	Avoids overburdening top managers, in terms of workload and stress.
Senior managers can take a wider view of problems and consequences.	Improves motivation of more junior managers who are given responsibility.

Pro centralisation	Pro decentralisation/delegation
Senior management can balance the interests of different functions – eg by deciding on the resources to allocate to each.	Greater awareness of local problems by decision makers. (Geographically dispersed organisations are often decentralised on a regional/area basis for this reason.)
Quality of decisions is (theoretically) higher due to senior managers' skills and experience.	Greater speed of decision making, and response to changing events, since no need to refer decisions upwards. This is particularly important in rapidly changing markets.
Possibly cheaper, by reducing number of managers needed and so lower costs of overheads.	Helps develop the skills of junior managers: supports managerial succession.
Crisis decisions are taken more quickly at the centre, without need to refer back.	Separate spheres of responsibility can be identified: controls, performance measurement and accountability are better.
Policies, procedures and documentation can be standardised organisation-wide.	Communication technology allows decisions to be made locally, with information and input from head office if required.

6 Stability or flexibility?

6.1 Burns and Stalker: mechanistic and organic organisation

FAST FORWARD

Burns and Stalker noted that **mechanistic** (or **bureaucratic**) organisations are stable and efficient in conditions of slow change, but that **organic** organisation is required for adaptation and responsiveness in fast-change environments.

The terms 'mechanistic' and 'organic' were coined by Burns and Stalker to describe forms of organisation which are:

(a) Stable, efficient and suitable for slow-changing operating environments (mechanistic organisations, or 'bureaucracies'), and

(b) Flexible, adaptive and suitable for fast-changing or dynamic operating environments (organic organisations)

Factor	Mechanistic	Organic
The job	Tasks are **specialised** and broken down into sub-tasks.	Specialist knowledge and expertise is understood to contribute to the **common task** of the concern.
How the job fits in	People are concerned with completing the task **efficiently**, but are not concerned with how the task can be made to improve organisational **effectiveness**.	Each task is seen and understood to be set by the **total situation** of the firm: people are concerned with the task insofar as it contributes to **organisational effectiveness**.

Factor	Mechanistic	Organic
Co-ordination	**Managers** are responsible for co-ordinating tasks.	People adjust and redefine their tasks through interaction with others. This is rather like co-ordination by **mutual adjustment**.
Job description	There are **precise** job descriptions and delineations of responsibility.	Job descriptions are **less precise**: it is harder to pass the buck.
Commitment	**Doing the job** takes priority over serving the interests of the organisation.	**Commitment to the organisation** spreads beyond any technical definition.
Legal contract vs common interest	**Hierarchical** structure of control. An individual's performance and conduct derive from a **contractual relationship** with an impersonal organisation.	**Network structure** of control. An individual's performance and conduct derive from a supposed **community of interest** between the individual and the organisation, and the individual's colleagues.
Decisions	Decisions are taken by **senior managers** who are assumed to know everything.	Relevant technical and commercial knowledge can be located **anywhere**.
Communication patterns	Communication is mainly **vertical** (up and down the scalar chain), and takes the form of **commands** and obedience.	Communication is **lateral** or networked, and communication between people of different rank represents **consultation**, rather than command.
Content of communications	Operations and working behaviour are governed by **instructions** issued by superiors.	Communication consists of **information and advice** rather than instructions and decisions.
Mission	Insistence on **loyalty** to the concern and **obedience** to superiors.	Commitment to the organisation's **mission** is more highly valued than loyalty as such.
Internal vs external expertise	**Internal knowledge** (eg of the organisation's specific activities) is more highly valued than general knowledge.	'Importance and prestige attach to affiliations and expertise valid in the industrial, technical and commercial milieus **external** to the firm.'

6.2 Mechanistic organisations: bureaucracy

FAST FORWARD

> **Bureaucracy** is 'a continuous organisation of official functions bound by rules' (Weber). It is a form of mechanistic organisation.

6.2.1 Legitimate authority (Weber)

The German writer **Max Weber** regarded an organisation as an **authority structure** in which people obey instructions because their superiors have authority that is legitimate and rational. He was interested in why individuals obeyed commands, and he identified three grounds on which **legitimate authority** could exist.

(a)   **Charismatic leadership**: the leader is regarded as having some special power or attribute.

(b)   **Traditional, or patriarchal leadership**: authority is bestowed by tradition or hereditary entitlement, as in the family firm. Decisions and actions are bound by precedent.

(c)   **Bureaucracy**: authority is bestowed by dividing an organisation into jurisdictional areas (production, marketing, sales and so on) each with specified duties. Authority to carry them out is given to the officials in charge, and rules and regulations are established in order to ensure their achievement. Leadership is therefore of a **'rational-legal'** nature: managers get things done because their orders are accepted as legitimate and justified.

6.2.2 What is bureaucracy?

Key term

> A **bureaucracy** is 'a continuous organisation of official functions bound by rules' (Weber).
>
> - **Continuous organisation**. The organisation does not disappear if people leave: new people will fill their shoes.
>
> - **Official functions**. The organisation is divided into areas (eg production, marketing) with specified duties. Authority to carry them out is given to the officials in charge.
>
> - **Rules**. A rule defines and specifies a course of action that must be taken under given circumstances.

Weber was inclined to regard **bureaucracy** as the ideal form of organisation, because it is impersonal and rational, based on a set pattern of behaviour and work allocation, and not allowing personal issues to get in the way of achieving goals.

The characteristics of bureaucracy can be summarised as follows.

Characteristic	Description
Hierarchy	An organisation exists even before it is filled with people. Each lower office is under the control and supervision of a higher one.
Specialisation and training	There is a high degree of specialisation of labour. Employment is based on ability, not personal loyalty.
Professional nature of employment	Officials are full-time employees; promotion is according to seniority and achievement; pay scales are prescribed according to the position or office held in the organisation structure.
Impersonal nature	Employees work within impersonal rules and regulations and act according to formal, impersonal procedures.
Rationality	The jurisdictional areas of the organisation are determined rationally. The hierarchy of authority and office structure is clearly defined. Duties are established and measures of performance set.

Characteristic	Description
Uniformity in the performance of tasks	Procedures ensure that, regardless of who carries out tasks, they should be executed in the same way.
Technical competence	All officials are technically competent. Their competence within the area of their expertise is rarely questioned.
Stability	The organisation rarely changes in response to environmental pressures.

6.2.3 Bureaucracy: good or bad?

It is common to think of bureaucracy as an old-fashioned and dysfunctional form of organisation, but it has some **advantages**.

(a) Bureaucracies are ideal for **standardised, routine tasks**. For example, processing driving license applications is fairly routine, requiring systematic work.

(b) Bureaucracies can be very **efficient**. Weber considered them the most effective organisational form, in stable environments.

(c) Rigid adherence to procedures may be necessary for **fairness**, adherence to the **law**, **safety** and **security** (eg procedures for data protection).

(d) Some people are suited to the structured, predictable environment. Bureaucracies tend to be long-lived because they select and retain bureaucratically-minded people.

Rosemary **Stewart** suggests that bureaucracy became the dominant organisational model because it was **supported** by increasing organisation size and complexity (requiring formalisation and standardisation) and increasing worker demands for equitable treatment (requiring impersonality).

In swiftly-changing environments, however, the **dysfunctions** of bureaucracy become apparent.

(a) It results in **slow decision-making**, because of the rigidity and length of authority networks.

(b) Uniformity creates **conformity**, inhibiting the personal development of staff.

(c) Bureaucracies suppress **innovation**: they can inhibit creativity and initiative.

(d) Bureaucracies find it hard to **learn** from their mistakes, because of the lack of feedback (especially upwards).

(e) Bureaucracies are **slow to change**. *Crozier* stated that 'a system of organisation whose main characteristic is its rigidity will not adjust easily to change and will tend to resist change as much as possible'. Environmental change therefore causes severe trauma.

(f) **Communication** is restricted to established channels, ignoring opportunities for networking, upward feedback and suggestions that contribute to customer service and innovation.

Question	Rules and procedures

Using Mintzberg's model, what component part of the organisation is responsible for designing rules and procedures?

Answer

The technostructure.

6.3 Organic organisations

FAST FORWARD ▶▶

Organic organisations are controlled by mechanisms such as commitment and culture.

Organic organisations have their own structures and control mechanisms.

Feature	Description
Status	Although organic systems are not hierarchical in the way that bureaucracies are, there are **differences of status**, determined by people's greater expertise, experience and so forth.
Commitment	The degree of **commitment** employees have to the goals of the firm and the team is more **extensive** in organic than in mechanistic systems.
Shared values and culture	Hierarchical control is replaced by the development of **shared beliefs and values**. In other words, corporate **culture** becomes a powerful guide to behaviour.

6.4 Beyond organic organisation?

Huczynski and Buchanan describe an even more fluid, flexible and adaptable organisation design called 'adhocracy'.

Key term

Adhocracy is 'a type of organisation design which is temporary, adaptive, creative – in contrast to bureaucracy, which tends to be permanent, rule-driven and inflexible'.

Adhocracy is associated with creative thinking, innovation and organisational learning. It would typically involve the use of a loose network of flexible, temporary, cross-functional project teams. While ideally suited to turbulent business environments, it also presents a challenge for managers and employees, since it means living with disorder, ambiguity and loss of security and identity.

7 Technology and structure

Two important research programmes, which took place in England in the 1950s, showed how production technology influences the way work is organised.

7.1 Joan Woodward: type of production system

FAST FORWARD ▶▶

Technology has a significant impact on the way work is organised.

Joan Woodward investigated specific features of organisation structure, such as span of control and the division of functions among specialists. She discovered considerable differences between firms, and suggested that the differences were related to the type of production technology in use.

(a) Production systems may be divided into three main categories, ranging from least to most **complex**.

    (i) Unit production: eg production of simple units to customer orders, assembly of complex units in stages, or small batches

    (ii) Mass production: eg production of components in large batches, assembly line type production

    (iii) Process production: where 'workers do not touch the product, but monitor machinery and the automated production process, for example chemical plants and oil refineries' (Huczynski & Buchanan)

(b) The main point of difference was the **degree of control** possible over the output of the system. In the case of one-off production to customers' requirements, it is very difficult to predict the results of development work, while in continuous flow production, the equipment can be set for a given result.

Some aspects of the organisation vary directly as the technology varies. For instance, the length of the scalar chain increases as complexity increases. However, other variables, such as span of control, do not vary linearly. Woodward found that span of control was greatest in mass production systems, while small work groups with more personal relationships with their supervisors were typical of both unit and process systems.

7.2 Socio-technical systems: Trist and Bamforth

FAST FORWARD

The organisation may be seen as a **socio-technical system**.

Trist and Bamforth studied the effect of the introduction of new technology in coal mining.

Case Study

The traditional method was based upon a small, integrated work group consisting of a skilled man, his mate and one or two labourers. There was a high degree of autonomy at the work group level and close working relationships. It was usual for the group to be paid for its work as a group. The work was hard, the conditions unpleasant and there was often conflict, and even violence between work groups. However, 'The system as a whole contained its bad in a way that did not destroy its good'.

The introduction of large-scale coal-cutting machinery created a need for larger, more specialised groups. A single cycle of mechanised production might extend over three 7 ½ shifts, each performing a separate process and made up of 10 to 20 men. The members of each shift would be spread over about 200 yards of coal face tunnel. This physical dispersion and the spread of the work over three shifts destroyed the previous close working relationships. Many symptoms of social stress appeared, including scapegoating across shifts, formation of cliques and absenteeism.

Trist studied the new technology and found that it was possible to organise its use in such a way that some of the social characteristics of the traditional method were preserved. The use of this new method led to greater productivity, lower cost, considerably less absenteeism and accidents, and greater work satisfaction.

Trist introduced the concept of the organisation as a **socio-technical system**, with at least two major sub-systems:

(a) **Technology**, including task organisation and methods (not just machinery and tools) and

(b) **People** and their social arrangements: personal factors and interpersonal interactions.

The socio-technical systems approach to organisation suggested that organisations should aim to find a 'fit' that will maximise efficiency (through use of technology) while at the same time ensuring member satisfaction and commitment (through meeting workers' social and psychological needs).

7.3 Information and Communication Technology (ICT)

The global explosion of **ICT** has also had a major impact on work organisation.

In particular, ICT has created the concept of **virtual teams** and even **virtual organisations**. Virtual teams are interconnected groups of people who may not be present in the same office or organisation (and may even be in different areas of the world) but who:

- Share information and tasks (eg technical support provided by a supplier)
- Make joint decisions (eg on quality assurance or staff training) and
- Fulfil the collaborative (working together) function of a team.

ICT has facilitated this kind of collaboration, simulating team working via teleconferencing, video-conferencing, networked computers and the World Wide Web.

(a)   Dispersed individuals and units can use such technology to access and share up-to-date research, product, customer, inventory and delivery information (eg using Web-based databases and data tracking systems).

(b)   Electronic meeting management systems allow virtual meeting participants to talk and listen to each other on teleconference lines, while sharing data and using electronic 'white boards' on their PCs.

This has enabled organisations to:

(a)   **Outsource** areas of organisational activity to other organisations and freelance workers (even 'off-shore' in countries where skilled labour is cheaper), without losing control or co-ordination.

(b)   **Organise 'territorially'** without the overhead costs of local offices, and without the difficulties of supervision, communication and control. Dispersed centres are linked to a 'virtual office' by communications technology and can share data freely.

(c)   **Centralise** shared functions and services (such as data storage and retrieval, technical support or secretarial services) without the disadvantages of 'geographical' centralisation, and with the advantages of decentralised authority. Databases and communication (eg via e-mail) create genuine interactive sharing of, and access to, common data.

(d)   **Adopt flexible cross-functional and multi-skilled working**, by making expertise available across the organisation. A 'virtual team' co-opts the best people for the task – regardless of location.

Question

Virtual teams

What areas of your own organisation's activities are currently 'outsourced' to other organisations, consultants or freelance workers?

Answer

Organisations often outsource activities such as recruitment and selection (for appropriate types of staff), sales (eg telemarketing) or research and development. You may have noted the use of external call centres for technical support, sales and customer service functions: these are often in overseas locations where labour is cost-effective (such as India) – but location is increasingly irrelevant to customers because of the technology available.

Chapter Roundup

- **Organisations** achieve results which individuals cannot achieve by themselves.

- An organisation is a **social arrangement** which pursues collective goals and controls its own performance.

- Organisations **differ** according to their: ownership, control, activity, orientation, size, legal status, funding and technology.

- **Organisation structure** is formed by the grouping of people into departments or sections and the allocation of responsibility and authority.

- **Mintzberg** suggests that all organisation structures have **five components: strategic apex, middle line** and **operating core**, plus **technostructure** and **support staff**.

- Classical organisations are based on the principle of **hierarchy**. There is a line of decision making power from the top of the organisation to the bottom. This **scalar chain** is intimately connected to the concept of **span of control**, which is the number of individuals under the direct supervision of any one person.

- Modern management theory stresses **flexibility** as a key value, and organisational measures such as matrix and horizontal structures, multi-skilling, empowerment and flexible labour deployment are currently being explored.

- **Contingency theory** suggests that there is no one best way to structure (or manage) an organisation. 'It all depends ...' on a number of variables.

- An organisation can be viewed as an **open system**, interacting with its environment.

- **Span of control** or **'span of management'** refers to the number of subordinates responsible to a superior.

- Recent trends have been towards **delayering** organisations of levels of management. In other words, **tall organisations** (with many management levels, and narrow spans of control) are turning into **flat organisations** (with fewer management levels, wider spans of control) as a result of technological changes and the granting of more decision making power to front line employees.

- Organisations can be **departmentalised** on a **functional** basis (with separate departments for production, marketing, finance etc), a **geographical** basis (by region, or country), a **product** basis (eg world wide divisions for product X, Y etc), a **brand** basis, or a **matrix** basis (eg someone selling product X in country A would report to both a product X manager and a country A manager). Organisation structures often feature a variety of these types, as **hybrid** structures.

- In a **divisional structure** some activities are **decentralised** to business units or regions.

- A **centralised** organisation is one in which authority is concentrated in one place.

- **Centralisation** offers greater control and co-ordination; decentralisation offers greater flexibility.

- Burns and Stalker noted that **mechanistic** (or **bureaucratic**) organisations are stable and efficient in conditions of slow change, but that **organic** organisation is required for adaptation and responsiveness in fast-change environments.

- **Bureaucracy** is 'a continuous organisation of official functions bound by rules' (Weber). It is a form of mechanistic organisation.

- **Organic organisations** are controlled by mechanisms such as commitment and culture.

- **Technology** has a significant impact on the way work is organised.

- The organisation may be seen as a **socio-technical system**.

- The global explosion of **ICT** has also had a major impact on work organisation.

Quick Quiz

1 List Fayol's principles of organisation.

2 List Mintzberg's methods of co-ordination.

3 'Span of control' refers to the number of layers in the organisation hierarchy. *True or false*?

4 What is delayering?

5 What is functional organisation?

6 What is a matrix organisation?

7 Which of the following is not a type of legitimate authority identified by Max Weber?

    A   Charismatic
    B   Technostructure
    C   Traditional
    D   Bureaucratic

8 'Horizontal' structures (Peters) would be an example of which type of organisation?

    A   Mechanistic
    B   Organic

Answers to Quick Quiz

1 Division of work; authority and responsibility; discipline; unity of command; unity of direction; subordination of individual interests; remuneration; scalar chain.

2 Mutual adjustment, direct supervision; standardisation (of work process, outputs, skills and knowledge).

3 False. It is the number of subordinates immediately reporting to a given official.

4 The reduction in the number of management levels.

5 People are grouped together as they do similar work.

6 A matrix organisation crosses functional boundaries and involves overlapping chains of command.

7 B: 'Technostructure' is a term drawn from Mintzberg's model of organisational components.

8 B: Organic. Horizontal structures aim at flexibility.

Now try the question below from the Exam Question Bank

Number	Level	Marks	Time
Q1	Examination	15	27 mins

The role of management and supervision

Topic list	Syllabus reference
1 The purpose of management	1 (c)
2 Classical writers on management	1 (b)
3 Modern writers on management	1 (b), 1 (c)
4 Management and supervision	1 (c)
5 The manager's role in organising work	1 (c)

Introduction

In this chapter, we attempt to get an overview of the manager's task. What is management? How should people be managed? What do managers actually do?

Sections 2 and 3 trace the **development of management theory** from its focus on efficiency and control (classical and scientific management), through a recognition of the importance of people factors (human relations and neo-human relations), to a more complex understanding that a variety of factors influence the managerial role.

In **Section 4**, we note the difference between a manager and a **supervisor**: the interface between managerial and non-managerial levels of the organisation.

In **Section 5**, we look at briefly at the management of resources, activities and projects.

Any of the theories discussed in this chapter may be examined, but some (such as Fayol's five functions of management, and Mintzberg's managerial roles) are also particularly useful as a framework for discussing management in general. The major challenge of this topic is learning the various theories in detail.

In today's organisations, managers are also called upon to be 'leaders'. We explore leadership as separate function (and skill-set) of management, in Chapter 14: just bear in mind that if you get a question on management, it is worth thinking about leadership as well...

Study guide

Section 2 – The role of management

- Identify and explain the contribution made by modern writers on management: Drucker, Kanter, Mintzberg, Ouchi, Peters

- Identify and explain the contribution made by classical writers on management: Fayol, Stewart, Taylor, Mayo, Weber

- Identify the differences between classical and modern theories of management

- Outline areas of management authority and responsibility

Section 3 – The role of management

- Explain the role of the manager in the organisation of work
- List the management tasks involved in organising the work of others
- Illustrate the role of the manager in achieving tasks
- Identify the responsibilities of the supervisor

Exam guide

You need a thorough grasp of the work of the writers summarised in Sections 2 – 4 of this chapter. Even simple models (such as Ouchi's Theory Z and Peters and Waterman's 'excellence') have come up in exams, and you should be able to refer to relevant theories to support your answers to a range of questions on the nature of management. You may have to explain theory, or apply your knowledge in scenario format.

1 The purpose of management

FAST FORWARD

Management is responsible for using the organisation's resources to meet its goals. It is accountable to the owners: shareholders in a business, or government in the public sector.

Why is it that organisations have to be managed, and what is the purpose of management?

Key term

Management may be defined, most simply, as 'getting things done through other people' (Stewart).

An organisation has been defined as 'a social arrangement for the controlled performance of collective goals.' This definition suggests the need for management.

(a) **Objectives** have to be set for the organisation.

(b) Somebody has to **monitor progress and results** to ensure that objectives are met.

(c) Somebody has to communicate and sustain **corporate values**, ethics and operating principles.

(d) Somebody has to look after the interests of the **organisation's owners** and other **stakeholders**.

Question

John, Paul, George and Ringo set up in business together as repairers of musical instruments. Each has contributed £5,000 as capital for the business. They are a bit uncertain as to how they should run the business, and, when they discuss this in the pub, they decide that attention needs to be paid to planning what they do, reviewing what they do and controlling what they do.

Suggest two ways in which John, Paul, George and Ringo can manage the business assuming no other personnel are recruited.

Answer

The purpose of this exercise has been to get you to separate the issues of management functions from organisational structure and hierarchy. John, Paul, George and Ringo have a number of choices. Here are some extreme examples.

(a)   All the management activities are the job of one person.

       In this case, Paul, for example, could plan direct and control the work and the other three would do the work.

(b)   Division of management tasks between individuals (eg: repairing drums *and* ensuring plans are adhered to would be Ringo's job, and so on).

(c)   Management by committee. All of them could sit down and work out the plan together etc. In a small business with equal partners this is likely to be the most effective.

Different organisations have different structures for carrying out management functions. For example, some organisations have separate strategic planning departments. Others do not.

In a **private sector business**, managers act, ultimately, on behalf of shareholders. In practical terms, shareholders rarely interfere, as long as the business delivers profits year on year.

In a **public sector organisation**, management acts on behalf of the government. Politicians in a democracy are in turn accountable to the electorate. More of the objectives of a public sector organisation might be set by the 'owners' – ie the government – rather than by the management. The government might also tell senior management to carry out certain policies or plans, thereby restricting management's discretion.

2 Classical writers on management

| FAST FORWARD | The classical writers on management and organisation were largely concerned with **efficiency**. |

2.1 Henri Fayol: five functions of management   6/02

| FAST FORWARD | **Fayol** was an administrator and proposed universal principles of organisation. |

Henri Fayol (1841-1925) was a French industrialist who put forward and popularised the concept of the '**universality of management principles**': in other words, the idea that all organisations could be structured and managed according to certain rational principles. Fayol himself recognised that applying such principles in practice was not simple: 'Seldom do we have to apply the same principles twice in identical conditions; allowance must be made for different and changing circumstances.'

Fayol classified five **functions of management** which apply to any organisation.

Function	Comment
Planning	This involves determining **objectives**, and strategies, policies, programmes and procedures for achieving those objectives, for the organisation and its sub-units.
Organising	Establishing a **structure of tasks** which need to be performed to achieve the goals of the organisation; grouping these tasks into jobs for individuals or teams; allocating jobs to sections and departments; **delegating** authority to carry out the jobs; and providing **systems of information** and communication, for the co-ordination of activities.
Commanding	Giving **instructions** to subordinates to carry out tasks, for which the manager has authority (to make decisions) and responsibility (for performance).
Co-ordinating	**Harmonising** the goals and activities of individuals and groups within the organisation. Management must reconcile differences in approach, effort, interest and timing, in favour of overall (or 'super-ordinate') shared goals.
Controlling	**Measuring** and **correcting** the activities of individuals and groups, to ensure that their performance is in accordance with plans. Deviations from plans are identified and corrected.

You may be struck by two key 'omissions' from Fayol's classification, from a more modern viewpoint.

(a) '**Motivating**' is not mentioned. It is assumed that subordinates will carry out tasks when 'commanded' or instructed to do so, regardless of whether or how far they may 'want' to.

(b) '**Communicating**' is not mentioned, although it is implied by the process of commanding (giving instructions), co-ordinating (sharing information) and controlling (giving feedback).

This reflects the classical view of the function of management as a matter of controlling resources and processes rather than people: an awareness of management as first of all an *interpersonal* process, involving communication and influence, only developed later, as we will see.

Exam focus point

Although Fayol's 'managerial functions' may seem like a minor topic – and rather old-fashioned – it is a foundational model. The five functions are a helpful framework or starting point for discussing the nature of management and supervision – even if you go on to propose more modern alternatives such as Mintzberg's more fluid managerial roles (discussed in Section 3) or more interpersonally-based interpretations (including 'leadership', discussed in Chapter 14). A question on Fayol, and the roles of the manager and supervisor, was set in the June 2002 exam.

2.2 F W Taylor: scientific management

FAST FORWARD

Taylor was an engineer and sought the most efficient methods.

Frederick W Taylor (1856-1915) pioneered the **scientific management** movement in the USA. He was among the first to argue that management should be based on 'well-recognised, clearly defined and fixed principles, instead of depending on more or less hazy ideas.' Taylor was a very skilled engineer and he took an engineering efficiency approach to management.

Principles of scientific management include the following.

(a)   The development of a true **science of work**. 'All knowledge which had hitherto been kept in the heads of workmen should be gathered and recorded by management. Every single subject, large and small, becomes the question for scientific investigation, for reduction to law.'

(b)   The **scientific selection** and **progressive development** of workers: workers should be carefully trained and given jobs to which they are best suited.

(c)   The application of techniques to **plan**, **measure and control work** for maximum productivity.

(d)   The constant and intimate **co-operation between management and workers**: 'the relations between employers and men form without question the most important part of this art'.

In practice, scientific management techniques included the following key elements.

(a)   Work study techniques were used to analyse tasks and establish the most efficient methods to use. No variation was permitted in the way work was done, since the aim was to use the 'one best way'.

(b)   Planning and doing were separated. It was assumed that the persons who were intellectually equipped to do a particular type of work were probably unlikely to be able to plan it to the best advantage.

(c)   Jobs were micro-designed: divided into single, simple task components which formed a whole specialised 'job' for an individual, rather than permitting an individual to perform whole or part-task processes. (Task 'meaning' and 'significance', now considered essential to job satisfaction, had not yet emerged as important values.)

(d)   Workers were paid incentives on the basis of acceptance of the new methods and output norms; the new methods greatly increased productivity and profits. Pay was assumed to be the only important motivating force.

Scientific management as practised by Taylor and contemporaries such as Gilbreth and Gantt was very much about **manual work**. However, elements of scientific management are still practised today, whenever there is a concern for productivity and efficiency.

 Case Study

Persistent Taylorism?

It has been argued that elements of Taylorism – maximising managerial control through the micro-design of jobs, automation and close supervision – can be seen in the management of junior staff in businesses such as:

- Large fast-food franchises (such as McDonalds)

- Call-centres, where calls are scripted, timed and monitored – and (in some reported cases) staff must ask permission to leave the 'floor' to go to the toilet.

2.3 Elton Mayo: human relations

Mayo and his colleagues investigated individual and group behaviour at work, as a factor in productivity.

In the 1920s, research began to show that managers needed to consider the complexity of **human behaviour**. It was recognised that an exclusive focus on technical competence (under scientific management) had resulted in social incompetence: managers were not taught how to manage people. At the same time, it emerged that being a 'small cog in the machine' was experienced as alienating and demoralising by workers – whatever the financial incentives offered. A more complex picture of human motivation began to emerge.

Elton Mayo was Professor of Industrial Research at the Harvard Business School. He was involved in a series of large scale studies at the Western Electric Company's Hawthorne works in Chicago between 1924 and 1932. These studies were originally firmly set in the context of scientific management in that they began with an experiment into the effect of lighting on work output. However, it rapidly became apparent that **worker attitudes** and **group relationships** were of greater importance in determining the levels of production achieved than the lighting itself.

An important element in the Hawthorne studies was the investigation of the dynamics of work groups. The group was very effective in enforcing its behavioural norms in such matters as 'freezing out' unpopular supervisors and restricting output. It was concluded that people are motivated at work by a variety of psychological needs, including social or 'belonging' needs. This became the basis of the **human relations school** of management theory.

2.3.1 Neo-human relations

Later writers (such as Maslow and Herzberg) focused on a wider variety of worker's 'higher-order' needs, including the need for challenge, responsibility and personal development in the job. This became known as the **neo-human relations school**, which proposed important theories of motivation and job satisfaction.

The human relations approaches contributed an important awareness of the influence of the human factor at work (and particularly in the work group) on organisational performance. Most of its theorists attempted to offer guidelines to enable practising managers to satisfy and motivate employees and so (theoretically) to obtain the benefits of improved productivity.

However, the approach tends to emphasise the importance of work to the workers without really addressing the economic issues: there is still no proven link between job satisfaction and motivation, or either of these and productivity or the achievement of organisational goals, as we will see in Chapter 13.

3 Modern writers on management

Subsequent writers have taken a more **flexible** view of what managers do.

In the second half of the twentieth century, writing on management became more diverse.

(a)   The early emphasis on the organisation of work has been continued in the field of **supervisory studies** and the development of specific management techniques such as **project management.** The search for efficiency continues in the field of **work study** and **industrial engineering.**

(b)   Human relations theory has been enhanced by developments in the study of motivation, group and individual behaviour, leadership and other aspects of **industrial psychology**.

(c)   There has been much new writing on the nature of the **manager's task**: what it is to be a manager and what managers do, in increasingly complex and chaotic business environments.

3.1 Peter Drucker: the management process

Drucker emphasised the economic objective of managers in businesses.

Peter Drucker worked in the 1940s and 1950s as a business adviser to a number of US corporations. He was also a prolific writer on management.

Drucker argued that the manager of a business has one basic function – **economic performance**. In this respect, the business manager is different from the manager of any other type of organisation. Management can only justify its existence and its authority by the economic results it produces, even though as a consequence of its actions, significant non-economic results occur as well.

3.1.1 Management tasks

Drucker described the jobs of management within this basic function of economic performance as follows.

(a) **Managing a business.** The purposes of the business are to create a customer and innovation.

(b) **Managing managers**. The requirements here are:

- Management by objectives (or performance management)
- Proper structure of managers' jobs
- Creating the right spirit (culture) in the organisation
- Making a provision for the managers of tomorrow (managerial succession)
- Arriving at sound principles of organisation structure

(c) **Managing workers and work**

A manager's performance in all areas of management, including management of the business, can be enhanced by a study of the principles of management, the acquisition of 'organised knowledge' (eg management techniques) and systematic self-assessment.

3.1.2 Management processes

Later, Drucker grouped the work of the manager into five categories.

(a) **Setting objectives for the organisation**. Managers decide what the objectives of the organisation should be and quantify the targets of achievement for each objective. They must then communicate these targets to other people in the organisation.

(b) **Organising the work**. The work to be done in the organisation must be divided into manageable activities and manageable jobs. The jobs must be integrated into a formal organisation structure, and people must be selected to do the jobs.

(c) **Motivating** employees and communicating information to them to enable them to do their work.

(d) **The job of measurement**. Management must:

(i) Establish **objectives** or yardsticks of performance for all personnel

(ii) Analyse **actual performance**, appraise it against the objectives or yardsticks which have been set, and analyse the comparison

(iii) **Communicate** the findings and explain their significance both to subordinate employees and also to superiors

(e) **Developing people**. The manager 'brings out what is in them or he stifles them. He strengthens their integrity or he corrupts them'.

Every manager performs all five functions listed above, no matter how good or bad a manager (s)he is. However, a bad manager performs these functions badly, whereas a good manager performs them well. Unlike Fayol, Drucker emphasised the importance of **communication** in the functions of management.

3.2 Ouchi: Theory Z   12/02

> **Ouchi** combined the American and Japanese ways of management in an ideal 'Theory Z' approach.

Douglas McGregor labelled two extreme sets of managerial approaches 'Theory X' and 'Theory Y' (see Chapter 13 of this Study Text). When the Japanese economy was performing well, a generation ago, it became fashionable to study Japanese management methods and promote them as a solution to the West's then seemingly intractable industrial problems. Profiling American management culture as 'Theory A' and typical Japanese management as 'Theory J', **William Ouchi** sought to synthesise the two, to propose a form of Japanese-style management that could be successfully applied in Western contexts. Ouchi called these methods 'Theory Z'.

The characteristics of a Theory Z organisation offer some interesting contrasts with the Western way of doing things, notably in key Japanese values such as consensus decision-making and mutual loyalty in the employment relationship.

Ouchi described the Theory Z organisation as being characterised by:

(a)   Long-term employment, with slow-progressing managerial career paths (as in the Japanese system, but with a more Western specialisation of skills)

(b)   Broad concern for employee welfare, both inside and outside the work context (not just work performance, as in the Western system): commitment to the 'organisation family'

(c)   Implicit informal controls (such as guiding values) alongside explicit, formal measures

(d)   Collective consensus decision-making processes (Japanese), but with individual retention of ultimate responsibility for defined areas of accountability (Western)

(e)   Industrial relations characterised by trust, co-operation and mutual adjustment, rather than unionisation, demarcation and artificial status barriers

Exam focus point

An essay question was set in the December 2002 exam about Theory Z and the applicability to Western organisations of Theory Z principles. This demonstrates the need to revise each management theory in detail. Although the naming of 'Theory Z' reflects McGregor's 'Theory X and Theory Y' (covered in Chapter 13), note that they are not related and do not describe the same things! Make sure you distinguish all terms clearly.

Theory Z was welcomed as a more human and therefore more effective way of managing employee relations: Marks and Spencer in the UK has been cited as an organisation operating on principles akin to Theory Z. Elements of the approach have been incorporated into the 'Human Resource Management' (HRM) orientation to management, which regards committed people as the key resource of a business. However, it is less easy to transfer cultural values to foreign contexts than it is to apply methods and techniques: employee development programmes and quality circles have been adopted without necessarily being underpinned by Theory Z values.

3.3 Peters and Waterman: excellence

Peters and Waterman set out the characteristics (supposedly) common to excellent organisations, and pioneered the concept of organisation culture.

Peters and Waterman *(In Search of Excellence)* designated certain companies as **excellent** because over a 20 year period they had given an above average return on investment and they had a reputation for innovation. Although some of these companies subsequently failed, the cultural values associated with excellence have remained influential as an accessible set of the characteristics of successful companies.

Peters and Waterman identified eight attributes of excellent or *successful firms*.

- **A bias for action** rather than analysis: not getting stuck in 'analysis paralysis', but doing something to keep improving.

- **Closeness to customers**: listening to their needs, wants, values and feedback.

- **Autonomy and entrepreneurship**: encouraging employees to take initiative, spot and seize opportunities (especially to win and please customers and enhance quality).

- **Productivity through people**: valuing employee commitment as the key resource of the business.

- **Hands-on, value driven**: commitment to shared corporate values, at all levels.

- **Stick to the knitting**: not diversifying the business into areas for which it lacks expertise.

- **Simplicity**: avoiding the over-complication of structures and processes.

- **Simultaneous loose-tight properties**: few rules and procedures (loose) but strong values guiding behaviour (tight) as a means of control.

The key contribution of Peters and Waterman was perhaps their finding that the dominance and coherence of a **corporate culture** was an essential feature of the 'excellent' companies they observed. A 'handful of guiding values' was more powerful than manuals, rule books, norms and controls formally imposed (and resisted). This is discussed further in Chapter 3.

Excellence theories are accessible and appealing, but they have also been criticised. Key problems are:

(a) Many 'excellent' companies, such as IBM, have stumbled since the original studies.

(b) Excellence concentrates on operational issues rather than long term strategy.

(c) Strong cultures can impede necessary change, as well as support it.

(d) Excellence appears to propose that there is 'one best way' to succeed, contrary to prevailing contingency theories which suggest that 'it all depends' on a range of internal and external factors.

3.4 Rosabeth Moss Kanter: managers and innovation

Kanter was concerned with innovation and its demands on managers.

Many large companies seek to retain some of the innovation and flexibility supposedly characteristic of small firms. They move towards a balance between bureaucracy (the old order) and entrepreneurial innovation (the new order) based on **synergies**, **alliances** and '**newstreams**'.

(a) A **synergy** is a combination of businesses, internal services and organisation structures which means that the whole is worth more in value than the sum of the parts. People at all levels focus on doing what they do best.

(b) Organisations are also seeking to extend their reach without increasing their size by forming closer working relationships or **strategic alliances** with other organisations. This involves partnerships, joint ventures, outsourcing functions to sub-contractors, and other forms of business networking.

(c) A **newstream** is a flow of new business possibilities within the organisation. Instead of relying on innovation just happening, **official mechanisms are used to speed the flow of new ideas such as special funds, creativity centres and incentives**. This implies a management approach which is sensitive, flexible, persistent and autonomous.

In *When Giants Learn to Dance*, Kanter described some of the impossible or incompatible demands made on managers when seeking improved performance and excellence through innovation.

DEMANDS MADE ON MANAGERS

Be entrepreneurial and risk taking	*but*	Don't lose money
Invest in the future	*but*	Keep profitable now
Do everything you're doing now but even better	*but*	Spend more time communicating, on teams and new projects
Lead and direct	*but*	Participate, listen, co-operate
Know everything about your business	*but*	Delegate more
Work all hours	*but*	Keep fit
Be single-minded in your commitment to ideas	*but*	Be flexible and responsive

DEMANDS MADE ON ORGANISATIONS

Be 'lean and mean'	*but*	Be a good employer
Be creative and innovative	*but*	'Stick to the knitting'
Decentralise to small, simple autonomous units	*but*	Centralise to be efficient and integrative
Have a sense of urgency	*but*	Deliberately plan for the future

3.5 Mintzberg: the manager's role

FAST FORWARD

Mintzberg described managerial roles, arguing that management is a disjointed, non-systematic activity.

Henry Mintzberg (1989) did a study of a relatively small sample of US corporations to see how senior managers actually spend their time. He suggests that in their daily working lives, managers fulfil three **types** of managerial role.

Role category	Role	Comment
Interpersonal Based on manager's formal authority or position	**Figurehead** (or ceremonial)	A large part of a Chief Executive's time is spent representing the company at dinners, conferences and so on.
	Leader	Hiring, firing and training staff, motivating employees, and reconciling individual goals with the objectives of the organisation.
	Liaison	Making contacts outside the vertical chain of command. Some managers spend up to half their meeting time with their peers rather than with their subordinates.
Informational Based on managers' access to: Upward and downward channels Many external contacts	**Monitor**	The manager monitors the environment, and receives information from subordinates, superiors and peers in other departments. Much of this information is of an informal nature, derived from the manager's network of contacts.
	Spokesperson	The manager provides information on behalf of the unit and/or organisation to interested parties.
	Disseminator	The manager disseminates relevant information to subordinates.
Decisional Based on the manager's formal authority and access to information, which allow him to take decisions relating to the work of the department as a whole.	**Entrepreneur**	A manager initiates projects to improve the department or to help it react to a changed environment.
	Disturbance handler	A manager has to respond to unexpected pressures, taking decisions when there is deviation from plan.
	Resource allocator	A manager takes decisions relating to the mobilisation and distribution of limited resources to achieve objectives.
	Negotiator	Both inside and outside the organisation, negotiation takes up a great deal of management time.

Mintzberg's research challenged the classical view of the manager as separate to, or above, the routine demands of day-to-day work.

(a)   Managers are not always able to be reflective, systematic planners.

(b)   Managerial work is disjointed and discontinuous.

(c)   Managers do have routine duties to perform, especially of a ceremonial nature (receiving important guests) or related to authority (signing cheques as a signatory) –contrary to the myth that all routine work is done by juniors.

(d)   Managers prefer verbal and informal information to the formal output of management information systems. Verbal information is 'hotter' and probably easier to grasp.

(e)   Management cannot be reduced to a science or a profession. According to Mintzberg, managerial processes cannot be analysed scientifically or codified into an examinable body of theory.

Mintzberg states that general management is, in practice, a matter of **judgement and intuition**, gained from **experience** in **particular situations** rather than from abstract principles. 'Fragmentation and verbal communication' characterise the manager's work.

Question	Mintzberg and classical management theory

'Mintzberg's findings completely invalidate the notion that there are distinct management functions'. Discuss.

Answer

Managers still perform functions (in the way Fayol suggested, say): Mintzberg's findings merely show that the functions are not as clear cut, or performed as systematically, as might be supposed from the classical literature.

4 Management and supervision   6/02

There are different levels of management in most organisations. A finance department in an organisation might be headed by the finance director (A) supported by a chief financial accountant (B) and chief management accountant (C). Lower down in the hierarchy assistant accountants might report to (B) and (C).

> **FAST FORWARD**   **Supervision** is the interface between the operational core (non-managerial workers) and management.

4.1 The supervisor's role

The supervisor is the lowest level of management, at the **interface** between managerial and non-managerial staff.

The key features of supervision are as follows.

(a)   A supervisor is usually a **front-line manager**, dealing with the levels of the organisation where the bread-and-butter work is done. (S)he will deal with matters such as staffing and health and safety at the day-to-day operational level, where a manger might deal with them at a policy-making level.

(b)   A supervisor does not spend all his or her time on the managerial aspects of his job. Much of the time will be spent doing **technical/operational work**.

(c)   A supervisor is a **gatekeeper** or filter for communication between managerial and non-managerial staff, both **upward** (conveying reports and suggestions) and **downward** (conveying policies, instructions and feedback).

(d)   The supervisor monitors and controls work by means of **day-to-day, frequent and detailed information:** higher levels of management plan and control using longer-term, less frequent and less detailed information, which must be 'edited' or selected and reported by the supervisor.

Above the supervisor there may be several levels of management. Authority, responsibility and the timescale for decision-making all increase as the scalar chain is ascended. However, all managerial work may be considered to have some elements of similarity: it may be argued that supervisors carry out Fayol's five functions of management at a lower level.

Question

Bert Close has decided to delegate the task of identifying the reasons for machine 'down' time (when machines are not working) over the past three months to Brenda Cartwright. This will involve her in talking to operators, foremen and supervisors and also liaising with other departments to establish the effects of this down time. What will Bert need to do to delegate this task effectively? List at least four items he will need to cover with Brenda.

Answer

- Identify task objectives
- Explain limits within which Brenda will work
- Deadlines
- Formats of reporting results
- Progress monitoring

5 The manager's role in organising work

FAST FORWARD

Managers have **key roles** in work planning, resource allocation and project management.

5.1 Work planning

Work planning is the establishment of work methods and practices to ensure that predetermined objectives are efficiently met at all levels.

(a) **Task sequencing** or **prioritisation** ie considering tasks in order of importance for achieving objectives and meeting deadlines.

(b) **Scheduling** or **timetabling tasks**, and allocating them to different individuals within appropriate time scales.

(c) Establishing **checks and controls** to ensure that:

  (i)   Priority deadlines are being met and work is not 'falling behind'
  (ii)   Routine tasks are achieving their objectives

(d) **Contingency plans:** arrangements for what should be done if changes or problems occur, eg computer system failure or industrial action.

(e) **Co-ordinating** the efforts of individuals: integrating plans and schedules so that data and work flows smoothly from one stage of an operation to another.

Some jobs (eg assembly line work) are entirely routine, and can be performed one step at a time, but for most people, some kind of on-going planning and adjustment will be required.

5.2 Assessing where resources are most usefully allocated

In broad terms, managers and supervisors have access to the following resources, which can be allocated or deployed to further the unit's objectives.

(a) **Human resources:** staff time and skills

(b) **Material resources**, including raw materials, equipment, machine time, office space and so on

(c) **Financial resources**, within budget guidelines

(d) **Information**

The first three of these are sometimes called 'the 4Ms': Manpower, Machine capacity, Materials and Money.

A manager or supervisor may be responsible for allocating resources between:

(a) Different ways to achieve the same objective (eg to increase total profits, sell more – or cut costs)

(b) Competing areas, where total resources are limited

A piece of work will be **high priority** in the following cases.

- If it has to be completed by a certain time (ie a deadline)
- If other tasks depend on it
- If other people depend on it
- If it has important potential consequence or impact

Routine priorities or regular peak times (eg tax returns) can be planned ahead of time, and other tasks planned around them.

Non-routine priorities occur when unexpected demands are made. Thus planning of work should cover routine scheduled peaks and contingency plans for unscheduled peaks and emergencies.

5.3 Projects

Key term

> A **project** is 'an undertaking that has a beginning and an end and is carried out to meet established goals within cost, schedule and quality objectives' (Haynes, *Project Management*).

The main difference between project planning and other types of planning is that a project is not generally a repetitive activity. Projects generally:

- Have specific start and end points
- Have well-defined objectives, cost and time schedules
- Cut across organisational and functional boundaries

The relocation of offices, the introduction of a new information system or the launch of a new product may be undertaken as a project. Other examples include building/capital projects, such as factory construction or bridge building.

5.3.1 Project management

The job of **project management** is to foresee as many contingencies as possible and to plan, organise, co-ordinate and control activities.

Management task	Comment
Outline project planning	• Developing project targets such as overall costs or timescale (eg project should take 20 weeks) • Dividing the project into activities (eg analysis, programming, testing), and placing these activities into the right sequence, often a complicated task if overlapping • Developing the procedures and structures, managing the project (eg plan weekly team meetings, performance reviews etc)
Detailed planning	Identifying the tasks and resource requirements; network analysis for scheduling
Teambuilding	The project manager has to meld the various people into an effective team
Communication	The project manager must let superiors know what is going on, and ensure that members of the project team are properly briefed
Co-ordinating project activities	Between the project team and clients/users, and other external parties (eg suppliers of hardware and software)
Monitoring and control	The project manager should determine causes of any departure from the plan, and take corrective measures
Problem-resolution	Unforeseen problems may arise, and it falls upon the project manager to sort them out, or to delegate the responsibility for so doing to a subordinate.

Chapter Roundup

- **Management** is responsible for using the organisation's resources to meet its goals. It is accountable to the owners: shareholders in a business, or government in the public sector.

- The classical writers on management and organisation were largely concerned with **efficiency.**

- **Fayol** was an administrator and proposed universal principles of organisation.

- **Taylor** was an engineer and sought the most efficient methods.

- **Mayo** and his colleagues investigated individual and group behaviour at work, as a factor in   productivity.

- **Subsequent writers** have taken a more **flexible** view of what managers do.

- **Drucker** emphasised the economic objective of managers in businesses.

- **Ouchi** combined the American and Japanese ways of management in an ideal 'Theory Z' approach.

- **Peters and Waterman** set out the characteristics (supposedly) common to excellent organisations and pioneered the concept of organisation culture.

- **Kanter** was concerned with innovation and its demands on managers.

- **Mintzberg** described managerial roles, arguing that management is a disjointed, non-systematic activity.

- **Supervision** is the interface between the operational core (non-managerial workers) and management.

- Managers have **key roles** in work planning, resource allocation and project management.

Quick Quiz

1   Which of the following is *not* one of Fayol's five functions of management?

    A   Commanding
    B   Controlling
    C   Communicating
    D   Co-ordinating

2   State Taylor's principles of scientific management.

3   What advance did the Hawthorne studies make in the management of people?

4   The overriding responsibility of the management of a business, according to Drucker, is employee development. *True or false?*

5   What managerial roles did Mintzberg describe and what categories did he group them into?

6   Ouchi's synthesis of Japanese management culture for Western contexts is called:

    A   Theory X
    B   Theory Y
    C   Theory Z
    D   Theory J

7   What criticisms have been made of Peters and Waterman's ideas about excellence?

Answers to Quick Quiz

1   C: Communicating

2   The development of a true science of work; the scientific selection and progressive development of workers; the bringing together of the science and the workers; constant and intimate co-operation between management and workers.

3   Individual attitudes and group relationships help determine the level of output.

4   False: The overriding responsibility is economic performance.

5   *Category*   *Roles*

    Interpersonal: Figurehead; Leader; Liaison
    Informational: Monitor; Spokesperson; Disseminator
    Decisional   Entrepreneur; Disturbance handler; Resource allocator; Negotiator

6   C: Theory Z

7   Many excellent companies have stumbled. Long term strategy is ignored. Strong culture can impede change. It supports a single solutions to success

Now try the question below from the Exam Question Bank

Number	Level	Marks	Time
Q2	Examination	10	18 mins

Organisation culture

Topic list	Syllabus reference
1 What is culture?	1 (d)
2 Organisation culture	1 (d)
3 Culture and structure	1 (d)
4 The impact of national culture	1 (d)
5 The informal organisation	1 (d)

Introduction

Organisation culture is, broadly, the distinctive way an organisation does things: its particular 'style'. We explore how this reveals itself in **Sections 1 and 2** of this chapter.

Like **structure**, the concept of **culture** gives us a way of talking about how organisations 'work'. Particular structures suit particular cultures – as we see in **Section 3**: this is a useful model, which should be learned in detail.

The impact of national culture on organisational culture **(Section 4)** is not specifically mentioned in the syllabus, but you may want to bear it in mind when discussing management in multi-national and cross-cultural contexts. With increasing globalisation and workforce diversity, this is useful awareness.

This chapter underpins much that follows in the Study Text. The objectives, policies, procedures and management/leadership style of an organisation will all be influenced (in part) by its culture – and it is worth noting this in exam answers.

Study guide

Section 4 – Individual and group behaviour

- Explain the concept of organisation culture

Exam guide

Like the material in Chapter 1, the contents of this chapter could form part of the background to questions on most parts of the syllabus. Think about the kind of cultural values portrayed in a case study, for example.

1 What is culture?

1.1 Spheres of culture

 **Culture** is 'the collective programming of the mind which distinguishes the members of one category of people from another' (Hofstede). It may be identified as ways of behaving, and ways of understanding, that are shared by a group of people.

Hofstede (1984) summed up culture as 'the collective programming of the mind which distinguishes the members of one category of people from another'.

Culture may therefore be identified as ways of behaving, and ways of understanding, that are shared by a group of people. Schein referred to it as: 'The way we do things round here.'

Culture can be discussed on many different levels. The 'category' or 'group' of people whose shared behaviours and meanings may constitute a culture include:

- A nation, region or ethnic group
- Women versus men ('gender culture')
- A social class (eg 'working class culture')
- A profession or occupation
- A type of business (eg 'advertising culture')
- An organisation ('**organisational culture**')

If you are a male (or female) accountant in an organisation operating in a given business sector in a particular region of your country of residence (which may not be your country of origin), you may be influenced by all these different spheres of culture!

1.2 Elements of culture

 **Elements of culture** include:

- Observable behaviour, artefacts, rituals and symbols
- Underlying values and beliefs which give meaning to the observable elements
- Hidden assumptions which unconsciously shape values and beliefs

Trompenaars (1993) suggested that in fact there are different levels at which culture can be understood.

    (a)   The **observable**, expressed or 'explicit' elements of culture include:

- **Behaviour**: norms of personal and interpersonal behaviour; customs and rules about behaviours that are 'acceptable' or unacceptable.

- **Artefacts**: concrete expressions such as art and literature, architecture and interior design (eg of office premises), dress codes, symbols and 'heroes' or role models.

- **Rituals**: patterns of collective behaviour which have traditional or symbolic value, such as greeting styles, business formalities, social courtesies and ceremonies.

(b) Beneath these observable phenomena lie **values and beliefs** which give the behaviours, artefacts and rituals their special meaning and significance. For example, the design of office space (artefact) may imply status and honour, or reflect the importance of privacy, or reflect spiritual beliefs (as in feng shui) within a culture: it 'means' more than the observable features. Values and beliefs may be overtly expressed in sayings, mottos and slogans.

(c) Beneath values and beliefs lie **assumptions**: foundational ideas that are no longer consciously recognised or questioned by the culture, but which 'programme' its ways of thinking and behaving. Examples include the importance of the individual in many Western cultures: this is taken for granted in designing HR (human resources) policies, for example.

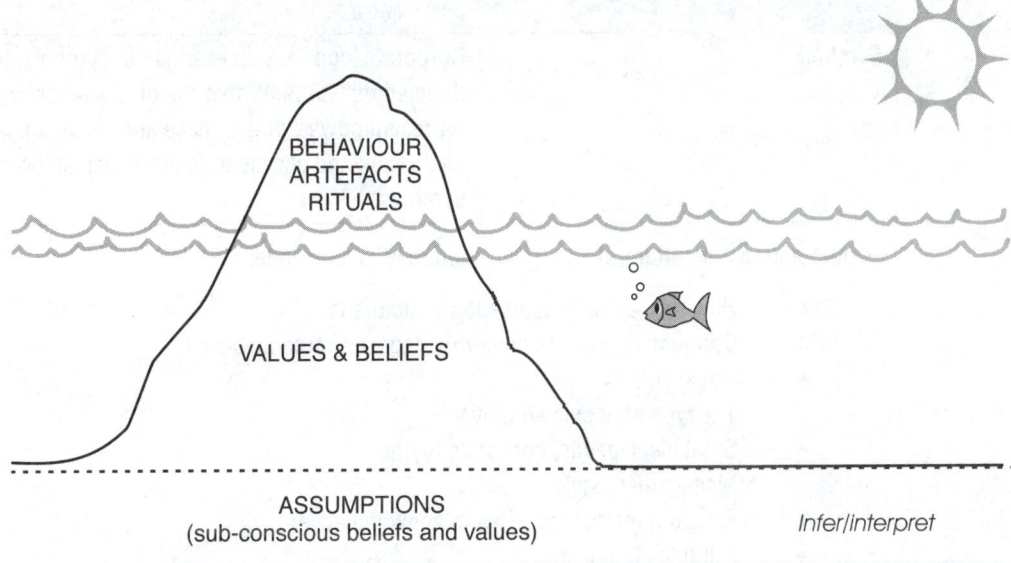

BEHAVIOUR
ARTEFACTS
RITUALS

VALUES & BELIEFS

ASSUMPTIONS
(sub-conscious beliefs and values)

Infer/interpret

Cultural assumptions, values and beliefs influence the behaviour of individuals, groups and organisations. They create a shared 'style' of operating within a given culture – but also the potential for misunderstanding and conflict *between* different cultural groups.

2 Organisation culture   12/04

Key term

> **Organisation culture** may be defined as:
>
> - 'The collection of traditions, values, policies, beliefs and attitudes that constitute a pervasive context for everything we do and think in an organisation' (Mullins)
>
> - 'A pattern of beliefs and expectations shared by the organisation's members, and which produce norms which powerfully shape the behaviour of individuals and groups in the organisation' (Schwartz & Davies)
>
> - 'The way we do things around here' (Handy)
>
> (These are the definitions cited by the ACCA in their suggested answers.)

2.1 Manifestations of culture in organisations

Organisation culture is **'the way we do things round here'**.

Examples of organisation culture, following Trompenaars' elements, include the following.

Item	Example
Beliefs and values, which are often unquestioned	'The customer is always right'
Behaviour	In the City of London, standard business dress is still generally taken for granted and even 'dress down Fridays' have their rules.
Artefacts	Microsoft encourages communication between employees by setting aside spaces for the purpose.
Rituals	In some firms, sales people compete with each other, and there is a reward, given at a ceremony, for the salesperson who does best in any period.
Symbols	Corporate logos are an example of symbols, but they are directed outwards. Within the organisation, symbols can represent power: dress, make and model of car, office size and equipment and access to facilities can all be important symbols.

Manifestations of culture in an organisation may thus include:

- How formal the organisation structure is
- Communication: are senior managers approachable?
- Office layout
- The type of people employed
- Symbols, legends, corporate myths
- Management style
- Freedom for subordinates to show initiative
- Attitudes to quality
- Attitudes to risk
- Attitudes to the customer
- Attitudes to technology

Question

Manifestations of culture

What do you think would differentiate the culture of:

- A regiment in the Army
- An advertising agency?

Answer

Here are some hints. The Army is very disciplined. Decisions are made by officers; behaviour between ranks is sometimes very formal. The organisation values loyalty, courage and discipline and team work. Symbols and artefacts include uniforms, medals, regimental badges and so on. Rituals include corporate expressions such as parades and ceremonies.

An advertising agency, with a different mission, is more fluid. Individual flair and creativity, within the commercial needs of the firm, is expected. Artefacts may include the style of creative offices, awards or prizes, and the agency logo. Rituals may include various award ceremonies, team meetings and social gatherings.

2.2 What shapes organisation culture?

Influences on organisational culture include:

(a) The organisation's **founder**. A strong set of values and assumptions is set up by the organisation's founder, and even after he or she has retired, these values have their own momentum. Or, to put it another way, an organisation might find it hard to shake off its original culture.

(b) The organisation's **history**.

    (i) Culture reflects the **era when the organisation was founded**.

    (ii) The effect of history can be determined by **stories, rituals and symbolic behaviour**. They legitimise behaviour and promote priorities.

(c) **Leadership and management style**. An organisation with a strong culture recruits managers who naturally conform to it, who perpetuate the culture.

(d) The **organisation's environment**. As we have seen, nations, regions, occupations and business types have their own distinctive cultures, and these will affect the organisation's style.

2.3 The importance of culture

FAST FORWARD

Cultural values can be used to guide organisational processes without the need for tight control. They can also be used to motivate employees, by emphasising the heroic dimension of the task. Culture can also be used to drive change, although – since values are difficult to change, it can also be a powerful force for preserving the status quo.

In 1982, Tom Peters and Robert Waterman published *In Search of Excellence*. Using an anecdotal approach, they set about describing and analysing what it was that made successful companies successful.

Excellent companies, according to Peters and Waterman, are good at two things:

- Producing commercially viable **new products**
- Responding to **changes in their environment**

A feature of excellent companies (as discussed in Chapter 2) was their use of **cultural values** to guide business processes and motivate employees.

(a) Cultural norms can replace rules and guidelines, focusing on output values such as quality and customer service, and freeing employees to make more flexible decisions in pursuit of those values.

(b) Valued cultural symbols can be used as rewards and incentives, to help employees feel 'heroic' in pursuing organisational aims.

(c) Cultural values can be used to drive organisational change, on the basis that if values change, behaviour will follow.

Exam focus point

If asked in an exam about Peters (or Peters and Waterman), as in December 2003, you might draw on a number of different areas: Peters and Waterman's attitudes of 'excellent' companies (see Chapter 2); their ideas about organisational culture (outlined above); or Peters' work on new organisation structures for turbulent business environments (see Chapter 1). Select whatever material is relevant.

3 Culture and structure

12/04

FAST FORWARD

Harrison classified four types of culture, to which Handy gave the names of Greek deities.

- **Power** culture (Zeus) is shaped by one individual
- **Role** culture (Apollo) is a bureaucratic culture shaped by rationality, rules and procedures
- **Task** culture (Athena) is shaped by a focus on outputs and results
- **Existential** or person culture (Dionysus) is shaped by the interests of individuals.

Writing in 1972, **Roger Harrison** suggested that organisations could be classified into four types. His work was later popularised by Charles Handy in his book *'Gods of Management'*. The four types are differentiated by their structures, processes and management methods. The differences are so significant as to create **distinctive cultures**, to each of which Handy gives the name of a Greek God.

Zeus Power culture	**Apollo** Role culture
The organisation is controlled by a key central figure, owner or founder. Power is direct, personal, informal. Suits small organisations where people get on well.	Classical, rational organisation: bureaucracy (see page 8). Stable, slow-changing, formalised, impersonal. Authority based on position and function.
Athena Task culture	**Dionysus** Person culture
Management is directed at outputs: problems solved, projects completed. Team-based, horizontally-structured, flexible, valuing expertise – to get the job done.	The purpose of the organisation is to serve the interests of the individuals who make it up: management is directed at facilitating, administering.

3.1 Power culture

Zeus is the god representing the **power culture** or **club culture**. Zeus is a dynamic entrepreneur who rules with snap decisions. Power and influence stem from a central source, perhaps the owner-directors or the founder of the business. The degree of formalisation is limited, and there are few rules and procedures. Such a firm is likely to be organised on a functional basis.

(a) The organisation is capable of adapting quickly to meet change.

(b) Personal influence decreases as the size of an organisation gets bigger. The power culture is therefore best suited to smaller entrepreneurial organisations, where the leaders have direct communication with all employees.

(c) Personnel have to get on well with each other for this culture to work. These organisations are clubs of 'like-minded people introduced by the like-minded people, working on empathetic initiative with personal contact rather than formal liaison.'

3.2 Role culture

Apollo is the god of the **role culture** or **bureaucracy**. There is a presumption of logic and rationality.

(a) These organisations have a formal structure, and operate by well-established rules and procedures.

(b) Individuals are required to perform their job to the full, but not to overstep the boundaries of their authority. Individuals who work for such organisations tend to learn an expertise without experiencing risk; many do their job adequately, but are not over-ambitious.

(c) The bureaucratic style, as we have seen, can be very efficient in a stable environment, when the organisation is large and when the work is predictable.

3.3 Task culture

Athena is the goddess of the **task culture**. Management is seen as completing a succession of projects or solving problems.

(a) The task culture is reflected in project teams and task forces. In such organisations, there is no dominant or clear leader. The principal concern in a task culture is to get the job done. Therefore the individuals who are important are the experts with the ability to accomplish a particular aspect of the task.

(b) Performance is judged by results.

(c) Task cultures are expensive, as experts demand a market price.

(d) Task cultures also depend on variety, and to tap creativity requires a tolerance of perhaps costly mistakes.

3.4 Person culture

Dionysus is the god of the **existential** or **person culture**. In the three other cultures, the individual is subordinate to the organisation or task. An existential culture is found in an organisation whose purpose is to serve the interests of the individuals within it. These organisations are rare, although an example might be a partnership of a few individuals who do all the work of the organisation themselves (with perhaps a little secretarial or clerical assistance): for example, barristers (in the UK) work through chambers.

Management positions in these organisations are often lower in status than the professionals and are labelled secretaries, administrators, bursars, registrars or clerks.

The organisation depends on the talent of the individuals; management is derived from the consent of the managed, rather than the delegated authority of the owners.

Exam focus point

The December 2004 exam offered 12 marks for describing Handy's cultural types. Less directly, the December 2003 exam case study portrayed a 'traditional, bureaucratic, formal ... type' of organisation, and asked what aspects of the organisation's culture might be contributing to its problems: you were expected to recognise this as a role culture – and you could then link this to the dysfunctions of bureaucracy discussed in Chapter 1. Don't neglect the key link between *culture* and *structure*!

3.5 A contingency approach

When thinking about these four types of culture, remember that they do not necessarily equate to specific organisation types, though some styles of organisation culture may accompany particular organisation structures. Also, it is quite possible for different cultures to prevail in different parts of the same organisation, especially large ones with many departments and sites. In other words, as the contingency approach says: 'it all depends'.

Case Study

Handy cites a pharmaceutical company which at one time had all its manufacturing subcontracted, until the turnover and cost considerations justified a factory of its own. The company hired nine talented individuals to design and run the factory. Result:

(a)   The *design team* ran on a task culture, with a democratic/consultative leadership style, using project teams for certain problems. This was successful while the factory was being built.

(b)   After its opening, the *factory*, staffed by 400, was run on similar lines. There were numerous problems. Every problem was treated as a project, and the workforce resented being asked to help sort out 'management' problems. In the end, the factory was run in a slightly more autocratic way. Handy states that this is a classic case of a task culture (to set something up) being superseded by a role culture (to run it). Different cultures suit different businesses.

Handy also matched appropriate cultural models to Robert **Anthony's** classification of managerial activity.

(a)   **Strategic management** (carried out by senior management) is concerned with direction-setting, policy making and crisis handling. It therefore suits a **power culture**.

(b)   **Tactical management** (carried out by middle management) is concerned with establishing means to the corporate ends, mobilising resources and innovating (finding new ways of achieving goals). It therefore suits a **task culture**.

(c)   **Operational management** (carried out by supervisors and operatives) is concerned with routine activities to carry out tactical plans. It therefore suits a **role culture**.

Question

Classifications of culture

Review the following statements. Ascribe each of them to one of Handy's four corporate cultures.

People are controlled and influenced by:

(a)   The personal exercise of rewards, punishments or charisma

(b)   Impersonal exercise of economic and political power to enforce procedures and standards of performance

(c)   Communication and discussion of task requirements leading to appropriate action motivated by personal commitment to goal achievement

(d)   Intrinsic interest and enjoyment in the activities to be done, and/or concern and caring for the needs of the other people involved

Answer

(a)   Zeus/power culture
(b)   Apollo/role culture
(c)   Athena/task culture
(d)   Dionysus/person culture

4 The impact of national culture

National culture influences organisation culture in various ways. One model of these effects is the 'Hofstede model' which describes four dimensions on which cultures differ:

- Power distance
- Uncertainty avoidance
- Individuality/collectivity
- Masculinity/femininity

Different countries have different ways of doing business, and different cultural values and assumptions which influence business and management styles.

Case Study

'French managers see their work as an intellectual challenge, requiring the remorseless application of individual brainpower. They do not share the Anglo-Saxon view of management as an interpersonally demanding exercise, where plans have to be constantly "sold" upward and downward using personal skills. 'Selection interviewers need to allow for cultural influences on interviewees' behaviour. For instance, Chinese applicants in Singapore tend to defer to the interviewer, whom they treat as 'superior', and to focus on the group or family, besides avoiding self-assertion… Hence, applicants from a Chinese background may be disadvantaged when being interviewed for jobs with multi-national companies that are heavily influenced by Anglo-American culture.' (Guirdham)

(Harvard Business Review)

4.1 The Hofstede model

Hofstede (1984) carried out cross-cultural research at 66 national offices of IBM and formulated one of the most influential models of work-related cultural differences.

The Hofstede model describes four main dimensions of difference between national cultures, which impact on all aspects of management and organisational behaviour: motivation, team working, leadership style, conflict management and HR policies.

(a) **Power distance**: the extent to which unequal distribution of power is accepted.

    (i) *High* PD cultures (as in Latin, near Eastern and less developed Asian countries) accept greater centralisation, a top-down chain of command and closer supervision. Subordinates have little expectation of influencing decisions.

    (ii) *Low* PD cultures (as in Germanic, Anglo and Nordic countries) expect less centralisation and flatter organisational structures. Subordinates expect involvement and participation in decision-making. (Japan is a medium PD culture.)

(b) **Uncertainty avoidance**: the extent to which security, order and control are preferred to ambiguity, uncertainty and change

    (i) *High* UA cultures (as in Latin, near Eastern and Germanic countries and Japan) respect control, certainty and ritual. They value task structure, written rules and regulations, specialists and experts, and standardisation. There is a strong need for consensus: deviance and dissent are not tolerated. The work ethic is strong.

    (ii) *Low* UA cultures (as in Anglo and Nordic countries) respect flexibility and creativity. They have less task structure and written rules; more generalists and greater variability. There is more tolerance of risk, dissent, conflict and deviation from norms.

(c)   **Individualism**: the extent to which people prefer to live and work in individualist (focusing on the 'I' identity) or collectivist (focusing on the 'we' identity) ways.

    (i)   *High* Individualism cultures (as in Anglo, more developed Latin and Nordic countries) emphasise autonomy and individual choice and responsibility. They prize individual initiative. The organisation is impersonal and tends to defend business interests: task achievement is more important than relationships. Management is seen in an individual context.

    (ii) *Low* Individualism (or Collectivist) cultures (as in less developed Latin, near Eastern and less developed Asian countries) emphasise interdependence, reciprocal obligation and social acceptability. The organisation is seen as a 'family' and tends to defend employees' interests: relationships are more important than task achievement. Management is seen in a team context. (Japan and Germany are 'medium' cultures on this dimension.)

(d)   **Masculinity**: the extent to which social gender roles are distinct. (Note that this is different from the usual sense in which the terms 'masculine' and 'feminine' are used.)

    (i)   *High* Masculinity cultures (as in Japan and Germanic and Anglo countries) clearly differentiate gender roles. Masculine values of assertiveness, competition, decisiveness and material success are dominant. Feminine values of modesty, tenderness, consensus, focus on relationships and quality of working life are less highly regarded, and confined to women.

    (ii) *Low* Masculinity (or Feminine) cultures (as in Nordic countries) minimise gender roles. Feminine values are dominant – and both men and women are allowed to behave accordingly.

Question

National culture and management style

According to the Hofstede model, what issues might arise in the following cases?

(a)   The newly-appointed Spanish (more developed Latin) R & D manager of a UK (Anglo) firm asks to see the Rules and Procedures Manual for the department.

(b)   A US-trained (Anglo) manager attempts to implement a system of Management by Objectives in Thailand (less developed Asian).

(c)   A Dutch (Nordic) HR manager of a US (Anglo) subsidiary in the Netherlands is instructed to implement downsizing measures.

Answer

(a)   A high-UA manager, expecting to find detailed and generally adhered-to rules for everything, may be horrified by the ad-hocracy of a low-UA organisation: if (s)he attempts to impose a high-UA culture, there may be resistance from employees and management.

(b)   A high-individuality manager may implement MbO on the basis of individual performance targets, results and rewards: this may fail to motivate collectivist workers, for whom group processes and performance is more important.

(c)   A low-masculinity manager may try to shelter the workforce from the effects of downsizing, taking time for consultation, retraining, voluntary measures and so on: this may seem unacceptably 'soft' to a high-masculinity parent firm.

5 The informal organisation

5.1 What is the 'informal organisation?

An **informal organisation** always exists alongside the formal one. This consists of social relationships, informal communication networks, behavioural norms and power/influence structures, all of which may 'by-pass' formal organisational arrangements. This may be detrimental or beneficial to the organisation, depending how it is managed.

An **informal organisation** exists side by side with the formal one. When people work together, they establish social relationships and customary ways of doing things. Unlike the formal organisation, the **informal organisation** is loosely structured, flexible and spontaneous. It embraces such mechanisms as:

(a) Social relationships and groupings (eg cliques) within – or across – formal structures

(b) The 'grapevine', 'bush telegraph', or informal communication which by-passes the formal reporting channels and routes

(c) Behavioural norms and ways of doing things, both social and work-related, which may circumvent formal procedures and systems (for good or ill). New members must 'learn the ropes' and get used to 'the way we do things here'

(d) Power/influence structures, irrespective of organisational authority: informal leaders are those who are trusted and looked to for advice

5.2 Benefits of the informal organisation

Benefits of the informal organisation for managers include the following.

(a) **Employee commitment.** The meeting of employees' social needs may contribute to morale and job satisfaction, with benefits in reduced absenteeism and labour turnover.

(b) **Knowledge sharing.** The availability of information through informal networks can give employees a wider perspective on their role in the task and the organisation, potentially stimulating 'big picture' problem-solving, cross-boundary co-operation and innovation.

(c) **Speed.** Informal networks and methods may sometimes be more efficient in achieving organisational goals, where the formal organisation has rigid procedures or lengthy communication channels, enabling decisions to be taken and implemented more rapidly.

(d) **Responsiveness.** The directness, information-richness and flexibility of the informal organisation may be particularly helpful in conditions of rapid environmental change, facilitating both the mechanisms and culture of anti-bureaucratic responsiveness.

(e) **Co-operation.** The formation and strengthening of interpersonal networks can facilitate teamworking and co-ordination across organisational boundaries. It may reduce organisational politics – or utilise it positively by mobilising effective decision-making coalitions and by-passing communication blocks.

5.3 Managerial problems of informal organisation

Each of the positive attributes of informal organisation could as easily be detrimental if the power of the informal organisation is directed towards goals unrelated to, or at odds with, those of the formal organisation.

(a) Social groupings may act collectively against organisational interests, strengthened by collective power and information networks. Even if they are aligned with organisational goals, group/network maintenance may take a lot of time and energy away from tasks.

(b)   The grapevine is notoriously inaccurate and can carry morale-damaging rumours.

(c)   The informal organisation can become too important in fulfilling employees' needs: individuals can suffer acutely when excluded from cliques and networks.

(d)   Informal work practices may 'cut corners', violating safety or quality assurance measures.

Managers can **minimise problems** by:

(a)   Meeting employees' **needs** as far as possible via the *formal* organisation: providing information, encouragement, social interaction and so on

(b)   Harnessing the **dynamics** of the informal organisation – for example by using informal leaders to secure employee commitment to goals or changes

(c)   Involving **managers** themselves in the informal structure, so that they support information sharing, the breaking down of unhelpful rules and so on

Question	Informal organisation structures

What 'informal organisation' structures are *you* involved in at work? How are they beneficial or detrimental to your work? What other satisfactions do they offer you?

Exam focus point

Culture impacts on other topics, such as motivation, leadership and teams. It is also an important and fashionable topic in its own right – including the influence of national cultures, with increasingly globalised management. Informal organisation would also lend itself to an essay question, so do not neglect these areas in your revision programme.

Chapter Roundup

- **Culture** is 'the collective programming of the mind which distinguishes the members of one category of people from another' (Hofstede). It may be identified as ways of behaving, and ways of understanding, that are shared by a group of people.

- **Elements of culture** include:

    - Observable behaviour, artefacts, rituals and symbols
    - Underlying values and beliefs which give meaning to the observable elements
    - Hidden assumptions which unconsciously shape values and beliefs

- Organisation culture is **'the way we do things round here'**.

- **Cultural values** can be used to guide organisational processes without the need for tight control. They can also be used to motivate employees, by emphasising the heroic dimension of the task. Culture can also be used to drive change, although – since values are difficult to change, it can also be a powerful force for preserving the status quo.

- Harrison classified four types of culture, to which Handy gave the names of Greek deities.

    - **Power** culture (Zeus) is shaped by one individual
    - **Role** culture (Apollo) is a bureaucratic culture shaped by rationality, rules and procedures
    - **Task** culture (Athena) is shaped by a focus on outputs and results
    - **Existential** or person culture (Dionysus) is shaped by the interests of individuals.

- **National culture** influences organisation culture in various ways. One model of these effects is the 'Hofstede model' which describes four dimensions on which cultures differ:

    - Power distance
    - Uncertainty avoidance
    - Individuality/collectivity
    - Masculinity/femininity

- An **informal organisation** always exists alongside the formal one. This consists of social relationships, informal communication networks, behavioural norms and power/influence structures, all of which may 'by-pass' formal organisational arrangements. This may be detrimental or beneficial to the organisation, depending how it is managed.

Quick Quiz

1   What are the elements of culture, according to Trompenaars?

2   'Bureaucracy' is another name for a:

    A   Power culture
    B   Role culture
    C   Task culture
    D   Existential culture

3   A project team is most likely to be a role culture. *True or false?*

4   List the four dimensions of cultural difference according to the Hofstede model.

5   Quality circles are likely to be a manifestation of:

    A   Low power distance
    B   Low individuality
    C   Neither A nor B
    D   Both A and B

6   List the potential benefits of the informal organisation.

Answers to Quick Quiz

1   Observable phenomena (behaviour, artefacts, rituals), values and beliefs, assumptions

2   B

3   False: it is most likely to be a task culture

4   Power distance, uncertainty avoidance, individuality, masculinity

5   D: quality circles suit employee responsibility and shared decision-making

6   Meeting of employee needs offering morale and job satisfaction; knowledge sharing; speed of operation; responsiveness to change; support for teamworking and co-ordination

Now try the question below from the Exam Question Bank

Number	Level	Marks	Time
Q3	Examination	15	27 mins

Individuals, groups and teams

Topic list	Syllabus reference
1 Individuals	1 (d)
2 Groups	1 (d)
3 Teams	1 (d), 1 (e)
4 Team member roles	1 (d)
5 Team development	1 (d), 1 (e)
6 Building a team	1 (e)
7 Successful teams	1 (d)

Introduction

It is a useful reminder that managers do not just manage activities, processes and resources: they manage *people*. Organisations (as we saw in Chapter 3) are made up of individuals and groups, with their own goals, needs and ways of seeing things.

In **Section 1**, we look at some useful concepts for understanding the behaviour of **individuals** at work, and how it can be managed.

In **Sections 2-5**, we look at how people behave in informal *groups* and in the more structured environment of **teams**. In particular, we consider how to create and maintain effective teams at work.

One of the key points to grasp is that an **effective team** is one which not only achieves its task objectives, but satisfies the needs of its members as well. As you will see in this chapter, **teamwork** involves both *task* functions (getting the job done) and *maintenance* functions (keeping the team together).

Teamwork is one of the hottest concepts in modern management – and it often comes up in the exam in some form or another. Fortunately, there are some useful models which can be learned: perhaps the major challenge of this topic is to get their details straight in your mind.

61

Study guide

Section 2 – The role of management

- Identify the difference between individual and group contribution to work performance

Section 4 – Individual and group behaviour

- Discuss the differences between individual and group behaviour
- Outline the contribution of individuals and teams to organisational success
- Identify individual and team approaches to work
- Understand perception and role theory

Section 5 – Team management

- Explain the role of the manager in building the team and developing individuals
- Define the purpose of a team
- Outline the composition of successful teams: Belbin, Peters and Waterman
- Explain the development of a team: Tuckman
- List team building tools
- Examine ways of rewarding a team
- Identify methods to evaluate team performance

Exam guide

Relationships within a team and the management of teams often figure in the examination, including named models such as Tuckman and Belbin. 'Perception and role theory' (among other aspects of individual behaviour and approaches to work) has not yet been examined – but it could be!

1 Individuals

1.1 Personality

FAST FORWARD

> **Personality** is the total pattern of an individual's thoughts, feelings and behaviours. It is shaped by a variety of factors, both inherited and environmental.

In order to identify, describe and explain the differences between people, psychologists use the concept of **personality**.

Key term

> **Personality** is the total pattern of characteristic ways of thinking, feeling and behaving that constitute the individual's distinctive method of relating to the environment.

1.1.1 Describing personality

Attempts to describe the 'components' of personality, or the ways people differ, focus on two broad concepts: traits and types.

(a) Personality **traits** are relatively stable, enduring qualities of an individual's personality which cause a tendency to behave in particular ways. If we say that someone is 'impulsive', for example, we are identifying one of his personality traits. This trait will make him tend to respond to situations in habitual ways: for example, by making rapid decisions and taking immediate liking to people.

Trait theories of personality account for individual differences by identifying the particular combination and strength of traits possessed by individuals.

(b)   Personality **types** are distinct clusters of personality characteristics, which reflect the psychological preferences of the individual. If we say that someone is an 'extravert', for example, we may be suggesting that she is sociable, expressive, impulsive, practical and active. An 'introvert', by contrast, is unsociable, inhibited, controlled, reflective and inactive.

Type theories of personality account for individual differences by identifying the particular mix of preferences within personality types. Carl Jung suggested that 'People tend to develop behaviours, skills and attitudes associated with their type, and those with types different from yours will probably be opposite to you in many ways.'

The well-known **Myers Briggs Type Inventory**™ is based on detailed analysis of personality types. The aim of the inventory (and the value of personality theories to managers) is:

(a)   To provide a shared language with which people can discuss and explore individual uniqueness (their own natural style) and ways of developing to their full potential

(b)   To help people to understand areas of difference which might otherwise be the source of misunderstanding and mis-communication

(c)   To encourage people to appreciate diversity by highlighting the value and complementary contributions of all personality types

Question   Personality

How is your personality 'cut out' to be an accountant? This is not a technical question: it merely invites you to think about your personality traits – and stereotypes about the 'type of person' who chooses to be an accountant or makes a good accountant. (This will be useful when we look at recruitment and selection later in the Study Text.)

1.1.2 Managing personality

An individual's personality should be compatible with his or her work requirements in three ways.

Compatibility	Comments
With the **task**	Different personality types suit different types of work. A person who appears unsociable and inhibited will find sales work, involving a lot of social interactions, intensely stressful – and will probably not be very good at it.
With the **systems** and **management culture** of the organisation	Some people hate to be controlled, for example, but others want to be controlled and dependent in a work situation, because they find responsibility threatening.
With other **personalities** in the team	Personality clashes are a prime source of conflict at work. An achievement-oriented personality, for example, tends to be a perfectionist, is impatient and unable to relax, and will be unsociable if people seem to be getting in the way of performance: such a person will clearly be frustrated and annoyed by laid-back sociable types working (or not working) around him.

Where incompatibilities occur, the manager or supervisor has three options.

(a)   **Restore compatibility**. This may be achieved by reassigning an individual to tasks more suited to his personality type, for example, or changing management style to suit the personalities of the team.

(b)   **Achieve a compromise**. Individuals should be encouraged to:

(i)   understand the nature of their differences. Others have the right to be themselves (within the demands of the team): personal differences should not be taken personally, as if they were adopted deliberately to annoy;

(ii)   modify their behaviour if necessary.

(c)   **Remove the incompatible personality**. In the last resort, obstinately difficult or disruptive people may simply have to be weeded out of the team.

1.2 Perception

FAST FORWARD

Perception is the process by which the brain selects and organises information in order to make sense of it. People behave according to what they perceive – not according to what really is.

Different people see things differently and human beings behave in (and in response to) the world, not as it really is, but as they see it.

Key term

Perception is the psychological process by which stimuli or in-coming sensory data are selected and organised into patterns which are meaningful to the individual.

1.2.1 Processes of perception

The process of **perceptual selection** deals with how we gather and filter out incoming data. Perception may be determined by any or all of the following.

(a)   **The context**. People see what they want to see: whatever is necessary or relevant in the situation in which they find themselves. You might notice articles on management in the newspapers while studying this module which normally you would not notice, for example.

(b)   **The nature of the stimuli**. Our attention tends to be drawn to large, bright, loud, contrasting, unfamiliar, moving and repeated (not repetitive) stimuli. Advertisers know it.

(c)   **Internal factors**. Our attention is drawn to stimuli that match our personality, needs, interests, expectations and so on. If you are hungry, for example, you will pick the smell of food out of a mix of aromas.

(d)   **Fear or trauma.** People are able to avoid seeing things that they *don't* want to see: things that are threatening to their security or self-image, or things that are too painful for them.

A complementary process of **perceptual organisation** deals with the interpretation of the data which has been gathered and filtered.

1.2.2 Managing perception

People do not respond to the world as it really is, but as they perceive it to be. If people act in ways that seem illogical or contrary to you, it is probably not because of stupidity or defiance, but because they simply do not see things in the same way you do. In order to manage differences in perception:

(a)   Consider whether you might be misinterpreting the situation

(b)   Consider whether others might be misinterpreting the situation or interpreting it differently from you

(c)   When tackling a task or a problem get the people involved to **define the situation** as they see it

(d)   Be aware of the most common clashes of perception at work.

    (i)   **Managers and staff.** The experience of work can be very different for managerial and non-managerial personnel. Efforts to bridge the gap may be viewed with suspicion.

    (ii)   **Work cultures**. Different functions in organisations may have very different time-scales and cultures of work, and will therefore perceive the work, and each other, in different ways.

    (iii)   **Race, sex** and **religious beliefs.** A joke, comment or gesture that one person may see as amusing may be offensive – and construed as harassment under UK law – to another.

Question

Perception

Identify the perceptual problem(s) in the following case.

A woman has just been promoted to the management team. At the first management meeting, the chairman introduces her to her new colleagues – all male – and says: 'At least we'll get some decent tea in these meetings from now on, eh?' Almost everyone laughs. For some reason, the woman does not contribute much in the meeting, and the chairman later tells one of his colleagues: 'I hope we haven't made a mistake. She doesn't seem to be a team player at all.'

Answer

The chairman thinks he is being funny. Maybe he is only joking about the woman making the tea – but he may really perceive her role that way. He lacks the perception that his new colleague may find his remark offensive. From the woman's point of view, she is bound to be sensitive and insecure in her first meeting and with all male colleagues: small wonder that, joke or not, she perceives the chairman's comment as a slap in the face. The chairman later fails to perceive the effect his joke has had on her, assuming that her silence is a sign of poor co-operation or inability to communicate.

1.3 Attitudes

FAST FORWARD

People develop **attitudes** about things, based on what they think, what they feel and what they want to do about it. Attitudes are formed by perception, experience and personality which in turn are shaped by wider social influences.

Attitudes are our general standpoint on things: the positions we have adopted in regard to particular issues, things and people, as we perceive them.

Key term

An **attitude** is 'a mental state … exerting a directive or dynamic influence upon the individual's response to all objects and situations with which it is related.'

Attitudes are thought to contain three basic components.

- Knowledge, beliefs or disbeliefs, perceptions
- Feelings and desires (positive or negative)
- Volition, will or the intention to perform an action

Behaviour in a work context will be influenced by:

(a) **Attitudes to work:** the individual's standpoint on working, work conditions, colleagues, the task, the organisation and management

(b) **Attitudes at work:** all sorts of attitudes which individuals may have about other people, politics, education or religion (among other things), and which they bring with them into the work place – to act on, agree, disagree or discuss

Positive, negative or neutral attitudes to other workers, or groups of workers, to the various systems and operations of the organisation, to learning – or particular training initiatives – to communication or to the task itself will obviously influence performance at work. In particular, they may result in varying degrees of:

- Co-operation or conflict between individuals and groups, or between departments
- Co-operation with or resistance to management
- Success in communication – interpersonal and organisation wide
- Commitment and contribution to the work

Question
Attitude

Suggest four elements which would make up a positive attitude to work. (An example might be the belief that you get a fair day's pay for a fair day's work.)

Answer

Elements of a positive attitude to work may include a willingness to:

(a) Commit oneself to the objectives of the organisation, or adopt personal objectives that are compatible with those of the organisation

(b) Accept the right of the organisation to set standards of acceptable behaviour for its members

(c) Contribute to the development and improvement of work practices and performance

(d) Take advantages of opportunities for personal development at work

1.4 Intelligence

Intelligence is a wider and more complex concept than the traditional view of 'IQ'. It includes useful attributes such as:

(a) **Analytic intelligence**: traditionally measured by IQ tests, including mental agility, logical reasoning and verbal fluency

(b) **Spatial intelligence**: the ability to see patterns and connections, most obvious in the creative artist or scientist

(c) **Practical intelligence**: practical aptitude, handiness

(d) **Intra-personal intelligence**: self awareness, self expression, self-control, handling stress

(e) **Inter-personal intelligence**: empathy, understanding of the emotional needs of others, influence, conflict resolution, assertiveness, co-operation

Intra- and inter-personal intelligence have recently attracted attention, through the work of Daniel **Goleman** (and others) as **emotional intelligence** (EQ). EQ is considered particularly important in managing people effectively, since it enables a person to manage the emotional components of situations, behaviour and communication.

1.5 Role theory

Role theory suggests that people behave in any situation according to other people's expectations of how they should behave in that situation.

A role may be seen as a part you play: people sometimes refer to wearing 'different hats' in different situations or groups of people.

(a) A **role set** is a group of people who respond to you in a given role. Staff in the accounts department will relate to the account manager in his role as professional and superior – rather than as a father or husband (within the role set of the family) or friend (in the role set of non-work peers) and so on. Individuals need to be aware of which role set they are operating in, in order to behave appropriately for the role.

(b) **Role ambiguity** may occur if you do not know what role you are operating in at a given time. If a manager tries to be 'friends' with staff, this may create ambiguity and people will not know where they stand.

(c) **Role incompatibility** or **role conflict** occurs when you are expected to operate in two roles at once: for example, if you have to discipline a member of staff (in your role as superior) with whom you have become informally friendly (in your role as sociable person).

(d) **Role signs** indicate what role you are in at a given moment, so that others relate to you in that role without ambiguity or confusion. Role signs at work have traditionally included such things as style of dress (signalling professionalism) and styles of address (signalling respect and relative status).

(e) **Role models** are the individuals you aspire to be like: people you look up to and model your own behaviour on.

Question
Roles

Choose one role in which your regularly interact with other people. (The role of 'student', say?)

(a) Identify your role set and role signs.

(b) Identify any areas of ambiguity, compatibility or conflict the role presents. What could be done about each (if anything)? Could the other members of your role set help?

Answer

Your answer might be along the following lines.

(a) If you chose 'student' your role set might consist of fellow students, lecturers, tutor, and library and administrative staff. Your role signs may include dressing and acting informally with your colleagues, but being rather more formal with the others.

(b) Lecturers who dress and act informally with their students may have problems asserting authority when they need to. Mature students with partners and children may find their roles incompatible when study interferes with personal life.

2 Groups

6/02

As an employee your relationship with the organisation is as an individual: the employment contract is with you as an individual, and you are recruited as an individual. In your working life, though, you will generally find yourself working as part of a group or **team**. If you are a supervisor or a manager, you may direct a **team**.

2.1 What are groups?

> **FAST FORWARD**
>
> A **group** is a collection of individuals who perceive themselves as a group. It thus has a sense of **identity**.

Key term

> A **group** is any collection of people who perceive themselves to be a group.

Groups have certain attributes that a random crowd does not possess.

(a) **A sense of identity**. There are acknowledged boundaries to the group which define who is in and who is out, who is us and who is them.

(b) **Loyalty to the group,** and acceptance within the group. This generally expresses itself as conformity or the acceptance of the norms of behaviour and attitudes that bind the group together and exclude others from it.

(c) **Purpose and leadership.** Most groups have an express purpose, whatever field they are in: most will, spontaneously or formally, choose individuals or sub-groups to lead them towards the fulfilment of those goals.

2.2 Why form groups?

Any organisation is composed of many groups, with attributes of their own. People in organisations will be **drawn together into groups** by a variety of forces.

- A preference for small groups, where closer relationships can develop
- The need to belong and to make a contribution that will be noticed and appreciated
- Familiarity: a shared office or canteen
- Common rank, specialisms, objectives and interests
- The attractiveness of a particular group activity (joining an interesting club, say)
- Resources offered to groups (for example sports facilities)
- Power greater than the individuals could muster alone (trade union, pressure group)
- Formal directives

2.3 Formal and informal groups

Informal groups will invariably be present in any organisation. Informal groups include workplace cliques, and networks of people who regularly get together to exchange information, groups of 'mates' who socialise outside work and so on. They have a constantly fluctuating membership and structure.

Formal groups will be intentionally organised by the organisation, for a task which they are held responsible – they are task oriented, and become **teams**. Although many people enjoy working in teams, their popularity in the work place arises because of their effectiveness in fulfilling the organisation's work.

 Question

Small groups

What groups are you a member of in your study or work environment(s)? How big are these groups? How does the size of your class, study group, work team – or whatever:

(a)   affect your ability to come up with questions or ideas?

(b)   give you help and support to do something you couldn't do alone?

Answer

Your primary groups are probably your tutor group or class. If at work, it would be the section in which you work. If the groups are large, you may feel reluctant to put forward ideas or ask questions, but even within a large group you should feel there is support and that help is at hand if you need it.

Exam focus point

Teams and groups often come up in the exams (generally alternating with management roles or authority issues as the question from this area of the syllabus). Aspects examined so far include the distinction between teams and groups; factors in team success; Belbin's team roles and Tuckman's team development model (both the subject of the compulsory question in December 2004). Revise teambuilding (Section 6) carefully: it is another key issue.

2.4 Individual and group contribution

FAST FORWARD

People **contribute differently in groups** (due to group dynamics and synergy) than they do individually. This may have a positive or negative effect.

People contribute different skills and attributes to the organisation as individuals than they do as group members, because:

(a)   Human behaviour is different in groups than in solo or interpersonal situations: **group dynamics** have an effect on performance.

(b)   Groups offer **synergy**: 2 + 2 = 5. The pooling and stimulation of ideas and energies in a group can allow greater contribution than individuals working on their own. ('None of us is as smart as all of us', *Blanchard*.)

(c)   Group dynamics and synergy may also be **negative**: distracting the individual, stifling individual responsibility and flair and so on. Individuals may contribute more and better in some situations.

Question   Individual and group contribution

Identify some differences between your contribution as an individual to your organisation and your contribution as a team member.

Answer

Individuals contribute:	Groups contribute:

Individuals contribute:

- A set of skills
- Objectives set by manager
- A point of view
- Creative ideas related to the individual's expertise
- 'I can't be in two places at once'
- Limited opportunity for self-criticism

Groups contribute:

- A mix of skills
- Some teams can set their own objectives under the corporate framework
- A number of different points of view, enabling a swift overview of different ways of looking at a problem
- Creative ideas arising from new combinations of expertise
- Flexibility as team members can be deployed in different ways
- Opportunity for exercising control

3 Teams

> **FAST FORWARD**
>
> A **team** is more than a group. It has joint **objectives** and **accountability** and may be set up by the organisation under the supervision or coaching of a team leader, although **self-managed teams** are growing in popularity.

Key term

> A **team** is a small number of people with complementary skills who are committed to a *common purpose*, performance *goals* and approach for which they hold themselves basically accountable.
>
> *(Katzenbach and Smith)*

3.1 Strengths of team working

> **FAST FORWARD**
>
> Teamworking may be used for: **organising** work; **controlling** activities; **generating** ideas; **decision-making**; pooling **knowledge.**

Teams are particularly well-adapted to the following purposes.

Type of role	Comments
Work organisation	Teams combine the skills of different individuals.
	Teams are a co-ordinating mechanism: they avoid complex communication between different business functions.
Control	Fear of letting down the team can be a powerful motivator: team loyalty can be used to control the performance and behaviour of individuals.
Ideas generation	Teams can generate ideas, eg through brainstorming and information sharing.
Decision making	Decisions are evaluated from more than one viewpoint, with pooled information. Teams make fewer, but better-evaluated, decisions than individuals.

3.2 Limitations of team working

Problems with teams include **conflict** on the one hand, and **groupthink** (excessive cohesion) on the other.

Teams and teamworking are very much in fashion, but there are potential **drawbacks**.

- (a) Teamworking is not suitable for all jobs – although some managers do not like to admit this.

- (b) Teamwork should be introduced because it leads to better performance, not because people feel better or more secure.

- (c) Team processes (especially seeking consensus) can delay decision-making. The team may also produce the compromise decision, not the right decision.

- (d) Social relationships might be maintained at the expense of other aspects of performance.

- (e) Group norms may restrict individual personality and flair.

- (f) 'Group think' (Janis): team consensus and cohesion may prevent consideration of alternatives or constructive criticism, leading the team to make risky, ill-considered decisions.

- (g) Personality clashes and political behaviour within a team can get in the way of effective performance.

3.3 Organising team work

Multi-disciplinary teams contain people from different departments, pooling the skills of specialists.

Multi-skilled teams contain people who themselves have more than one skill.

A team may be called together temporarily, to achieve specific task objectives (**project team**), or may be more or less permanent, with responsibilities for a particular product, product group or stage of the production process (a **product or process team**).

There are two basic approaches to the organisation of team work: multi-skilled teams and multi-disciplinary teams.

3.3.1 Multi-disciplinary teams

Multi-disciplinary teams bring together individuals with different skills and specialisms, so that their skills, experience and knowledge can be pooled or exchanged.

Multi-disciplinary teams can:

- (a) Increase workers' awareness of their overall objectives and targets

- (b) Aid co-ordination between different areas of the business

- (c) Help to generate solutions to problems, and suggestions for improvements, since a multi-disciplinary team has access to more pieces of the jigsaw

3.3.2 Multi-skilled teams

A multi-skilled team brings together a number of individuals who can perform any of the group's tasks. These tasks can then be shared out in a more flexible way between group members, according to who is available and best placed to do a given job at the time it is required. Multi-skilling is the cornerstone of team empowerment, since it cuts across the barriers of job descriptions and demarcations to enable teams to respond flexibly to changing demands.

3.3.3 Virtual teams

As discussed in Chapter 1, virtual teams bring together individuals working in remote locations, reproducing the social, collaborative and information-sharing aspects of team working using Information and Communications Technology (ICT).

3.3.4 Task force teams

Peters and Waterman *(In Search of Excellence)* suggest that successful task force project teams have certain key cultural attributes.

- (a)   They should be **small**, requiring the trust of those who are not involved.

- (b)   They should be of **limited duration** and work under the 'busy member theorem': 'get off the damn task force and back to work'!

- (c)   They should be **voluntary**, which ensures that the business is 'real'.

- (d)   They should have **informal** structure and documentation: no bulky paperwork, open communication.

- (e)   They should be **action oriented**, with swift follow up of proposals and decisions.

4 Team member roles

4.1 Who should belong in the team?

Team members should be selected for their potential to contribute to getting things done (**task performance**) and establishing good working relationships (**group maintenance**). This may include:

- (a)   **Specialist skills**. A team might exist to combine expertise from different departments.

- (b)   **Power** in the wider organisation. Team members may have influence.

- (c)   **Access to resources**

- (d)   The **personalities and goals** of the individual members of the team. These will determine how the group functions.

The blend of the individual skills and abilities of its members will (ideally) **balance** the team.

4.2 Belbin: team roles   6/02

FAST FORWARD

> Ideally team members should perform a balanced mix of **roles**. **Belbin** suggests: co-ordinator, shaper, plant, monitor-evaluator, resource-investigator, implementer, team-worker, completer-finisher and specialist.

R Meredith **Belbin** (1981) researched business game teams at the Henley Management College and drew up a widely-used framework for understanding roles within work groups.

Belbin insisted that a distinction needs to be made between:

- (a)   **Team (process) role** ('a tendency to behave, contribute and interrelate with others at work in certain distinctive ways'), and

- (b)   **Functional role** ('the job demands that a person has been engaged to meet by supplying the requisite technical skills and operational knowledge')

His model of nine roles addresses the mix of team/process roles required for a fully functioning team.

BPP
PROFESSIONAL EDUCATION

4.2.1 Nine team roles

Belbin identifies nine team roles.

Role and description	Team-role contribution	Allowable weaknesses
Plant Creative, imaginative, unorthodox	Solves difficult problems	Ignores details, too preoccupied to communicate effectively
Resource investigator Extrovert, enthusiastic, communicative	Explores opportunities, develops contacts	Over-optimistic, loses interest once initial enthusiasm has passed
Co-ordinator (chairman) Mature, confident, a good chairperson	Clarifies goals, promotes decision-making, delegates well	Can be seen as manipulative, delegates personal work
Shaper Challenging, dynamic, thrives on pressure	Has the drive and courage to overcome obstacles	Can provoke others, hurts people's feelings
Monitor evaluator Sober, strategic and discerning	Sees all options, judges accurately	Lacks drive and ability to inspire others, overly critical
Team worker Co-operative, mild, perceptive and diplomatic	Listens, builds, averts friction, calms the waters	Indecisive in crunch situations, can be easily influenced
Implementer (company worker) Disciplined, reliable, conservative and efficient	Turns ideas into practical actions	Somewhat inflexible, slow to respond to new possibilities
Completer – Finisher Painstaking, conscientious, anxious	Searches out errors and omissions, delivers on time	Inclined to worry unduly, reluctant to delegate, can be a nitpicker
Specialist Single-minded, self-starting, dedicated	Provides knowledge and skills in rare supply	Contributes only on a narrow front, dwells on technicalities, overlooks the 'big picture'

4.2.2 A balanced team

These team roles are not fixed within any given individual. Team members can occupy more than one role, or switch to 'backup' roles if required: hence, there is no requirement for every team to have nine members. However, since role preferences are based on personality, it should be recognised that:

- Individuals will be naturally inclined towards some roles more than others
- Individuals will tend to adopt one or two team roles more or less consistently
- Individuals are likely to be more successful in some roles than in others

The nine roles are complementary, and Belbin suggested that an 'ideal' team should represent a mix or balance of all of them. If managers know employees' team role preferences, they can strategically select, 'cast' and develop team members to fulfil the required roles.

Question

The following phrases and slogans project certain team roles: identify which. (Examples are drawn from Belbin, 1993.)

(a)   The small print is always worth reading.
(b)   Let's get down to the task in hand.
(c)   In this job you never stop learning.
(d)   Without continuous innovation, there is no survival.
(e)   Surely we can exploit that?
(f)   When the going gets tough, the tough get going.
(g)   I was very interested in your point of view.
(h)   Has anyone else got anything to add to this?
(i)   Decisions should not be based purely on enthusiasm.

Answer

(a)   Completer – finisher
(b)   Implementer/company worker
(c)   Specialist
(d)   Plant
(e)   Resource investigator
(f)   Shaper
(g)   Teamworker
(h)   Co-ordinator/Chairman
(i)   Monitor evaluator

4.3 How do people contribute?

FAST FORWARD

Team members make different types of **contribution** (eg proposing, supporting, blocking) in the areas of **task performance** and **team maintenance**.

In order to evaluate and manage team dynamics, it may be helpful for the team leader to:

(a)   Assess who (if anybody) is performing each of Belbin's **team roles**. Who is the team's plant? monitor-evaluator? and so on. There should be a mix of people performing task and team maintenance roles.

(b)   Analyse the **frequency and type of individual members' contributions** to group discussions and interactions.

   (i)   Identify which members of the team habitually make the most contributions, and which the least. (You could do this by taking a count of contributions from each member, during a sample 10-15 minutes of group discussion.)

   (ii)   If the same people tend to dominate discussion *whatever* is discussed (ie regardless of relevant expertise), the team has a problem in its communication process.

Neil Rackham and Terry Morgan have developed a helpful categorisation of the types of contribution people can make to team discussion and decision-making, including the following.

Category	Behaviour	Example
Proposing	Putting forward suggestions, new concepts or courses of action	'Why don't we look at a flexi-time system?'
Supporting	Supporting another person or his/her proposal.	'Yes, I agree, flexi-time would be worth looking at.'
Seeking information	Asking for more facts, opinions or clarification.	'What exactly do you mean by "flexi-time"?'
Giving information	Offering facts, opinions or clarification.	'There's a helpful outline of flexi-time in this article.'
Blocking/ difficulty stating	Putting obstacles in the way of a proposal, without offering any alternatives.	'What if the other teams get jealous? It would only cause conflict.'
Shutting-out behaviour	Interrupting or overriding others; taking over.	'Nonsense. Let's move onto something else – we've had enough of this discussion.
Bringing-in behaviour	Involving another member; encouraging contribution.	'Actually, I'd like to hear what Fred has to say. Go on, Fred.'
Testing understanding	Checking whether points have been understood.	'So flexi-time could work over a day or a week; have I got that right?'
Summarising	Drawing together or summing up previous discussion.	'We've now heard two sides to the flexi-time issue: on the one hand, flexibility; on the other side possible risk. Now … '

Each type of behaviour may be appropriate in the right situation at the right time. A team may be low on some types of contribution – and it may be up to the team leader to encourage, or deliberately adopt, desirable behaviours (such as bringing-in, supporting or seeking information) in order to provide balance.

4.4 Team communication patterns 12/03

4.4.1 Basic patterns

In a well-known laboratory test, **Leavitt** (1951) examined the effectiveness of different communication patterns between members of a small group.

(a)   The **circle**: each member could communicate with only two others in the information 'loop'.

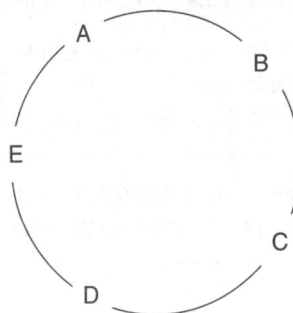

(b)   The **chain**:

A ——— B ——— C ——— D ——— E

(c)   The **Y**: one individual co-ordinates some of the communication within the group.

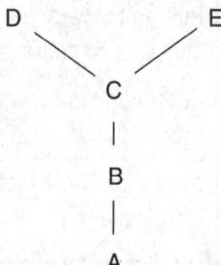

(d)   The **wheel**: one individual acts as a central hub for all communications.

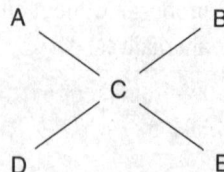

The experiment found that in **speed of problem-solving**, the wheel was fastest and the circle slowest (thanks to the co-ordinating, facilitating function of the 'hub' of the wheel).

4.4.2 All-channel communication

Shaw (1978) added an **'all-channel'** pattern, in which all members could communicate with each other.

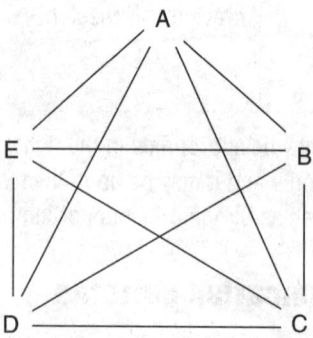

While slower than the circle for simple problem solving, the All-Channel pattern provided the best solutions to complex problems (because of its information-pooling style). It also provides fairly high group member satisfaction (because of the opportunity to share leadership) compared to the other systems. Under pressure, however, the All-Channel pattern tends to disintegrate – or a communication hub (group leader) emerges and the pattern becomes a wheel.

Bear in mind that these are only laboratory experiments. The communication was in *writing* only, and groups had to stick to specific patterns: in practice, and with the complexity of oral, face-to-face communication, the dynamics are likely to be more fluid.

Exam focus point

These communication patterns were tested as part of a communication question in the December 2003 exam, which indicates the level of detail (and theoretical knowledge) the examiner may be interested in!

5 Team development

6/03, 12/04

You probably have had experience of being put into a group of people you do not know. Many teams are set up this way and it takes some time for the team to become effective.

FAST FORWARD

A team develops in **stages**: forming, storming, norming, performing (**Tuckman**) and dorming or mourning/adjourning.

5.1 Tuckman's stages of group development

Four stages in group development were identified by **Tuckman** (1965).

Step 1   **Forming**

The team is just coming together. Each member wishes to impress his or her personality on the group. The individuals will be trying to find out about each other, and about the aims and norms of the team. There will at this stage probably be a wariness about introducing new ideas. The objectives being pursued may as yet be unclear and a leader may not yet have emerged.

Step 2   **Storming**

This frequently involves more or less open conflict between team members. There may be changes agreed in the original objectives, procedures and norms established for the group. If the team is developing successfully this may be a fruitful phase, as more realistic targets are set and trust between the group members increases.

Step 3   **Norming**

A period of settling down: there will be agreements about work sharing, individual requirements and expectations of output. Norms and procedures may evolve which enable methodical working to be introduced and maintained.

Step 4   **Performing**

The team sets to work to execute its task. The difficulties of growth and development no longer hinder the group's objectives.

Later writers added two stages to Tuckman's model.

(a)   **Dorming**. Once a group has been performing well for some time, it may get complacent, and fall back into self-maintenance functions, at the expense of the task.

(b)   **Mourning/adjourning**. The group sees itself as having fulfilled its purpose – or, if it is a temporary group, is due to physically disband. This is a stage of confusion, sadness and anxiety as the group breaks up. There is evaluation of its achievements, and gradual withdrawal of group members. If the group is to continue, going on to a new task, there will be a re-negotiation of aims and roles: a return to the forming stage.

Exam focus point

A full 15-mark essay question was set on Tuckman's model in the June 2003 exam, and Tuckman and Belbin were the focus of the 40-mark question in December 2004. Worth getting to grips with these major models: the examiner often uses them to test candidates' preparation – as you can't get by with 'common sense' in such a question!

Note also that the Section A 'teams' question in December 2004 followed an article on the topic by the examiner, in October's *Student Accountant*! This has been a pattern in recent years: take the hint!

Read the following descriptions of team behaviour and decide to which category they belong (forming, storming, norming, performing, dorming).

(a)   Two of the group arguing as to whose idea is best
(b)   Progress becomes static
(c)   Desired outputs being achieved
(d)   Shy member of group not participating
(e)   Activities being allocated

Answer

Categorising the behaviour of group members in the situations described results in the following: (a) storming, (b) dorming, (c) performing, (d) forming, (e) norming.

6 Building a team

In Section 5, we suggested that teams have a natural evolutionary life cycle, and that four stages can be identified. Not all teams develop into mature teams and might be stuck, stagnating, in any one of the stages.

So, it often falls to the supervisor or manager to build the team. There are three main issues involved in team building.

Issues	Comments
Team identity	Get people to see themselves as part of this group
Team solidarity	Encourage loyalty so that members put in extra effort for the sake of the team
Shared objectives	Encourage the team to commit itself to shared work objectives and to co-operate willingly and effectively in achieving them.

FAST FORWARD

Team development can be facilitated by active **team building** measures to support team identity, solidarity and commitment to shared objectives.

6.1 Team 'building blocks'

Woodcock refers to blockages and building blocks in the team building process. Adapted, these are as follows.

Issue	Blockage	Building block
Leadership	Inappropriate	The leader can adopt a suitable leadership style (See Chapter 10)
Membership	Insufficient mix of skills and personalities	Ensure team members are suitably qualified; if necessary, get them to adopt another role than what they would normally
Climate	Unconstructive	Strive to achieve an atmosphere of co-operation
Objectives	Not clear	The team has been brought together for some organisational purpose, so this can be clarified and developed into sub-objectives which are agreed
Achievement	Poor achievement	Performance is improved in a climate of trust and learning
Work methods	Ineffective	Develop sensible procedures for carrying out the team's business
Communications	Not open; people are afraid to challenge or confront key issues	Develop a climate in which people can speak their minds, constructively
Individuals	Development needs not attended to	Individuals are given opportunities to grow or develop within the team; easier in multi-skilled teams
Creativity	Low	Techniques such as brainstorming can enhance creativity, but a lot depends on how new ideas are treated
Interpersonal relations	Poor and unconstructive	Some people will never get on or have much in common, but they can still work together effectively. Exercises might be needed to break the ice
Review and control	Non-existent	The performance of the team can be reviewed at regular intervals

We can now discuss some of the techniques for building team identity, team solidarity and the commitment to shared-objectives. But first try the question below.

Question

Why might the following be effective as team-building exercises?

(a)   Sending a project team (involved in the design of electronic systems for racing cars) on a recreational day out karting

(b)   Sending two sales teams on a day out playing 'War Games', each being an opposing combat team trying to capture the other's flag, armed with paint guns

(c)   Sending a project team on a conference at a venue away from work, with a brief to review the past year and come up with a vision for the next year

(These are actually commonly-used techniques. If you are interested, you might locate an activity centre or company near you which offers outdoor pursuits, war games or corporate entertainment and ask them about team-building exercises and the effect they have on people.)

Answer

(a)   Recreation helps the team to build informal relationships: in this case, the chosen activity also reminds them of their tasks, and may make them feel special, as part of the motor racing industry, by giving them a taste of what the end user of their product does.

(b)   A team challenge forces the group to consider its strengths and weaknesses, to find its natural leader. This exercise creates an 'us' and 'them' challenge: perceiving the rival team as the enemy heightens the solidarity of the group.

(c)   This exercise encourages the group to raise problems and conflicts freely, away from the normal environment of work and also encourages brainstorming and the expression of team members' dreams for what the team can achieve in the future.

6.2 Team identity

A manager might seek to reinforce the sense of identity of the group. Arguably this is in part the creation of boundaries, identifying who is in the team and who is not.

(a)   **Name**. Staff at McDonald's restaurants are known as the Crew. In other cases, the name would be more official describing what the team actually does (eg Systems Implementation Task Force)

(b)   **Badge or uniform**. This often applies to service industries, but it is unlikely that it would be applied within an organisation

(c)   Expressing the team's **self-image:** teams often develop their own jargon, especially for new projects

(d)   Building a team **mythology** – in other words, stories from the past ('classic mistakes' as well as successes)

(e)   **A separate space**: it might help if team members work together in the same or adjacent offices, but this is not always possible

6.3 Team solidarity

Team solidarity implies cohesion and loyalty inside the team. A team leader might be interested in:

(a) **Expressing** solidarity

(b) Encouraging **interpersonal relationships** – although the purpose of these is to ensure that work does get done

(c) Dealing with **conflict** by getting it out into the open; disagreements should be expressed and then resolved

(d) **Controlling competition**. The team leader needs to treat each member of the team fairly and to be seen to do so; favouritism undermines solidarity.

(e) Encouraging some **competition with other groups**, if appropriate. For example, sales teams might be offered a prize for the highest monthly orders; London Underground runs best-kept station competitions.

Question

Group cohesion

Can you see any dangers in creating a very close-knit group? Think of the effect of strong team cohesion on:

(a) What the group spends its energies and attention on
(b) How the group regards outsiders, and any information or feedback they supply
(c) How the group makes decisions

What could be done about these dangerous effects?

Answer

Problems may arise in an ultra close-knit group because:

(a) The group's energies may be focused on its own maintenance and relationships, instead of on the task.

(b) The group may be suspicious or dismissive of outsiders, and may reject any contradictory information or criticism they supply; the group will be blinkered and stick to its own views, no matter what; cohesive groups thus often get the impression that they are infallible: they can't be wrong – and therefore can't learn from their mistakes.

(c) The group may squash any dissent or opinions that might rock the boat. Close-knit groups tend to preserve a consensus – falsely, if required – and to take risky decisions, because they have suppressed alternative facts and viewpoints.

This phenomenon is called '**groupthink**' (Janis). In order to limit its effect, the team must be encouraged:

(a) Actively to seek outside ideas and feedback
(b) To welcome self-criticism within the group, and
(c) Consciously to evaluate conflicting evidence and opinions

81

6.4 Commitment to shared objectives

Getting commitment to the team's shared objectives may involve a range of leader activity.

- Clearly setting out the objectives of the team

- Allowing the team to participate in setting objectives

- Giving regular feedback on progress and results with constructive criticism

- Getting the team involved in providing performance feedback

- Offering positive reinforcement (praise etc) for co-operative working and task achievement by the team as a whole (rather than just 'star' individuals)

- Championing the success of the team within the organisation

7 Successful teams

A team can be evaluated on the basis of quantifiable and qualitative factors, covering its **operations** and its **output**, and team member **satisfaction**.

7.1 Evaluating team effectiveness

The task of the team leader is to build a 'successful' or 'effective' team. The criteria for team effectiveness include:

(a) **Task performance**: fulfilment of task and organisational goals

(b) **Team functioning**: constructive maintenance of team working, managing the demands of team dynamics, roles and processes, *and*

(c) **Team member satisfaction**: fulfilment of individual development and relationship needs.

There are a number of factors, both quantitative and qualitative, that may be assessed to decide whether or how far a team is operating effectively. Some factors cannot be taken as evidence on their own, but may suggest underlying problems: accident rates may be due to poor safety systems, for example – but may also suggest poor morale and lack of focus due to team problems.

Some of the characteristics of effective and ineffective teams may be summarised as follows.

Factor	Effective team	Ineffective team
Quantifiable		
Labour turnover	Low	High
Accident rate	Low	High
Absenteeism	Low	High
Output and productivity	High	Low
Quality of output	High	Low
Individual targets	Achieved	Not achieved
Stoppages and interruptions to the work flow	Low	High (eg because of misunderstandings, disagreements)
Qualitative		
Commitment to targets and organisational goals	High	Low
Understanding of team's work and why it exists	High	Low
Understanding of individual roles within the team	High	Low
Communication between team members	Free and open	Mistrust
Ideas	Shared for the team's benefit	'Owned' (and hidden) by individuals for their own benefit
Feedback	Constructive criticism	Point scoring, undermining
Problem-solving	Addresses causes	Only looks at symptoms
Interest in work decisions	Active	Passive acceptance
Opinions	Consensus	Imposed solutions
Job satisfaction	High	Low
Motivation in leader's absence	High	'When the cat's away…'

7.2 Rewarding effective teams

FAST FORWARD

Team-based rewards may be used to encourage co-operation and mutual accountability.

Organisations may try to encourage effective team performance by designing reward systems that recognise team, rather than individual success. Indeed, individual performance rewards may act *against* team co-operation and performance.

(a) They emphasise individual rather than team performance.

(b) They encourage team leaders to think of team members only as individuals, rather than relating to them as a team.

For **team rewards** to be effective, the team must have certain characteristics.

- Distinct roles, targets and performance measures (so the team knows what it has to do to earn the reward)

- Significant autonomy and thus influence over performance (so the team perceives that extra effort will be rewarded)

- Maturity and stability

- Co-operation

- Interdependence of team members (so that the team manages member contribution, everyone 'pulls their weight', no-one feels they could earn higher rewards on their own)

Reward schemes which focus on team (or organisation) performance include:

(a) **Profit sharing** schemes, based on the distribution of a pool of cash related to profit

(b) **Gainsharing** schemes, using a formula related to a suitable performance indicator, such as added value. Improvements in the performance indicator must be perceived to be within the employees' control, otherwise there will be no incentive to perform.

(c) **Employee share option** schemes, giving staff the right to acquire shares in the employing company at an attractive price

We cover these in more detail in Chapter 13.

Chapter Roundup

- **Personality** is the total pattern of an individual's thoughts, feelings and behaviours. It is shaped by a variety of factors, both inherited and environmental.

- **Perception** is the process by which the brain selects and organises information in order to make sense of it. People behave according to what they perceive – not according to what really is.

- People develop **attitudes** about things, based on what they think, what they feel and what they want to do about it. Attitudes are formed by perception, experience and personality which in turn are shaped by wider social influences.

- **Role theory** suggests that people behave in any situation according to other people's expectations of how they should behave in that situation.

- A **group** is a collection of individuals who perceive themselves as a group. It thus has a sense of **identity**.

- People **contribute differently in groups** (due to group dynamics and synergy) than they do individually. This may have a positive or negative effect.

- A **team** is more than a group. It has joint **objectives** and **accountability** and may be set up by the organisation under the supervision or coaching of a team leader, although **self-managed teams** are growing in popularity.

- Teamworking may be used for: **organising** work; **controlling** activities; **generating** ideas; **decision-making**; pooling **knowledge.**

- Problems with teams include **conflict** on the one hand, and **group think** (excessive cohesion) on the other.

- **Multi-disciplinary** teams contain people from different departments, pooling the skills of specialists.

- **Multi-skilled** teams contain people who themselves have more than one skill.

- Ideally team members should perform a balanced mix of **roles**. **Belbin** suggests: co-ordinator, shaper, plant, monitor-evaluator, resource-investigator, implementer, team-worker, completer-finisher and specialist.

- Team members make different types of **contribution** (eg proposing, supporting, blocking) in the areas of **task performance** and **team maintenance**.

- A team develops in **stages**: forming, storming, norming, performing (**Tuckman**) and dorming or mourning/adjourning.

- Team development can be facilitated by active **team building** measures to support team identity, solidarity and commitment to shared objectives.

- A team can be evaluated on the basis of quantifiable and qualitative factors, covering its **operations** and its **output**, and team member **satisfaction**.

- **Team-based rewards** may be used to encourage co-operation and mutual accountability.

Quick Quiz

1   List three factors for a manager to consider in managing 'personality' at work.

2   Give three examples of areas where people's perceptions commonly conflict.

3   What is a team?

4   List Belbin's nine roles for a well-rounded team.

5   Who described the stages of group development?

    A   Woodcock
    B   Belbin
    C   Tuckman
    D   Rackham and Morgan

6   List the teambuilding issues identified by Woodcock.

7   Suggest five ways in which a manager can get a team 'behind' task objectives.

8   List six of Rackham and Morgan's categories of contribution to group discussion.

9   High labour turnover is a characteristic of effective teams. *True or false?*

Answers to Quick Quiz

1   The compatibility of an individual's personality with the task, with the systems and culture of the organisation and with other members of the team.

2   Managers and staff, work culture, race and gender.

3   A small number of people with complementary skills who are committed to a common purpose, performance goals and approach for which they hold themselves basically accountable.

4   Co-ordinator (or chairman), shaper, plant, monitor-evaluator, resource-investigator, implementer (or company worker), team worker, completer-finisher, specialist.

5   C: Tuckman. You should be able to identify the team-relevant theories of Woodcock and Belbin and Rackham and Morgan as well.

6   Leaders, Members, Climate, Objectives, Achievement, Work methods, Communications, Individuals, Creativity, Interpersonal communications, Review and control.

7   Set clear objectives, get the team to set targets/standard, provide information and resources, give feedback, praise and reward, and champion the team in the organisation.

8   Proposing, building, supporting, seeking information, giving information, disagreeing.

9   False.

Now try the question below from the Exam Question Bank

Number	Level	Marks	Time
Q4	Examination	15	27 mins

Authority, power and delegation

Topic list	Syllabus reference
1 Power and authority	1 (g)
2 Responsibility and accountability	1 (g)
3 Delegation	1 (g)
4 Empowerment	1 (g)

Introduction

This is a straightforward but crucial chapter. The structure of the organisation (Chapter 1) and the role of management (Chapter 2) are both defined by how authority is distributed and used.

In **Section 1**, we look at **power** and **authority**: the source of a manager's right to make decisions and expect them to be carried out.

In **Section 2**, we look at the other side of that coin: **responsibility**, whereby the manager is liable to be held to account for the decisions (s)he has made.

In **Section 3**, we look at how authority 'flows' down from the top of the organisation, via **delegation.** This is a highly practical matter of how managers give tasks to their subordinates – and why they often don't!

Finally, we look at **empowerment**: the trend towards giving more authority and responsibility to lower levels of the organisation.

Study guide

Section 7 – Authority, responsibility and delegation

- Define the items authority, responsibility and delegation
- Explain the term legitimised power: Weber
- Describe the process of determining authority and responsibility
- Examine the case of responsibility without authority

Exam guide

This is an important topic because power and authority are features of all organisations. A specific question was set on this area in the June 2002 exam. Ensure that you can distinguish clearly between the various terms: this is perhaps the major potential pitfall.

1 Power and authority

Organisations have a large number of different activities to be co-ordinated, and large numbers of people whose co-operation and support is necessary for a manager to get anything done. As you have probably noticed if you have worked for any length of time, organisations rarely run as clockwork, and all depend on the directed energy of those within them.

1.1 Power

FAST FORWARD

> **Power** is the ability to get things done. There are many types of power in organisations: position or **legitimate power**, expert power, personal power, resource power and negative power are examples.

Key term

Power is the **ability** to get things done.

Power is not something a person 'has' in isolation: it is exercised over other individuals or groups, and – to an extent – depends on their *recognising* the person's power over them.

1.1.1 Types of power

French and Raven (followed by Charles Handy) classified power into six types or sources.

Type of power	Description
Coercive power	The power of physical force or punishment. Physical power is rare in business organisations, but intimidation may feature, eg in workplace bullying.
Reward (or resource) power	Based on access to or control over valued resources. For example, managers have access to information, contacts and financial rewards for team members. The amount of resource power a person has depends on the scarcity of the resource, how much the resource is valued by others, and how far the resource is under the manager's control.
Legitimate (or position) power	Associated with a particular position in the organisation. For example, a manager has the power to authorise certain expenses, or issue instructions, because the authority to do so has been formally delegated to her. (In Chapter 1, Section 6, we looked at Weber's definition of legitimate authority; note that this is slightly different.)

BPP
PROFESSIONAL EDUCATION

Type of power	Description
Expert power	Based on experience, qualifications or expertise. For example, accountants have expert power because of their knowledge of the tax system. Expert power depends on others recognising the expertise in an area which they need or value.
Referent (or personal) power	Based on force of personality, or 'charisma', which can attract, influence or inspire other people.
Negative power (*Handy*)	The power to disrupt operations: for example, by industrial action, refusal to communicate information, or sabotage.

1.2 Authority   6/02

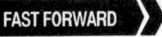

> **Authority** is related to position power. It is the right to take certain decisions within certain boundaries.

Key term

> **Authority** is the **right** to do something, or to ask someone else to do it and expect it to be done. Authority is thus another word for position or legitimate power.

Managerial authority is exercised in such areas as:

(a) **Making decisions within the scope of authority** given to the position. For example, a supervisor's authority is limited to his/her team and with certain limits. For items of expenditure more than a certain amount, the supervisor may have to go to someone else up the hierarchy.

(b) **Assigning tasks** to subordinates, and expecting satisfactory performance of these tasks.

Question   Types of power

What types of power are being exercised in the following case?

Marcus is an accountant supervising a team of eight technicians. He has to submit bank reconciliation statements every week to the chief accountant. However, the company runs four different bank accounts and Marcus gets a team member, Dave, to do it for him. Marcus asks Isabella to deal with the purchase ledger – the company obtains supplies from all over the world, and Isabella, having worked once for an international bank, is familiar with letters of credit and other documentation involved with overseas trade. Isabella has recently told Marcus that Maphia Ltd, a supplier, should not be paid because of problems with the import documentation, even though Marcus has promised Maphia to pay them. Marcus is getting increasingly annoyed with Sandra, who seems to be leaving his typing until last, although she says she has piles of other work to do. 'Like reading the newspaper,' thinks Marcus, who is considering pulling rank by giving her an oral warning.

Answer

Marcus exercises position power because he has the right, given to him by the chief accountant, to get staff members, such as Dave, to do bank reconciliations. Dave does not do bank recs because of Marcus's personality or expertise, but because of the simple fact that Marcus is his boss. Marcus also exercises position power by getting Isabella to do the purchase ledger. However, Isabella exercises expert power because she knows more about import/export documentation than Marcus. She does not have the authority to stop the payment to Maphia, and Marcus can ignore what she says, but that would be a bad decision. Sandra is exercising negative power as far as Marcus is concerned, although she is claiming, perhaps, to exercise resource power – her time is a scarce resource.

1.2.1 Line and staff authority

When analysing the types of authority which a manager or a department may have, the terms **line**, **staff** and **functional authority** are often used.

Key terms

> **Line authority** is the authority a manager has over a subordinate, down the vertical chain (or line) of command.
>
> **Staff authority** is the authority one manager or department may have in giving specialist advice to another manager or department, over which there is no line authority. Staff authority does not entail the right to make or influence decisions in the advisee department. An example might be the HR department advising the Accounts Manager on selection interviewing methods.
>
> **Functional authority** is a hybrid of line and staff authority, whereby the technostructure manager or department has the authority, in certain circumstances, to direct, design or control activities or procedures of another department. An example is where a finance manager has authority to require timely reports from line managers.

Question

Line and staff authority

What sort of authority is exercised:

(a)   by the financial controller over the chief accountant?
(b)   by the production manager over the production workforce?
(c)   by the financial controller over the production manager?

Answer

(a) and (b) are both examples of line authority.
(c) is staff or perhaps functional authority.

There are inevitable tensions involved in asserting staff authority.

Problem	Possible solution
The technostructure can **undermine** the **line managers'** authority, by empire building.	Clear demarcations of line, staff and functional authority should be created.
Lack of seniority: middle line managers may be more senior in the hierarchy than technostructure advisers.	Use functional authority (via policies and procedures). Experts should be seen as a resource, not a threat.
Expert managers may **lack realism**, going for technically perfect, but commercially impractical solutions.	Technostructure planners should be fully aware of operational issues and communicate regularly with the middle line.
Technostructure experts **lack responsibility** for the success of their ideas.	Technostructure experts should be involved in implementing their suggestions and share accountability for outcomes.

2 Responsibility and accountability

2.1 Responsibility

Responsibility is the obligation a person has to fulfil a task (s)he has been given. Responsibility can be delegated, but the person delegating responsibility still remains accountable to his or her boss for completion of the task.

Key terms

Responsibility is the **obligation** a person has to fulfil a task, which (s)he has been given.

Accountability is a person's **liability** to be called to account for the fulfilment of tasks they have been given.

The definitions given above are useful because the term 'responsibility' is used in two ways.

(a) A person is said to be responsible *for* a piece of work when he or she is required to ensure that the work is done.

(b) The same person is said to be responsible *to* a superior when he or she is given work by that superior: in this sense, the term 'accountable' is often used.

One is thus accountable *to* a superior *for* a piece of work for which one is responsible.

The principle of **delegation** (which we discuss in the next section) is that a manager may make subordinates **responsible for** work, but remains **accountable to** his or her own superior for ensuring that the work is done. Appropriate decision-making **authority** must be delegated alongside the delegated responsibility.

2.2 Responsibility authority mismatch

Authority/responsibility mismatch or **ambiguity** is stressful for the individual.

In practice, matters are rarely clear-cut, and in many organisations responsibility and authority are:

	Comments
Not clear	When the organisation is doing something new or in a different way, its existing rules and procedures may be out of date or unable to cope with the new development. Various people may try to 'empire build'. The managers may not have designed the organisation very well.
Shifting	In large organisations there may be real conflict between different departments; or the organisation may, as it adapts to its environment, need to change.

Authority without responsibility is a recipe for arbitrary and irresponsible behaviour: the person has the right to make decisions – without being held accountable for them.

Responsibility without authority places a subordinate in an impossible and stressful position: (s)he is held accountable for results over which (s)he has no control.

Question   Responsibility and authority

You have just joined a small accounts department. The financial controller keeps a very close eye on expenditure and, being prudent, believes that nothing should be spent that is not strictly necessary. She has recently gone on a three week holiday to Venezuela. You have been told that you need to prepare management accounts, and for this you have to obtain information from the payroll department in two weeks' time. This is standard procedure. However, there are two problems. One of the other people in your department has gone sick, and a temporary replacement will be needed very shortly. The personnel department say: 'We need a staff requisition from the Financial Controller before we can get in a temp. Sorry, you'll just have to cancel your weekend'. The payroll department is happy to give you the information you need – except directors' salaries, essential for the accounts to be truly accurate.

What is the underlying cause of the problem and what, in future, should you ask the Financial Controller to do to put it right?

Answer

The immediate problem is that the Financial Controller should have considered these issues before she went to Venezuela. The underlying cause, as far as you are concerned, is that you have responsibility to do a task but without the authority – to obtain all the information you need and to hire a temp – to do the job. In future the Financial Controller should, when delegating the task, delegate the authority to do it.

3 Delegation   6/02

Key term

> **Delegation** of authority is the process whereby a superior gives to a subordinate part of his or her own authority to make decisions.

Note that delegation can only occur if the superior initially possesses the authority to delegate; a subordinate cannot be given organisational authority to make decisions unless it would otherwise be the superior's right to make those decisions.

3.1 Why delegate?

FAST FORWARD

> **Delegation** is necessary for division of labour and technical/managerial specialisation.

Managers must delegate some authority for three reasons.

(a)   There are **physical and mental limitations** to the work load of any individual or group in authority.

(b)   Managers need time to concentrate on **higher-level tasks** (such as planning), which only they are competent (and paid) to do.

(c)   The **increasing size and complexity** of some organisations calls for specialisation, both managerial and technical.

(d)   Delegated authority contributes to the job satisfaction and development of ??? levels of employees.

However, by delegating authority to assistants, the manager takes on two extra tasks:

- **Monitoring** their performance
- **Co-ordinating** the efforts of different assistants.

3.2 How to delegate

FAST FORWARD

> **Successful delegation** requires that people have the right skills and the authority to do the job, and are given feedback.

The process of delegation can be outlined as follows.

Step 1   **Specify performance:** the goals and standards expected of the subordinate, keeping in mind his or her level of expertise

Step 2   **Formally assign tasks** to the subordinate, who should formally agree to do them

Step 3   **Allocate resources and authority** to the subordinate to enable him or her to carry out the delegated tasks at the expected level of performance

Step 4   **Back off** and allow the subordinate to perform the delegated tasks

Step 5   **Maintain contact,** to review progress made, make constructive criticism and be available to give help and advice if requested

3.3 When to delegate

The decision of when to delegate is equally important.

(a) Is the acceptance of staff affected required for morale, relationships or ease of implementation of the decision? (If so, it may be worth involving them in the decision.)

(b) Is the quality of the decision most important? (Many technical financial decisions may be of this type, and should be retained by the manager if he or she alone has the knowledge and experience to make them.)

(c) Is the expertise or experience of assistants relevant or necessary to the task, and will it enhance the quality of the decision? (If so, it may be worth involving them in the decision.)

(d) Can trust be placed in the competence and reliability of the assistants? (If not, it will be difficult to delegate effectively.)

3.4 Upward delegation

In instances where **reference upwards** to the manager's own superior (upward delegation) may be necessary, the manager should consider:

(a) Whether the decision is relevant to the superior: will it have any impact on the boss's area of responsibility, such as strategy, staffing, or the departmental budget?

(b) Whether the superior has authority or information relevant to the decision that the manager does not possess: for example, authority over issues which affect other departments or interdepartmental relations, or information only available at senior levels.

(c) The political climate of the organisation: will the superior expect to be consulted, and resent any attempt to make the decision without his authority?

Exam focus point

> An exam question in June 2002 covered authority, responsibility and delegation. Surprisingly, a major pitfall in this topic is being able to distinguish accurately between the three terms: make sure you can do so. You should also be able to outline important practical considerations, such as *how* to delegate effectively, and what might happen if there is a mismatch between authority, power and responsibility.

3.5 Problems of delegation

FAST FORWARD   Successful delegation requires skill training, cultural support and resolution of the **'trust-control' dilemma**.

Many managers are **reluctant to delegate** and attempt to handle many routine matters themselves in addition to their higher-level tasks, because of:

(a)   **Low confidence and trust** in the abilities of their staff: the suspicion that 'if you want it done well, you have to do it yourself'.

(b)   The burden of **accountability for the mistakes of subordinates**, aggravated by (a) above.

(c)   A **desire to 'stay in touch'** with the department or team – both in terms of workload and staff – particularly if the manager does not feel 'at home' in a management role.

(d)   **Feeling threatened.** An unwillingness to admit that assistants have developed to the extent that they could perform some of the manager's duties. The manager may feel threatened by this sense of 'redundancy'.

(e)   **Poor control and communication systems** in the organisation, so that the manager feels he has to do everything himself, if he is to retain real control and responsibility for a task, and if he wants to know what is going on.

(f)   An **organisational culture** that has failed to reward or recognise effective delegation, so that the manager may not realise that delegation is positively regarded (rather than being seen as shirking responsibility).

(g)   **Lack of understanding** of what delegation involves – ie *not* giving assistants total control, or making the manager himself redundant.

(h)   **Lack of training** and development of managers in delegation skills and related areas (such as assertiveness and time management).

Handy (1993) describes a **trust-control dilemma** in a superior-subordinate relationship as:

$T + C = Y$

where   T   =   the trust the superior has in the subordinate, and the trust which the subordinate feels the superior has in him

C   =   the degree of control exercised by the superior over the subordinate

Y   =   a constant, unchanging value.

The less the superior feels able to trust the subordinate, the more control (s)he will exercise. The more trustworthy the subordinate, the less control will be needed.

3.6 Overcoming the reluctance of managers to delegate

Encouraging managers to delegate therefore partly involves increasing trust.

(a)   **Train the subordinates** so that they are capable of handling delegated authority in a responsible way.

(b)   Have a system of **open communications** between the manager and subordinates. If the subordinate is given all the information needed to do the job, and if the manager is kept informed of progress or problems:

(i)   The subordinate will make better-informed decisions.
(ii)   The manager will not need to exercise constant close control.

(c)   **Ensure that a system of control is established**. If responsibility and accountability are monitored at all levels of the management hierarchy, the risks of relinquishing authority and control to subordinates are significantly lessened.

In addition, managers should be trained (or coached by their own superiors) in delegation skills, and should be recognised and rewarded for positive and effective delegation.

Question |

You are the manager of an accounts section of your organisation and have stopped to talk to one of the clerks in the office to see what progress he is making. He complains bitterly that he is not learning anything. He gets only routine work to do and it is the same routine. He has not even been given the chance to swap jobs with someone else. You have picked up the same message from others in the office. You discuss the situation with Jean Howe, the recently appointed supervisor of the section. She appears to be very busy and harassed. When confronted with your observations she says that she is fed up with the job. She is worked off her feet, comes early, goes late, takes work home and gets criticised behind her back by incompetent clerks.

What has gone wrong? What will you do about it?

Answer

The problem appears to be that the new supervisor is taking too much of the department's work on to herself. While she is overworked, her subordinates are apparently not being stretched and as a result motivation and morale amongst them are poor. The supervisor herself is unhappy with the position and there is a danger that declining job satisfaction will lead to inefficiencies and eventually staff resignations.

There could be a number of causes contributing to the problem.

(a)   Jean Howe may have been badly selected, ie she may not have the ability required for a supervisory job.

(b)   She may be unaware that the supervisor's role includes managing subordinates; she is not required to shoulder all the detailed technical work herself.

(c)   Jean Howe regards her clerks as incompetent: this attitude may arise from interpersonal hostility. (Another possibility is that her staff actually are incompetent.)

(d)   Jean may not understand delegation: what or how to delegate, or how delegation can improve the motivation and job satisfaction of subordinates.

As manager, you have already gone some way towards identifying the actual causes of the problem: you have spoken to Jean and some of the subordinates. You could supplement this by a review of personnel records, to discover how Jean's career has progressed so far and what training she had received (if any) in the duties of a supervisor. You may then be in a position to determine which of the possible causes of the problems are operating in this case.

4 Empowerment

Empowerment takes the process of delegation further. Its advantages are not simply that it releases managers to do more important things, but that front line staff closest to customers are able to take decisions concerning them.

Empowerment and delegation are related.

Key term

> **Empowerment** is the current term for making workers (and particularly work teams) responsible for achieving, and even setting, work targets, with the freedom to make decisions about how they are to be achieved.

4.1 The context of empowerment

Empowerment goes in hand in hand with:

(a) **Delayering**, or cutting the number of levels (and managers) in the chain of command, since responsibility previously held by middle managers is, in effect, being given to operational workers.

(b) **Flexibility**, since giving responsibility to the people closest to the products and customer encourages responsiveness – and cutting out layers of communication, decision-making and reporting speeds up the process.

(c) **New technology**, since there are more 'knowledge workers'. Such people need less supervision, being better able to identify and control the means to clearly understood ends. Better information systems also remove the mystique and power of managers as possessors of knowledge and information in the organisation.

4.2 The effects of empowerment

The change in organisation structure and culture as a result of empowerment can be shown in the diagram below.

Traditional hierarchical structure: fulfilling management requirements

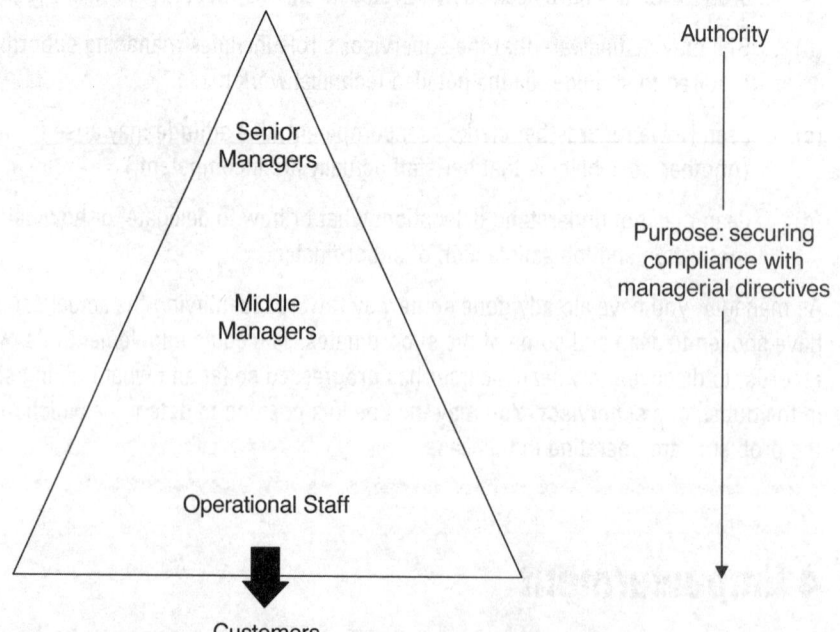

Empowerment structure: supporting workers in serving the customer

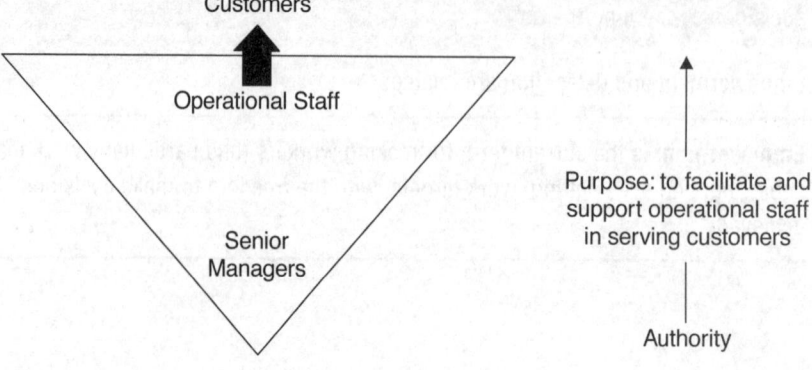

The argument for empowerment, in a nutshell, is that by empowering workers (or 'decentralising' control of business units, or devolving/delegating responsibility, or removing levels in hierarchies that restrict freedom), not only will the job be done more effectively, but the people who do the job will get more out of it.

'The people lower down the organisation possess the knowledge of what is going wrong with a process but lack the authority to make changes. Those further up the structure have the authority to make changes, but lack the profound knowledge required to identify the right solutions. The only solution is to change the culture of the organisation so that everyone can become involved in the process of improvement and work together to make the changes.' (*Max Hand*)

Case Study

The validity of this view and its relevance to modern trends appears to be borne out by the approach to empowerment adopted by *Harvester Restaurants*, as described in *Personnel Management*. The management structure comprises a branch manager and a 'coach', while everyone else is a team member. Everyone within a team has one or more 'accountabilities' (these include recruitment, drawing up rotas, keeping track of sales targets and so on) which are shared out by the team members at their weekly team meetings. All the team members at different times act as 'co-ordinator': the person responsible for taking the snap decisions that are frequently necessary in a busy restaurant. Apparently all of the staff involved agree that empowerment has made their jobs more interesting and has hugely increased their motivation and sense of involvement.

Chapter Roundup

- **Power** is the ability to get things done. There are many types of power in organisations: position or **legitimate power**, expert power, personal power, resource power and negative power are examples.

- **Authority** is related to position power. It is the right to take certain decisions within certain boundaries.

- **Responsibility** is the obligation a person has to fulfil a task (s)he has been given. Responsibility can be delegated, but the person delegating responsibility still remains accountable to his or her boss for completion of the task.

- **Authority/responsibility mismatch** or **ambiguity** is stressful for the individual.

- **Delegation** is necessary for division of labour and technical/managerial specialisation.

- **Successful delegation** requires that people have the right skills and the authority to do the job, and are given feedback.

- Successful delegation requires skill training, cultural support and resolution of the '**trust-control' dilemma**.

- **Empowerment** takes the process of delegation further. Its advantages are not simply that it releases managers to do more important things, but that front line staff closest to customers are able to take decisions concerning them.

Quick Quiz

1 Power arising from an individual's formal position in the organisation is called:

    A   Referent power
    B   Legitimate power
    C   Expert power
    D   Resource power

2 Give an example of negative power.

3 Why might functional authority be a good thing for the organisation?

4 Why can't accountability be delegated?

5 Why are there problems in determining authority and responsibility?

6 List the stages in the process of delegation.

7 List some problems in delegation.

8 'Empowerment' is equivalent to the centralisation of authority. *True or false?*

Answers to Quick Quiz

1 B (or 'position' power).

2 Going on strike; refusal to communicate; withhold information; delaying etc.

3 Because it is exercised impersonally, impartially and automatically.

4 Because the delegator has been given the task by his/her own boss.

5 Because the boundaries are often unclear and/or shifting.

6 Specify performance levels; formally assign task; allocate resources and authority; back off; give feedback.

7 Low trust, low competence, fear, worry about accountability.

8 False: empowerment implies decentralised (delegated) authority.

Now try the question below from the Exam Question Bank

Number	Level	Marks	Time
Q5	Examination	15	27 mins

Performance, objectives and targets

Topic list	Syllabus reference
1 Introducing control systems	1 (f)
2 Organisational objectives and targets	1 (f)
3 Ethics and social responsibility	1 (f)
4 Personal objectives and targets	1 (h)
5 Performance management	1 (h)

Introduction

In Chapter 1, we noted that an organisation's basic purpose is 'the **controlled performance** of **collective goals**'. In this chapter, we look at what this means in practice.

We start with the basic cycle of **planning and control**: a useful framework for looking at all kinds of management activity.

In **Section 2**, we look at the different levels and types of goals an organisation might have.

It is important to grasp the variety of organisational objectives – and the potential tension between them. It's not just about maximising profit! (In **Section 3**, for example, we look at the emerging area of **corporate social responsibility** and **ethics.**)

Another key point is the **hierarchy** of objectives flowing from the overall corporate mission right down to the detailed day-to-day plans of individuals and teams: this is what keeps all the activity heading in the same direction. In **Sections 4 and 5**, we look at two practical (and highly examinable) approaches: Management by Objectives and Performance Management.

Study guide

Section 6 – Objective setting

- Explain the importance of objective setting

- Compare and contrast profit and other objectives: Drucker, Cyert and March, Marginalist Theories, Simon

- Explain the behavioural theories of objective setting

- Explain the importance of understanding ethics and social responsibility

- Compare and contrast the difference between corporate objectives and personal objectives

- Illustrate the difference between quantitative and qualitative target setting

- Outline the management role in identifying performance standards and accountability

- Identify methods to measure achievement of objectives

Section 8 – Standard setting and performance management

- Define the term performance management
- Identify a process for establishing work standards and performance management
- Outline a method to establish performance indicators

Exam guide

This topic could form the background to questions on a variety of management topics. Questions might come up on areas such as the behavioural purposes of objective-setting, or business ethics and responsibility, or performance management (as in the June 2003 exam). Social responsibility has not yet come up in the exam – but it *is* an area of interest to the examiner: in his December 2004 report, he noted that one of the reasons why it is so important for students to get to grips with 'correct' procedures (in all sorts of areas of HR management) is to ensure the fair and equitable treatment of employees and other stakeholders. (You might want to demonstrate your awareness of this when discussing otherwise 'dry' procedures …)

1 Introducing control systems

Achieving organisational goals requires a system of **planning and control**: deciding what should be done (aims and objectives), how it is to be done (plans and standard-setting), reviewing what is actually done, comparing actual outcome with plans, and taking corrective action.

Because organisations have **goals** they want to satisfy, they need to direct their activities by:

- Deciding what they want to achieve

- Deciding how and when to do it and who is to do it

- Checking that they do achieve what they want, by monitoring what has been achieved and comparing it with the plan

- Taking action to correct any deviation

The overall framework for this is a system of **planning and control**. This is best demonstrated by means of a diagram.

Control system

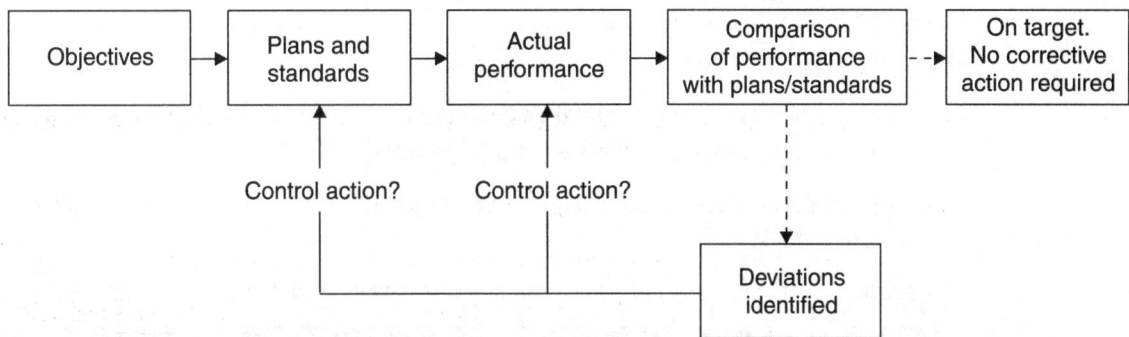

Where there is a deviation from plan, a decision has to be made as to whether to adjust the plan (eg it was unachievable) or the performance (eg it was sub-standard).

2 Organisational objectives and targets

2.1 Mission

FAST FORWARD

> The **mission** is the organisation's overall purpose and reason for existence. It has implications for the commercial strategy, the values of the organisation, and policies and actual standards of behaviour of the people within it.

Overall, the main direction of an organisation is set by its mission.

Key term

> **Mission** describes 'the organisation's basic function in society'.

Mission has four elements.

Elements	Comments
Purpose	Why does the organisation exist and for whom (eg shareholders)?
Strategy	Mission provides the operational logic for the organisation: • What do we do? • How do we do it?
Policies and standards of behaviour	Mission should influence what people actually do and how they behave: the mission of a hospital is to save lives, and this affects how doctors and nurses interact with patients.
Values	What the organisation believes to be important: that is, its principles.

Even though the mission can be very general, you can see it should have real implications for the policies and activities of the organisation, and how individuals go about what they do.

2.2 Goals, aims and objectives

FAST FORWARD

> **Goals** give flesh to the mission. They can be quantified (**objectives**) or not quantified (**aims**). Most organisations use a combination of both. Quantified or specific objectives have SMART characteristics.

Different terminology is used in this area. We will distinguish between terms, for clarity.

Key term

> **Goals**: 'The intentions behind decision or actions' (Henry Mintzberg) or 'a desired end result' (Shorter Oxford English Dictionary)

There are two types of goal.

- Non-operational, **qualitative** goals (**aims**)
- Operational, **quantitative** goals (**objectives**)

Aims are qualitative goals. For example, a university's may be: 'to seek truth'. (You would not see: 'increase truth by 5%')

Objectives are operational goals, which can be expressed in quantitative (numerical) form.

Characteristics	Example
Objectives are SMART - Specific - Measurable - Achievable - Relevant - Time-bounded	- Operational goal: cut costs - Objective: reduce budgeted expenditure on office stationery by 5% by 31 December 2006

In practice, people often use the words goals, aims and objectives interchangeably.

 Question

Aims and objectives

Most organisations establish closed or quantifiable objectives. Give reasons why aims (non-operational goals) might still be important.

Answer

Aims can be just as helpful: customer satisfaction, for example, is not something which is achieved just once. Some goals are hard to measure and quantify, for example 'to retain technological leadership'. Quantified objectives are hard to change when circumstances change, as changing them looks like an admission of defeat: aims may support greater flexibility.

2.3 The purpose of organisational objective setting

'Objectives are needed in every area where performance and results directly and vitally affect the survival and prosperity of the business' (*Drucker*). Objectives in these key areas should enable management to:

(a) **Implement** the mission, by outlining what needs to be achieved

(b) **Publicise** the direction of the organisation to managers and staff, so that they know where their efforts should be directed

(c) **Appraise** the validity of decisions about **strategies** (by assessing whether these are sufficient to achieve the stated objectives)

(d) **Assess and control actual performance**, as objectives can be used as targets for achievement.

2.4 The hierarchy of objectives

FAST FORWARD

There is **hierarchy of objectives**. A primary objective of a business might be profit; secondary objectives relate to ways to achieve it.

There is a **hierarchy of objectives/goals**, with one primary corporate objective (restricted by certain constraints on corporate activity) and a series of subordinate objectives/goals which should combine to ensure the achievement of the overall objective.

2.4.1 Primary objectives

People might disagree on the choice of the overall corporate objective, although for a business it must be a **financial objective,** such as profitability, return on capital employed or earnings per share.

(a)   **Profit**, in its broadest sense, measures the creation of value, the relationship of inputs to outputs. It thus integrates cost behaviour and revenue performance for the whole organisation.

(b)   Profit also is a key indicator for shareholders.

(c)   Profit is one of several measures that can be compared across organisations.

2.4.2 Secondary objectives

Secondary or subordinate goals and objectives support the primary goal. They can be listed under the following broad headings.

(a)   **Market position**

Total market share of each market; growth of sales, customers or potential customers; the need to avoid relying on a single customer for a large proportion of total sales; what markets should the company be in?

(b)   **Product development**

Bring in new products; develop a product range; investment in research and development; provide products of a certain quality at a certain price level.

(c)   **Technology**

Improve productivity; reduce the cost per unit of output; exploit appropriate technology.

(d)   **Employees and management**

Train employees in certain skills; reduce labour turnover; create an innovative, flexible culture; employ high quality leaders.

Question · **Primary and secondary objectives**

Review the list of secondary objectives above. How do you think of each of them relates to the financial objectives suggested in the preceding section?

Answer

(a)   Markets are customers. Customers are source of revenue. Markets are where organisations compete with each other. Gaining market share *now* helps future profitability – but may be expensive in the short term.

(b)   Product development is another way of competing, to make profits to satisfy the corporate objectives.

(c)   and (d) are to do with organising the production process, making operations efficient and effective.

2.5 The tension between profit maximisation and other objectives

> **Profit maximisation** is assumed to be the primary goal of business organisations, but other objectives and stakeholder interest also influence managerial decision-making.

Profit maximisation is assumed to be the goal of business organisations. Where the entrepreneur is in full managerial control of the firm, as in the case of a small owner-managed company or partnership, this assumption would seem to be very reasonable. Even in companies owned by shareholders, but run by non-shareholding managers, we might expect that the profit maximisation assumption would be close to the truth. However, some writers have suggested that objectives other than profit maximisation might be pursued by firms.

Managers will not necessarily make decisions that will maximise profits.

(a)   They may have **no personal interest** in the size of profits earned, except in so far as they are accountable to shareholders.

(b)   There may be a **lack of competitive pressure** in the market to be efficient, minimise costs and maximise profits, for example where there are few firms in the market.

Price and output decisions might be taken by managers with **managerial objectives** in mind rather than the aim of profit maximisation. The profit level must be satisfactory and so acceptable to shareholders, and must provide enough retained profits for future investment in growth. But rather than seeking to maximise profits, managers may choose to achieve a satisfactory profit for a firm: this is called **'satisficing'**.

2.5.1 Baumol's sales maximisation model

One managerial model of the firm assumes that the firm acts to **maximise sales revenue** in order to maintain or increase its market share, ensure survival, and discourage competition. Managers benefit personally because of the prestige of running a large and successful company, and also because salaries and other benefits are likely to be higher in bigger companies than in smaller ones.

2.5.2 Drucker's multiple objectives

Management writer Peter **Drucker** points out that:

'To manage a business is to balance a variety of needs and goals.... The very nature of business enterprise requires multiple objectives'. He suggests that objectives are needed in eight key areas.

- **Market standing**: this includes market share, customer satisfaction, size of product range and distribution resources

- **Innovation** in all major aspects of the organisation

- **Productivity**
- **Physical and financial resources**
- **Profitability**
- **Manager performance and development**
- **Worker performance and attitude**
- **Public responsibility**

2.5.3 Simon

Simon has pointed out that for many members of an organisation, decisions are taken without reference to the profit goal. This is not because they are ignoring profit, but because profit is not the most important **constraint** in their business. This is perhaps seen most clearly in areas where ethical constraints apply, such as staff relations or environmental protection. It may also be seen, as Drucker also argued, in the need to satisfy customers with quality products and service – which may lower profit margins.

2.5.4 Cyert and March's organisational coalition model

The American management writers **Cyert and March** suggest that traditional ideas on organisational objectives are too simplistic and do not recognise managerial and economic reality.

(a) The firm is **an organisational coalition** of stakeholders: shareholders, managers, employees, suppliers and customers.

(b) This network has **potentially competing goals and interests**. There is a need for 'political' compromise in establishing the goals of the firm. Each group must settle for less than it would ideally want to have. Shareholders must settle for less than maximum profits, managers for less than maximum utility, and so on.

(c) Organisations have *responsibilities* to (and constraints imposed by) various stakeholder groups. These may be internal considerations, based on stakeholder influence and the organisation's values. They may also be *external* considerations, such as legislation. (We will look at this further.)

Cyert and March conclude that 'organisations cannot have objectives, only people have objectives'.

2.6 Plans and standards

 **FAST FORWARD**

Standards and targets are used in the **control system** to monitor whether performance is in fact proceeding according to plan.

Plans state *what should be done to achieve the objectives*. Standards and targets specify a *desired level of performance*. Here are some examples.

(a) **Physical standards** eg units of raw material per unit produced.

(b) **Cost standards**. These convert physical standards into a money measurement by the application of standard prices. For example, the standard labour cost of making product X might be 4 hours at £5 per hour = £20.

(c) **Capital standards**. These establish some form of standard for capital invested (eg the ratio of current assets to current liabilities) or a desired share price.

(d) **Revenue standards**. These measure expected performance in terms of revenue earned (such as turnover per square metre of shelf space in a supermarket).

(e)   **Deadlines for programme completion**. Performance might be measured in terms of actual completion dates for parts of a project compared against a budgeted programme duration.

(f)   The **achievement of stated goals** (eg meeting profit objective).

(g)   **Intangible standards**. Intangible standards might relate to employee motivation, quality of service, customer goodwill, corporate image, product image etc. It is possible to measure some of these by attitude surveys, market research etc.

3 Ethics and social responsibility

FAST FORWARD
Ethical and **social responsibility** are two key areas in which businesses have adopted non-financial objectives, partly in response to political and consumer pressure.

Key terms

Ethics are the moral principles by which people act or do business.

Social responsibility comprises those values and actions which the organisation is not obliged to adopt for business reasons, which it adopts for the good and well-being of stakeholders within and outside the organisation.

3.1 Why be socially responsible?

FAST FORWARD
There is pressure towards **corporate social responsibility (CSR)** from law and regulation, market forces and the stakeholder perspective.

Managers need to take into account the effect of organisational outputs into the market and the wider **social community**, for several reasons.

(a)   The modern **marketing concept** says that in order to survive and succeed, organisations must satisfy the needs, wants and values of customers and potential customers. Communication and education have made people much more aware of issues such as the environment, the exploitation of workers, product safety and consumer rights. Therefore an organisation may have to be seen to be responsible in these areas in order to retain public support for its products.

(b)   There are skill shortages in the labour pool and employers must compete to attract and retain high quality employees. If the organisation gets a reputation as a socially responsible employer it will find it easier to do this, than if it has a poor '**employer brand**'.

(c)   A business itself is a **social system**, not just an economic machine (*Mintzberg*). Organisations **rely** on the society and local community of which they are a part, for access to facilities, business relationships, media coverage, labour, supplies, customers and so on. Organisations which acknowledge their responsibilities as part of the community may find that many areas of their operation are facilitated.

(d)   Social responsibility recognises **externalities**: the costs imposed by businesses on other people. For example, it is recognised that industrial pollution is bad for health. Law, regulation and Codes of Practice **impose** certain social responsibilities on organisations, in areas such as employment protection, equal opportunities, environmental care, health and safety, product labelling and consumer rights. There are financial and operational **penalties** for organisations which fail to comply.

The **stakeholder view** of organisations emphasises that they are not solely 'self interested': other parties have an interest or 'stake' in the performance and practices of an organisation.

> A **stakeholder** is an individual or group who has an interest or 'stake' in the organisation's performance and impacts. Examples include: the owners, managers and employees of the organisation; its customers, suppliers and business partners; government and its agencies; interest groups (eg environmental or social justice groups); trade unions; and the community in which the organisation operates.

The stakeholder approach acknowledges that such parties have a **legitimate interest** – and may also have **influence** over the organisation. (Workers can withhold labour; customers can withhold business.) The objectives of the organisation should therefore take into account the needs and claims of influential stakeholder groups.

3.2 Areas of social responsibility

The perceived social responsibilities of a business, depending on the nature of its operations, may include the following matters.

(a) The impact of its operations on the **natural environment**

(b) Its **human resource management policies**: for example, the hiring and promotion of people from minority groups, policies on sexual harassment, refusal to exploit cheap labour in developing countries

(c) Non-reliance on contracts with **adverse political connotations**: sustainable business practices in developing countries, compliance with sanctions imposed by the international community and so on

(d) **Charitable support** and activity in the local community or in areas related to the organisation's field of activity

(e) **Above-minimum (legal) standards** of workplace health and safety, product safety and labelling, and so on.

Question   Socially responsible activities

See if you can come up with examples of socially responsible activities, in line with (a) to (e) above.

Answer

Examples (our suggestions only) include:

(a) The Body Shop (among others) not using animal testing for ingredients, Shell (as a *negative* example) being held responsible for environmental devastation in Nigeria's river deltas, recyclable packaging

(b) British Airways extension of married employees' benefits to homosexual partners, voluntary, non-ageist recruitment policies, the Body shop (again) building economic infrastructures in rural communities

(c) Sanctions or boycotts of countries such as (in the past) South Africa or Iraq

(d) Major supermarkets and retailers such as WH Smith often sponsor community facilities, charities and sporting events

(e) Some organisations have very stringent quality standards, and immediate no-strings product recall policies.

3.3 Limits of corporate social responsibility

According to Milton **Friedman** and Elaine **Sternberg**, 'the social responsibility of business is profit maximisation': in other words, the only responsibility of a *business* organisation, as opposed to a public sector one, is to maximise wealth for its owners over the long term.

(a)   Business profits are shareholders' wealth. Spending on other objectives *not* related to shareholders' wealth maximisation is irresponsible.

(b)   The public interest is served because the state levies taxes: the state is a better arbiter of the public interest than a business.

(c)   Without the discipline of shareholders, managers will simply favour their own pet interests. 'Managers who are accountable to everyone are accountable to none.'

'Consequently, the only justification for social responsibility is **enlightened self interest'** (Friedman) on the part of the organisation. Socially responsible behaviour should be pursued for its *benefits* in: employee recruitment, retention and commitment; customer retention; and public relations.

3.4 Business ethics

FAST FORWARD

> **Business ethics** are the values underlying what an organisation understands by socially responsible behaviour.

An organisation may have values to do with non-discrimination, fairness and integrity. It is very important that managers understand:

- The importance of ethical behaviour
- The differences in what is considered ethical behaviour in different cultures

Theorist Elaine Sternberg suggests that two **ethical values** are particularly pertinent for business, because without them business could not operate at all. These are:

(a)   **Ordinary decency.** This includes respect for property rights, honesty, fairness and legality.

(b)   **Distributive justice**. This means that organisational rewards should be proportional to the contributions people make to organisational ends. The supply and demand for labour will influence how much a person is actually paid, but if that person is worth employing and the job worth doing, then the contribution will justify the expense.

Business ethics in a **global market place**, are, however, far from clear cut. If you are working outside the UK, you will need to develop – in line with whatever policies your organisation may have in place – a kind of 'situational' ethic to cover various issues.

(a)   **Gifts** may be construed as bribes in Western business circles, but are indispensable in others.

(b)   Attitudes to **women** in business vary according to ethnic traditions and religious values.

(c)   The use of **cheap labour** in very poor countries (eg through off-shoring) may be perceived as 'development' – or as 'exploitation'.

(d)   The expression and nature of **agreements** varies according to cultural norms.

A business may operate on principles which strive to be:

- Ethical and legal (eg The Body Shop)
- Unethical but legal (eg arms sales to repressive regimes)
- Ethical but illegal (eg publishing stolen documents on government mismanagement)
- Unethical and illegal (eg the drugs trade, employing child labour)

3.4.1 Applying ethical principles

Assuming a firm wishes to act ethically, it can embed ethical values in its decision processes in the following ways.

(a) Include **value statements** in corporate culture, policy and codes of practice

(b) Ensure that **HR systems** (appraisal, training and rewards) are designed to support ethical behaviour

(c) Identify ethical objectives in the **mission statement**, as a public declaration of what the organisation stands for

Exam focus point

> Social responsibility and ethics has not (at the time of writing) been directly examined in this paper, although it underpinned a major case study question on equal opportunities and diversity: organisational policies over and above legal requirements, in areas such as these, fulfil responsibility objectives. Keep an eye on this topic: it is well suited to an essay question.

4 Personal objectives and targets

4.1 Behavioural theories of objective setting

FAST FORWARD

> In order for learning and motivation to be effective, it is essential that **people** know exactly what their **objectives** are.

People are purposive: that is, they act in pursuit of particular goals or purposes. Individual objectives influence:

(a) **Perception**, since we filter out messages not relevant to our goals, and select those which are relevant

(b) **Behaviour**, since people behave in such a way as to satisfy their goals

(c) **Motivation**, since organisations can motivate people by offering them the means to fulfil their goals

(d) **Learning**, which is a process of adapting our behaviour so that our goals may be more effectively met 'next time'.

In order for learning and motivation to be effective , it is essential that people know exactly what their objectives are. This enables them to:

(a) **Plan and direct their effort** towards the objectives

(b) **Monitor their performance** against objectives and adjust (or learn) if required

(c) Experience the **reward of achievement** once the objectives have been reached

(d) Feel that their tasks have **meaning and purpose**, which is an important element in job satisfaction

(e) Experience the **motivation of a challenge:** the need to expend energy and effort in a particular direction in order to achieve something

(f) Avoid the **de-motivation** of impossible or inadequately rewarded tasks: if objectives are vague, unrealistic or unattainable, there may be little incentive to pursue them: hence the importance of SMART objectives.

We will be discussing specific behavioural theories in relation to motivation and learning in later chapters.

4.2 Individual and organisational objectives

Individual objectives must be directed towards, or **'dovetailed with'**, organisational goals.

Individual objectives must be directed towards, or **'dovetailed with'**, organisational goals.

(a) **Direction**. Each job is directed towards the same organisational goals. Each managerial job must be focused on the success of the business as a whole, not just one part of it.

(b) **Target**. Each manager's targeted performance must be derived from targets of achievement for the organisation as a whole.

(c) **Performance measurement**. A manager's results must be measured in terms of his or her contribution to the business as a whole.

(d) **Each manager must know** what his or her targets of performance are.

The hierarchy of objectives which emerges may be shown as follows.

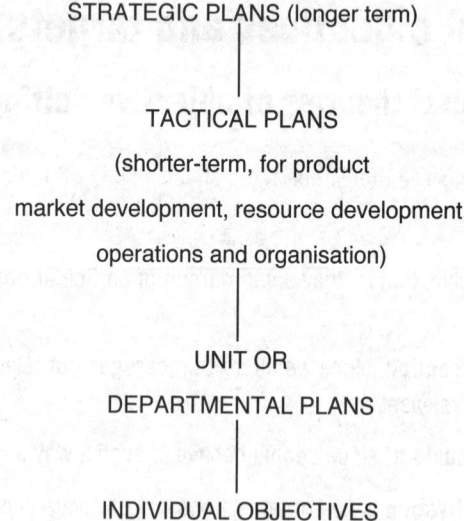

STRATEGIC PLANS (longer term)

TACTICAL PLANS

(shorter-term, for product

market development, resource development,

operations and organisation)

UNIT OR

DEPARTMENTAL PLANS

INDIVIDUAL OBJECTIVES

4.3 Types of objectives for individuals and teams

Different types of objectives include:

(a) **Work objectives**

(i) At team level, these relate to the purpose of the team and the contribution it is expected to make to the goals of the department and the organisation.

(ii) At individual level, these are related specifically to the job. They clarify what the individual is expected to do and they enable the performance of the individual to be measured.

(b) **Standing aims and objectives**

(i) **Qualitative aims** cover issues such as promptness and courtesy when dealing with customer requests.

(ii) A **quantified target** for a sales team would be to ensure that all phone calls are picked up within three rings.

(c) **Output or improvement targets**

A sales person may be given a target of increasing the number of sales made in a particular district in a certain time. Many firms have targets which involve reducing the number of defects in goods produced, or seek to find ways of working more efficiently.

(d) **Developmental goals**

These deal with how an individual can improve his/her own performance and skills. These goals are often set at the appraisal interview and are part of the performance management system. In the control model outlined in Section 1, setting developmental goals would be an example of action taken to improve the individual's and the organisation's performance.

4.4 Management by Objectives   6/04

FAST FORWARD

Techniques have been suggested to break down organisational goals into targets for departments and individuals. **Management by Objectives** is one such technique.

The diagram of the hierarchy of objectives in Section 4.2 shows a cascade of objectives from the organisation to the individual. Integrating all these objectives is not always easy to achieve. However, a method of doing so was suggested by proponents of **Management by Objectives**.

Exam focus point

15 marks were available for describing 'seven key stages' in an MbO programme. You should bear in mind that, depending what specific model the examiner had in mind, the question might have asked for five or six stages, or eight. Don't panic if this happens in the exam, and the question asks for a different number of stages than the model you know. The basics will be the same. Just adjust the steps to fit the number asked for in the question.

4.4.1 Stages in MbO

Management by Objectives (MbO) is a process whereby individual goals are integrated with the corporate plan, as part of an on-going programme of goal-setting and performance review involving all levels of management. The stages in developing such a programme are as follows.

Step 1 Clarifying **organisational goals and objectives**: MbO will only be effective within the framework of a coherent strategic plan.

Step 2 Collaboratively defining each individual's major **areas of responsibility** and their purpose within the corporate plan.

Step 3 Jointly defining and agreeing the **key tasks** which are directly related to the achievement of objectives, and in which any performance shortfall would negatively impact on the organisation's effectiveness.

Step 4 Jointly defining and agreeing **key results** (which must be achieved in order for the key tasks to be successfully performed and objectives met) and methods of monitoring and measuring performance in these areas.

Step 5 Agreeing individual **performance improvement plans** for a defined planning period: selecting specific improvement objectives for each key task and formulating an action plan to achieve those objectives. This will include measures to be taken by the job-holder, resources to be provided by superiors (eg guidance, training) and dates for review.

Step 6 **Monitoring, self-evaluation and review** of performance at agreed intervals, with revision of objectives, targets and action plans as required.

Step 7 **Periodic review of performance** against individual improvement objectives and key results (reflected at the organisation level in a review of performance against the corporate plan).

A fresh cycle of planning and control would then continue the process.

4.4.2 Evaluating MbO

Advantages and disadvantages of an MbO programme may be identified as follows.

There are a number of **advantages** to an MbO program.

(a) Clarifying organisational and sub-unit **goals**. This is crucial in establishing direction and co-ordination. It helps to focus organisation structures according to defined responsibilities. The goal clarification exercise may also encourage the flow of multi-directional communication and identify needs for innovation, change and development.

(b) Focusing organisational attention on **key tasks**, results and problem areas, for more efficient targeting of effort.

(c) Systematically converting strategic plans into **co-ordinated** managerial action plans and budgets. Each individual manager knows clearly what is expected of him or her, while retaining a big-picture perspective and unity of purpose.

(d) Securing the **commitment** of individuals to defined targets and areas of accountability, as well as potentially improving morale and motivation through greater involvement and discretion in performing tasks (within defined targets).

(e) **Systematic information** for managerial planning and control, individual performance appraisal, reward and development planning.

There are **disadvantages** too.

(a) Potential rigidity: individual objectives must be set and, once set, are not changed because the overall plan is difficult to revise. There must be **flexibility**, especially:

    (i) In flexible working environments where individual 'jobs' are no longer rigidly defined

    (ii) Where individual results are less relevant (or measurable) because of teamworking

    (iii) Where a less hierarchical management authority structure is preferred (eg self-managed teamworking)

    (iv) Where jobs are less amenable to measurement and the setting of specific quantitative targets (eg interpersonal roles such as counselling)

(b) Potential requirement for a significant **change** in attitudes, the style of leadership and organisation structure. This may involve time and labour costs of change management – and may ultimately be unsuccessful if not supported (and sustained) by senior management.

(c) Potential for **conflict** and de-motivation: staff may perceive increasing accountability for defined results as a command-and-control pressure tactic, thinly disguised as involvement/empowerment.

4.5 Performance measures for individuals

FAST FORWARD **Standards of performance** set for individuals should be job related, controllable and observable.

Some principles for devising performance measures are as follows.

Principle	Comment
Job-related	They should be related to the actual job, and the key tasks outlined in the job description (see Chapter 7)
Controllable	People should not be assessed according to factors which they cannot control
Objective and observable	This is contentious. Certain aspects of performance can be measured, such as volume sales, but matters such as courtesy or friendliness which are important to some businesses are harder to measure
Data must be available	There is no use identifying performance measures if the data cannot be collected efficiently

Question   Performance indicators

A senior sales executive has a job which involves: 'building the firm's sales' and maintaining 'a high degree of satisfaction with the company's products and services'. The firm buys sports equipment, running machines and so on, which it sells to gyms and individuals. The firm also charges fees to service the equipment. Service contracts are the sales executive's responsibility, and he has to manage that side of the business.

Here some possible performance indicators to assess the sales executive's performance in the role. What do you think of them? Are they any good?

(a)   Number of new customers gained per period
(b)   Value of revenue from existing customers per period
(c)   Renewal of service contracts
(d)   Record of customer complaints about poor quality products
(e)   Regular customer satisfaction survey

Answer

These measures do not all address the key issues of the job.

(a)   *Number of new customers.* This is helpful as far as it goes but omits two crucial issues: how much the customers actually spend and what the potential is. Demand for this service might be expanding rapidly, and the firm might be increasing sales revenue but losing market share.

(b)   *Revenue from existing customers* is useful – repeat business is generally cheaper than gaining new customers, and it implies customer satisfaction.

(c)   *Renewal of service contracts* is very relevant to the executive's role.

(d)   *Customer complaints about poor quality products.* As the company does not make its own products, this is not really under the control of the sales manager. Instead the purchasing manager should be more concerned. Complaints about the service contract are the sales executive's concern.

(e)   *Customer satisfaction survey.* This is a tool for the sales manager to use as well as a performance measure, but not everything is under the sales executive's control.

5 Performance management

FAST FORWARD

> **Performance management** suggests that people must agree performance standards, that the responsibility for performance management is principally that of line management, and that it is a conscious commitment to developing and managing people in organisations. It is a continuous process.

Key term

> **Performance management** is: 'a means of getting better results…by understanding and managing performance within an agreed framework of planned goals, standards and competence requirements. It is a process to establish a shared understanding about what is to be achieved, and an approach to managing and developing people … [so that it] … will be achieved' (Armstrong, *Handbook of Personnel Management Practice*).

Exam focus point

> The definition is long, but it is worth learning, because the ability to define performance management is explicitly mentioned in the ACCA's Teaching Guide. The stages of performance management (see Section 5.2 below) were the subject of a 15-mark essay question in June 2003.

5.1 Features of performance management

Armstrong expands on this definition, and describes some other features of performance management.

Aspect	Comment
Agreed framework of goals, standards and competence requirements	As in MbO, the manager and the employee agree about a standard of performance, goals and the skills needed.
Shared understanding	People need to understand the nature of high levels of performance, so they can work towards them.
Approach to managing and developing people	(1) How managers work with their teams (2) How team members work with managers and each other (3) Developing individuals to improve their performance
Achievement	The aim is to enable people to realise their potential and maximise their contribution to the organisation's well being.
Future-based	Performance management is forward-looking, based on the organisation's future needs and what the individual must do to satisfy them.

5.2 The process of performance management

The process of performance management may be outlined as follows.

Step 1 From the **business plan**, identify the requirements and competences required to carry it out.

Step 2 Draw up a **performance agreement**, defining the expectations of the individual or team, covering standards of performance, performance indicators and the skills and competences people need.

Step 3 Draw up a **performance and development plan** with the individual. These record the actions needed to improve performance, normally covering development in the current job. They are discussed with job holders and will cover, typically:

- The areas of performance the individual feels in need of development
- What the individual and manager agree is needed to enhance performance
- Development and training initiatives

Step 4 **Manage performance continually throughout the year,** not just at appraisal interviews done to satisfy the personnel department. Managers can review actual performance, with more informal interim reviews at various times of the year.

(a) High performance is reinforced by praise, recognition, increasing responsibility. Low performance results in coaching or counselling.

(b) Work plans are updated as necessary.

(c) Deal with performance problems, by identifying what they are, establish the reasons for the shortfall, take control action (with adequate resources) and provide feedback.

Step 5 **Performance review**. At a defined period each year, success against the plan is reviewed, but the whole point is to assess what is going to happen in future.

| Question | Performance management |

What are the advantages to *employees* of introducing such a system?

| Answer |

The key to performance management is that it is forward looking and constructive. Objective-setting gives employees the security in knowing exactly what is expected of them, and this is agreed at the outset with the manager, thus identifying unrealistic expectations. The employee at the outset can indicate the resources needed.

Organisations are introducing such systems for much the same reason as they pursued management by objectives, in other words, to:

- Tie in individual performance with the performance of the organisation
- Indicate where training and development may be necessary

Many of the issues covered in this brief outline are explored in later chapters. The purpose of introducing it here is to show how the wider goals and expectations of the organisation depend on how individuals work together.

Chapter Roundup

- Achieving organisational goals requires a system of **planning and control**: deciding what should be done (aims and objectives), how it is to be done (plans and standard-setting), reviewing what is actually done, comparing actual outcome with plans, and taking corrective action.

- The **mission** is the organisation's overall purpose and reason for existence. It has implications for the commercial strategy, the values of the organisation, and policies and actual standards of behaviour of the people within it.

- **Goals** give flesh to the mission. They can be quantified (**objectives**) or not quantified (**aims**). Most organisations use a combination of both. Quantified or specific objectives have SMART characteristics.

- There is **hierarchy of objectives**. A primary objective of a business might be profit; secondary objectives relate to ways to achieve it.

- **Profit maximisation** is assumed to be the primary goal of business organisations, but other objectives and stakeholder interest also influence managerial decision-making.

- Standards and targets are used in the **control system** to monitor whether performance is in fact proceeding according to plan.

- **Ethical** and **social responsibility** are two key areas in which businesses have adopted non-financial objectives, partly in response to political and consumer pressure.

- There is pressure towards **corporate social responsibility (CSR)** from law and regulation, market forces and the stakeholder perspective.

- **Business ethics** are the values underlying what an organisation understands by socially responsible behaviour.

- In order for learning and motivation to be effective, it is essential that **people** know exactly what their **objectives** are.

- Individual objectives must be directed towards, or **'dovetailed with'**, organisational goals.

- Techniques have been suggested to break down organisational goals into targets for departments and individuals. **Management by Objectives** is one such technique.

- **Standards of performance** set for individuals should be job related, controllable and observable.

- **Performance management** suggests that people must agree performance standards, that the responsibility for performance management is principally that of line management, and that it is a conscious commitment to developing and managing people in organisations. It is a continuous process.

Quick Quiz

1   How can organisations direct their activities?

2   What are the elements of a control system?

3   What are four elements of mission?

4   What do you understand by the acronym SMART?

5   Socially responsible behaviour is a constraint on managerial decision-making, without significant business benefit. *True or false*?

6   List four types of objectives for an individual.

7   How must objectives be interlocked?

8   Fill in the blanks in the following definition. Performance management is 'a means of getting better _____ ... by _____ and managing performance within an agreed framework of planned _____, standards and _____ requirements. It is a process to establish a _____ understanding about what is to be achieved, and an approach to managing and _____ people ... [so that it] ... will be achieved'.   (Armstrong, *Handbook of Personnel Management Practice*)

9   List five steps in performance management.

10 How can managers and staff become more committed to objectives, according to supporters of MbO and performance management?

Answers to Quick Quiz

1 By deciding what should be done, how it should be done, reviewing outcomes, and monitoring performance

2 Plans and standards; sensor to detect actual performance; comparator to compare performance with plans and standards; effector to take control action where necessary. Feedback is information about performance.

3 Purpose; business strategy; policies and standards of behaviour; values

4 Specific, measurable, achievable, relevant, agreed, time-bounded

5 False. Social responsibility allows businesses to retain and attract customers and employees and community support.

6 Work-based; standing; output or improvement; developmental

7 Vertically; horizontally (across departments); over time

8 Performance management is 'a means of getting better **results**…by **understanding** and managing performance within an agreed framework of planned **goals**, standards and **competence** requirements. It is a process to establish a **shared** understanding about what is to be achieved, and an approach to managing and **developing** people..[so that it]…will be achieved'.

9 **Step 1** From the business plan, identify the requirements and competences required to carry it out.

Step 2 Develop a performance agreement.

Step 3 Draw up a performance and development plan with the individual.

Step 4 Manage performance continually throughout the year,

Step 5 Performance review.

10 By participating in setting them

Now try the question below from the Exam Question Bank

Number	Level	Marks	Time
Q6	Intermediate (question part)	10	18 mins

BPP
PROFESSIONAL EDUCATION

Part B
Recruitment and selection

Recruitment

7

Topic list	Syllabus reference
1 Recruitment and selection	2 (a)
2 Responsibility for recruitment and selection	2 (a)
3 The recruitment process	2 (a)
4 Job analysis	2 (d)
5 Job description	2 (c)
6 Person specification	2 (c)
7 Advertising vacancies	2 (b)

Introduction

Recruitment and selection are two core activities in the field of Human Resource Management (HRM). Together, they are broadly aimed at ensuring that the organisation has the human resources (labour and skills) it needs, when it needs them, in order to fulfil its objectives.

In this chapter, we explore the process of **recruitment**, which is about **obtaining candidates**: defining the skills and attributes needed (**Sections 4-6**), and advertising the vacancy in the labour market (**Section 7**).

Chapter 8 goes on to cover the process of **selection**, which is about deciding which of the applicants is the **right candidate**.

Sections 1-3 of this chapter are designed to give you an overview of the process. The examiner has pointed out the importance of a **systematic approach** to HR systems and procedures – not least in order to ensure that they are fair and consistently applied.

Perhaps the major challenge of HR topics is to distinguish the procedures and documents that deal with *jobs* (such as job descriptions) and those that deal with *people* (such as person specifications). Bear this in mind as you read on.

Study guide

The full detail of all these Study Guide sessions can be found in the introductory pages to this Study Text.

Exam guide

A question requirement on recruitment may be combined with a requirement relating to **selection**, so you should treat this chapter and the next as a unity. Some aspects of recruitment and/or selection will inevitably come up in the exam, from 'overview' questions (as in June 2002 and December 2004) to detailed questions, such as the decision whether to recruit internally or externally (December 2002); or recruitment advertising (December 2003). Recruitment and selection also lends itself to case studies: be prepared to integrate learning from all areas of this topic.

1 Recruitment and selection

The process of recruitment should be part of the organisation's human resource plan. People are a major organisational resource and must be managed as such.

1.1 Overview of recruitment and selection

FAST FORWARD

Effective recruitment practices ensure that a firm has enough **people with the right skills**.

The **overall aim of the recruitment and selection process** in an organisation is to obtain the quantity and quality of employees required to fulfil the objectives of the organisation.

This process can be broken down into three main stages.

(a) **Defining requirements**, including the preparation of job descriptions, job specifications and person specifications (or personnel specifications).

(b) **Attracting applicants**, including the evaluation and use of various methods for reaching appropriate sources of labour (both within and outside the organisation).

(c) **Selecting** the appropriate candidates for the job, or the appropriate job for the candidate.

Key terms

Recruitment is the part of the process concerned with finding applicants: it is a positive action by management, going into the labour market (internal and external), communicating opportunities and information, generating interest.

Selection is the part of the employee resourcing process which involves choosing between applicants for jobs: it is largely a 'negative' process, eliminating unsuitable applicants.

In times of low unemployment, employers have to compete to *attract* desirable categories of labour. In times of high unemployment, and therefore plentiful supply, 'the problem is not so much of attracting candidates, but in deciding how best to *select* them' (Cole, *Personnel Management Theory and Practice*). In times of low demand for labour, however, socially responsible employers may have the additional policy of using *existing staff* (internal recruitment) rather than recruiting from outside, in order to downsize staff levels through natural wastage and redeployment.

1.2 The important of recruitment and selection

The founding belief of the human resources management (HRM) approach is that employees represent a scarce and crucial resource which must be obtained, retained, developed and mobilised for organisational success.

(a) Recruitment (and training) issues are central to the business strategy.

(b) Organisations need to deploy skills in order to succeed. Although the labour market might seem a 'buyer's market', in practice there are:

(i) Skill shortages in key sectors (eg computing services) and local areas

(ii) Mismatches between available skill supply and the demands of particular markets and organisations

Even in conditions of high overall employment, particular skill shortages still exist and may indeed be more acute because of recessionary pressures on education and training. Engineers and software designers, among other specialist and highly trained groups, are the target of fierce competition among employers, forcing a revaluation of recruitment and retention policies.

2 Responsibility for recruitment and selection

FAST FORWARD

> The recruitment process involves **personnel specialists** and **line managers**, sometimes with the help of recruitment **consultants**.

Question

Recruitment procedures

Think back to when you started work or when you obtained your current position. How many people did you have to see? Were you interviewed by your immediate boss or someone else?

Answer

In many organisations, the trend is towards decentralising selection to the line managers of recruiting departments. For higher volume, more general recruitment, the process may be standardised and centralised, with interviewing carried out by personnel/HR specialists or even recruitment consultants. You may wish to use your own experience as an illustration/example (naming the organisation, where appropriate) of a theoretical point. However, you are advised not to *rely* on your own experience alone: you will need to show evidence of reading and study!

The people involved in recruitment and selection vary from organisation to organisation.

2.1 Senior managers

Senior managers/directors may be involved in recruiting people – from within or outside the organisation – for **senior positions**, or in authorising key appointments. For most other positions, they will not be directly involved. However, they are responsible for **human resources (HR) planning**: identifying the overall skill needs of the organisation, and the types of people it wishes to employ (perhaps as part of the corporate mission statement).

2.2 The personnel/human resources department

Some firms employ specialists to manage their recruitment and other (HR) activities, often under the authority of **personnel manager** or **human resources manager**.

The role of the human resources (HR) function in recruitment and selection may include:

- Assessing needs for human resources (HR planning)
- Maintaining records of people employed
- Keeping in touch with trends in the labour market
- Advertising for new employees
- Ensuring the organisation complies with equal opportunities and other legislation
- Designing application forms
- Liaising with recruitment consultants
- Preliminary interviews and selection testing

2.3 Line managers

In many cases the recruit's prospective boss will be involved in the recruitment.

(a)   In a small business (s)he might have sole responsibility for recruitment.

(b)   In larger organisations, line managers may be responsible for:

- Asking for more human resources: notifying vacancies or issuing a job requisition
- Advising on skill requirements and attributes required
- Selection interviewing (perhaps collaborating with HR specialists)
- Having a final say in the selection decision

The current trend is towards devolving recruitment and selection (among other Human Resource Management activities) increasingly to line management.

2.4 Recruitment consultants

Specialist recruitment consultants or agencies may be contracted to perform some recruitment tasks on the organisation's behalf, including:

(a)   Analysing, or being informed of, the requirements

(b)   Helping to draw up, or offering advice on, job descriptions, person specifications and other recruitment and selection aids

(c)   Designing job advertisements (or using other, informal methods and contacts, eg by 'head hunting')

(d)   Screening applications, so that those most obviously unsuitable are weeded out immediately

(e)   Helping with short-listing for interview

(f)   Advising on, or conducting, first-round interviews

(g)   Offering a list of suitable candidates with notes and recommendations

2.4.1 Factors in the outsourcing decision

The decision of whether or not to use consultants will depend on a number of factors.

(a)   **Cost**.

(b)   The level of expertise, specialist knowledge and contacts which the consultant can bring to the process.

(c) The level of recruitment expertise available **within the organisation**.

(d) Whether there is a need for **impartiality** which can only be filled by an outsider trained in objective assessment. If fresh blood is desired in the organisation, it may be a mistake to have insiders selecting clones of the common organisational type.

(e) Whether the use of an outside agent will be supported or resented/rejected by in-house staff.

(f) Whether the organisation culture supports in-house staff in making HR decisions. (Consultants are not tied by status or rank and can discuss problems freely at all levels.)

(g) **Time**. Consultants will need to learn about the vacancy, the organisation and its requirements.

(h) **Supply of labour**. If there is a large and reasonably accessible pool of labour from which to fill a post, consultants will be less valuable. If the vacancy is a standard one, and there are ready channels for reaching labour (such as professional journals), the use of specialists may not be cost-effective.

3 The recruitment process

FAST FORWARD

Recruitment is a systematic **process** of (a) identifying and defining skill needs and (b) attracting suitably skilled candidates.

3.1 A systematic approach

The recruitment process is part of a wider whole which is outlined below.

(a) Detailed **human resource planning** defines what resources the organisation needs to meet its objectives, and what sources of labour (internal and external) are available. The organisation's skill requirements may be met through recruitment – but there may also be plans for reducing staff numbers, redeployment, training and development, promotion, retention (to reduce loss of skills through staff turnover) and so on.

(b) **Job analysis** produces two outputs.

   (i) A **job description**: a statement of the component tasks, duties, objectives and standards involved in a job.

   (ii) A **person specification**: a reworking of the job description in terms of the kind of person needed to perform the job.

(c) Recruitment as such *begins with the identification of vacancies*, from the requirements of the human resource plan or by a **job requisition** from a department that has a vacancy.

(d) Preparation and publication of **recruitment advertising** will have three aims.

   (i) Attract the attention and interest of potentially suitable candidates

   (ii) Give a favourable (but accurate) impression of the job and the organisation

   (iii) Equip those interested to make an appropriate application (how and to whom to apply, desired skills, qualifications and so on)

(e) Recruitment merges into **selection** when processing applications and assessing candidates.

(f) **Notifying applicants** of the results of the selection process is the final stage of the combined recruitment and selection process.

Exam focus point

A question in the December 2004 exam asked you to identify the stages in recruitment and selection. The examiner was surprised that candidates began with job analysis. It is worth bearing in mind that *establishing* a formal recruitment process begins with job analysis, but more usually, this will already have been carried out. Recruiting for specific *vacancies* therefore starts with a job requisition, followed by reference to (existing) job descriptions and so on. If in doubt, make sure that you *explain your assumptions* at the start of your answer!

The diagram on the next page shows recruitment activities in more detail.

3.2 Recruitment policy

FAST FORWARD

Detailed procedures for recruitment should only be devised and implemented within the context of a fair, consistent and coherent **policy**, or code of conduct.

A typical recruitment policy might deal with:

- Internal advertisement of vacancies, where possible
- Efficient and courteous processing of applications
- Fair and accurate provision of information to potential recruits
- Selection of candidates on the basis of suitability, without discrimination

As an example the Institute of Personnel and Development has issued a Recruitment Code.

The IPD Recruitment Code

1   Job advertisements should state clearly the form of reply desired, in particular whether this should be a formal application form or by curriculum vitae. Preferences should also be stated if handwritten replies are required.

2   An acknowledgement of reply should be made promptly to each applicant by the employing organisation or its agent. If it is likely to take some time before acknowledgements are made, this should be made clear in the advertisement.

3   Applicants should be informed of the progress of the selection procedures, what they will be (eg group selection, aptitude tests etc), the steps and time involved and the policy regarding expenses.

4   Detailed personal information (eg religion, medical history, place of birth, family background, etc) should not be called for unless it is relevant to the selection process.

5   Before applying for references, potential employers must secure permission of the applicant.

6   Applications must be treated as confidential.

The code also recommends certain courtesies and obligations on the part of the applicants.

Detailed procedures should be devised in order to make recruitment activity **systematic** and **consistent** throughout the organisation (especially where it is decentralised in the hands of line managers). Apart from the human resourcing requirements which need to be effectively and efficiently met, there is a **marketing** aspect to recruitment, as one 'interface' between the organisation and the outside world: applicants who feel they have been unfairly treated, or recruits who leave because they feel they have been misled, do not enhance the organisation's reputation in the labour market or the world at large.

The Recruitment Process

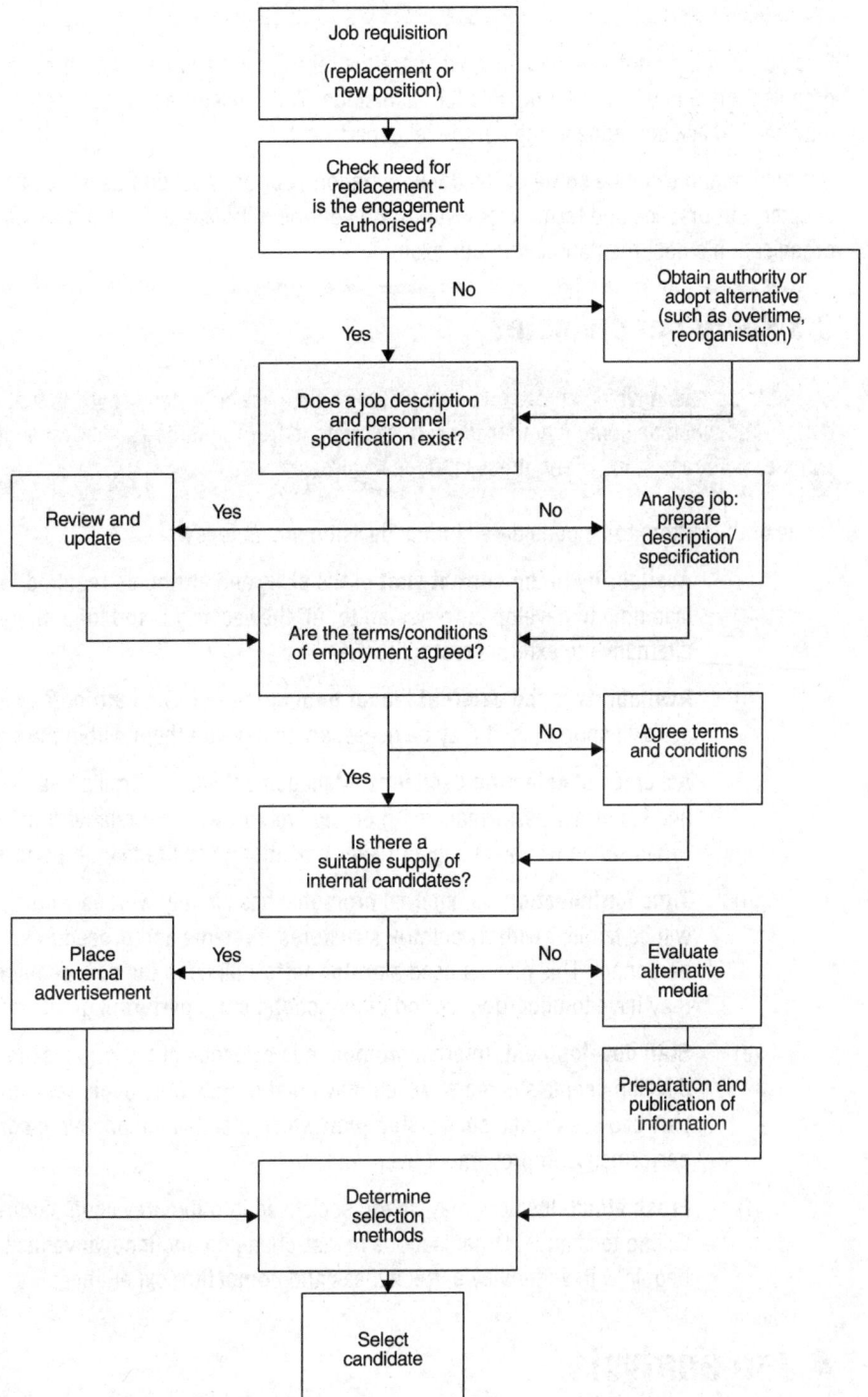

Find out, if you do not already know, what are the recruitment and selection procedures in your organisation, and who is responsible for each stage. The procedures manual should set this out, or you may need to ask someone in the personnel department.

Get hold of and examine some of the documentation your organisation uses. We show specimens in this chapter, but practice and terminology varies, so your own 'house style' will be invaluable. Compare your organisation's documentation with our example.

3.3 Recruit or promote?   12/02

FAST FORWARD

One of the areas in which an organisation will formulate a recruitment policy is that of the factors to be considered when deciding whether to **recruit** someone from **outside** to fill a vacancy *or* to **promote** or **transfer** someone from within the existing workforce.

Some of the factors to be considered in this decision are as follows.

(a)   **Availability in the current staff** of the skills and attributes required to fill the vacancy. If the lead time to develop current staff to 'fit' the vacancy is too long, there may be no immediate alternative to external recruitment.

(b)   **Availability in the external labour pool** of the skills and attributes required. Where there are skill shortages, it may be necessary to develop them within the organisation.

(c)   **Accuracy of selection decisions**. Management will be familiar with an internal promotee and his or her performance. An outside recruit will be a relatively unknown quantity and the organisation will be taking a greater risk attempt to predict job performance.

(d)   **Time for induction**. An internal promotee has already worked within the organisation and will be familiar with its culture, structures, systems and procedures, objectives and other personnel. This gives a head start for performance in the new position. An external recruit may have to undergo a period of induction before performing effectively.

(e)   **Staff development**. Internal promotion is evidence of the organisation's willingness to develop people's careers, which may build morale (and avoid resentments). It may also be part of a systematic **succession plan** which maintains managerial continuity and individual performance improvement over time.

(f)   **Fresh blood**. Insiders may be too socialised into the prevailing culture to see faults or be willing to change. Organisations in fast-changing and innovative fields may require new people with wider views, fresh ideas and competitor experience.

4 Job analysis   12/04

FAST FORWARD

A **job analysis** identifies the nature and content of each job, as a basis for determining specific requirements of the job holder.

Key term

Job analysis is: 'the process of collecting, analysing and setting out information about the content of jobs in order to provide the basis for a job description and data for recruitment, training, job evaluation and performance management. Job analysis concentrates on what job holders are expected to do.' (*Armstrong*)

The firm has to know what people are doing (or should be doing) in order to recruit effectively.

4.1 Information obtained from job analysis

Information that might be obtained from a job analysis includes the following.

Information	Comments
Purpose of the job	Set in the context of the organisation as a whole.
Content of the job	The detailed duties and responsibilities of the job.
Accountabilities	The results for which the job holder must account to his or her superior.
Performance criteria	Measures of acceptable performance in the job.
Responsibility	Scope of the job holder's authority, discretion to take decisions, responsibility for budget and so on.
Organisational factors	Reporting and liaison relationships in the organisation structure.
Developmental factors	Opportunities for skill, career and personal development (training, promotion paths etc).
Environmental factors	Working conditions, security and safety issues, equipment and so on.

The product of job analysis is usually a **job description**: a detailed statement of the activities (mental and physical) involved in the job, and other relevant factors in the social and physical environment. (See Section 5.) This has many uses in personnel management.

Exam focus point

A 15 mark question in the December 2004 exam addressed the definition, stages and information requirements of job analysis. In his report, the examiner highlighted a common pitfall: job analysis (like job evaluation, covered in Chapter 11) is about the *content of the job – not* the person who occupies that position. Ensure that you demonstrate your understanding of such fundamental points by defining your terms at the beginning of your exam answers.

4.2 Carrying out a job analysis

FAST FORWARD

Job analysis may be carried out using **interviews**, **questionnaires**, **observation** and **documentary evidence**.

A systematic approach to job analysis may be as follows.

Step 1 **Obtain documentary information** such as procedures manuals and written instructions relating to the job

Step 2 **Ask managers** about more general aspects such as the job's purpose, the main activities, the responsibilities involved and the relationships with others

Step 3 **Ask job holders** questions about their jobs – perceptions might differ

Step 4 **Observe** job holders to see what they actually do.

Various techniques may be used in job analysis.

4.2.1 Interviews

Interviews establish basic facts about the job from the job holder's point of view. There are two sorts of information.

(a) **Basic facts** about the job, such as the job title, the job holder's manager or team leader, people reporting to the jobholder, the main tasks or duties, official targets or performance standards.

(b) More **subjective issues**, which are harder to measure, but which are still important.

- The amount of supervision a person receives
- How much freedom a person has to take decisions
- How hard the job is
- The skills/qualifications needed to carry out the job
- How the job fits within the business process
- How work is allocated

The advantages and disadvantages of interviewing as a job analysis technique can be summarised as follows.

Advantages	Disadvantages
Interactive, flexible: follow-on questions can be asked in the light of information received	Time consuming and labour intensive (and therefore also costly)
Easy to organise and carry out	Hard to analyse data provided in narrative form.
	Subjective and subject to factors such as interviewer bias, interviewee defensiveness.

4.2.2 Questionnaires

Questionnaires are sometimes used in job analysis. Their success depends on the willingness of people to complete them accurately.

- They gather purely factual relevant information (if questions are well designed)
- They can cover large numbers of staff cost-effectively
- They provide a structure to the process of information gathering

4.2.3 Checklists and inventories

The job holder marks down the importance and relevance in the job of a list of activities/characteristics.

Activity description	Time spent on activity		Importance of activity	
Processes sales invoices	☐	Less than 10%	☐	Unimportant
	☐	10% to 20%	☐	Not very important
	☐	20-30%	☐	Important
	…and so on			

4.2.4 Other methods of data-gathering

Other methods of data gathering include:

(a)   **Observation**. People are watched doing the job. This may be used for jobs which can be easily observed (eg physical tasks), but is less suitable for knowledge-based work.

(b)   **Self description**. Jobholders are asked to prepare their own job descriptions. People often find it hard to stand back from what they are doing, but they are also most familiar with the reality of their jobs.

(c)   **Diaries and logs**. People keep records of what they do over a period of time, and these can be used by the analyst to develop job descriptions.

4.2.5 Which method should be used?

It depends – and a given job analysis exercise might involve a variety of methods. Questionnaires or checklists save time. Interviews give a better idea of the detail. Self-description shows how people *perceive* their jobs, which may be very different from how managers perceive them. Diaries and logs are useful for management jobs, in which a lot is going on.

Case Study

Workset is a job analysis system developed by Belbin. Workset uses colour coding to classify work and working time into seven types.

1	Blue: tasks the job holder carries out in a prescribed manner to an approved standard
2	Yellow: individual responsibility to meet an objective (results, not means)
3	Green: tasks that vary according to the reactions and needs of others
4	Orange: shared rather than individual responsibility for meeting an objective
5	Grey: work incidental to the job, not relevant to the four core categories
6	White: new or creative undertaking outside normal duties
7	Pink: demands the presence of the job holder but leads to no useful results

The manager gives an outline of the proportion of time which the manager expects the jobholder to spend on each 'colour' of work. The job holder then briefs the manager on what has actually been done. This highlights differences: between managers' and job-holders' perceptions of jobs; between the perceptions of different jobholders in the same nominal position, who had widely different ideas as to what they were supposed to do.

Important issues arise when there is a gap in perception. Underperformance in different kinds of work can be identified, and people can be steered to the sort of work which suits them best.

Question   Workset job classification

Analyse your own working time according to the Workset classification above. Do the results surprise you?

4.3 Competences

In recent years, recruiters have been using the **competences** as a means to select candidates. Work-based competences directly relate to the job (eg the ability to prepare a trial balance); behavioural competences relate to underlying issues of personality.

A more recent approach to job analysis is the definition and analysis of **competences**.

Key term

> **Competence** is 'a capacity that leads to behaviour that meets the job demands within the parameters of the organisational environment and that, in turn, brings about desired results' (Boyzatis). Some take this further and suggest that a competence embodies the ability to transfer skills and knowledge to new situations within the occupational area.

Different sorts of competences include the following.

(a) **Behavioural/personal** competences: underlying personal characteristics people bring to work (eg interpersonal skills); personal characteristics and behaviour for successful performance, for example, 'ability to relate well to others'. Most jobs require people to be good communicators.

(b) **Work-based/occupational competences** refer to 'expectations of workplace performance and the outputs and standards people in specific roles are expected to obtain'. This approach is used in NVQ standards. They cover what people have to do to achieve the results of the job. For example, a competence of a Certified Accountant includes 'produce financial and other statements and report to management'.

These competences can be elaborated by identifying **positive** and **negative** indicators, or **performance criteria**.

5 Job description   12/01, 6/05

A **job description** outlines the **tasks** of the job and its place within the organisation.

Key term

> **Job description** is a detailed statement of the activities (mental and physical) involved in the job, and other relevant factors in the social and physical environment.

5.1 Uses of job descriptions

Job descriptions can be used for a number of purposes in human resource management.

(a) In **recruitment**, to set out the demands of the job and what it offers: a useful basis for advertising vacancies, interviewing candidates, assessing candidates against requirements and so on

(b) In **reward management**: to set pay rates fair for the job

(c) In **induction**, giving new recruits a clear guide to job requirements

(d) In **appraisal** and **training/development**, to suggest areas in which job requirements need to be more effectively met

(e) In **job design**, to indicate where areas of responsibility are ambiguous, or inflexible; where there could be greater challenge or task variety and so on.

5.2 Contents of a job description

Typical contents of a job description include the following.

(a) **Job title** (eg Assistant Financial Controller).

(b) **Reporting to** (eg the Assistant Financial Controller reports to the Financial Controller), in other words the person's immediate boss.

(c) **Subordinates** directly reporting to the job holder (if any)

(d) **Overall purpose** of the job, distinguishing it from other jobs

(e) **Principal accountabilities or main tasks**

    (i) Group the main activities into a number of broad areas

    (ii) Define each activity as a statement of accountability: what the job holder is expected to achieve (eg tests new systems to ensure they meet agreed systems specifications)

(f) **Terms and conditions** of employment, working conditions and special demands (eg hazards)

The following is an example of a simple job description.

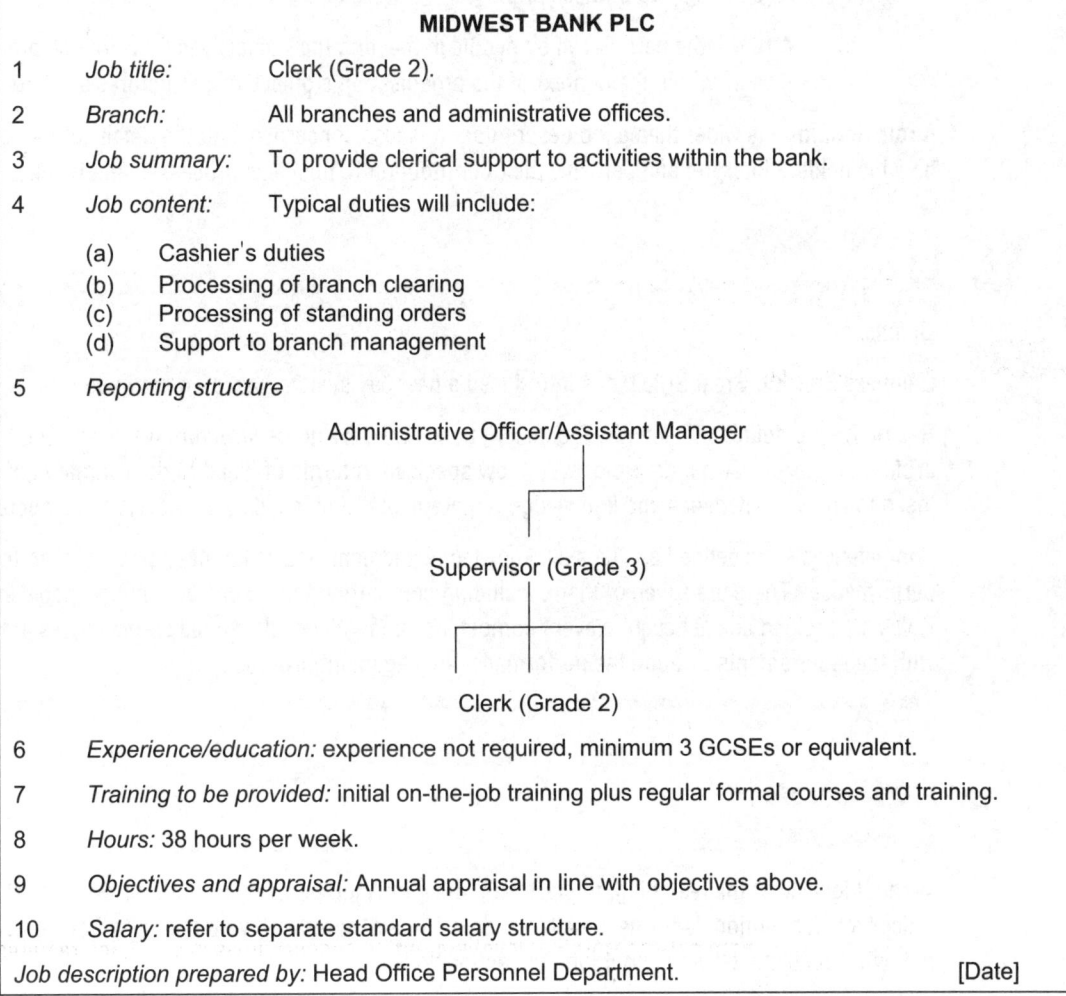

		MIDWEST BANK PLC
1	*Job title:*	Clerk (Grade 2).
2	*Branch:*	All branches and administrative offices.
3	*Job summary:*	To provide clerical support to activities within the bank.
4	*Job content:*	Typical duties will include:

    (a) Cashier's duties
    (b) Processing of branch clearing
    (c) Processing of standing orders
    (d) Support to branch management

5   *Reporting structure*

Administrative Officer/Assistant Manager

Supervisor (Grade 3)

Clerk (Grade 2)

6   *Experience/education:* experience not required, minimum 3 GCSEs or equivalent.

7   *Training to be provided:* initial on-the-job training plus regular formal courses and training.

8   *Hours:* 38 hours per week.

9   *Objectives and appraisal:* Annual appraisal in line with objectives above.

10   *Salary:* refer to separate standard salary structure.

Job description prepared by: Head Office Personnel Department.   [Date]

5.3 Limitations of job descriptions

Townsend (*Up the Organisation*) suggested that job descriptions are of limited use.

(a)   They are only suited for jobs where the work is largely repetitive and predictable.

(b)   Management jobs are likely to be constantly changing as external influences impact upon them, so a job description is constantly out of date.

(c)   Difficulties arise when job descriptions are taken too literally, and cause demarcation disputes and costly over-manning practices.

A job description is a static 'snapshot' of a job at a given time: it requires flexibility and constant, negotiated revision. It must also be remembered that job descriptions are 'the map' – not 'the territory': they are designed as a tool for management, not a constraint.

5.4 Alternatives to job descriptions

It has been suggested that job descriptions should be written in terms of the **outputs and performance levels** expected. Some firms are moving towards **accountability profiles** in which outputs and performance are identified explicitly.

Armstrong suggests a crucial difference between:

(a)   **A job** – a group of tasks *and*

(b)   **A role** – the part played by people in meeting their objectives by working competently and flexibly within the context of the organisation's objectives, structures and processes.

A **role definition** is wider than a job description. It is less concerned with the details of the job content, but how job holders interpret and perceive their contribution to business processes and results.

 Case Study

Guinness

Guinness Brewing Great Britain has introduced a new pay system based on competences.

Restrictive job definitions, lengthy job descriptions and a 24-grade structure were replaced by broad role profiles and three pay bands. Roles were now specified in terms of 'need to do' (primary accountabilities), 'need to know' (experience and knowledge requirements) and 'need to be' (levels of competence).

Competences were defined as 'the skill, knowledge and behaviours that need to be applied for effective performance'. There are seven of them, including commitment to results and interpersonal effectiveness. Roles are profiled against each relevant competence and individuals' actual competences are compared with the requirements through the performance management process.

 Question   Job description

Without looking at the real thing, to start with, draw up a job description for your own job. Now look at the official job description. Is it true, detailed and up-to-date, compared with the actual job as you saw it? If not, what does this tell you about job descriptions?

6 Person specification

12/01, 6/05

A **person specification** identifies the characteristics of the ideal job holder. The Seven Point Plan and Five Point Pattern are examples of person specification formats.

Key term

'A **person specification** sets out the education, qualifications, training, experience personal attributes and competences a job holder requires to perform her or his job satisfactorily.' (*Armstrong*)

The job description outlines the **job**: the person (or personnel) specification describes the **person** needed to do the job, or the ideal job holder.

Exam focus point

The similarity of terms in this area is a potential exam pitfall. You were asked to distinguish between job description and person specification in the December 2001 exam – but make sure you can also distinguish these terms from job analysis, job evaluation, performance appraisal and other like-sounding concepts!

6.1 Frameworks for person specification

6.1.1 The Seven Point Plan

The **Seven Point Plan** put forward by Professor **Rodger** in 1951 draws the selector's attention to seven points about the candidate.

- **Physical attributes** (such as neat appearance, ability to speak clearly)
- **Attainment** (including educational qualifications)
- **General intelligence**
- **Special aptitudes** (such as neat work, speed and accuracy)
- **Interests** (practical and social)
- **Disposition** (or manner: friendly, helpful and so on)
- Background **circumstances**

6.1.2 The Five Point Pattern

Munro-Fraser's Five Point Pattern is an alternative classification. It focuses attention on:

- **Impact on others**: physical attributes, speech, manner

- **Acquired knowledge** and qualifications

- **Innate abilities**: ability to learn, mental agility

- **Motivation**: What sort of goals the individual sets, how much effort goes into achieving them, how successful

- **Adjustment**: emotional stability, tolerance of slips

6.1.3 Competence definitions

The two methods described above have been in use for many years. Recruiters are increasingly using **competences** (see Section 4.3) in designing person specifications.

6.2 Preparing person specifications

Each feature in the person specification should be classified as essential, desirable or contra-indicated (undesirable) for competent performance in the job.

PERSON SPECIFICATION: Customer Accounts Manager			
	ESSENTIAL	DESIRABLE	CONTRA-INDICATED
Physical attributes	Clear speech Well-groomed Good health	Age 25-40	Age under 25 Chronic ill-health and absence
Attainments	2 'A' levels GCSE Maths and English Thorough knowledge of retail environment	Degree (any discipline) Marketing training 2 years' experience in supervisory post	No experience of supervision or retail environment

PERSON SPECIFICATION: Customer Accounts Manager cont'd			
	ESSENTIAL	DESIRABLE	CONTRA-INDICATED
Intelligence	High verbal intelligence		
Aptitudes	Facility with numbers Attention to detail and accuracy Social skills for customer relations	Analytical abilities (problem solving) Understanding of systems and IT	No mathematical ability Low tolerance of technology
Interests	Social: team activity		Time-consuming hobbies 'Solo' interests only
Disposition	Team player Persuasive Tolerance of pressure and change	Initiative	Anti-social Low tolerance of responsibility
Circumstances	Able to work late, take work home	Located in area of office	

6.3 Limitations of person specifications

Care must be taken in the design and use of person specifications, for a number of reasons.

(a) If the specification is not used **flexibly**, and fails to evolve as business and employment conditions change, it may swiftly lose its relevance.

(b) **Attainments** are often focused on educational achievements, since there has traditionally been a strong correlation between management potential and higher education. However, graduate recruitment is now in crisis, as more people enter higher education, with more diverse educational backgrounds, and more diverse educational standards.

(c) **Physical attributes** and **background circumstances** may suggest criteria which can now be interpreted as discriminatory (on grounds of sex, race, disability and so on).

(d) The category of **general intelligence** has traditionally been based on IQ, a narrow definition of intelligence as mental dexterity: measures such as emotional intelligence (EQ) may also need to be taken into account.

In addition, person specifications were explicitly developed to match the aptitudes of job applicants to the requirements of an occupation. If employees are recruited and deployed on a **project** or **consultancy basis**, a different package of attributes will be required for each project in each organisation.

7 Advertising vacancies

FAST FORWARD

Job advertising is aimed at attracting quality applicants and aiding self-selection.

The object of recruitment advertising is to attract suitable candidates and deter unsuitable candidates.

7.1 Qualities of a good job advertisement

Job advertisements should be:

(a) **Concise**, but comprehensive enough to be an accurate description of the job, its rewards and requirements

(b) **Attractive** to the maximum number of the right people

(c) **Positive and honest** about the organisation. Disappointed expectations will be a prime source of dissatisfaction when an applicant actually comes into contact with the organisation.

(d) **Relevant and appropriate to the job and the applicant**. Skills, qualifications and special aptitudes required should be prominently set out, along with special features of the job that might attract – on indeed deter – applicants, such as shiftwork or extensive travel.

7.2 Contents of a job advertisement

Typical contents of an advertisement targeted at external job seekers would include information about:

(a) The **organisation**: its main business and location, at least

(b) The **job**: title, main duties and responsibilities and special features

(c) **Conditions**: special factors affecting the job

(d) **Qualifications and experience** (required, and preferred); other attributes, aptitudes and/or knowledge required

(e) **Rewards**: salary, benefits, opportunities for training, career development, and so on

(f) **Application process**: how to apply, to whom, and by what date

It should encourage a degree of **self-selection**, so that the target population begins to narrow itself down. The information contained in the advertisement should deter unsuitable applicants as well as encourage potentially suitable ones.

Question | Job advertisement

Dealing with individuals demands a certain... ...um...

You've heard the old line...
'You don't have to be mad to work here, but it helps'. It's like that at AOK, but in the nicest possible way. We believe that our Personnel Department should operate for the benefit of our staff, and not that staff should conform to statistical profiles. It doesn't make for an easy life, but dealing with people as individuals, rather than numbers, certainly makes it a rewarding one.

We're committed to an enlightened personnel philosophy. We firmly believe that our staff are our most important asset, and we go a long way both to attract the highest quality of people, and to retain them.

AOK is a company with a difference. We're a highly progressive, international organisation, one of the world's leading manufacturers in the medical electronics field.

...Character

As an expanding company, we now need another experienced Personnel Generalist to join us at our UK headquarters in Reigate, Surrey.

Essentially we're looking for an individual, a chameleon character who will assume an influential role in recruitment, employee relations, salary administration, compensation and benefits, or whatever the situation demands. The flexibility to interchange with various functions is vital. Within your designated area, you'll experience a large degree of independence. You'll be strong in personality, probably already experienced in personnel management in a small company. Whatever your background you'll certainly be someone who likes to help people help themselves and who is happy to get involved with people at all levels within the organisation.

Obviously, in a fast growing company with a positive emphasis on effective personnel work, your prospects for promotion are excellent. Salaries are highly attractive and benefits are, of course, comprehensive.

So if you're the kind of personnel individual who enjoys personal contact, problem solving, and will thrive on the high pace of a progressive, international organisation, such as AOK, get in touch with us by writing or telephoning, quoting ref: 451/BPD, to AOK House, Reigate, Surrey.

What do you think of this advertisement? How can you improve it?

Answer

(a)   *Good points about the advertisement and points for improvement*

(i)   It is attractively designed in terms of page layout.

(ii)   The tone of the headline and much of the body copy is informal, colloquial and even friendly. It starts with a joke, implying that the company has a sense of humour.

(iii)   The written style is fluent and attractive.

(iv)   It appears to offer quite a lot of information about the culture of the company – how it feels about personnel issues, where it's going etc – as well as about the job vacancy.

(b)   *Improvements that could be made*

(i)   There is too much copy. Readers may not have the patience to read through so much (rather wordy) prose.

(ii) There are many words and expressions which sound good, and seem to *imply* good things, but are in fact empty of substance, and commit the organisation to nothing. They are usually the 'stock' expressions like 'committed to an enlightened personnel philosophy': what does that actually *mean*?

(iii) There are confusing contradictions, eg between the requirements for flexibility, 'interchange with various functions', do 'whatever the situation demands' etc and the more cautious 'within your designated area ...'.

(iv) The advertisement does not give enough 'hard' information to make effective response likely – and then fails to do its job of facilitating response at all! Despite the invitation to telephone, no number is given. No named correspondent is cited, merely a reference number – despite the claimed emphasis on people as people, not numbers.

7.3 Advertising media

FAST FORWARD

A number of print, electronic and interpersonal **media** are used for job **advertising**.

Media for recruitment advertising include the following.

(a) **In-house magazine, noticeboards**, e-mail or intranet. An organisation might invite applications from employees who would like a transfer or a promotion to the particular vacancy advertised, from within the internal labour pool.

(b) **Professional and specialist newspapers or magazines,** such as *Accountancy Age, Marketing Week* or *Computing.*

(c) **National newspapers:** often used for senior management jobs or vacancies for skilled workers, where potential applicants will not necessarily be found through local advertising.

(d) **Local newspapers:** suitable for jobs where applicants are sought from the local area.

(e) **Local radio, television and cinema**. These are becoming increasingly popular, especially for large-scale campaigns for large numbers of vacancies.

(f) **Job centres**. Vacancies for unskilled work (rather than skilled work or management jobs) are advertised through local job centres, although in theory any type of job can be advertised here.

(g) **School and university careers offices**. Ideally, the manager responsible for recruitment in an area should try to maintain a close liaison with careers officers. Some large organisations organise special meetings or **careers fairs** in universities and colleges, as a kind of showcase for the organisation and the careers it offers.

(h) The **Internet**. Many businesses advertise vacancies on their websites, or register vacancies with on-line databases. The advantages of '*e-recruitment*' include:

   (i) Large audience, reached at low cost

   (ii) Interactivity with links to information, downloadable application forms, email contacts and so on

   (iii) Pre-selection of people with Internet skills

7.4 Choosing

The choice of advertising medium depends on criteria such as **reach, targeting** and **cost.**

There is a variety of advertising media available to recruiters. Factors influencing the choice of medium include the following.

(a) **The type of organisation**. A factory is likely to advertise a vacancy for an unskilled worker in a different way to a company advertising for a member of the Institute of Personnel and Development for an HRM position.

(b) **The type of job**. Managerial jobs may merit national advertisement, whereas semi-skilled jobs may only warrant local coverage, depending on the supply of suitable candidates in the local area. Specific skills may be most appropriately reached through trade, technical or professional journals, such as those for accountants or computer programmers.

(c) **The cost of advertising**. It is more expensive to advertise in a national newspaper than on local radio, and more expensive to advertise on local radio than in a local newspaper etc.

(d) The **readership and circulation** (type and number of readers/listeners) of the medium, and its suitability for the number and type of people the organisation wants to reach.

(e) The **frequency** with which the organisation wants to advertise the job vacancy, and the duration of the recruitment process.

Exam focus point

A 15-mark essay question was set in December 2003 on recruitment advertising: factors to be taken into account (see Sections 7.1-7.2 for example) and factors which will influence the choice of advertising media (see Section 7.4 above). This is a 'classic' question: you might identify other topics that have clear 'factors influencing ...', 'benefits and limitations of ...' and so on.

Chapter Roundup

- Effective recruitment practices ensure that a firm has enough **people with the right skills**.

- The recruitment process involves **personnel specialists** and **line managers**, sometimes with the help of recruitment **consultants**.

- **Recruitment** is a systematic **process** of (a) identifying and defining skill needs and (b) attracting suitably skilled candidates.

- Detailed procedures for recruitment should only be devised and implemented within the context of a fair, consistent and coherent **policy**, or code of conduct.

- One of the areas in which an organisation will formulate a recruitment policy is that of the factors to be considered when deciding whether to **recruit** someone from **outside** to fill a vacancy *or* to **promote** or **transfer** someone from within the existing workforce.

- A **job analysis** identifies the nature and content of each job, as a basis for determining specific requirements of the job holder.

- Job analysis may be carried out using **interviews, questionnaires, observation** and **documentary evidence.**

- In recent years, recruiters have been using the **competences** as a means to select candidates. Work-based competences directly relate to the job (eg the ability to prepare a trial balance); behavioural competences relate to underlying issues of personality.

- A **job description** outlines the **tasks** of the job and its place within the organisation.

- A **person specification** identifies the characteristics of the ideal job holder. The Seven Point Plan and Five Point Pattern are examples of person specification formats.

- **Job advertising** is aimed at attracting quality applicants and aiding self-selection.

- A number of print, electronic and interpersonal **media** are used for job **advertising.**

- The choice of advertising medium depends on criteria such as **reach, targeting** and **cost**.

Quick Quiz

1   What is the underlying principle of human resources management?

2   What, in brief, are the stages of the recruitment and selection process?

3   What is the role of line managers in the recruitment process?

4   List the factors determining whether a firm should use recruitment consultants.

5   The process of describing the ideal candidate for a job is called:

   A   Job analysis
   B   Job description
   C   Person specification
   D   Job evaluation

6   What is a currently fashionable approach to drawing up job analyses and descriptions?

7   'General Intelligence' is a component of the Five Point Pattern. *True or False?*

8   What are the characteristics of a good job advertisement?

Answers to Quick Quiz

1   People are a scarce resource and need to be managed effectively.

2   Identifying/defining requirements; attracting potential employees; selecting candidates.

3   It depends – making a requisition, identifying departmental needs, interviewing, reviewing the job analysis, job description etc.

4   Cost: expertise; impartiality; organisation structure and politics; time; supply of labour.

5   C: make sure you can define the other terms as well.

6   The use of competences – work based and behavioural.

7   False: it is a component of the Seven Point Pattern. The Five Point Plan or Pattern includes impact on others; acquired knowledge and qualifications; innate abilities; motivation; adjustment.

8   Concise; reaches the right people; gives a good impression; relevant to the job, identifying skills required etc.

Number	Level	Marks	Time
Q7	Examination	15	27 mins

Now try the question below from the Exam Question Bank

BPP
PROFESSIONAL EDUCATION

Selection

Topic list	Syllabus reference
1 A systematic approach to selection	2 (a)
2 Application methods	2 (a)
3 Selection methods in outline	2 (e)
4 Interviews	2 (f)
5 Selection testing	2 (e)
6 Other selection methods	2 (e)
7 Evaluating recruitment and selection practices	2 (a)

Introduction

Once candidates have been attracted to apply (Chapter 7), there needs to be a systematic process to separate out those who are most suitable for the job.

This chapter looks at how selection decisions are made. Again, we start with an overview of the **process** – and this is in itself one of the key learning points.

In **Section 2**, we look at effective formats for gathering information about applicants.

In **Sections 3 – 6**, we examine a range of selection tools. **Interviews** are the most popular – but not necessarily the most effective in its ability to predict future job performance! Organisations are increasingly using 'back-up' methods such as tests and group assessments.

In **Section 7**, we complete the planning and control cycle by suggesting how a manager might **evaluate** the effectiveness of the recruitment and selection process – and what might be done to improve it where necessary.

While you learn the detailed procedural aspects (as the examiner requires), bear in mind what they are designed to *do*: identify the best person for the job *and* ensure fair treatment for all potential applicants. (This issue will be explored in detail in Chapter 9.)

Study guide

Section 13 – Selection methods

Section 14 – Selection interview

The full details of these sessions can be found in the introductory pages to this Study Text.

Exam guide

Bear in mind that there are a number of procedures and techniques involved in selection. Questions have so far focused specifically on selection interviews and selection testing – but 'other techniques' might equally form the basis of a case study or essay question.

1 A systematic approach to selection

> The process of **selection** begins when the recruiter receives details of candidates interested in the job. A systematic approach includes short-listing, interviewing (and other selection methods), decision-making and follow-up.

A systematic approach to selection may be outlined as follows.

Step 1 Deal with responses to job advertisements. This might involve sending **application forms** to candidates.

Step 2 Assess each application against **key criteria** in the job advertisement and specification. Critical factors may include age, qualifications, experience or whatever.

Step 3 **Sort applications** into 'possible', 'unsuitable' and 'marginal. 'Possibles' will then be more closely scrutinised, and a shortlist for interview drawn up. Ideally, this should be done by both the personnel specialist and the prospective manager of the successful candidate.

Step 4 Invite candidates **for interview.**

Step 5 Reinforce interviews with **selection testing,** if suitable.

Step 6 **Review** un-interviewed 'possibles', and 'marginals', and put potential future candidates on hold, or in reserve.

Step 7 Send **standard letters** to unsuccessful applicants, and inform them simply that they have not been successful. Reserves will be sent a holding letter: 'We will keep your details on file, and should any suitable vacancy arise in future…'.

Step 8 Make a **provisional offer** to the successful candidate.

2 Application methods

Many firms require candidates to fill out an **application form**. This is standardised and the firm can ask for specific information about work experience and qualifications, as well as other personal data. Alternatives include CVs with a covering letter.

2.1 Application forms

Job advertisements usually ask candidates to fill in a **job application form**, or to send information about themselves and their previous job experience (their **curriculum vitae** or CV), usually with a covering letter briefly explaining why they think they are qualified to do the job.

Application forms are a cost-efficient, standardised way of gathering data which will help to identify suitable candidates and weed out unsuitable candidates. They do this in two ways.

(a) **Asking specific, relevant questions.** A good application form will be designed around the person specification. So if a certain number of GCSEs are needed, the applicant will be asked to list educational qualifications, for example.

(b) **Finding out more.** Candidates may be given the opportunity to write at more length about themselves, their ambitions, and why they want the job. Some application forms ask people to write about key successes and failures. This gives information about the candidate's underlying personality as well as matters such as neatness, literacy and ability to communicate in writing.

A sample application form is shown on the next two pages.

Question

Application forms

Suggest four possible design faults in job application forms. You may be able to draw on your own personal experience.

Answer

(a) Boxes too small to contain the information asked for

(b) Forms which are (or look) so lengthy or complicated that a prospective applicant either completes them perfunctorily or gives up (and applies to another employer instead)

(c) Illegal (eg discriminatory) or offensive questions

(d) Lack of clarity as to what (and how much) information is required

2.2 CVs

Many firms are too small to use standard application forms. The requirements of a business employing, say, 30 people, are very different from a large employer such as the Civil Service or British Airways. This is why many job advertisements ask for a CV and a covering letter.

How a CV is presented tells a great deal about the candidate – not only the information on the CV but the candidate's neatness and ability to structure information.

Application forms have the merit of being standardised, so that all candidates are asked the same information. Gaps can thus be identified clearly, and essential information can be asked for. CVs, on the other hand, are designed to showcase the best attributes of the candidate, and may need to be checked and even challenged at the interview and reference-checking stages of selection.

2.3 Screening applications

For some jobs, hundreds or even thousands of people might apply, so recruiters can often use structured ways of sifting the data. Some firms use computers to match items on CVs or application forms to key criteria, in order to rank the candidates or generate a shortlist.

			Page 1

AOK PLC

APPLICATION FORM

Post applied for ....

PERSONAL DETAILS

Surname Mr/ Mrs/ Miss/Ms

First name

Address

Post code

Telephone   (Daytime)   (Evenings)

Date of birth

Nationality

Education (latest first)

Date		Institution	Exams passed/qualifications
From	To		

TRAINING AND OTHER SKILLS

Please give details of any specialised training courses you have attended.

Please note down other skills such as languages (and degree of fluency), driving licence (with endorsements if any), keyboard skills (familiarity with software package).

EMPLOYMENT		Page 2	
Dates		Employer	Title
From	To	name and address	and duties

Current salary and benefits:

INTERESTS

Please describe your leisure/hobby/sporting interests.

YOUR COMMENTS

Why do you think you are suitable for the job advertised?

ADDITIONAL INFORMATION

Do you have any permanent health problems? If so, please give details.

When would you be able to start work?

REFERENCES

Please give two references. One should be a former employer.

Name Name

Address   Address

Position   Position

Signed   Date

3 Selection methods in outline

All **selection methods** are **limited** in their ability to predict future job performance!

3.1 A range of methods

We will briefly list the main selection methods here. The more important are discussed in the following sections.

Methods	Examples
Interviewing	• Individual (one-to-one) • Interview panels • Selection boards
Selection tests	• Intelligence • Aptitude • Personality • Proficiency • Medical
Reference checking	• Job references • Character references
Work sampling	• Portfolios • Trial periods or exercises
Group selection methods	• Assessment centres

3.2 Which method is best?

Smith and Abrahamsen developed a scale that plots selection methods according to how accurately they predict a candidate's future performance in the job. This is known as a **predictive validity** scale. The scale ranges from 1 (meaning that a method is right every time) to 0 (meaning that a method is no better than chance).

Method	% use by firms	Predictive validity
Interviews	92	0.17
References	74	0.13
Work sampling	18	0.57
Assessment centres	14	0.40
Personality tests	13	0.40
Cognitive tests	11	0.54
Biodata (biography analysis)	4	0.40
Graphology (handwriting analysis)	3	0.00

The results surprisingly show a pattern of employers relying most heavily on the *least* accurate selection methods. Interviews in particular (and for the reasons given earlier) seem not much better than tossing a coin.

4 Interviews

Most firms use selection **interviews**, on a one-to-one or panel basis. Interviews have the advantage of flexibility, but have limitations as predictors of job performance.

Most firms use the interview as the main basis for selection decisions.

4.1 Purposes of selection interviews

Purposes of the selection interview include:

(a) Finding the best person for the job, by giving the organisation a chance to assess applicants (and particularly their interpersonal and communication skills) directly

(b) Making sure that applicants understand what the job involves, what career prospects there are, and other aspects of the employment relationship on offer

(c) Giving the best possible impression of the organisation as a prospective employer

(d) Offering fair treatment to all applicants, whether they get the job or not: in the UK, this is covered by anti-discrimination legislation, but it is also part of the organisation's 'employer brand' and reputation in the labour market

4.2 Preparation of the interview

Candidates should be given clear instructions about the date, time and location of the interview.

The layout of the interview room should be designed to create the desired impression of the organisation, and to create the atmosphere for the interview. In most cases, it will be designed to put the candidate at ease and facilitate communication (eg removing unnecessary formal barriers) – but it may also be used to create pressures on the candidate, to test his or her response to stress.

The agenda and questions should be at least partly prepared in advance, based on *documentation* such as:

(a) The job description (which sets out the requirements of the job)
(b) The person specification (which describes the ideal candidate)
(c) The application form and/or the applicant's CV (which outline the candidate's claim to suitability)

4.3 Conduct of the interview

Questions should be paced and put carefully. The interviewer should not be trying to confuse the candidate, plunging immediately into demanding questions or picking on isolated points; neither, however, should the interviewee be allowed to digress or gloss over important points. The interviewer must retain control over the information-gathering process.

Type of question	Comment
Open questions	('Who…? What…? Where…? When…? Why….?) These force candidates to put together their own responses in complete sentences. This encourages them to talk, keeps the interview flowing, and is most revealing ('Why do you want to be an accountant?')
Probing questions	These aim to discover the deeper significance of the candidate's answers, especially if they are initially dubious, uninformative, too short, or too vague. ('But what was it about accountancy that *particularly* appealed to you?')
Closed questions	Invite only 'yes' or 'no' answers: ('Did you…?', 'Have you…?'). (a) They elicit an answer *only* to the question asked. This may be useful where there are points to be pinned down ('Did you pass your exam?') (b) Candidates cannot express their personality, or interact with the interviewer on a deeper level. (c) They make it easier for candidates to conceal things ('You never *asked* me…'). (d) They make the interviewer work very hard.
Problem solving questions	Present the candidate with a situation and ask him/her to explain how s(he) would deal with it. ('How would you motivate your staff to do a task that they did not want to do?') Such questions are used to establish whether the candidate will be able to deal with the sort of problems that are likely to arise in the job.
Leading questions	Encourage the candidate to give a certain reply. ('We are looking for somebody who likes detailed figure work. How much do you enjoy dealing with numbers?' or 'Don't you agree that…?' 'Surely…?). The danger with this type of question is that the candidate will give the answer that he thinks the interviewer wants to hear.

Question

Identify the type of question used in the following examples, and discuss the opportunities and constraints they offer the interviewee who must answer them.

(a)   'So, you're interested in a Business Studies degree, are you, Jo?

(b)   'Surely you're interested in Business Studies, Jo?'

(c)   'How about a really useful qualification like a Business Studies degree, Jo? Would you consider that?'

(d)   'Why are you interested in a Business Studies degree, Jo?

(e)   'Why particularly Business Studies, Jo?'

Answer

(a) Closed. (The only answer is 'yes' or 'no', unless Jo expands on it, at his or her own initiative.)

(b) Leading. (Even if Jo was not interested, (s)he should get the message that 'yes' would be what the interviewer wanted, or expected, to hear.)

(c) Leading closed multiple! ('Really useful' leads Jo to think that the 'correct' answer will be 'yes': There is not much opportunity for any other answer, without expanding on it unasked.)

(d) Open. (Jo has to explain, in his or her own words.)

(e) Probing. (If Jo's answer has been unconvincing, short or vague, this forces a specific answer.)

Evaluating the response to questions requires another set of interpersonal skills.

(a) The interviewer must **listen carefully** to the responses and evaluate them so as to judge what the candidate is:

- Wanting to say
- Trying not to say
- Saying, but does not mean, or is lying about
- Having difficulty saying

(b) In addition, the interviewer will have to be aware when (s)he is hearing:

- Something (s)he needs to know

- Something (s)he *doesn't* need to know

- Only what (s)he *expects* to hear

- Inadequately – when his or her own attitudes, perhaps prejudices, are getting in the way of an objective response to the candidate

Candidates should also be given the opportunity to ask questions. The choice of questions might well have some influence on how the interviewers assess a candidate's interest in and understanding of the job. Moreover, there is information that the candidate will need to know about the organisation, the job, and indeed the interview process.

Exam focus point

> A 15-mark essay question was set in June 2003 on the purpose of selection interviewing and the advantages and disadvantages of face-to-face and panel interviews (see below).

4.4 Types of interview

4.4.1 Individual interviews

Individual, one-to-one or face-to-face interviews are the most common selection method.

Advantages include:

(a) Direct face-to-face communication, with opportunities for the interviewer to use both verbal and non-verbal cues to assess the candidate.

(b) Rapport between the candidate and the interviewer: each has to give attention solely to the other, and there is potentially a relaxed atmosphere, if the interviewer is willing to establish an informal style.

(c) Flexibility in the direction and follow-up of questions.

Disadvantages include:

(a)   The candidate may be able to disguise lack of knowledge in a specialist area of which the interviewer knows little.

(b)   The interviewer's perception may be selective or distorted, and this lack of objectivity may go unnoticed and unchecked.

(c)   The greater opportunity for personal rapport with the candidate may cause a weakening of the interviewer's objective judgement.

4.4.2 Panel interviews

Panel interviews are designed to overcome such disadvantages. A panel may consist of two or three people who together interview a single candidate: most commonly, an HR specialist and the departmental manager who will have responsibility for the successful candidate. This saves the firm time and enables better assessment.

4.4.3 Selection boards

Large formal panels, or **selection boards**, may also be convened where there are a number of individuals or groups with an interest in the selection.

Advantages include:

(a)   A number of people see candidates, and share information about them at a single meeting.

(b)   Similarly, they can compare their assessments on the spot, without a subsequent effort at liaison and communication.

Drawbacks include:

(a)   Questions tend to be more varied, and more random, since there is no single guiding force behind the interview strategy. The candidate may have trouble switching from one topic to another so quickly, especially if questions are not led up to, and not clearly put – as may happen if they are unplanned.

(b)   If there is a dominating member of the board, the interview may have greater continuity – but that individual may also influence the judgement of other members.

(c)   Some candidates may not perform well in a formal, artificial situation such as the board interview, and may find such a situation extremely stressful.

(d)   Research shows that board members rarely agree with each other in their judgements about candidates.

4.5 Advantages of interviews

Interviews in general are by far the most popular selection method used by organisations. They offer some significant advantages.

(a)   They are highly interactive, allowing flexible question and answers. This allows candidates opportunities to ask questions, and allows questions and responses to be adapted to the direction and style of the interview.

(b)   They offer opportunities to use non-verbal communication, which might confirm or undermine spoken answers (eg a candidate looking hesitant or embarrassed when making competence claims). This is particularly helpful to interviewers when challenging or probing in relation to inconsistencies or gaps in a candidate's application or answers.

(c)   They offer opportunities to assess a candidate's personal appearance (relevant in areas such as grooming), interpersonal and communication skills.

(d)   They offer initial opportunities to evaluate rapport between the candidate and his or her potential colleagues/bosses.

4.6 The limitations of interviews

Interviews are criticised, however, because **they fail to provide accurate predictions** of how a person will perform in the job, partly because of the nature of interviews, partly because of errors of judgement by interviewers.

Problem	Comment
Scope	An interview is too brief to 'get to know' candidates in the kind of depth required to make an accurate prediction of work performance.
Artificiality	An interview is an artificial situation: candidates may be on their best behaviour or, conversely, so nervous that they do not do themselves justice. Neither situation reflects what the person is really like.
The halo effect	A tendency for people to make an initial general judgement about a person based on a single obvious attribute, such as being neatly dressed or well-spoken. This single attribute will colour later perceptions, and make an interviewer mark the person up or down on every other factor in their assessment.
Contagious bias	The interviewer changes the behaviour of the applicant by suggestion. The applicant might be led by the wording of questions, or non-verbal cues from the interviewer, to change what (s)he is doing or saying in response.
Stereotyping	Stereotyping groups together people who are assumed to share certain characteristics (women, say, or vegetarians), then attributes certain traits to the group as a whole. It then assumes that each individual member of the supposed group will possess that trait.
Incorrect assessment	Qualitative factors such as motivation, honesty or integrity are very difficult to define and assess objectively.
Logical error	For example, an interviewer might decide that a young candidate who has held two or three jobs in the past for only a short time will be unlikely to last long in any job.
Inexperienced interviewers	<ul><li>Inability to evaluate information about a candidate properly</li><li>Failure to compare a candidate against the job description or person specification</li><li>Failure to take control of the direction and length of the interview</li><li>Using inappropriate question types to elicit data or put candidates at ease</li><li>A reluctance to probe into facts or challenge statements where necessary</li></ul>

Question

What assumptions might an interviewer make about *you*, based on your:

(a) Accent, or regional/national variations in your spoken English?

(b) School?

(c) Clothes and hair-style?

(d) Stated hobbies, interest, 'philosophies'?

(e) Taste in books and TV programmes?

For objectivity, you might like to conduct this activity in class. What assumptions do you make about the person sitting next to you?

Exam focus point

Interviews are relevant to many areas of personnel management. Many of the issues described above may be relevant to appraisal interviews, disciplinary interviews and so on.

The limitations of interviews as a selection method is a particularly contentious issue which would lend itself to essay discussion.

Selection tests were also tested specifically in June 2004.

5 Selection testing

6/04

FAST FORWARD

Selection tests can be used before or after interviews. Intelligence tests measures the candidate's general intellectual ability, and personality tests identify the type of person. Other tests are more specific to the job (eg proficiency tests)

5.1 Types of selection test

In some job selection procedures, an interview is supplemented by some form of **selection test**. Tests must be:

(a) **Sensitive** enough to discriminate between different candidates

(b) **Standardised** on a representative sample of the population, so that a person's results can be interpreted meaningfully

(c) **Reliable**: in that the test should measure the same thing whenever and to whomever it is applied

(d) **Valid**: measuring what they are supposed to measure

There are two basic types of test.

(a) **Proficiency and attainment** tests measure an individual's demonstrated competence in particular job-related tasks.

(b) **Psychometric** tests measure such psychological factors as aptitude, intelligence and personality.

5.1.1 Proficiency, attainment or competence tests

Proficiency tests are designed to measure an individual's current ability to perform particular tasks or operations relevant to the job: for example, giving a secretarial candidate a typing test. **Attainment** (or competence) tests are a similar measurement of the standard an individual has reached at a particular skill. There is a wide range of proficiency testing material available, including 'in-tray' exercises (simulating work tasks). **Work sampling** requires the candidate to demonstrate work outputs: selectors may observe the candidate working, or the candidate may bring a portfolio of past work.

5.1.2 Intelligence tests

Tests of general intellectual ability typically test memory, ability to think quickly and logically, and problem solving skills. Most people have experience of IQ tests and the like, and few would dispute their validity as good measure of general intellectual capacity. However, there is no agreed definition of intelligence, and tests have now been devised to measure emotional intelligence factors (such as self-awareness, interpersonal ability and self-control).

5.1.3 Aptitude tests

Aptitude tests are designed to measure and predict an individual's potential for performing a job or learning new skills.

- **Reasoning**: verbal, numerical and abstract
- **Spatio-visual ability**: practical intelligence, non-verbal ability and creative ability
- **Perceptual speed and accuracy**: clerical ability
- **'Manual' ability**: mechanical, manual, musical and athletic

5.1.4 Personality tests

Personality tests may measure a variety of characteristics, such as an applicant's skill in dealing with other people, his ambition and motivation or his emotional stability. Examples include the 16PF, the Myers-Briggs Type Indicator™ and the Minnesota Multiphasic Personality Inventory (MMPI).

The validity of such tests has been much debated, but is seems that some have been shown by research to be valid predictors of job performance, so long as they are used properly.

5.2 Limitations of testing

Despite current enthusiasm for selection testing, it has its limitations.

(a) There is not always a direct relationship between ability in the test and **ability in the job**: the job situation is very different from artificial test conditions.

(b) The **interpretation of test results** is a skilled task, for which training and experience is essential. It is also highly subjective (particularly in the case of personality tests), which belies the apparent scientific nature of the approach.

(c) Additional difficulties are experienced with particular kinds of test. For example:

   (i) An aptitude test measuring arithmetical ability would need to be constantly revised or its content might become known to later applicants.

   (ii) Personality tests can often give misleading results because applicants seem able to guess which answers will be looked at most favourably.

   (iii) It is difficult to design intelligence tests which give a fair chance to people from different cultures and social groups and which test the kind of intelligence that the organisation wants from its employees: the ability to score highly in IQ tests does not necessarily correlate with desirable traits such as mature judgement or creativity, merely mental ability.

   (iv) Most tests are subject to coaching and practice effects.

(d)   It is difficult to exclude **bias** from tests. Many tests (including personality tests) are tackled less successfully by women than by men, or by some candidates born overseas than by indigenous applicants because of the particular aspect chosen for testing.

6 Other selection methods

6.1 Group selection methods (assessment centres)

FAST FORWARD

Group selection methods might be used by an organisation as the final stage of a selection process, as a more 'natural' and in-depth appraisal of candidates.

Group assessments (sometimes called **assessment centres**) tend to be used for posts requiring leadership, communication or teamworking skills: advertising agencies often use the method for selecting account executives, for example.

6.1.1 Methods used in group selection

Assessment centres consist of a series of tests, interviews and group situations over a period of two days, involving a small number of candidates for a job. After an introductory session to make the candidates feel at ease, they will be given one or two tests, one or two individual interviews, and several group scenarios in which the candidates are invited to discuss problems together and arrive at solutions as a management team.

A variety of tools and techniques are used in group selection, including:

(a)   **Group role-play exercises**, in which they can explore (and hopefully display) interpersonal skills and/or work through simulated managerial tasks

(b)   **Case studies**, where candidates' analytical and problem-solving abilities are tested in working through described situations/problems, as well as their interpersonal skills, in taking part in (or leading) group discussion of the case study

6.1.2 Advantages of group selection

These group sessions might be useful for the following reasons.

(a)   They give the organisation's selectors a longer opportunity to study the candidates.

(b)   They reveal more than application forms, interviews and tests alone about the ability of candidates to persuade others, negotiate with others, explain ideas to others, investigate problems efficiently and so on. These are typically management skills.

(c)   They reveal more about how the candidate's personality and skills will affect the work team and his own performance in the job.

6.2 Reference checking   6/05

FAST FORWARD

References provide further information about the prospective employee.

This may be of varying value, as the subjectivity and reliability of all but the most factual information provided by chosen reference sources must be questioned. A reference should contain two types of information.

(a)   Straightforward **factual information.** This confirms the nature of the applicant's previous job(s), period of employment, pay, and circumstances of leaving.

(b)   **Opinions** about the applicant's personality and other attributes. These should obviously be treated with some caution. Allowances should be made for prejudice (favourable or unfavourable), charity (withholding detrimental remarks), and possibly fear of being actionable for libel (although references are privileged, as long as they are factually correct and devoid of malice).

At least two **employer** references are desirable, providing necessary factual information, and comparison of personal views. **Personal** references tell the prospective employer little more than that the applicant has a friend or two.

Written references save time, especially if a standardised letter or form has been pre-prepared. A simple letter inviting the previous employer to reply with the basic information and judgements required may suffice. A standard form may be more acceptable, and might pose a set of simple questions about:

- Job title
- Main duties and responsibilities
- Period of employment
- Pay/salary
- Attendance record

If a judgement of character and suitability is desired, it might be most tellingly formulated as the question: 'Would you re-employ this individual? (If not, why not?)'

Telephone references may be time-saving if standard reference letters or forms are not available. They may also elicit a more honest opinion than a carefully prepared written statement. For this reason, a telephone call may also be made to check or confirm a poor or grudging reference which the recruiter suspects may be prejudiced.

Question   References

At the end of a recent selection process one candidate was outstanding, in the view of everyone involved. However, you have just received a very bad reference from her current employer. What do you do?

Answer

It is quite possible that her current employer is desperate to retain her. Disregard the reference, or question the employer by telephone, and seek a reference from another previous employer if possible.

7 Evaluating recruitment and selection practices

FAST FORWARD

The effectiveness and cost-effectiveness **of recruitment and selection** should be systematically **evaluated**, using a variety of measures.

7.1 How effective are recruitment and selection?

To get a clear idea of how efficient their recruitment and selection practices are, firms can ask themselves these questions.

- Can we identify human resources requirements from the business plans?
- How fast do we respond to demands from line managers for human resources?
- Do we give/receive good advice on labour market trends?
- Do we select the right advertising media to reach the market?
- How effective (and cost effective) is our recruitment advertising?
- How do our recruits actually perform – do we end up employing the right people?
- Do we retain our new recruits?

Recruitment and selection practices can be reviewed in various ways.

Review	Comment
Performance indicators	Each stage of the process can be assessed by performance indicators, for example the time it takes to process an application. Data can be collected to check any deviation from standard.
Cost-effectiveness	For example, number of relevant responses per recruitment ad, or cost of various advertising media per application elicited (or person employed).
Monitoring the workforce	High staff turnover, absenteeism and other problems (particularly among new recruits) may reflect poor recruitment and selection. Lack of workforce diversity may highlight discriminatory practices.
Attitude surveys	The firm can ask its recruits what they thought of the process.
Actual individual job performance	A person's actual performance can be compared with what was expected when (s)he was recruited.

7.2 Improving recruitment and selection procedures

A systematic model has been proposed in this chapter. If it is considered that recruitment and selection procedures need to be improved, attention may be given to matter such as:

(a) Improvement of **policies and guidelines** for selectors: eg in equal opportunities and recruit/promote decisions

(b) Establishment of **systematic procedures** for all stages of the process

(c) Improved **education and training** of selectors: eg in interviewing skills and testing techniques

(d) **Auditing of job advertising** content and media, in order to improve the attractiveness and realism of the organisation's offerings and the cost-effectiveness of advertising

(e) Widening the organisation's **repertoire of selection techniques**, to aim for the highest possible accuracy in predicting job performance and confirming candidate claims

(f) The possible use of external recruitment and selection **agencies and consultants**

Chapter Roundup

- The process of **selection** begins when the recruiter receives details of candidates interested in the job. A systematic approach includes short-listing, interviewing (and other selection methods), decision-making and follow-up.

- Many firms require candidates to fill out an **application form**. This is standardised and the firm can ask for specific information about work experience and qualifications, as well as other personal data. Alternatives include CVs with a covering letter.

- All **selection methods** are **limited** in their ability to predict future job performance!

- Most firms use selection **interviews**, on a one-to-one or panel basis. Interviews have the advantage of flexibility, but have limitations as predictors of job performance.

- **Selection tests** can be used before or after interviews. Intelligence tests measures the candidate's general intellectual ability, and personality tests identify the type of person. Other tests are more specific to the job (eg proficiency tests)

- **Group selection methods** might be used by an organisation as the final stage of a selection process, as a more 'natural' and in-depth appraisal of candidates.

- **References** provide further information about the prospective employee.

- The effectiveness and cost-effectiveness of **recruitment and selection** should be systematically **evaluated**, using a variety of measures.

Quick Quiz

1   What should application forms achieve?

2   Why are bio-data techniques useful?

3   What factors should be taken into account in an organisation's interview strategy?

4   The question 'Did you complete your accountancy qualification?' is:

    A   An open question
    B   A closed question
    C   A leading question
    D   A probing question

5   Why do interviews fail to predict performance accurately?

6   List the desirable features of selection tests.

7   Give examples of group selection methods.

8   'Personality and cognitive tests are more reliable predictors of job performance than interviews.' True or False?

9   What should be obtained in a reference?

10   How can firms improve their recruitment and selection practices?

Answers to Quick Quiz

1   They should give enough information to identify suitable candidates and weed out no-hopers, by asking specific questions and by getting the candidate to volunteer information.

2   Bio-data techniques enable data in application forms/CVs to be weighted and scored, making it easier to sift candidates' applications.

3   In brief, giving the right impression on the organisation and obtaining a rounded, relevant assessment of the candidate.

4   B. (You might try to rephrase this question as the other types, for extra practice.)

5   Brevity and artificiality of interview situation combined with the bias and inexperience of interviewers.

6   Sensitive; standardised; reliable; valid.

7   Role play exercises; case studies.

8   True.

9   Facts, corroborating other data supplied by the candidate; opinions about the candidate.

10   Clearly identifying what they want from the candidate; not relying on interviews alone. (For a fuller answer, see Section 7.2.)

Now try the question below from the Exam Question Bank

Number	Level	Marks	Time
Q8	Examination	15	27 mins

Diversity and equal opportunities

Topic list	Syllabus reference
1 Discrimination at work	2 (g)
2 Equal pay	2 (g)
3 Equal opportunity	2 (g)
4 The practical implications	2 (g)
5 Diversity	2 (g)

Introduction

This chapter addresses a key issue in recruitment and selection (following on from Chapters 7 & 8), but it also has wider implications for HR policy and practice.

Sexual and racial discrimination has become such a high-profile issue that you should be aware of obvious abuses: 'White Anglo Protestant Males only need apply' is *not* an acceptable recruitment pitch! However, recent years have seen the range of discrimination issues widen.

Employers are slowly starting to realise that equal opportunity policies have social and business benefits (as discussed in **Section 1**) and are seeking not just to comply with the legal framework **(Sections 2 and 3)**, but to develop positive action initiatives **(Section 4)**.

It is also being recognised that the workforce is increasingly **diverse** – and not just in the rather 'obvious' ways referred to by equal opportunities. Managing diversity is discussed in **Section 5**.

This chapter refers to the UK framework. Non-UK students may choose to use this material or may prefer to make use of their knowledge of similar matters in their own countries.

Study guide

Section 15 – Equal opportunities and the management of diversity

- Understanding equal opportunities
- Measuring equal value
- Appreciate the legal position
- Explain the appropriateness of managing diversity in the workplace
- Identify individual circumstances and differences

Exam guide

Discrimination and equal opportunities are topics of great importance for managers in real life. We include them in this part of the Study Text because that is where the syllabus puts them. However, you should be aware that they are relevant to all aspects of people management and therefore, potentially to **any question** in the examination. A whole Section A compulsory question was devoted to this topic in the December 2002 exam.

1 Discrimination at work

1.1 Equal opportunities

> **Equal opportunities** is an approach to the management of people at work based on equal access to benefits and fair treatment.

Key term

> Equal opportunities is an approach to the management of people at work based on equal access and fair treatment, irrespective of gender, race, ethnicity, age, disability, sexual orientation or religious belief.

Equal opportunities employers will seek to redress inequalities (eg of access to jobs, training, promotion, pay or benefits) which are based around differences, where they have no relevance to work performance.

Certain aspects of equal opportunities (such as discrimination on the basis of sex, race or disability) are enshrined in law; others (such as, currently, discrimination on the basis of age) rely upon models of good practice.

1.1.1 Why is equal opportunities an issue?

Despite the fact that women have contributed directly to the national product since medieval times, the acceptance of women in paid employment, on equal terms to men, has been a slow process. Many assumptions about women's attitudes to work, and capabilities for various types of work, have only recently been re-examined. Meanwhile, earnings surveys report that across all occupations, women are still earning 60-70% of male earnings in the same occupational group.

The TUC reports that the level of unemployment for black and Asian communities in the UK is significantly higher than for the white population. There is also ethnic segregation in the labour market, with a concentration of minority (male) employees in comparatively low-paying sectors. Meanwhile, the proportion of ethnic minority employees falls sharply at higher levels of the organisation (only 1% of senior managers in FTSE 100 companies).

The choice of jobs for the disabled is often restricted, resulting in higher and longer unemployment rates than the general population. Jobs are concentrated in plant/machine operative jobs, which tend to be low-paid.

Despite demographic and educational changes (and associated skill shortages among the younger population) a certain amount of discrimination is still directed at mature-age workers.

1.1.2 Why is equal opportunity an issue for employers?

FAST FORWARD

Sound business arguments can be made for equal opportunities policy.

Reasons argued for adopting non- or anti-discrimination measures include the following.

(a) Common decency and fairness, in line with business ethics

(b) Good HR practice, to attract and retain the best people for the job, regardless of race or gender

(c) Compliance with relevant legislation and Codes of Practice, which are used by employment tribunals

(d) Widening the recruitment pool in times of skill shortages

(e) Other potential benefits to the business through its image as a good employer, and through the loyalty of customers who benefit from (or support) equality principles

The Chairman of the Campaign for Racial Equality, however, has criticised companies that did nothing except use 'equal opportunities designer labels' to make recruitment advertisements look good.

| Question | Personal discrimination |

Have you ever felt discriminated against at school, work or your university/ college? On what grounds: your sex, colour, age, background? What was the effect of the discrimination on your plans and attitudes?

2 Equal pay

FAST FORWARD

Specific legislation (Equal Pay Act 1970) covers the offer of **equal pay** to a woman for work that is:
- Similarly evaluated in a job evaluation scheme
- 'The same or broadly similar' to the man's
- 'Of equal value' (Equal Pay (Amendment) Regulations)

2.1 Equal Pay Act 1970

The Equal Pay Act was the first major attempt to tackle sexual discrimination. It was intended 'to prevent discrimination as regards terms and conditions of employment between men and women'.

(a) Where there is an element of sex discrimination in a collective agreement, this must be removed to offer a unisex pay rate.

(b) Where a job evaluation scheme is operated to determine pay rates (as discussed in Chapter 11), a woman can claim equal pay for a job which has been rated as equivalent under the scheme.

(c) Where job evaluation is not used, a women can claim equal pay for work that is 'the same or broadly similar' as the work of a man in the same establishment, ('broadly similar' having to be interpreted in the courts, in many cases. The defending employer must show differences of 'practical importance' in the two jobs).

2.2 Equal pay for work of equal value

The Equal Pay (Amendment) Regulations 1984 established the right to equal pay for 'work of equal value', so that a woman would no longer have to compare her work with that of a man in the same or broadly similar work, but could establish that her work has equal value to that of a man in the same establishment.

The Equal Opportunities Commission issued a 1997 Code of Practice on Equal Pay, covering definitions, pay systems, methods of identifying discrimination, job evaluation methods and a model policy.

3 Equal opportunity

FAST FORWARD

Discrimination of certain types is illegal in the UK on grounds of:

- Sex and marital status (Sex Discrimination Act 1986)
- Colour, race, nationality and ethnic or national origin (Race Relations Act 1996)
- Disability (Disability Discrimination Act 1995)
- Sexual orientation and religious beliefs (Employment Equality Regulations 2003)

3.1 The legal framework on sex and race

In Britain, several main Acts have been passed to deal with inequality of opportunity.

(a)   The **Sex Discrimination Act 1986,** and the **Sex Discrimination and Equal Pay (Miscellaneous Amendments) Regulations 1996**, outlawing certain types of discrimination on the grounds of sex, marital status and sex change

(b)   The **Race Relations Act 1996**, outlawing certain types of discrimination on grounds of colour, race, nationality, or ethnic or national origin. The **Race Relations (Amendment) Act 2000** added the requirement that larger public organisations (more than 150 employees) must draw up detailed plans for achieving racial equality in all employment practices.

3.1.1 Types of discrimination

FAST FORWARD

Employers should note the implications of the Acts for both:

- **Direct discrimination** – less favourable treatment of a protected group
- **Indirect discrimination** – when requirements or conditions cannot be justified on non-racial grounds and work to the detriment of a protected group.

There are three types of discrimination under the Acts.

Key terms

> **Direct discrimination** occurs when one interested group is treated less favourably than another (except for exempted cases). It is unlikely that a prospective employer will practise direct discrimination unawares.
>
> **Indirect discrimination** occurs when a policy or practice is fair in form, but discriminatory in operation: for example, if requirements or conditions are imposed, with which a substantial proportion of the interested group cannot comply, to their detriment.
>
> **Victimisation** occurs when a person is penalised for giving information or taking action in pursuit of a claim of discrimination.

In addition, **harassment** is the use of threatening, intimidatory, offensive or abusive language or behaviour. This is covered by UK law in relation to race, religious belief and sexual orientation: sexual harassment will also be covered in forthcoming legislation.

An employer must, if challenged, justify apparently discriminatory conditions on non-gender grounds. It is often the case that employers are not aware that they are discriminating indirectly, and this concept was a major breakthrough when introduced by the Acts.

Question	Indirect discrimination

Suggest four examples of practices that would constitute indirect discrimination on the grounds of sex.

Answer

(a)   Advertising a vacancy in a primarily male environment, where women would be less likely to see it.

(b)   Offering less favourable terms to part-time workers (given that most of them are women).

(c)   Specifying age limits which would tend to exclude women who had taken time out of work for child-rearing.

(d)   Asking in selection interviews about plans to have a family (since this might be to the detriment of a woman, but not a man).

3.1.2 Applying the law

In both Acts, the obligation of non-discrimination applies to all aspects of employment, including advertisements, recruitment and selection programmes, access to training, promotion, disciplinary procedures, redundancy and dismissal.

In both Acts, too, there are certain exceptions ('genuine occupational qualifications'), in which discrimination of a sort may be permitted. For example, a firm may prefer a man over a women if there are reasons of physiology (not strength), privacy/decency (closely defined) or legal restrictions, eg work outside the UK, where 'laws or customs are such that the duties could not, or could not effectively, be performed by a woman'.

The legislation does not (except with regard to training) permit **positive discrimination**: actions which give preference to a protected person, regardless of genuine suitability and qualification for the job.

Exam focus point

> Bear in mind that the above provisions apply in the UK. Other countries, for reasons of social policy, may have different legislative measures in place. Be ready to cite legislation in your own country – where relevant – in the exam.

Training may be given to particular groups exclusively, if the group has in the preceding year been substantially under-represented. It is also permissible to encourage such groups to apply for jobs where such exclusive training is offered; and to apply for jobs in which they are under-represented.

The Equal Opportunities Commission and Commission for Racial Equality have powers, subject to certain safeguards, to investigate alleged breach of the Acts, to serve a 'non-discrimination notice', and to follow-up the investigation until satisfied that undertakings given (with regard to compliance and information of persons concerned) are carried out.

3.2 The legal framework on disability

The **Disability Discrimination Act 1995** contains the following key points.

(a) A disabled person is defined as a person who has a physical or mental impairment that has a substantial and long-term (more than 12 months) adverse effect on his ability to carry out normal day to day activities. Severe disfigurement is included, as are progressive conditions such as HIV even though the current effect may not be substantial.

(b) The effect includes mobility, manual dexterity, physical co-ordination, and lack of ability to lift or speak, hear, see, remember, concentrate, learn or understand or to perceive the risk of physical danger.

(c) The Act makes it unlawful for an employer (of more than 20 employees) to discriminate against a disabled person/employee in three respects.

    (i) In deciding who to interview or who to employ, or in the terms of an employment offer

    (ii) In the terms of employment and the opportunities for promotion, transfer, training or other benefits, or by refusing the same

    (iii) By dismissal or any other disadvantage

(d) The employer has a duty to make reasonable adjustments to working arrangements or to the physical features of premises where these constitute a disadvantage to disabled people.

Question	Disability

Examine any large shop (like a supermarket) you know well. What facilities have been provided for disabled people (staff and customers)? What problems remain? Are there any disabled people on the staff? If so, what are their jobs?

3.3 Sexual orientation and religious beliefs

The **Employment Equality Regulations 2003** outlawed discrimination and harassment on grounds of sexual orientation and religious belief. Employers can be held responsible for conduct deemed offensive or harassing (including inappropriate jokes) in regard to either issue. In addition, firms may need to review policies on staff benefits (for gay partners as well as married couples), dress codes (to allow religious expressions) and staff absence (to allow for religious holidays).

3.4 Age discrimination

The 1999 Voluntary Code of Practice on Age Diversity in Employment (currently used as guidance for employment tribunals) states that employers should:

(a) Recruit on the basis of skills and abilities; refrain from using age limits or phrases that imply restrictions (such as 'newly-qualified' or 'recent graduate') in job advertisements; refrain from asking for medical references only from older applicants

(b) Select on merit and use, where possible, a mixed-age panel of interviewers, trained to avoid decisions based on prejudices and stereotypes

(c) Promote on the basis of ability, having openly advertised opportunities

(d) Train and develop all employees and regularly review training to avoid age being a barrier

(e) Base redundancy decisions on job-related criteria and ensure that retirement schemes are applied fairly.

The UK is required to implemxent legislation on this area, under EU directive, by October 2006: watch this space!

3.5 Watch for developments!

Age discrimination and **sexual harassment** are to be the subject of specific legislation in the next few years.

In 2002, the EU announced new provisions to combat **sex discrimination**, which will eventually result in changes to the Sex Discrimination Act, including:

(a) The adoption of a statutory definition of **sexual harassment**. Currently, this is defined (by the EU) as 'unwanted conduct of a sexual nature, or other conduct based on sex, affecting the dignity of men and women at work': it includes unwanted sexual contact, innuendo, jokes or insults. It is not yet covered by UK law, although it has been ruled unlawful as a form of sexual discrimination.

(b) The re-definition of indirect discrimination

(c) Encouragement to employers to promote equal treatment for men and women in a planned and systematic way and

(d) Encouragement to employers to produce regular equality reports for the benefit of staff and employee representatives.

European social policy dealing with discrimination on the grounds of **age** is due to be enacted into UK law over the next two years.

There are also plans for a *merged body*, in the UK, to oversee all forms of discrimination and equal opportunity.

Watch out for updates on these issues in the quality press and professional journals.

Exam focus point

> Although the legal framework is clearly important, because of the organisation's compliance obligations, you should be aware of the wider implications of equal opportunity. Think about the ethical and business arguments for eliminating discrimination. Think about the components of a proactive and positive sexual and racial equality policy. These matters formed the core of a major case study question in the December 2002 exam.

4 The practical implications   12/02

The practical implications of the legislation for employers are set out in **Codes of Practice**, issued by the Commission for Racial Equality and the Equal Opportunities Commission. These do not have the force of law, but may be taken into account by employment tribunals, where discrimination cases are brought before them.

4.1 Formulating an effective equal opportunities policy

Many organisations now establish their own **policy statements** or **codes of practice on equal opportunities**: apart from anything else, a statement of the organisation's position may provide some protection in the event of complaints.

Some organisations make minimal efforts to avoid discrimination, paying lip-service to the idea only to the extent of claiming 'We are an Equal Opportunities Employer' on advertising literature. To turn such a claim into reality, the following are needed.

(a)   **Support** from the top of the organisation for the formulation of a practical policy

(b)   A **working party** drawn from – for example – management, unions, minority groups, the HR function and staff representatives. This group's brief will be to produce a draft Policy and Code of Practice, which will be approved at senior level

(c)   **Action plans and resources** (including staff) to implement and monitor the policy, publicise it to staff, arrange training and so on

(d)   **Monitoring**. The numbers of women and ethnic minority staff can easily be monitored

- On entering (and applying to enter) the organisation
- On leaving the organisation
- On applying for transfers, promotions or training schemes

(It is less easy to determine the ethnic origins of the workforce through such methods as questionnaires: there is bound to be suspicion about the question's motives, and it may be offensive to some workers.)

(e)   **Positive action**: the process of taking active steps to encourage people from disadvantaged groups to apply for jobs and training, and to compete for vacancies. (Note that this is not positive discrimination.) Examples might be: using ethnic languages in job advertisements, or implementing training for women in management skills. In addition, there may be awareness training, counselling and disciplinary measures to manage sexual, racial and religious harassment.

4.2 Recruitment and selection

FAST FORWARD

Recruitment and selection are areas of particular **sensitivity** to claims of discrimination – as well as genuine (though often unintended) inequality.

There is always a risk that a disappointed job applicant, for example, will attribute his lack of success to discrimination, especially if the recruiting organisation's workforce is conspicuously lacking in representatives of the same ethnic minority, sex or group.

(a)   **Advertising**

(i)   Any wording that suggests preference for a particular group should be avoided (except for genuine occupational qualifications).

(ii)   Employers must not indicate or imply any 'intention to discriminate'.

(iii)   Recruitment literature should state that the organisation is an Equal Opportunities employer.

(iv)   The placing of advertisements only where the readership is predominantly of one race or sex is construed as indirect discrimination. This includes word-of-mouth recruiting from the existing workforce, if it is not broadly representative.

(b)   **Recruitment agencies**. Instructions to an agency should not suggest any preference.

(c)   **Application forms**. These should include no questions which are not work-related (such as domestic details) and which only one group is asked to complete.

(d)   **Interviews**

(i)   Any non-work-related question must be asked of all subjects, if at all, and even then, some types of question may be construed as discriminatory. (You cannot, for example, ask only women about plans to have a family or care of dependants, or ask – in the most offensive case – about the Pill or PMT.)

(ii)   It may be advisable to have a witness at interviews, or at least to take detailed notes, in the event that a claim of discrimination is made.

(e) **Selection tests**. These must be wholly relevant, and should not favour any particular group. Even personality tests have been shown to favour white male applicants.

(f) **Records**. Reasons for rejection, and interview notes, should be carefully recorded, so that in the event of investigation the details will be available.

4.3 Other initiatives

In addition to responding to legislative provisions, some employers have begun to address the **underlying problems** of equal opportunities.

Measures such as the following may be used as positive action initiatives.

(a) Putting equal opportunities **higher on the agenda** by appointing Equal Opportunities Managers (and even Directors) who report directly to the Personnel Director.

(b) **Flexible hours** or part-time work, term-time or annual hours contracts (to allow for school holidays) to help women to combine careers with family responsibilities. Terms and conditions, however, must not be less favourable.

(c) **Career-break or return-to-work** schemes for women.

(d) **Fast-tracking school-leavers**, as well as graduates, and posting managerial vacancies internally, giving more opportunities for movement up the ladder for groups (typically women and minorities) currently at lower levels of the organisation.

(e) **Training for women-returners** or women in management to help women to manage their career potential. Assertiveness training may also be offered as part of such an initiative.

(f) **Awareness training** for managers, to encourage them to think about equal opportunity policy.

(g) **Counselling and disciplinary policies** to raise awareness and eradicate sexual, racial and religious harassment.

(h) **Positive action** to encourage job and training applications from minority groups.

5 Diversity

The concept of **'managing diversity'** is based on the belief that the dimensions of individual difference on which organisations currently focus are crude and performance-irrelevant classifications of the most obvious differences between people.

The concept of 'managing diversity' is based on the belief that the dimensions of individual difference on which organisations currently focus are crude and performance-irrelevant classifications of the most obvious differences between people.

Diversity in employment, as a concept, goes further than equal opportunities.

The *ways in which people meaningfully differ* in the work place include not only race and ethnicity, age and gender, but personality, preferred working style, individual needs and goals and so on Managing diversity

5.1 Managing diversity

A 'managing diversity' orientation implies the need to be proactive in managing the needs of a diverse workforce in areas (beyond the requirements of equal opportunity and discrimination regulations) such as:

(a) Tolerance of individual differences

(b) Communicating effectively with (and motivating) ethnically diverse work forces

(c)   Managing workers with increasingly diverse family structures and responsibilities

(d)   Managing the adjustments to be made by an increasingly aged work force

(e)   Managing increasingly diverse career aspirations/patterns and ways of organising working life (including flexible working)

(f)   Confronting issues of literacy, numeracy and differences in qualifications in an international work force

(g)   Managing co-operative working in ethnically diverse teams.

5.2 Diversity policy

Ingham (2003) suggests the following key steps in implementing a *diversity policy* taking into account all the equal opportunity requirements.

Step 1   **Analyse your business environment**

(a)   Internally – does the diversity of the organisation reflect the population in its labour market?

(b)   Externally – does the diversity of the workforce mirror that of the customer base?

Step 2   **Define diversity and its business benefits**

(a)   Legal, moral and social benefits

(b)   Business benefits: better understanding of market segments; positive employer brand; attraction and retention of talent

(c)   Employee benefits: more representative workforce; value and respect for people; opportunity to contribute fully; enhanced creativity

Step 3   **Introduce diversity policy into corporate strategy**

Weave diversity into corporate values and mission.

Step 4   **Embed diversity into core HR processes and system**

Review and refocus recruitment and selection, induction, reward and recognition, career management and training and development.

Step 5   **Ensure leaders implement policy**

(a)   Leaders and top management need to provide long-term commitment and resources

(b)   Use diversity as a key factor in coaching, awareness training and development of managers.

Step 6   **Involve staff at all levels**

- Educate the workforce through awareness training
- Create a 'diversity handbook'
- Set up diversity working parties and councils
- Establish mentoring schemes

Step 7   **Communicate, communicate, communicate**

- Communicate diversity policy and initiatives clearly
- Internally: updates, briefings, training, intranet pages
- Externally: to boost employer brand and recruitment

Step 8 **Understand your company's needs**

(a) Match resources to the size of the organisation and the scale of change required.

(b) Consider using diversity consultants or best practice representatives to provide advice, support and training.

Step 9 **Evaluate**

- Benchmark progress at regular intervals
- Internally: diversity score cards, employee climate surveys
- Externally: focus groups, customer/supplier surveys

Chapter Roundup

- **Equal opportunities** is an approach to the management of people at work based on equal access to benefits and fair treatment.

- Sound business arguments can be made for equal opportunities policy.

- Specific legislation (Equal Pay Act 1970) covers the offer of **equal pay** to a woman for work that is:

  - Similarly evaluated in a job evaluation scheme
  - 'The same or broadly similar' to the man's
  - 'Of equal value' (Equal Pay (Amendment) Regulations)

- **Discrimination** of certain types is illegal in the UK on grounds of:

  - Sex and marital status (Sex Discrimination Act 1986)
  - Colour, race, nationality and ethnic or national origin (Race Relations   Act 1996)
  - Disability (Disability Discrimination Act 1995)
  - Sexual orientation and religious beliefs (Employment Equality Regulations 2003)

- Employers should note the implications of the Acts for both:

  - **Direct discrimination** – less favourable treatment of a protected group
  - **Indirect discrimination** – when requirements or conditions cannot be justified on non-racial grounds and work to the detriment of a protected group.

- **Age discrimination** and **sexual harassment** are to be the subject of specific legislation in the next few years.

- Many organisations now establish their own **policy statements** or **codes of practice on equal opportunities**: apart from anything else, a statement of the organisation's position may provide some protection in the event of complaints.

- Recruitment and selection are areas of particular **sensitivity** to claims of discrimination – as well as genuine (though often unintended) inequality.

- In addition to responding to legislative provisions, some employers have begun to address **the underlying problems** of equal opportunities.

- The concept of **'managing diversity'** is based on the belief that the dimensions of individual difference on which organisations currently focus are crude and performance-irrelevant classifications of the most obvious differences between people.

Quick Quiz

1   Matt Black and Di Gloss run a small DIY shop. They're recruiting an assistant. Matt puts up an ad on the notice board of his Men's Club. It says: 'Person required to assist in DIY shop. Fulltime. Aged under 28. Contact...' Two candidates turn up for interview the following day: a man and a woman (who's heard about the job by word of mouth, through Di). Matt interviews them both, asking work-related questions. He also asks the woman whether she has children and how much time she expects to spend dealing with family matters.

Under the Sex Discrimination Act, Matt has laid himself open to allegations of:

   A   One count of discrimination
   B   Two counts of discrimination
   C   Three counts of discrimination
   D   No discrimination at all

2   List four causes of high minority unemployment in the UK.

3   List five possible measures that might support an equal opportunities policy in an organisation.

4   What is sexual harassment?

5   Under Equal Pay legislation, women are entitled to equal pay for 'similar' jobs. *True or false?*

Answers to Quick Quiz

1   C. Advertising in a place where the readership is predominately male. Asking the women about (1) children and (2) time spent on family matters.

2   Low average age of minority populations; lack of UK recognised skills and qualifications; racial discrimination; concentrations of minority populations in places and industries with falling or static economic activity.

3   Support from top management; a policy and code of practice on equal opportunities; resources to implement the policy; monitoring of implementation; positive action to encourage minority applications.

4   Any unwanted conduct of a sexual nature, or based on sex, affecting the dignity of men and women at work.

5   False. This was the previous position: the benchmark is now 'jobs of equal value' as determined by job evaluation.

Now try the question below from the Exam Question Bank

Number	Level	Marks	Time
Q9	Examination	15	27 mins

Part C
Training and development

Employee development and training

10

Topic list	Syllabus reference
1 Development and training	3 (c)
2 Training needs and objectives	3 (c)
3 Training methods	3 (c)
4 The learning process	3 (a)
5 Responsibility for training and development	3 (b)
6 Evaluating training programmes	3 (c)
7 Development	3 (c)

Introduction

The development of people to meet current – and changing – job demands is a key leadership task.

In **Section 1**, we set out a **systematic approach** to training, and in **Sections 2-6**, we look at key aspects of this approach: identifying training needs, selecting training **methods**, designing training that suits how people **learn**, and **evaluating** the effectiveness of training.

There are detailed procedures and models to learn, but at the core of this topic is the need to ensure that trainee learning is **applied** in the work context. Bear this in mind as you explore training methods, in particular.

In **Section 7**, we look at the wider topic of **development**, which is about more than just improving job performance.

This topic looks forward to performance appraisal (Chapter 11) because that's one of the formal ways of identifying training needs and development potential.

175

Study guide

Section 16 – The learning process

Section 17 – Retention, training and development

Section 18 – Effective training and development

Full details of these sessions can be found in the introductory pages of this Study Text.

Section 8 – Standard setting and performance management

- Describe management contribution to personal development planning

Section 21 – Individual skills and development

- Identify the methods used to develop skills
- Outline how to plan a skills development programme
- Explain the role of mentoring in the process of skills development

Exam guide

Training and development could well form the basis of a complete case study question as it contains a wide range of examinable topics. It is also likely to be linked with appraisal and performance management, where training needs are identified.

1 Development and training

FAST FORWARD

In order to achieve its goals, an organisation requires a **skilled workforce**. This is partly achieved by training.

1.1 Factors affecting job performance

There are many factors affecting a person's performance at work, as shown in the diagram below. Training and development are one method by which an organisation may seek to improve the performance of its staff.

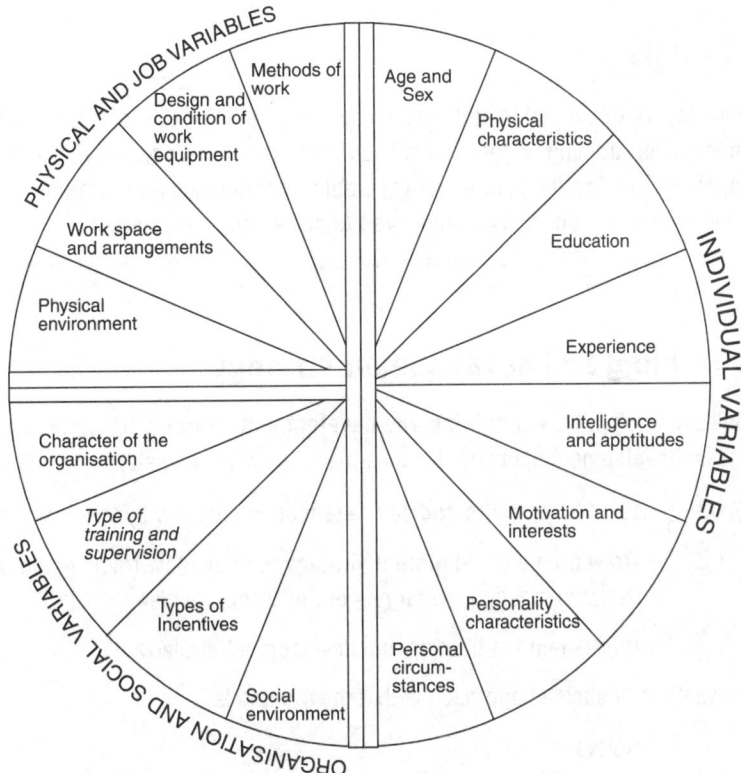

1.2 What are training and development?

The main **purpose** of training and development is to raise competence and therefore performance standards. It is also concerned with personal development, helping and motivating employees to fulfil their potential.

Key terms

Development is 'the growth or realisation of a person's ability and potential through the provision of learning and educational experiences'.

Training is 'the planned and systematic modification of behaviour through learning events, programmes and instruction which enable individuals to achieve the level of knowledge, skills and competence to carry out their work effectively'.

(Armstrong)

The overall purpose of employee development is:

- To ensure the firm meets current and future performance objectives by...
- Continuous improvement of the performance of individuals and teams, and...
- Maximising people's potential for growth (and promotion)

We will discuss development separately in Section 7 of this chapter.

Question

Self-appraisal

Note down key experiences which have developed your capacity and confidence at work, and the skills you are able to bring to your employer (or indeed a new employer!).

Answer

Few employers throw you in at the deep end – it is far too risky for them! Instead, you might have been given induction training to get acclimatised to the organisation, and you might have been introduced slowly to the job. Ideally, your employer would have planned a programme of tasks of steadily greater complexity and responsibility to allow you to grow into your role(s).

1.3 Training and development strategy

Organisations often have a **training and development strategy**, based on the overall strategy for the business. Development planning includes the following broad steps.

Step 1   Identify the **skills and competences** are needed by the business plan or HR plan.

Step 2   Draw up the **development strategy** to show how training and development activities will assist in meeting the targets of the corporate plan.

Step 3   **Implement** the training and development strategy.

The advantage of such an approach is that the training is:

- Relevant
- Problem-based (ie corrects a real lack of skills)
- Action-oriented
- Performance-related
- Forward-looking

1.4 Benefits of training   6/04

FAST FORWARD

Training offers significant **benefits** for both employers and employees – although it is *not* the solution to every work problem!

1.4.1 Benefits for the organisation

Training offers some significant benefits for the organisation.

Benefit	Comment
Minimise the costs of obtaining the skills the organisation needs	Training supports the business strategy.
Increased productivity, improving performance	Some people suggest that higher levels of training explain the higher productivity of German as opposed to many British manufacturers
Fewer accidents, and better health and safety	EU health and safety directives require a certain level of training.
Less need for detailed supervision	If people are trained they can get on with the job, and managers can concentrate on other things. Training is an aspect of empowerment.
Flexibility	Training ensures that people have the variety of skills needed – multi-skilling is only possible if people are properly trained.

Benefit	Comment
Recruitment and succession planning	Opportunities for training and development attract new recruits and ensure that the organisation has a supply of suitable managerial and technical staff for the future.
Retention	Training and development supports an internal job market (through transfer and promotion). It also helps to satisfy employees' self-development needs internally, without the need to change employers for task variety and challenge.
Change management	Training helps organisations manage change by letting people know why the change is happening and giving them the skills to cope with it.
Corporate culture	(1) Training programmes can be used to build the corporate culture or to direct it in certain ways, by indicating that certain values are espoused. (2) Training programmes can build relationships between staff and managers in different areas of the business
Motivation	Training programmes can increase commitment to the organisation's goals, by satisfying employees' self-actualisation needs (discussed in Part D)

Note, however, that training cannot do everything! (Look at the wheel in Section 1.1 again.) Training cannot by itself improve performance problems arising out of:

- Bad management
- Poor job design
- Poor equipment, workplace layout or work organisation
- Lack of aptitude or intelligence
- Poor motivation (training gives a person the ability, but not necessarily willingness)

Question

Limitations of training

Despite all the benefits to the organisation, many are still reluctant to train. What reasons can you give for this?

Answer

Cost: training can be costly. Ideally, it should be seen as an investment in the future or as something the firm has to do to maintain its position. In practice, many firms are reluctant to train because of poaching by other employers – trained staff are more marketable elsewhere. While some organisations encourage this 'employability' training, recognising their inability to offer employees long-term job security, others may experience it as a resource drain. In addition, it must be recognised that training by itself is not the solution to performance problems: it must be effectively planned and managed, as we will see later in this chapter.

1.4.2 Benefits for the employee

For the **individual employee**, the benefits of training and development are more clear-cut, and few refuse it if it is offered.

Benefit	Comment
Enhances portfolio of **skills**	Even if not specifically related to the current job, training can be useful in other contexts. The employee becomes more attractive in the labour market ('employability') and more profitable within the firm.
Psychological benefits	The trainee might feel reassured that (s)he is of continuing value to the organisation. A perception of competence also enhances self-esteem and confidence.
Social benefit	People's social needs can be met by training courses – they can also develop networks of contacts.
The job	Training can help people do their job better, thereby increasing job satisfaction, promotion and earning prospects.

Exam focus point

The 2004 exam illustrated a classic question type: 'Explain the advantages of training for the organisation … (and) for the individual'. Get into the habit of noting *both* view points for any given HR policy – and look out for 'ands' and 'ors' in the exam!

1.5 A systematic approach to training

FAST FORWARD

A **systematic approach** to training includes: need definition; objective setting; planning training programmes; delivering training; and evaluating results.

In order to ensure that training meets the real needs of the organisation, larger firms adopt a systematic approach.

Step 1   Identify and define (from the human resource plan) the **organisation's training needs**. (It may be that recruitment might be a better solution to skills shortfalls.)

Step 2   **Define the learning required** – in other words, specify the knowledge, skills or competences that have to be acquired. (For technical training, this is not difficult: for example, all finance department staff will have to become conversant with a new accounting system.)

Step 3   **Define training objectives** – what must be learnt and what trainees must be able to do after the training exercise.

Step 4   **Plan training programmes.** Training and development can be structured and implemented in a number of ways, as we shall discuss in Section 3. This covers:

- Who provides the training
- Where the training takes place
- Division of responsibilities between trainers, managers and the individual
- What training approaches, techniques, styles and technologies are used

Step 5   **Implement the training programme**

Step 6   **Monitor, review and evaluate** training. Has it been successful in achieving the learning objectives?

Step 7   Go back to Step 2 if more training is needed.

Question	Training plan

Draw up a training plan for introducing a new employee into your department. Repeat this exercise after you have completed this chapter to see if your chosen approach has changed.

We will now look at the stages of this process in more detail.

2 Training needs and objectives

A thorough analysis of **training needs** should be carried out to ensure that training programmes meet organisational and individual requirements.

2.1 Indicators of the need for training

Some training requirements will be obvious and 'automatic'.

(a) If a piece of legislation is enacted which affects the organisation's operations, training in its provisions will automatically be indicated. Thus, for example, personnel staff have needed training as various EU Directives have been enacted in UK law.

(b) The introduction of new technology similarly implies a training need: for relevant employees to learn how to use it.

Other training requirements may emerge in response to **critical incidents**: problems or events which affect a key area of the organisation's activity and effectiveness. A service organisation may, for example, receive bad press coverage because of a number of complaints about the rudeness of its customer service staff on the telephone. This might highlight the need for training in telephone skills, customer care, scheduling (for the team manager, if the rudeness was a result of unmanageable workloads) and so on.

Some **qualitative indicators** might be taken as symptoms of a need for training: absenteeism, high labour turnover, grievance and disciplinary actions, crises, conflict, poor motivation and performance. Such factors will need to be investigated to see what the root causes are, and whether training will solve the problem.

2.2 Assessment for training

Another alternative is **self-assessment** by the employee. This may be highly informal (a list of in-house or sponsored courses is posted on the notice board or intranet and interested employees are invited to apply) or more systematic (employees complete surveys on training needs). An example of a self-administered needs survey for managerial staff (suggested by Kramer, McGraw and Schuler) is as follows.

Self assessment of training needs

Please indicate in the blanks the extent to which you have a training need in each specific area. Use the following scale

Scale

1 ——————— 2 ——————— 3 ——————— 4 ——————— 5

(To no extent)   (To a very large extent)

To what extent do you need training in the following areas?

Basic management skills (organising, planning, delegating, problem-solving)

———— A   Setting goals and objectives
———— B   Developing realistic time schedules to meet work requirements
———— C   Identifying and weighing alternative solutions
———— D   Organising work activities

Interpersonal skills

———— A   Resolving interpersonal conflicts
———— B   Creating a development plan for employees
———— C   Identifying and understanding individual employee needs
———— D   Conducting performance appraisal reviews
———— E   Conducting a disciplinary interview

Administrative skills

———— A   Maintaining equipment, tools and safety controls
———— B   Understanding local agreements and shop rules
———— C   Preparing work flowcharts
———— D   Developing departmental budgets

Quality control

———— A   Analysing and interpreting statistical data
———— B   Constructing and analysing charts, tables and graphs
———— C   Using statistical software on the computer

The advantage of self-assessment, or self-nomination for training, is that it pre-supposes motivation on the part of the trainee and harnesses employees' knowledge of their own job requirements and skill weaknesses. The drawback, however, is that employees may be reluctant to admit to performance deficiencies.

A further alternative, therefore, is the use of **attitude surveys** and **360º feedback appraisal reports**, since the employee's superiors, subordinates, colleagues and customer contacts will be in a good position to identify performance deficiencies in areas that affect them: this will be particularly important in the case of customers.

Question	Types of power

What alerted you to a training need, to encourage you to undertake this course? What was the training need: what could you not yet do, or what did you not yet know, that you thought you needed? What help did you get in identifying your training needs? Have you defined them (or had them defined for you) in a helpful way?

2.3 Formal training need analysis

Other training requirements may only emerge from a formal learning gap (or training need) analysis.

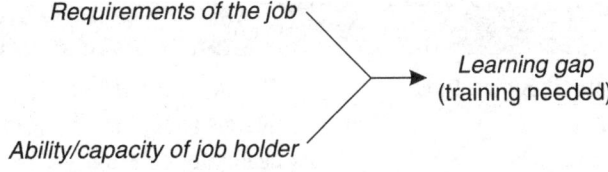

Requirements of the job

Learning gap (training needed)

Ability/capacity of job holder

Key term

> **Training needs** may be defined as the gap between what people should be achieving and what they actually are achieving. In other words:
>
> Required level of competence *minus* present level of competence = training need.

The **required level of competence for the job** can be determined by:

   (a)   **Job analysis**, identifying the elements of the task

   (b)   **Skills analysis**, identifying the skill elements of the task, such as:

       (i)   What senses (vision, touch, hearing etc) are involved?
       (ii)   What left-hand/right-hand/foot operations are required?
       (iii)   What interactions with other operatives are required?

   (c)   **Role analysis,** for managerial and administrative jobs requiring a high degree of co-ordination and interaction with others

   (d)   **Existing records**, such as job specifications and descriptions, person specifications, the organisation chart (depicting roles and relationships) and so on

   (e)   **Competence analysis** or existing competence frameworks, such as NVQs relevant to the job

The **present level of employees' competence** (which includes not only skill and knowledge, but the employee's inclination or willingness to work competently as well) can be measured by an appropriate **pre-training test** of skills, knowledge, performance, attitude and so on.

The ongoing system of **performance appraisal** (discussed in Chapter 11) will furnish some of this information. A **human resources audit** or **skills audit** may also be conducted for a more comprehensive account of the current level of competence, skill, knowledge (and so on) in the workforce.

2.4 Setting training objectives

FAST FORWARD

> Once training needs have been identified, they should be translated into **training objectives**.

If it is considered that training would improve work performance, training **objectives** can be defined. They should be clear, specific and related to observable, measurable targets, ideally detailing:

- **Behaviour** – What the trainee should be able to do
- **Standard** – To what level of performance?
- **Environment** – Under what conditions (so that the performance level is realistic)?

For example:

'At the end of the course the trainee should be able to describe ... or identify ... or distinguish x from y ... or calculate ... or assemble ...' and so on. It is insufficient to define the objectives of training as 'to give trainees a grounding in ...' or 'to encourage trainees in a better appreciation of ...': this offers no target achievement which can be measured.

Training objectives link the identification of training needs with the content, methods and technology of training. Some examples of translating training needs into learning objectives are given in *Personnel Management, A New Approach* by Torrington and Hall.

Training needs	Learning objectives
To know more about the Data Protection Act	The employee will be able to answer four out of every five queries about the Data Protection Act without having to search for details.
To establish a better rapport with customers	The employee will immediately attend to a customer unless already engaged with another customers.
	The employee will greet each customer using the customer's name where known.
	The employee will apologise to every customer who has had to wait to be attended to.
To assemble clocks more quickly	The employee will be able to assemble each clock correctly within thirty minutes.

Having identified training needs and objectives, the manager will have to decide on the best way to approach training: there are a number of approaches and techniques, which we will discuss below.

2.5 Incorporating training needs into an individual development programme

FAST FORWARD

Individuals can incorporate training and development objectives into a **personal development plan**.

Key term

A **personal development plan** is a clear developmental action plan for an individual which incorporates a wide set of developmental opportunities, including formal training.

The purposes of a personal development plan include:

- Improving performance in the existing job
- Developing skills for future career moves within and outside the organisation

2.5.1 Steps in personal development planning

Personal development planning includes the following basic steps.

Step 1 **Analyse the current position**. You could do a personal SWOT (strengths, weaknesses, opportunities, threats) analysis, or a **skills analysis** (as depicted in the following diagram).

		Performance	
		High	Low
Liking of skills	High	Like and do well	Like but don't do well
	Low	Dislike but do well	Dislike and don't do well

The aim is to try to incorporate more of the employees' interests into their actual roles.

Step 2 **Set goals** to cover performance in the existing job, future changes in the current role, moving elsewhere in the organisation, developing specialist expertise. Such goals should have the characteristic of SMART objectives (specific, measurable, achievable, relevant and time-bounded).

Step 3 **Draw up action plan** to achieve the goals, including:

- The objective
- Methods you will use to develop the identified skills (including learning experiences, opportunities to try and practise new behaviours and so on)
- Timescales for review of progress
- Methods of monitoring and reviewing progress and achievement of the objective

Question	Personal development planning

Draw up a personal development plan for yourself over the next month, the next year, and the next five years.

3 Training methods   12/03, 6/04

FAST FORWARD There are a variety of **training methods**. These include:

- Off-the-job education and training
- On-the-job training

3.1 Off the job training

FAST FORWARD **Off the job training** minimises risk but does not always support transfer of learning to the job.

Off the job training is formal training conducted outside the context of the job itself in special training rooms or off-site facilities.

(a) **Courses** may be run by the organisation's training department or may be provided by external suppliers. These may be:

   (i) **Day release**: the employee works in the organisation and on one day per week attends a local college or training centre for theoretical learning.

   (ii) **Distance learning, evening classes and correspondence courses**, which make demands on the individual's time outside work.

   (iii) **Revision courses** for examinations of professional bodies.

   (iv) **Block release** courses which may involve four weeks at a college or training centre followed by a period back at work.

   (v) **Sandwich courses**, which usually involve six months at college then six months at work, in rotation, for two or three years.

   (vi) A **sponsored full-time course** at a university for one or two years.

(b) **Computer-based training** involves interactive training via PC. The typing program *Mavis Beacon* is a good example.

(c) **E-learning**

   E-learning is computer-based learning through a network of computers or the Internet (rather than stand-alone CD-Rom or software). Learning support is available from online tutors, moderators and discussion groups. This is a major element of the UK government's Lifelong Learning initiative, through the University for Industry (UfI) and 'learndirect'.

(d)   **Techniques** used on the course might include lectures and seminars (theory and information) or role plays, case studies and in-tray exercises (to simulate work activities).

3.1.1 Evaluation of off-the-job training

The advantages and disadvantages of off-the-job training may be summarised as follows.

Advantages	Disadvantages
Allows exploration/experimentation without the risk of consequences for actual performance	May not be directly relevant or transferable to the job and/or job content
Allows focus on learning, away from distractions and pressures of work	May be perceived as a waste of working time
Allows standardisation of training Suits a variety of learning styles (depending on the method used)	Immediate and relevant feedback may not be available (eg if performance is assessed by exam)
May confer status, implying promotability	Tends to be more theoretical: does not suit 'hands on' learning styles
	May represent a threat, implying inadequacy

3.2 On the job training

FAST FORWARD

On the job training maximises transfer of learning by incorporating it into 'real' work.

On the job training utilises real work tasks as learning experiences. Methods of on the job training include the following.

(a)   **Demonstration/instruction:** show the trainee how to do the job and let them get on with it. It should combine **telling** a person what to do and **showing** them how, using appropriate media. The trainee imitates the instructor, and asks questions.

(b)   **Job rotation:** the trainee is given several jobs in succession, to gain experience of a wide range of activities. (Even experienced managers may rotate their jobs, to gain wider experience; this philosophy of job education is commonly applied in the Civil Service, where an employee may expect to move on to another job after a few years.)

(c)   **Temporary promotion:** an individual is promoted into his/her superior's position whilst the superior is absent. This gives the individual a chance to experience the demands of a more senior position.

(d)   **'Assistant to' positions (or work shadowing):** an employee may be appointed as assistant to a more senior or experienced person, to gain experience of a new or more demanding role.

(e)   **Action learning:** managers are brought together as a problem-solving group to discuss a real work issue. An 'advisor' facilitates, and helps members of the group to identify their interpersonal and problem-solving skills are effecting the process.

(f)   **Committees:** trainees might be included in the membership of committees, in order to obtain an understanding of inter-departmental relationships.

(g)   **Project work:** work on a project with other people can expose the trainee to other parts of the organisation.

3.2.1 Evaluation of on-the-job training

The advantages and disadvantages of on-the-job training may be summarised as follows.

Advantages	Disadvantages
Takes account of job context: high relevance and transfer of learning	Undesirable aspects of job context (group norms, corner-cutting) also learned
Suits 'hands on' learning styles: offers 'learning by doing'	Doesn't suit 'hands off' learning styles
No adjustment barriers (eg anti-climax after training) to application of learning on the job	Trial and error may be threatening (if the organisation has low tolerance of error!)
Develops working relationships as well as skills	Risks of throwing people in at the deep end with real consequences of mistakes
	Distractions and pressures of the workplace may hamper learning focus

Question

Training methods

Suggest a suitable training method for each of the following situations.

(a) A worker is transferred onto a new machine and needs to learn its operation.

(b) An accounts clerk wishes to work towards becoming qualified with the relevant professional body.

(c) An organisation decides that its supervisors would benefit from ideas on participative management and democratic leadership.

(d) A new member of staff is about to join the organisation.

Answer

Training methods for the various workers indicated are as follows.

(a) Worker on a new machine: on-the-job training, coaching

(b) Accounts clerk working for professional qualification: external course – evening class or day-release

(c) Supervisors wishing to benefit from participative management and democratic leadership: internal or external course. However, it is important that monitoring and evaluation takes place to ensure that the results of the course are subsequently applied in practice.

(d) New staff: induction training

3.3 Induction training

Induction is the process whereby a person is formally introduced and integrated into an organisation or system.

3.3.1 The purposes of induction

The purposes of induction are:

(a)   To help new recruits to find their bearings

(b)   To begin to socialise new recruits into the culture and norms of the team/organisation

(c)   To support recruits in beginning performance

(d)   To identify on-going training and development needs

(e)   To avoid initial problems at the 'induction crisis' stage of the employment lifecycle, when frustration, disorientation and disappointment may otherwise cause new recruits to leave the organisation prematurely

3.3.2 The process of induction

The immediate superior should commence the **on-going process of induction**.

Step 1   Pinpoint the areas that the recruit will have to learn about in order to start the job. Some things (such as detailed technical knowledge) may be identified as areas for later study or training.

Step 2   Introduce the recruit to the work premises and facilities, so (s)he can get his or her bearings.

Step 3   Briefing by the HR Manager on relevant policies and procedures: conditions of employment, sickness and holiday absences, health and safety and so on.

Step 4   Introduce the recruit to key people in the office: co-workers, health and safety officers, etc. One particular colleague may be assigned to recruits as a **mentor**, to keep an eye on them, answer routine queries, 'show them the ropes'.

Step 5   Introduce work procedures.

(a)   Explain the nature of the job, and the goals of each task

(b)   Explain hours of work

(c)   Explain the structure of the department: to whom the recruit will report, to whom s(he) can go with complaints or queries and so on.

Step 6   Plan and implement an appropriate training programme for whatever technical or practical knowledge is required. Again, the programme should have a clear schedule and set of goals so that the recruit has a sense of purpose, and so that the programme can be efficiently organised to fit in with the activities of the department.

Step 7   Monitor initial progress, as demonstrated by performance, as reported by the recruit's mentor, and as perceived by the recruit him or herself. This is the beginning of an on-going cycle of feedback, review, problem-solving and development planning.

Note that induction is an **on-going process**, embracing mentoring, coaching, training, monitoring and so on. It is not just a first day affair! After three months, six months or one year the performance of a new recruit should be formally appraised and discussed. Indeed, when the process of induction has been finished, a recruit should continue to receive periodic appraisals, just like every other employee in the organisation.

3.4 Coaching

Coaching is an approach whereby a trainee is put under the guidance of an experienced employee who shows the trainee how to perform tasks. It is also a fashionable aspect of leadership style and a feature of superior/subordinate relationships, where the aim is to *develop* people by providing challenging opportunities and guidance in tackling them.

Step 1   **Establish learning targets**. The areas to be learnt should be identified, and specific, realistic goals (eg completion dates, performance standards) stated by agreement with the trainee.

Step 2   **Plan a systematic learning and development programme.** This will ensure regular progress, appropriate stages for consolidation and practice.

Step 3   **Identify opportunities for broadening the trainee's knowledge and experience**, eg by involvement in new projects, placement on inter-departmental committees, suggesting new contacts, or simply extending the job, adding more tasks, greater responsibility etc.

Step 4   **Take into account the strengths and limitations of the trainee** in learning, and take advantage of learning opportunities that suit the trainee's ability, preferred style and goals.

Step 5   **Exchange feedback**. The coach will want to know how the trainee sees his or her progress and future. He or she will also need performance information in order to monitor the trainee's progress, adjust the learning programme if necessary, identify further needs which may emerge and plan future development for the trainee.

3.5 Mentoring

Key term

> **Mentoring** is a long-term relationship in which a more experienced person occupies a role as a coach/teacher, counsellor, role model, supporter and encourager, in order to foster the individual's personal and career development.

Mentoring differs from coaching in two main ways.

(a)   The mentor is not usually the protégé's immediate superior.

(b)   Mentoring covers a much wider range of functions, not necessarily related to immediate job performance.

Kram identifies two broad types of function for the mentor.

Career functions include:

- Sponsoring within the organisation and providing exposure at higher levels
- Coaching and influencing progress through appointments
- Protection
- Drawing up personal development plans
- Advice with administrative problems people face in their new jobs
- Help in tackling projects, by pointing people in the right direction

Psychosocial functions include:

- Creating a sense of acceptance and belonging
- Counselling and friendship
- Providing a role model

Organisational arrangements for coaching and mentoring will vary, but in general a coach needs to be an expert in the trainee's professional field. Mentors are often drawn from other areas of the organisation but

can open up lines of communication to those with power and influence across it. For this reason, a mentor is usually in a senior position.

Exam focus point

10 marks were available in the December 2003 exam for explaining coaching and mentoring.

4 The learning process

FAST FORWARD

There are different schools of thought as to **how people learn**.

4.1 Approaches to learning theory

There are different schools of learning theory which explain and describe how people learn.

(a)   **Behaviourist psychology** concentrates on the relationship between stimuli (input through the senses) and responses to those stimuli. 'Learning' is the formation of new connections between stimulus and response, on the basis of conditioning. We modify our responses in future according to whether the results of our behaviour in the past have been good or bad.

(b)   The **cognitive approach** argues that the human mind takes sensory information and imposes organisation and meaning on it: we interpret and rationalise. We use feedback information on the results of past behaviour to make rational decisions about whether to maintain successful behaviours or modify unsuccessful behaviours in future, according to our goals and our plans for reaching them.

4.2 Lessons from learning theory

Whichever approach it is based on, learning theory offers certain useful propositions for the design of **effective training programmes**.

Proposition	Comment
The individual should be **motivated** to learn.	The advantages of training should be made clear, according to the individual's motives – money, opportunity, valued skills or whatever.
There should be clear **objectives and standards** set, so that each task has some meaning.	Each stage of learning should present a challenge, without overloading the trainee or making them lose confidence. Specific objectives and performance standards will help the trainee in the planning and control process that leads to learning, and provide targets against which performance will constantly be measured.
There should be timely, relevant **feedback** on performance and progress.	This will usually be provided by the trainer, and should be concurrent – or certainly not long delayed. If progress reports or performance appraisals are given only at the year end, for example, there will be no opportunity for behaviour adjustment or learning in the meantime.

Proposition	Comment
Positive and negative **reinforcement** should be judiciously used.	Recognition and encouragement enhance individuals' confidence in their competence and progress: punishment for poor performance – especially without explanation and correction – discourages the learner and creates feelings of guilt, failure and hostility.
Active **participation** is more telling than passive reception (because of its effect on the motivation to learn, concentration and recollection).	If a high degree of participation is impossible, practice and repetition can be used to reinforce receptivity. However, participation has the effect of encouraging 'ownership' of the process of learning and changing – committing the individual to it as their own goal, not just an imposed process.

4.3 Learning styles: Honey and Mumford   12/02

FAST FORWARD

Different people have different **learning styles** or preferences.

The way in which people learn best will differ according to their psychological preferences. That is, there are **learning styles** which suit different individuals. Peter **Honey** and Alan **Mumford** have drawn up a popular classification of four learning styles.

(a) **Theorists** seek to understand basic principles and to take an intellectual, 'hands-off' approach based on logical argument. They prefer training to be:

- Programmed and structured
- Designed to allow time for analysis
- Provided by teachers who share their preference for concepts and analysis

(b) **Reflectors**

- Observe phenomena, think about them and then choose how to act
- Need to work at their own pace
- Find learning difficult if forced into a hurried programme
- Produce carefully thought-out conclusions after research and reflection
- Tend to be fairly slow, non-participative (unless to ask questions) and cautious

(c) **Activists**

- Deal with practical, active problems and do not have patience with theory
- Require training based on hands-on experience
- Are excited by participation and pressure, such as new projects
- Are flexible and optimistic, but tend to rush at something without due preparation

(d) **Pragmatists**

- Only like to study if they can see a direct link to real, practical problems
- Are good at learning new techniques through on-the-job training
- Aim to implement action plans and/or do the task better
- May discard good ideas which only require some development

Training programmes should ideally be designed to accommodate the preferences of all four styles, or to suit individual trainees (where feasible).

Question

With reference to the four learning styles drawn up by Honey and Mumford, which of these styles do you think most closely resembles your own? What implications has this got for the way you learn?

Answer

Depending on your answer you will learn most effectively in particular given situations. For example, the theorist will learn best from lectures and books, whereas the activist will get most from practical activities.

Exam focus point

> Learning styles appeared on the pilot paper and again in the December 2002 exam, together with the learning cycle. These are basic theories underpinning training. Bear in mind, though, that more practical aspects (such as training needs analysis and programme planning or the benefits of training), would be equally well suited to exam questions – especially a case study.

4.4 The learning cycle: Kolb

FAST FORWARD

> People can learn from everyday work experience, using the **learning cycle** of reflection, generalisation and application.

Another useful model is the **experiential learning cycle** devised by David **Kolb** and popularised by Honey and Mumford. Experiential learning involves doing and puts the learner in an active problem-solving role: a form of self-learning which encourages learners to formulate and commit themselves to their own learning objectives.

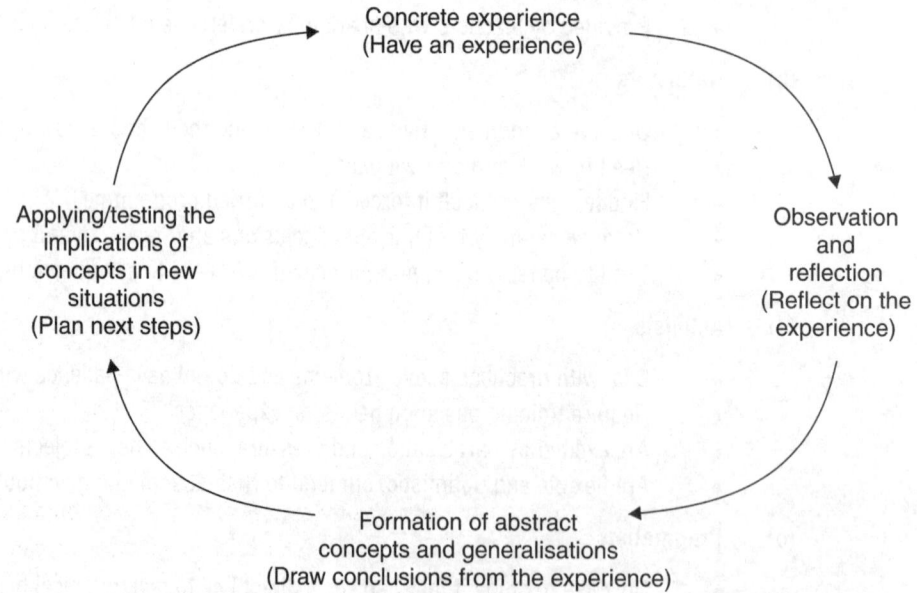

Suppose that an employee interviews a customer for the first time (concrete experience). He observes his own performance and the dynamics of the situation (observation) and afterwards, having failed to convince the customer to buy his product, the employee thinks about what he did right and wrong (reflection). He comes to the conclusion that he failed to listen to what the customer really wanted and feared, underneath his general reluctance: he realises that the key to communication is active listening (abstraction/ generalisation). He decides to apply active listening techniques in his next interview (application/testing). This provides him with a new experience with which to start the cycle over again.

Simplified, this **learning by doing** approach involves:

Act $\longrightarrow$ Analyse action $\longrightarrow$ Suggest principles $\longrightarrow$ Apply principles $\longrightarrow$ Act ... (etc)

4.5 Organisational learning

The **learning organisation** is an organisation that facilitates the learning of all its members (*Pedler, Burgoyne, Boydell*), by gathering and sharing knowledge, tolerating experience and solving problems analytically.

Pedler, Burgoyne and Boydell are the main proponents in the UK of the idea that some organisations are better adapted to continuous learning than others.

Key term

The **learning organisation** is an organisation that facilitates the acquisition and sharing of knowledge, and the learning of all its members, in order continuously and strategically to transform itself in response to a rapidly changing and uncertain environment.

The key dimensions of a learning organisation are:

- The generation and transfer of knowledge
- A tolerance for risk and failure as learning opportunities
- A systematic, on-going, collective and scientific approach to problem-solving

4.5.1 Strengths of learning organisations

Garvin suggests that learning organisations are good at certain key processes.

(a) **Experimentation**. Learning organisations systematically search for and test new knowledge. Decision-making is based on 'hypothesis-generating, hypothesis-testing' techniques: the plan-do-check-act cycle. Application of information and learning is key. Innovation is encouraged, with a tolerance for risk.

(b) **Learning from past experience**. Learning organisations freely seek and provide feedback on performance and processes: they review their successes and failures, assess them systematically and communicate lessons to all employees. Mistakes and failures are regarded as learning opportunities.

(c) **Learning from others**. Learning organisations recognise that the most powerful insights and opportunities come from looking 'outside the box' of the immediate environment. They encourage employees to seek information and learning opportunities outside the organisation as well as inside.

(d) **Transferring knowledge quickly and efficiently throughout the organisation.** Information is made available at all levels and across functional boundaries. Education, training and networking opportunities are constantly available.

4.5.2 Potential barriers to learning

According to Peter **Senge**, there are also sources of **learning disability** in organisations, which prevent them from attaining their potential – which trap them into 'mediocrity', for example, when they could be achieving 'excellence'.

(a) **'I am my position'**. When asked what they do for a living, most people describe the tasks they perform, not the purposes they fulfil; thus they tend to see their responsibilities as limited to the boundaries of their position.

(b) **'The enemy is out there'**. If things go wrong it is all too easy to imagine that somebody else 'out there' was at fault.

(c) **The fixation on events**. Conversations in organisations are dominated by concern about events (last month's sales, who's just been promoted, the new product from our competitor), and this focus inevitably distracts us from seeing the longer-term patterns of change.

(d) **The parable of the boiled frog**. If you place a frog in a pot of boiling water, it will immediately try to scramble out; but if you place the frog in room temperature water, he will stay put. If you heat the water gradually, the frog will do nothing until he boils: this is because 'the frog's internal apparatus for sensing threats to survival is geared to sudden changes in his environment, not to slow, gradual changes'. People ignore gradually building threats, rather than identifying learning needs.

(e) **The delusion of learning from experience.** We learn best from experience, but we never experience the results of our most important and significant decisions. Indeed, we never know what the outcomes would have been had we done something else.

Question	Learning disability

How far do Senge's learning disabilities apply to your own organisation, or to some other significant organisation with which you may be familiar?

For *individuals*, additional barriers to learning may be:

- 'A waste of time': people see no personal benefit from training
- Training programmes employ the wrong techniques for people's learning styles
- Unwillingness to change

5 Responsibility for training and development

FAST FORWARD

Increasingly, **responsibility for training and development** is being devolved to the individual learner, in collaboration with line managers and training providers.

5.1 The trainee

Many people now believe that the ultimate responsibility for training and development lies, not with the employer, but with the **individual**. People should seek to develop their own skills, to improve their own careers rather than wait for the organisation to impose training upon them. Why?

(a) Delayering means there are fewer automatic promotion pathways: individuals need to seek non-'vertical' paths to challenge in the job.

(b) Technological change means that new skills are always needed, and people who can learn new skills will be more employable.

5.2 The human resources (HR) department or training department

The human resources department is centrally concerned with developing people. larger organisations often have extensive learning and career planning programmes, managing the progression of individuals through the organisation, in accordance with the performance and potential of the individual and the needs of the organisation.

5.3 Line managers

Line managers bear some of the responsibility for training and development within the organisation by:

- Identifying the training needs of the department or section
- Assessing the current competences of the individuals within the department
- Identifying opportunities for learning and development on the job
- Coaching staff
- Offering performance feedback for on-the-job learning
- Organising training programmes where required

5.4 The training manager

The training manager is a member of staff appointed to arrange and sometimes run training. The training manager generally reports to the **human resources** or **personnel director**, but also needs a good relationship with line managers in the departments where the training takes place.

Responsibilities of the training manager include:

Responsibility	Comment
Liaison	With HR department and operating departments
Scheduling	Arranging training programmes at convenient times
Needs identification	Discerning existing and future skills shortages
Programme design	Developing tailored training programmes
Feedback	To the trainee, the department and the HR department

6 Evaluating training programmes

FAST FORWARD

Training results can be evaluated using **Hamblin's five-level model.**

Key terms

Validation of training means observing the results of the course and measuring whether the training objectives have been achieved.

Evaluation of training means comparing the costs of the scheme against the assessed benefits which are being obtained.

6.1 The five-level evaluation model: Hamblin

The effectiveness of a training scheme may be measured at different levels (*Hamblin*).

Level 1   **Trainees' reactions to the experience.** These are usually measured by post-training feedback forms ('Happy Sheets'), asking whether trainees enjoyed the course, found it relevant etc. This form of monitoring is rather inexact, and it does not allow the training department to measure the results for comparison against the training objective.

Level 2 **Trainee learning** (new skills and knowledge): measuring what the trainees have learned on the course usually by means of a test at the end of it.

Level 3 **Changes in job behaviour following training**: observing work practices and outputs (products, services, documents) to identify post-training differences. This is possible where the purpose of the course was to learn a particular skill, for example. It measures not just what trainees have learned, but how far they have been able to apply their learning to the job.

Level 4 **Impact of training on organisational goals/results**: seeing whether the training scheme has contributed to the overall objectives of the organisation, in terms of quality, productivity, profitability, employee retention and so on. This is a form of monitoring reserved for senior management, and would perhaps be discussed at board level. It is likely to be the main component of a cost-benefit analysis.

Level 5 **Ultimate value**: the impact of training on the wider 'good' of the organisation in terms of stakeholder benefits, greater social responsibility, corporate growth/survival and so on.

Exam focus point

You were asked to explain five criteria against which the effectiveness of training could be evaluated, in the December 2003 exam. These kinds of topics lend themselves to brief point lists for revision – or using BPP Passcards!

Question
Evaluating and validating training

Outline why it is important to evaluate and validate a training programme.

Answer

Validation of a new course is important to ensure that objectives have been achieved. Evaluation of it is more difficult, but at least as important because it identifies the value of the training programme to the organisation.

7 Development

Development includes a range of learning activities and experiences (not just training) to enhance employees' or managers' portfolio of competence, experience and capability, with a view to personal, professional or career progression.

7.1 What is development?

As we noted at the beginning of this chapter, development is a 'wider' approach to fulfilling an individual's potential than training. Development may include training, but may also include a range of learning experiences whereby:

(a) Employees gain **work experience** of increasing challenge and responsibility, which will enable them to other more senior jobs in due course of time

(b) Employees are given **guidance, support and counselling** to help them to formulate personal and career development goals

(c) Employees are given suitable **education and training** to develop their skills and knowledge

(d)   Employees are facilitated in **planning their future** and identifying opportunities open to them in the organisation

7.2 Approaches to development

Approaches to development include the following.

Approach	Comment
Management development	'An attempt to improve managerial effectiveness through a planned and deliberate learning process' (*Mumford*). This may include the development of management/leadership skills (or competences), management education (such as MBA programmes) and planned experience of different functions, positions and work settings, in preparation for increasing managerial responsibility.
Career development	Individuals plan career paths. The trend for delayered organisations has reduced opportunities for upward progression: opportunities may be planned for sideways/lateral transfers, secondments to project groups, short external secondments and so on, to offer new opportunities.
Professional development	Professional bodies offer structured programmes of continuing professional development (CPD). The aim is to ensure that professional standards are maintained and enhanced through educational, development and training self-managed by the individual. A CPD approach is based on the belief that a professional qualification should be the basis for a career lifetime of development *and* adherence to a professional code of ethics and standards.
Personal development	Businesses are increasingly offering employees wider-ranging development opportunities, rather than focusing on skills required in the current job. Personal development creates more rounded, competent employees who may contribute more innovatively and flexibly to the organisation's future needs. It may also help to foster employee job satisfaction, commitment and loyalty.

Chapter Roundup

- In order to achieve its goals, an organisation requires a **skilled workforce**. This is partly achieved by training.

- The main **purpose** of training and development is to raise competence and therefore performance standards. It is also concerned with personal development, helping and motivating employees to fulfil their potential.

- **Training** offers significant **benefits** for both employers and employees – although it is *not* the solution to every work problem!

- A **systematic approach** to training includes: need definition; objective setting; planning training programmes; delivering training; and evaluating results.

- A thorough analysis of **training needs** should be carried out to ensure that training programmes meet organisational and individual requirements.

- Once training needs have been identified, they should be translated into **training objectives**.

- Individuals can incorporate training and development objectives into a **personal development plan**.

- There are a variety of **training methods**. These include:

  - Off-the-job education and training
  - On-the-job training

- **Off the job training** minimises risk but does not always support transfer of learning to the job.

- **On the job training** maximises transfer of learning by incorporating it into 'real' work.

- **Induction** is the process whereby a person is formally introduced and integrated into an organisation or system.

- There are different schools of thought as to **how people learn**.

- Different people have different **learning styles** or preferences.

- People can learn from everyday work experience, using the **learning cycle** of reflection, generalisation and application.

- The **learning organisation** is an organisation that facilitates the learning of all its members (*Pedler, Burgoyne, Boydell*), by gathering and sharing knowledge, tolerating experience and solving problems analytically.

- Increasingly, **responsibility for training and development** is being devolved to the individual learner, in collaboration with line managers and training providers.

- Training results can be evaluated using **Hamblin's five-level model.**

- **Development** includes a range of learning activities and experiences (not just training) to enhance employees' or managers' portfolio of competence, experience and capability, with a view to personal, professional or career progression.

Quick Quiz

1   List examples of development opportunities within organisations.

2   List how training can contribute to:

    (a)   Organisational effectiveness
    (b)   Individual effectiveness and motivation

3   The formula 'required level of competence *minus* present level of competence describes
    .... '.

4   How should training objectives be expressed?

5   What does learning theory tell us about the design of training programmes?

6   Which of the following is not one of the learning styles defined by Honey and Mumford?

    A   Pragmatist
    B   Theorist
    C   Abstractor
    D   Reflector

7   List the four stages in Kolb's experiential learning cycle.

8   List the available methods of on-the-job training.

9   What are the levels of training validation/evaluation?

10 What is the supervisor's role in training?

Answers to Quick Quiz

1   Career planning, job rotation, deputising, on-the-job training, counselling, guidance, education and training.

2   (a)   Increased efficiency and productivity; reduced costs, supervisory problems and accidents; improved quality, motivation and morale.

          (b)   Demonstrates individual value, enhances security, enhances skills portfolio, motivates, helps develop networks and contacts.

3   Training needs.

4   Actively – 'after completing this chapter you should understand how to design and evaluate training programmes'.

5   The trainee should be motivated to learn, there should be clear objectives and timely feedback. Positive and negative reinforcement should be used carefully, to encourage active participation where possible.

6   C: the correct 'A' word (you may like to use the acronym PART or TRAP to remember the model) is 'Activist'.

7   Concrete experience, observation/reflection, abstraction/generalisation, application/testing.

8   Induction, job rotation, temporary promotion, 'assistant to' positions, project or committee work

9   Reactions, learning, job behaviour, organisational change, ultimate impact.

10   Identifying training needs of the department or section. Identifying the skills of the individual employee, and deficiencies in performance. Providing or supervising on-the-job training (eg coaching). Providing feedback on an individual's performance.

Now try the question below from the Exam Question Bank

Number	Level	Marks	Time
Q10	Examination	15	27 mins

11

Appraisal and competence assessment

Topic list	Syllabus reference
1 The purpose of appraisal	3 (d)
2 Job evaluation	3 (d)
3 The process of performance appraisal	3 (d), 3 (e), 3 (f)
4 Alternative approaches to appraisal	3 (d)
5 Barriers to effective appraisal	3 (d)
6 How effective is the appraisal scheme?	3 (d)

Introduction

The general purpose of performance appraisal is to improve the efficiency of the organisation by ensuring that individuals within it are performing to the best of their ability, and (perhaps) also developing their potential for improvement. (There is a clear link here to Chapter 10 on training and development.)

In this chapter, we look at the role of formal **appraisal (Section 1)** and distinguish it from **job evaluation (Section 2)**. Be sure that you're clear about this: job evaluation assesses the value of *jobs*, while appraisal assesses the performance of *people*.

In **Sections 3-4**, we look at various approaches and techniques of appraisal.

It's worth noting that appraisal has been poorly regarded (for various reasons which we explore in **Section 5**). In recent years, it has shifted towards a more proactive performance-management orientation.

The key challenge of this topic is perhaps to keep in mind the variations of what is being appraised and who is doing the appraising.

Study guide

Section 8 – Standard setting and performance management

- Illustrate ways of applying performance management

Section 19 – Competence assessment

Section 20 – Conducting the appraisal process

Section 21 – Individual skills and development

- Explain the link between the appraisal process and effective employee development
- Describe the role of the appraisee in the process
- Suggest ways in which self-development can be part of the process

Exam guide

The process of appraisal and the detailed procedures associated with it could form a question in either Section A (as in June 2004) or Section B.

1 The purpose of appraisal 12/01, 6/04

1.1 Main components of appraisal

FAST FORWARD

Appraisal can be used to **reward** but also to identify **potential**, and **training and development** needs.

The general purpose of any appraisal system is to improve the efficiency of the organisation by ensuring that the individuals within it are performing to the best of their ability and developing their potential for improvement. This has three main *components*.

(a) **Reward review**. Measuring the extent to which an employee is deserving of performance-related bonuses or pay increases

(b) **Performance review**, for planning and following-up training and development programmes: identifying training needs, validating training methods and so on

(c) **Potential review**, as an aid to planning career development and succession, by attempting to predict the level and type of work the individual will be capable of in the future

1.2 Specific objectives of appraisal

More specific objectives of appraisal may be summarised as follows.

(a) Establishing what **the individual has to do** in a job in order that the objectives for the section or department are realised

(b) Establishing the **key or main results** which the individual will be expected to achieve in the course of his or her work over a period of time

(c) **Comparing** the individual's level of performance against a standard, to provide a basis for remuneration above the basic pay rate

(d) Identifying the individual's **training and development needs** in the light of actual performance

(e) Identifying potential candidates **for promotion**

(f)   Identifying **areas for improvement**

(g)   Establishing an **inventory** of actual and potential performance within the undertaking, as a basis for human resource planning

(h)   Monitoring the undertaking's **selection procedures** against the subsequent performance of recruits

(i)   **Improving communication** about work tasks between different levels in the hierarchy

1.3 Why have formal appraisal?

Formal appraisal systems support objective, positive, relevant, consistent feedback by managers.

You may argue that managers gather performance evaluations, and give feedback, on an on-going basis, in the course of supervision. Why is a formal appraisal system required?

(a)   Managers and supervisors may obtain random impressions of subordinates' performance (perhaps from their more noticeable successes and failures), but rarely form a **coherent, complete and objective** picture.

(b)   They may have a fair idea of their subordinates' shortcomings – but may not have devoted time and attention to the matter of **improvement and development**.

(c)   Judgements are easy to make, but less easy to justify in detail, in writing, or to the subject's face.

(d)   Different assessors may be applying a **different set of criteria**, and varying standards of objectivity and judgement. This undermines the value of appraisal for comparison, as well as its credibility in the eyes of the appraisees.

(e)   Unless stimulated to do so, managers rarely give their subordinates adequate **feedback** on their performance.

In an article in *Student Accountant* (April 2004), the examiner set out the advantages of benefits for the individual and the organisation:

	Benefits
Individual	• Objectives are established in relation to the whole organisation
	• Key results and timescales are established
	• Compares past performance and future activities against standards
	• Basis for performance related pay schemes
Organisation	• Suitable promotion candidates are identified
	• Areas of improvement can be seen
	• Communication is improved
	• Basis for medium to long term HR planning

Question

Formal appraisal

List four disadvantages to the individual of not having a formal appraisal system.

Answer

Disadvantages to the individual of not having an appraisal system include: the individual is not aware of progress or shortcomings, is unable to judge whether s/he would be considered for promotion, is unable to identify or correct weaknesses by training and there is a lack of communication with the manager.

2 Job evaluation

12/01

FAST FORWARD

Job evaluation measures the value of a job to the organisation (for the purpose of salary planning): appraisal measures the performance of a given individual in the job.

This is often regarded as an aspect of performance appraisal, but in fact it is a systematic evaluation of the *job* – not the performance of the job holder.

Key term

Job evaluation is a systematic method of assessing the value or worth of a job to the organisation in order to determine wage or salary structures so that the rate of pay for a given job is fair in comparison to other jobs in the organisation.

Exam focus point

Approaches to 'job measurement' used in performance appraisal systems – specifically including the job evaluation methods discussed below – were examined in December 2001. Be clear in your mind, however, that job evaluation determines the worth of the *job*: it says nothing about the performance of individuals doing the job, which is the purpose of *performance appraisal*.

2.1 Methods of job evaluation

FAST FORWARD

Job evaluation methods may be non-analytical (whole job) or analytical (components). Only analytical method are acceptable in defending equal pay claims.

Non-analytical approaches to job evaluation make largely subjective judgements about the whole job, its difficulty, and its importance to the organisation relative to other jobs.

Analytical methods of job evaluation identify the component factors or characteristics involved in the performance of each job, such as:

- Skill
- Responsibility
- Experience
- Mental and physical effort required

Each component is separately analysed, evaluated and weighted. Degrees of each factor, and the importance of the factor within the job, are quantified.

Analytical methods are acceptable as a measurement of the 'value' of a job for the purposes of equal pay claims. They involve detailed analysis and a numerical basis for comparing jobs. However, there is still an element of subjectivity.

(a)   The factors for analysis are themselves qualitative, and not easy to measure.

(b)   Assessment of the importance and difficulty of a job cannot be divorced from the context of the organisation and job holder.

(i)   The relative importance of a job is a function of the culture and politics of the organisation.

(ii)   The difficulty of the job depends on the ability of the job holder and the favourability or otherwise of the environment/technology/work methods/ management.

(c)   The selection of factors and the assignment of monetary values to factors remain subjective judgements.

We shall briefly describe four methods of job evaluation.

- Ranking
- Classification
- Factor comparison
- Points rating

2.1.1 Ranking method

In a ranking system of job evaluation, each job is considered as a whole (rather than in terms of job elements) and ranked in accordance with its relative importance or contribution to the organisation. Having established a list of jobs in descending order of importance, they can be divided into groups, and jobs in each group given the same salary grade.

The advantage of the ranking method is that it is simple and unscientific. In a small organisation, it might be applied with fairness.

However, the job evaluators need to have a good personal knowledge of every job being evaluated and in a large organisation, they are unlikely to have it. Without this knowledge, the ranking method would not produce fair evaluations.

2.1.2 Classification method

This is similar to the ranking method, except that instead of ranking jobs in order of importance and then dividing them into grades, the classification method begins with deciding what grades there ought to be (say, grades A, B, C, D and E, with each grade carefully defined) and then deciding into which grade each individual job should be classified: is the job a grade C or a grade D job?

The advantages and disadvantages of this method are the same as those of ranking.

2.1.3 Factor comparison method

This is an analytical method of job evaluation. It begins with the selection of a number of qualitative factors on which each job will be evaluated. These qualitative factors might include, for example:

- Technical knowledge
- Physical skill
- Mental skill
- Responsibility for other people
- Responsibility for assets or working conditions

Key benchmark jobs are then taken, for which the rate of pay is considered to be fair (perhaps in comparison with similar jobs in other organisations). Each key job is analysed in turn, factor by factor, to decide how much of the total salary is being paid for each factor. So if technical skill is 50% of a benchmark job paying £10,000, the factor pay rate for technical skill (within that job) is £5,000. When this has been done for every benchmark job, all the different rates of pay for each factor are correlated, to formulate a ranking and pay scale for that factor.

Other (non-benchmark) jobs are then evaluated by analysing them factor by factor. In this way a salary or grading for the job can be built up. For example, analysis of a clerk's job factor by factor might look like this.

Factor	Proportion of job		Pay rate for factor (as established by analysis of benchmark jobs)	Job value £
Technical skills	50%	×	£12,000 pa	6,000
Mental ability	25%	×	£16,000 pa	4,000
Responsibility for others	15%	×	£10,000 pa	1,500
Other responsibilities	10%	×	£5,000 pa	500
				12,000

2.1.4 Points rating method

Points rating is probably the most popular method of formal job evaluation. It begins with listing a number of factors which are thought to represent the qualities being looked for in the jobs to be evaluated. (Remember that jobs are being evaluated, not job holders.) In a typical evaluation scheme, there might be about 8-12 factors listed. The factors will vary according to the type of organisation, but they might include the following.

- Skill – education, experience, dexterity, qualifications
- Initiative
- Physical or mental effort
- Dealing with others
- Responsibility for subordinates, or the safety and welfare of others
- Responsibility for equipment, for a process or product, for materials
- Job conditions – such as monotony of working, working in isolation, work hazards

A number of points is allocated to each factor, as a maximum score, reflecting its important to the organisation. Each job is then analysed, and a points score awarded for each factor according to the amount of each factor in the job. The scores are then added, to derive a total points score for the job. This provides the basis for ranking the jobs in order of importance, for grading jobs, if required, and for fixing a salary structure.

Points rating has the advantage of flexibility in that the factors selected are best suited for the particular types of job being evaluated, and the importance given to each factor is decided by the allocation of points. It provides a rank order of jobs, without determining the money value of the job – which can be set flexibly with reference to market rates and other factors.

3 The process of performance appraisal   6/04

3.1 Overview of the appraisal process

Three basic requirements of a **formal appraisal system** are: defining what is to be appraised, recording assessments, and getting the appraiser and appraisee together.

There are three basic requirements for a formal appraisal system.

(a) The **formulation of desired traits and standards** against which individuals can be consistently and objectively assessed.

(b) **Recording assessments**. Managers should be encouraged to utilise a standard framework, but still be allowed to express what they consider important, and without too much form-filling.

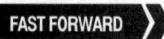

(c) **Getting the appraiser and appraisee together**, so that both contribute to the assessment and plans for improvement and/or development.

A systematic appraisal system would include the following stages.

Step 1 **Identification of criteria** for assessment, perhaps based on job analysis, performance standards, person specifications and so on.

Step 2 The preparation by the subordinate's manager of an **appraisal report**. In some systems both the appraisee and appraiser prepare a report. These reports are then compared.

Step 3 An **appraisal interview**, for an exchange of views about the appraisal report, targets for improvement, solutions to problems and so on.

Step 4 **Review of the assessment** by the assessor's own superior, so that the appraisee does not feel subject to one person's prejudices. Formal appeals may be allowed, if necessary to establish the fairness of the procedure.

Step 5 The preparation and implementation of **action plans** to achieve improvements and changes agreed.

Step 6 **Follow-up:** monitoring the progress of the action plan.

This can be depicted as a control system, as follows.

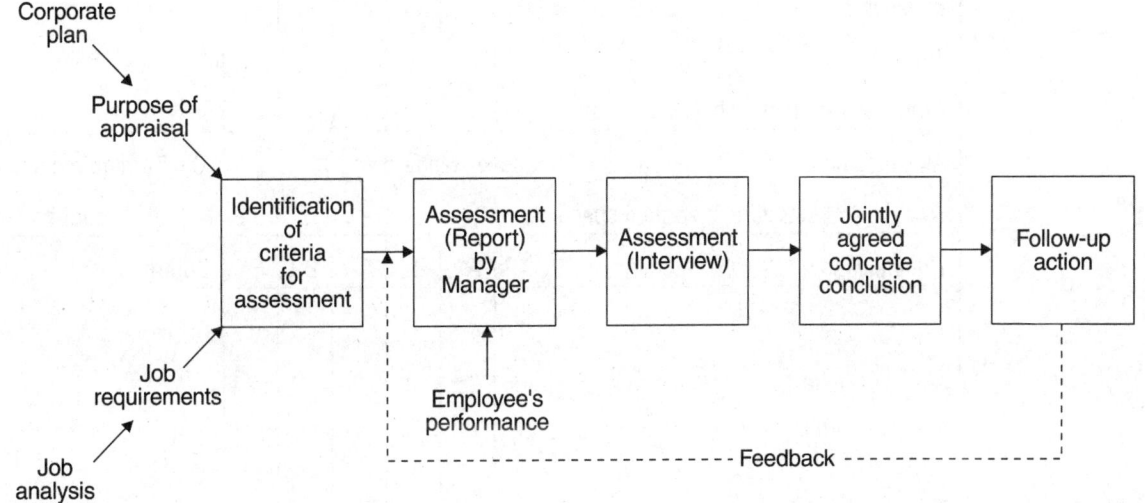

3.2 What is appraised?

Assessments must be related to a common standard, in order for comparisons to be made between individuals: on the other hand, they should be related to meaningful *performance criteria*, which take account of the critical variables in each different job.

Some basic criteria might appear in a simple appraisal report form as follows.

APPRAISAL REPORT						
Name:				Time in position		
Position:				Period of review:		
Company:				Age:		
	A	B	C	D	E	Comment
Overall assessment						
Job knowledge						
Effective output						
Co-operation						
Initiative						
Time-keeping						
Other relevant facts (specify)						
A= Outstanding B = above standard C = To required standard						
D = Short of standard in some respects E= Not up to required standard						
Potential	A	B	C	D	E	Comment
A = Overdue for promotion B = Ready for promotion C = Potential for promotion						
D = No evidence of promotion potential at present						
E = Has not worked long enough with me for judgement						
Training, if any, required						
Assessment discussed with employee?			Yes		No	
Signed			Date			
Confirmed			Date			

Question

Identify specific appraisal criteria which may be relevant to some jobs of your choice.

Answer

You might have identified such things as:

(a)   Numerical ability applicable to accounts staff, say, more than to customer contact staff

(b)   Ability to drive safely, essential for transport workers – not for desk-bound ones

(c)   Report-writing (not applicable to manual labour, say)

3.3 Appraisal techniques

FAST FORWARD

A variety of appraisal **techniques** can be used to measure different criteria in a different ways.

A variety of appraisal techniques may be used, measuring different criteria in different ways.

(a)   **Overall assessment**. The manager writes in narrative form his judgements about the appraisee. There will be no guaranteed consistency of the criteria and areas of assessment, however, and managers may not be able to convey clear, effective judgements in writing.

(b)   **Guided assessment**. Assessors are required to comment on a number of specified characteristics and performance elements, with guidelines as to how terms such as 'application', 'integrity' and 'adaptability' are to be interpreted in the work context. This is more precise, but still rather vague.

(c)   **Grading**. Grading adds a comparative frame of reference to the general guidelines, whereby managers are asked to select one of a number of levels or degrees to which the individual in question displays the given characteristic. These are also known as **rating scales**.

Numerical values may be added to ratings to give rating scores. Alternatively a less precise **graphic scale** may be used to indicate general position on a plus/minus scale.

Factor: job knowledge

High __✔__ Average ____ Low

(d)   **Behavioural incident methods**. These concentrate on employee behaviour, which is measured against typical behaviour in each job, as defined by common critical incidents of successful and unsuccessful job behaviour reported by managers.

(e)   **Results-orientated schemes**. This reviews performance against specific targets and standards of performance agreed in advance by manager and subordinate together.

(i)   The subordinate is more involved in appraisal because (s)he is able to evaluate his/her progress in achieving jointly-agreed targets.

(ii)   The manager is relieved of a critic's role, and becomes a counsellor.

(iii)   Clear and known targets help modify behaviour.

The effectiveness of the scheme will depend on the **targets set** (are they clearly defined? realistic?) and the **commitment** of both parties to make it work.

Question   Appraisal techniques

What sort of appraisal systems are suggested by the following examples?

(a)   The Head Teacher of Dotheboys Hall sends a brief report at the end of each term to the parents of the school's pupils. Typical phrases include 'a satisfactory term's work', and 'could do better'.

(b)   A firm of auditors assess the performance of their staff in four categories: technical ability, relationships with clients, relationships with other members of the audit team, and professional attitude. On each of these criteria staff are marked from A (= excellent) to E (= poor).

(c)   A firm of insurance brokers assesses the performance of its staff by the number of clients they have visited and the number of policies sold.

Answer

(a)   Overall assessment of the blandest kind
(b)   A grading system, based on a guided assessment
(c)   Results-orientated scheme

3.4 Self-appraisals

Self-appraisals occur when individuals carry out their own self-evaluation as a major input into the appraisal process.

Advantages include:

(a)   It **saves the manager time** as the employee identifies the areas of competence which are relevant to the job and his/her relative strengths.

(b)   It offers **increased responsibility** to the individual which may improve motivation.

(c)   This **reconciles the goals** of the individual and the organisation.

(d)   In giving the responsibility to an individual, the scheme may offer more **flexibility** in terms of the timing and relevance of the appraisal.

Disadvantages include:

(a)   People are often not the best judges of their own performance.

(b)   People may deliberately over- (or under-) estimate their performance, in order to gain approval or reward – or to conform to group norms.

Many schemes combine managerial and self appraisal (as we shall see in Section 4 below).

Exam focus point

An extensive 40 mark question was set on appraisal in June 2004. It covered: purposes of appraisal; benefits to the organisation and employees; barriers to effective appraisal; documentation used; interview approaches; and follow-up action.

Note: this followed an article in the April 2004 *Student Accountant* on this subject. There has been a steady pattern of Section A questions addressing topics covered by the examiner in such articles, 2-3 months before the exam. Take the hint!

3.5 The appraisal interview   6/04

The appraisal **interview** is an important stage in the process, as it can be used to encourage collaborative problem solving and improvement planning. A 'problem-solving' style is preferable to a 'tell and sell' or 'tell and listen' style (*Maier*).

The process of an appraisal interview may be as follows.

Step 1   Prepare

- Plan interview time and environment: the aim is to facilitate collaborative problem-solving and communication. Privacy is essential
- Prepare relevant documentation: job description, employee records, and statement of performance (or appraisal form)
- Review employee's history and self-appraisals/peer appraisals (if used)
- Prepare for the interview
- Prepare report. Review employee's self-appraisal

Step 2   Interview

- Select an appropriate style (see below): directional, persuasive or collaborative
- Encourage employee to talk, identify problems and solutions
- Be fair

Step 3   Agree

- Summarise to check understanding
- Gain employee commitment
- Agree plan of action

Step 4   Report

- Complete appraisal report, if not already prepared

Step 5   Follow up

- Take action as agreed
- Monitor progress
- Keep employee informed

3.5.1 Three approaches: Maier

Maier *(The Appraisal Interview)* identifies three types of approach to appraisal interviews. Most appraisees prefer the third of the alternatives suggested.

(a)   The **tell and sell style**. The manager tells the subordinate how (s)he has been assessed, and then tries to 'sell' (gain acceptance of) the evaluation and the improvement plan. This requires unusual human relations skills in order to convey constructive criticism in an acceptable manner, and to motivate the appraisee to alter his/her behaviour.

(b)   The **tell and listen style**. The manager tells the subordinate how (s)he has been assessed, and then invites the appraisee to respond. The manager therefore no longer dominates the interview throughout, and there is greater opportunity for counselling as opposed to pure direction.

(i)   The employee is encouraged to participate in the assessment and the working out of improvement targets and methods: it is an accepted tenet of behavioural theory that participation in problem definition and goal setting increases the individual's commitment to behaviour and attitude modification.

(ii)   This method does not assume that a change in the employee will be the sole key to improvement: the manager may receive helpful feedback about how job design, methods, environment or supervision might be improved.

(c)   The **problem-solving style**. The manager abandons the role of critic altogether, and becomes a helper. The discussion is centred not on the assessment, but on the employee's work problems. The employee is encouraged to think solutions through, and to commit himself to the recognised need for personal improvement. This approach encourages intrinsic motivation through the element of self-direction, and the perception of the job itself as a problem-solving activity. It may also stimulate creative thinking on the part of employee and manager alike, to the benefit of the organisation's adaptability and methods.

Exam focus point

Maier seems to be the accepted framework for discussing appraisal interviews: worth learning. Similarly, Lockett (see Section 5) is the commonly cited framework for appraisal problems. Use named authors where you can – but make sure that you name them correctly!

Question   **Appraisal interview**

What approach was taken at your last appraisal interview? Could it have been better?

3.6 Follow-up

After the appraisal interview, the manager may complete the report, with an overall assessment, assessment of potential and/or the jointly-reached conclusion of the interview, with **recommendations for follow-up action**. The manager should then discuss the report with the counter-signing manager (usually his or her own superior), resolving any problems that have arisen in making the appraisal or report, and agreeing on action to be taken. The report form may then go to the development adviser, training officer or other relevant people as appropriate for follow-up.

Follow-up procedures may include the following.

(a)   **Informing appraisees of the results** of the appraisal, if this has not been central to the review interview

(b)   **Carrying out agreed actions** on training, promotion and so on

(c)   **Monitoring the appraisee's progress** and checking that (s)he has carried out agreed actions or improvements

(d)   Taking necessary steps to **help the appraisee to attain improvement objectives**, by guidance, providing feedback, upgrading equipment, altering work methods and so on.

Question   **Follow-up**

What would happen without follow-up?

Answer

The appraisal would merely be seen as a pleasant chat with little effect on future performance, as circumstances change. Moreover the individual might feel cheated.

The appraisal can also be used as an input to the employee's **personal development plan**.

4 Alternative approaches to appraisal

FAST FORWARD

> **New techniques** of appraisal aim to monitor the appraisee's effectiveness from a number of perspectives. These techniques include upward, customer and 360-degree feedback and performance management.

4.1 Upward appraisal

A notable modern trend, adopted in the UK by companies such as BP and British Airways, is upward appraisal, whereby employees are not rated by their superiors but by their subordinates. The followers appraise the leader. This has a number of **advantages**.

    (a)   Subordinates tend to know their superior (particularly in the area of leadership skills) better than anyone.

    (b)   As multiple subordinates rate each manager, ratings may be more reliable: instead of the potential bias of a single rating, multiple ratings offer a representative view.

    (c)   Subordinates' ratings may have more impact because it is more unusual to receive upward feedback from subordinates.

Problems with upward feedback include fear of reprisals, vindictiveness, and extra form processing. Some bosses in strong positions might refuse to act, even if a consensus of staff suggested that they should change their ways.

4.2 Customer appraisal

In some companies, the appraisal process includes feedback from 'customers' (internal or external). At Rank-Xerox, for example, 30% of a manager's annual bonus is conditional upon satisfactory levels of 'customer' feedback. This is a valuable development, in that customers are the best judges of customer service, which is a key value in competitive business environments.

4.3 360 degree appraisal

Taking downwards, upwards and customer appraisals together, some firms have instituted **360 degree appraisal** (or *multi-source feedback*) by collecting feedback on an individual's performance from:

- The person's immediate boss
- People or groups of people who report to the appraisee
- Peers (co-workers)
- Customers (internal and external) and
- The manager personally by self-appraisal

Advantages include:

- More rounded picture of performance

- Multiple ratings may offset subjectivity/bias

- Increases task/results-related communication in the organisation

- Takes into account the views of subordinates (eg on leadership skills) and customers (eg on customer service): best viewpoint

- Indicates the seriousness with which appraisal is regarded

Disadvantages include:

- Peer appraisal may cause suspicion and hostility
- Upward appraisal is resisted
- Difficult to standardise criteria for all feedback sources
- Extra organisation and paperwork

4.4 Performance management   6/03

Performance management (discussed in Chapter 6) may be regarded as a new approach to appraisal. It has significant advantages, as:

(a)   It separates appraisal (for development/development planning) from pay awards, freeing the appraisal process from some of its inhibitions.

(b)   Collaboration in objective-setting gives employees the security and satisfaction of knowing what is expected of them, and participating in the process.

(c)   The process is positive and participatory: it removes the element of 'judgement' (on past performance) and focuses on eliminating obstacles, improvement and developments (in future).

(d)   It is an on-going process: not just an annual event.

(e)   Being results-oriented, it enhances focus and communication on key values such as quality, flexibility and customer satisfaction.

 Case Study

W H Smith supplemented their upwards appraisal system with 360 degree appraisal, starting with the personnel department.

Between eight and fifteen people filled in forms covering each manager's competences and personal objectives. The appraisers were asked to rate them on a scale of one to five and give anecdotal examples to support the marks. The forms were sent to an independent third party for collating.

The system was said to have sharpened the developmental aspects of W H Smiths' standard appraisal meetings. But there were also problems: a minimum of eight people commenting on 15 managers (in the personnel department alone) meant at least 120 forms – a significant increase in administration; many appraisers found it difficult to comment on the individual manager's objectives; and there was a reluctance to back up ratings with anecdotal comments.

5 Barriers to effective appraisal

Problems with appraisal are its implementation in practice and a range of misperceptions about it (*Lockett*).

5.1 Problems in practice

Lockett *(Effective Performance Management)* suggests that barriers to effective appraisal can be identified as follows.

Appraisal barriers	Comment
Appraisal as confrontation	Many people dread appraisals, or use them 'as a sort of show down, a good sorting out or a clearing of the air.' In this kind of climate: • There is likely to be a lack of agreement on performance levels and improvement needs. • The feedback may be subjective or exaggerated. • The feedback may be negatively delivered. • The appraisal may focus on negative aspects, rather than looking forward to potential for improvement and development.
Appraisal as judgement	The appraisal 'is seen as a one-sided process in which the manager acts as judge, jury and counsel for the prosecution'. This puts the subordinate on the defensive. Instead, the process of performance management 'needs to be jointly operated in order to retain the commitment and develop the self-awareness of the individual.'
Appraisal as chat	The appraisal is conducted as if it were a friendly chat 'without ... purpose or outcome ... Many managers, embarrassed by the need to give feedback and set stretching targets, reduce the appraisal to a few mumbled "well dones!" and leave the interview with a briefcase of unresolved issues.'
Appraisal as bureaucracy	Appraisal is a form-filling exercise, to satisfy the personnel department. Its underlying purpose, improving individual and organisational performance, is forgotten.
Appraisal as unfinished business	Appraisal should be part of a continuing future-focused process of performance management, not a way of 'wrapping up' the past year's performance issues.
Appraisal as annual event	Many targets set at annual appraisal meetings become irrelevant or out-of-date. Feedback, goal adjustment and improvement planning should be a continuous process.

The examiner, in a *Student Accountant* article (April 2004) suggests that: 'Perhaps the greatest problem with appraisals is that they are often regarded as a nuisance' by employees and managers alike.

5.2 Appraisal and pay

Another problem is the extent to which the appraisal system is related to the **pay and reward system**. Many employees consider that positive appraisals should be rewarded, but there are major drawbacks to this approach.

(a) **Funds available** for pay rises rarely depend on one individual's performance alone – the whole company has to do well.

(b) **Continuous improvement** should perhaps be expected of employees as part of their work and development, not rewarded as extra.

(c) Performance management is about a lot more than pay for *past* performance – it is often **forward looking** with regard to future performance.

Question	Appraisal in practice

This extensive activity shows some of the problems of operating appraisal schemes in practice.

It is time for Pauline Radway's annual performance appraisal and Steve Taylor, her manager, has sought your advice on two problem areas which he has identified as 'motivation' and 'the organisation's systems'.

The appraisal system has a six point rating scale:

1	Excellent	4	Acceptable
2	Outstanding	5	Room for improvement
3	Competent	6	Unacceptable

The annual pay increase is determined, in part, by the overall rating of the employee.

Pauline was recruited into Steve's section 18 months ago. She took about five months to learn the job and achieve competence. Accordingly, at last year's appraisal she and Steve agreed that an overall rating of '4' was appropriate.

Over the next six months Pauline worked hard and well and in effect developed her job so she was able to accept more responsibility and expand her range of activities into areas which were both interesting and demanding.

During the last six months the section has been 'rationalised' and the workforce has been reduced (although the workload has increased). Steve is under pressure to contain costs – particularly in the area of salary increases.

Steve now has to rely on Pauline performing her enriched job which, taking the past six months as a whole and given the increased pressure, she performs 'satisfactorily' rather than 'outstandingly'; there are aspects of her performance in this enriched job which she could improve.

When Steve met Pauline to agree the time for the appraisal interview she said – only half jokingly – 'I warn you, I'm looking forward to a respectable pay rise this year'.

Required

Outline the problems for Steve that arise from the above scenario:

(a) In relation to Pauline's feelings
(b) In relation to the organisation's systems

Answer

(a) **Pauline's feelings**

Pauline, not unreasonably, **makes a connection between performance and reward**. She feels she has worked hard and that this should be recognised in financial terms. Steve, on the other hand, is under pressure to keep costs under control. In fact, one of the reasons for Pauline's increased responsibility is the rationalisation of the department.

Pauline, however, does make a **crude assumption that effort equals performance**. She is highly motivated at the moment, but her performance is not outstanding. Her performance is only satisfactory in her changed job, and therefore it would not be appropriate to tell her otherwise. However, using **expectancy theory**, we can assert that a pay increase for her is an important motivating factor to get her to work hard.

Steve is thus faced with a **dilemma**. If she is not rewarded, it is likely that she will make less effort to perform well, and this would be suggested by expectancy theory. Steve will suffer, as the rationalised department depends on her continual hard work. In short, this is a **hygiene factor**.

Another factor is **fairness**. Pauline cannot expect special treatment, when compared to other workers, who may have made an equal effort. Over-rewarding average performance, despite the effort, might demotivate other staff who will accuse Steve of favouritism.

(b) **The organisation's systems**

It is clear that Steve is having to negotiate the requirements and failings of **four different systems** here.

    (i)   The budgetary control system, restricting pay rises
    (ii)   The appraisal system, which conflates effort and performance
    (iii)   The remuneration system, by which pay rises are awarded

Finally, Pauline's job is very different from what it was when she first started.

The source of the problem is the failure to recognise that **Pauline is now doing a different job**. Her job should have been re-evaluated. If this were the case, Steve could assess her reward on the basis of the performance in this re-evaluated job. She would have higher pay, commensurate with her enhanced responsibilities, but not an unfairly favourable grading.

However, Steve realises that the appraisal system is the one over which he has most direct control. He is in a position to reward her effort, but this would be anomalous as her performance in the new job is not exceptional. Her rating would not be appropriate to her performance. Yet her enhanced responsibilities need to be recognised somehow, although Steve, under pressure from the budgetary control system, may not be able to reward it financially.

There is little Steve can do about the budgetary factors, apart from stating to Pauline that everybody is in the same boat. There might be **non-financial rewards** that he can offer her. Pauline might like to have her own separate office space, for example, if it were available, or Steve might be able to offer her increased annual leave or a unique job title.

Pauline might also resent waiting for the outcome of a job re-evaluation exercise, as, from her point of view, that is the organisation's problem, not hers.

6 How effective is the appraisal scheme?

FAST FORWARD

New techniques of appraisal aim to monitor the appraisee's effectiveness from a number of perspectives. These techniques include upward, customer and 360-degree feedback and performance management.

6.1 Criteria for evaluating appraisal

The appraisal scheme should itself be evaluated (and regularly re-assessed) according to the following general criteria.

Criteria	Comment
Relevance	• Does the system have a useful purpose, relevant to the needs of the organisation and the individual?
	• Is the purpose clearly expressed and widely understood by all concerned, both appraisers and appraisees?
	• Are the appraisal criteria relevant to the purposes of the system?
Fairness	• Is there reasonable standardisation of criteria and objectivity throughout the organisation?
	• Is it reasonably objective?
Serious intent	• Are the managers concerned committed to the system – or is it just something the personnel department thrusts upon them?
	• Who does the interviewing, and are they properly trained in interviewing and assessment techniques?
	• Is reasonable time and attention given to the interviews – or is it a question of 'getting them over with'?
	• Is there a genuine demonstrable link between performance and reward or opportunity for development?
Co-operation	• Is the appraisal a participative, problem-solving activity – or a tool of management control?
	• Is the appraisee given time and encouragement to prepare for the appraisal, so that he can make a constructive contribution?
	• Does a jointly-agreed, concrete conclusion emerge from the process?
	• Are appraisals held regularly?
Efficiency	• Does the system seem overly time-consuming compared to the value of its outcome?
	• Is it difficult and costly to administer?

6.2 Methods of evaluation

Evaluating the appraisal scheme may involve:

(a) Asking appraisers and appraisees how they **felt** about the system (addressing issues of perceived usefulness, fairness and so on)

(b) Checking to see if there have been enhancements in **performance** by the individual and the organisation (as a result of problem solving and improvement planning)

(c) Reviewing other **indicative** factors, such as staff turnover or disciplinary problems, lack of management succession and so on

However, firms should not expect too much of the appraisal scheme. Appraisal systems, because they target the individual's performance, concentrate on the lowest level of performance feedback: they ignore the organisational and systems context of performance.

Chapter Roundup

- Appraisal can be used to **reward** but also to identify **potential**, and **training and development** needs.

- **Formal appraisal systems** support objective, positive, relevant, consistent feedback by managers.

- **Job evaluation** measures the value of a job to the organisation (for the purpose of salary planning): appraisal measures the performance of a given individual in the job.

- **Job evaluation methods** may be non-analytical (whole job) or analytical (components). Only analytical method are acceptable in defending equal pay claims.

- Three basic requirements of a **formal appraisal system** are: defining what is to be appraised, recording assessments, and getting the appraiser and appraisee together.

- A variety of appraisal **techniques** can be used to measure different criteria in a different ways.

- The appraisal **interview** is an important stage in the process, as it can be used to encourage collaborative problem solving and improvement planning. A 'problem-solving' style is preferable to a 'tell and sell' or 'tell and listen' style (Maier).

- **New techniques** of appraisal aim to monitor the appraisee's effectiveness from a number of perspectives. These techniques include upward, customer and 360-degree feedback and performance management.

- **Problems** with appraisal are its implementation in practice and a range of misperceptions about it (Lockett).

Quick Quiz

1   What are the purposes of appraisal?

2   What bases or criteria of assessment might an appraisal system use?

3   Outline a results-oriented approach to appraisal.

4   What is a 360-degree feedback, and who might be involved?

5   When a subordinate rates his or her manager's leadership skills, this is an example of:

    A   Job evaluation
    B   Job analysis
    C   Performance management
    D   Upward appraisal

6   What follow-up should there be after an appraisal?

7   How can appraisals be made more positive and empowering to employees?

8   What kinds of criticism might be levelled at appraisal schemes by a manager who thought they were a waste of time?

9   What is the difference between performance appraisal and performance management?

10 The most empowering style of appraisal interview, according to Maier, is the 'tell and listen' approach. *True or false?*

Answers to Quick Quiz

1   Identifying performance levels, improvements needed and promotion prospects; deciding on rewards; assessing team work and encouraging communication between manager and employee.

2   Job analysis, job description, plans, targets and standards.

3   Performance against specific mutually agreed targets and standards.

4   Refer to Section 4.3.

5   D. Make sure you can define all these terms clearly.

6   Appraisees should be informed of the results, agreed activity should be taken, progress should be monitored and whatever resources or changes are needed should be provided or implemented.

7   Ensure the scheme is relevant, fair, taken seriously, and co-operative.

8   The manager may say that he has better things to do with his time, that appraisals have no relevance to the job and there is no reliable follow-up action, and that they involve too much paperwork.

9   Appraisal *on its own* is a backward-looking performance review. But it is a vital input into performance management, which is forward-looking.

10   False. The most empowering style is 'problem solving'.

Now try the questions below from the Exam Question Bank

Number	Level	Marks	Time
Q11	Examination	15	27 mins
Q17	Examination	40 (scenario)	72 mins

The management
of health and safety

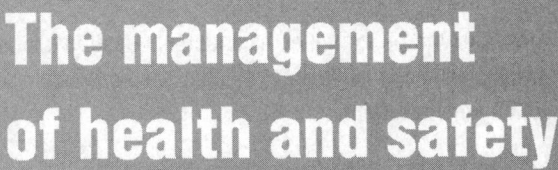

Topic list	Syllabus reference
1 Health and safety	3 (h)
2 The legal framework	3 (h)
3 Accidents and other workplace hazards	3 (h)
4 Summary	3 (h)

Introduction

In the ACCA syllabus, health and safety is included under training and development. As we will see in this chapter, training has a key role to play in educating and equipping employees to operate safely in the workplace.

However, it would be a mistake to see it exclusively as a training matter. All managers – and indeed all staff – have a direct responsibility for health and safety at work.

In **Section 1**, we examine why systematic attention to health and safety is important.

In **Section 2**, we look at some of the main UK law and regulation in this area. (If you are studying outside the UK, make sure that you stay up to date with key requirements in your own country.)

Section 3 takes a more practical look at managing a range of workplace health and safety hazards.

Perhaps the key challenge of this topic is to realise how complex the threats are. Accidents are caused by irresponsible behaviour as well as dangerous machines. There are health risks in lifting objects and using computers as well as handling toxic chemicals. Stress is a common cause of illness absence.

BPP
PROFESSIONAL EDUCATION

Study guide

Section 22 – The management of health and safety

- Identify preventative and protective measures
- Describe safety awareness and training
- Outline working conditions and hazards
- Explain the legal context and the obligation of management

Exam guide

The management of health and safety is perhaps most likely to be examined as a factual question in Section B. A knowledge of the basic various legal principles is advisable, but you also need practical awareness of the range of hazards in the typical working environment.

1 Health and safety

1.1 Why is health and safety important?

> **FAST FORWARD**
>
> **Health and safety** are important for both ethical and business reasons.

Health, safety and well-being at work are important for several reasons.

(a) Employees should – as human beings – be **protected** from needless pain and suffering!

(b) Employers and employees have **legal obligations** to take reasonable measures to promote healthy and safe working (discussed in Section 2 of this chapter).

(c) Accidents, illness and other causes of absence and impaired performance **cost** the organisation money.

(d) A business' **corporate image** and reputation as an employer (its **employer brand**) may suffer if its health and safety record is bad: this might alienate customers and potential employees.

1.2 Surely health and safety precautions are obvious?

> **FAST FORWARD**
>
> **Legislation** is not designed to represent best practice but offers a floor below which standards of conduct cannot drop, for the protection of employees.

In 1972, the Royal Commission on Safety and Health at Work reported that unnecessarily large numbers of days were being lost each year through industrial accidents, injuries and diseases, because of the 'attitudes, capabilities and performance of people and the efficiency of the organisational systems within which they work'.

Since 1972, **major legislation** has been brought into effect in the UK, most notably the Health and Safety at Work Act 1974, plus Regulations and Codes of Practice under the Act, which implement the provisions of EU directives on health and safety issues.

However, it would be wrong to paint too optimistic a picture of employers' performance on health and safety.

(a) **Legislation sets bare minimum standards** for (and levels of commitment to) health and safety. ('The law is a floor'). It does not represent satisfactory – let alone best – practice for socially responsible organisations.

(b) Health and safety are still a **low priority** in some organisation cultures. Provisions are costly, and have no immediately quantifiable benefit.

(c) **Positive discipline** (setting mechanisms and systems which theoretically prevent hazardous behaviour) only goes so far, and irresponsible or ignorant behaviour can still cause accidents.

(d) **New health and safety concerns** are constantly emerging, as old ones are eradicated.

   (i) New technology and ergonomics may make physical labour less stressful, but it creates new hazards and health risks, such as a sedentary, isolated lifestyle, and problems associated with working long hours at VDUs.

   (ii) New issues in health are constantly arising, such as passive smoking in the workplace or alcohol abuse, with the increasing stress of work in highly competitive sectors.

Question
Disaster costs

How many notorious workplace disasters can you think of? What were the main costs to the organisations concerned?

Answer

You may have thought of the Bhopal chemical plant explosion, Chernobyl reactor explosion, Kings Cross station fire, Piper Alpha oil rig disaster, various bombings by terrorist groups, and so on. The main costs are reconstruction, compensation for death and injury, lost production, and loss of reputation.

2 The legal framework

FAST FORWARD

Health and safety legislation requires that the systems, environment, equipment and conduct of organisations be such as to minimise the risk to the health and safety of employees and visitors alike.

2.1 The Health and Safety at Work Act (HSWA) 1974

FAST FORWARD

Employees **share responsibility** for health and safety with employers, although the latter take responsibility for the environment, systems, equipment and training.

In the UK, the Health and Safety at Work Act 1974 provides for the introduction of a system of approved Codes of Practice, prepared in consultation with industry, so that an employee, whatever his employment, should find that his work is covered by an appropriate code of practice.

Employers' responsibilities under the HSWA may be summarised as follows.

(a) To provide **safe systems** (work practices)

(b) To provide a **safe and healthy work environment** (well-lit, warm, ventilated, hygienic and so on)

(c) To maintain all **plant and equipment** to a necessary standard of safety

(d) To **support safe working practices** with information, instruction, training and supervision

(e)   To consult with **safety representatives** appointed by a recognised trade union

(f)   To appoint a **safety committee** to monitor safety policy, if asked to do so

(g)   To **communicate safety policy** and measures to all staff, clearly and in writing

An **employee's responsibilities** under the Act include:

(a)   Taking **reasonable care** of himself and others affected by his acts or omissions at work

(b)   **Co-operating** with the employer in carrying out his duties (including enforcing safety rules)

(c)   **Not interfering** intentionally or recklessly with any machinery or equipment provided in the interests of health and safety.

2.2 The Management of Health and Safety at Work Regulations 1992

These regulations impose additional responsibilities on **employers** as follows.

(a)   To carry out **risk assessment**, generally in writing, of all work hazards, on a continuous basis

(b)   To introduce **controls** to reduce risks

(c)   To assess the risks to anyone else affected by their work activities

(d)   To **share hazard and risk information** with other employers, including those on adjoining premises, other site occupiers and all subcontractors entering the premises

(e)   To initiate or revise **safety policies** in the light of the above

(f)   To identify employees who are especially **at risk** (other legislation cites pregnant women, young workers, shift-workers and part-time workers)

(g)   To provide **fresh and appropriate training** in safety matters

(h)   To provide **information to employees** (including temporary workers) about health and safety

(i)   To employ competent **safety and health advisors**

Employees have the additional responsibility under the regulations to inform the employer of any situation which may pose a danger to themselves or others.

2.3 Health and Safety (Consultation with Employees) Regulations 1996

Employers have the responsibility to consult all employees on health and safety matters, including the planning of health and safety training, changes in equipment and procedures which may substantially affect health and safety at work, or the health and safety consequences of introducing new technology.

| Question | Health, safety and productivity |

What aspects of your studying environment (if any) do you think are:

- A hindrance to your work?
- A source of dissatisfaction?
- A hazard to your health and/or safety?

2.4 The Workplace (Health, Safety and Welfare) Regulations 1992

These regulations provide for health and hygiene in work environments, including such aspects as the following.

(a) **Equipment** must be properly maintained.

(b) **Ventilation**. Air should be fresh or purified.

(c) **Temperature** must be 'reasonable' inside buildings during working hours.

(d) **Lighting** should be suitable and sufficient, and natural, if practicable.

(e) **Cleaning and decoration**. Floors, walls, ceilings, furniture, furnishings and fittings must be kept clean.

(f) **Room dimensions and space**. Each person should have at least 11 cubic metres of space.

(g) **Floors** must be properly constructed and maintained (without holes, not slippery, properly drained and so on).

(h) **Sanitary conveniences and washing facilities** must be suitable and sufficient.

(i) **Drinking water**. An adequate supply should be available with suitable drinking vessels.

| Question | Health, safety, productivity – and compliance! |

Reassess your answer to the previous Question in the light of these specific provisions.

2.5 The Manual Handling Operations Regulations 1992

The manual handling regulations cover heavy lifting – a major cause of industrial injury. They require employers, so far as is reasonably practicable, to avoid the need for employees to undertake any manual handling activities which will involve the risk of their becoming injured. However, if the cost of avoiding such risk is unreasonable the employer will be required to carry out an assessment of all manual handling operations, and to take steps to reduce the risks.

2.6 The Health and safety (Display Screen Equipment) Regulations 1992

If you have ever worked for a long period at a VDU you may personally have experienced some discomfort. Backache, eye strain and stiffness or muscular problems of the neck, shoulders, arms or hands are frequent complaints. The common, if somewhat inaccurate, term for this is Repetitive Strain Injury or RSI.

The regulations address areas such as:

(a) Minimisation of glare and flicker from VDU screens

(b) Arrangement and flexibility of screens, keyboards, desks and chairs to enable comfortable working

(c) The provision of breaks

(d) Training and consultation to improve work practices

3 Accidents and other workplace hazards

6/03

3.1 Causes of accidents

FAST FORWARD

Apart from obviously dangerous equipment in offices, there are many **hazards** to be found in the modern working environment.

Many accidents could be avoided by the simple application of common sense and consideration by employer and employee; and by safety consciousness encouraged or enforced by a widely acceptable and well-publicised safety policy.

Common causes of injury in administrative workplaces include falling/tripping, lifting and materials/equipment handling, related to hazards such as:

- Slippery or poorly maintained floors (eg frayed carpets)
- Trailing electric leads
- Obstacles in gangways or staircases
- Standing on chairs (particularly swivel chairs) to reach high shelving
- Lifting heavy items without bending properly
- Incorrect use of electrical machinery (including overloading power sockets)
- Removing the safety guard on a machine to free a blockage
- Incorrect labelling or storage of chemicals (which may burn, cause allergic reactions etc)

Exam focus point

The June 2003 exam asked you to identify three hazards to health and safety that might be found in the workplace, and to outline general policies for avoiding risks (see Section 3.5 below).

3.2 The cost of accidents

The costs of accidents to the employer are significant.

(a)   **Time lost** by the injured employee and other employees who choose to, or must of necessity, stop work at the time of or following the accident

(b)   Time lost by management and technical staff following the accident

(c)   A proportion of the cost of **first aid materials and officers**

(d)   The cost of **disruption to operations** at work

(e)   The cost of any **damage** to the equipment or any cost associated with the subsequent modification of the equipment

(f)   The costs associated with increased **insurance premiums**

(g)   **Reduced output** from the injured employee on return to work

(h)   The cost of possible **reduced morale**, increased absenteeism, increased labour turnover among employees

(i)   The cost of recruiting and training a **replacement** for the injured worker

(j)   The cost of **compensation payments** if employees sue for damages

Although the injured employee's damages may be reduced if his injury was partly a consequence of his own contributory **negligence**, due allowance is made for ordinary human failings.

(a) An employee is not deemed to consent to the risk of injury because he is aware of the risk. It is the employer's duty to provide a safe working system.

(b) Employees can become inattentive or careless in doing work which is monotonous or imposes stress. This factor too must be allowed for in the employer's safety precautions.

(c) It is not always a sufficient defence that the employer provided safety equipment and rules: the employer has some duty to encourage its proper use.

(d) Employees do not work continuously. The employer's duty is to take reasonable care for their safety in all acts which are normally and reasonably incidental to the day's work.

Question

Responsibility for safe working

If a person went to wash a tea-cup after use, at his or her office, and slipped on a slippery surface in the kitchen and was injured, who would be at fault?

Answer

This was a real case. It was held that the employee's injury had occurred in the course of her work, and that the employer had failed in his duty to take reasonable care to provide safe premises.

3.3 Preventing accidents

FAST FORWARD

The **prevention of accidents** requires efforts on the part of employees and management.

Some steps which might be taken to reduce the frequency and severity of accidents are as follows.

(a) Developing a **safety consciousness** among staff and workers and encouraging departmental pride in a good safety record: creating a culture of safety

(b) Developing effective **consultative participation** between management, workers and unions so that safety and health rules can be accepted and followed

(c) Giving **adequate instruction in safety rules** and measures as part of the training of new and transferred workers, or where working methods or speeds of operation are changed

(d) **Identified risks** (eg materials handling) to be minimised and designed as far as possible for safe operation

(e) Ensuring a **satisfactory standard** for both basic plant and auxiliary fittings (such as safety guards)

(f) **Proactive maintenance:** apart from making sound job repairs, temporary expedients to keep production going should not prejudice safety.

In general, the appropriate code of practice for the industry/work environment should be implemented in full.

Question

What hazards can you identify in the following office scene?

Answer

You may have spotted the following hazards (if not others as well...)

(a)   Heavy object on high (secure?) shelf
(b)   Standing on swivel chair
(c)   Lifting heavy object incorrectly
(d)   Trailing wires
(e)   Electric bar fire
(f)   Open drawers blocking passage and risk toppling cabinet
(g)   Unattended lit cigarette – passive smoking AND fire hazard
(h)   Over-full waste bin
(i)   Overloaded electric socket
(j)   Overloaded tray of hot liquids
(k)   Dangerous spike

3.4 Investigation and report of accidents

FAST FORWARD

> **Safety inspections** should be carried out to locate and define faults in the system that allow accidents to occur.

Safety inspections may be carried out as a comprehensive **audit**, working through a checklist, or by using **random spot checks**, regular checks of particular risk points or statutory inspections of particular areas, such as lifts, hoists, boilers or pipelines.

It is essential that checklists used in the inspection process should identify corrective action to be taken, and allocate responsibility for that action. There should be reporting systems and control procedures to ensure that inspections are taking place and that findings are being acted on.

Accident-reporting systems (eg using accident books) will be particularly important, but it must be emphasised to staff that the report is not an exercise in itself but a management tool, designed to:

- Identify problems
- Indicate corrective action

Serious accidents and dangerous occurrences (such as explosions) must be formally reported to the relevant authorities under the **Reporting of Injuries, Diseases and Dangerous Occurrences Regulations** (RIDDOR 1995).

3.5 Fire prevention

FAST FORWARD

Fire represents a further area for preventive action. The main causes of fire in industry and commerce tend to be associated with electrical appliances and installations, and smoking is a major source of fires in business premises.

The general regulations relating to fire have been summarised in the Fire Precautions (Workplace) Regulations 1997.

- There must be adequate means of escape, kept free from obstructions.
- All doors out of the building must be capable of opening from the inside.
- All employees should know the fire alarm signal and evacuation procedures.
- There must be an effective and regularly tested fire alarm system.
- There must be fire-fighting equipment easily available and in working order.

The Fire Protection Association (of the UK) suggests the following guidelines for fire prevention and control.

(a) Management should accept that fire prevention policies and practices must be established and reviewed regularly.

(b) Management should be aware of the possible effects and consequences of fires, in terms of loss of buildings, plant and output, damage to records, effects on customers and workers, and so on.

(c) Fire risks should be identified, particularly as regards sources of ignition, presence of combustible materials, and the means by which fires can spread.

(d) The responsibility for fire prevention should be established.

(e) A fire officer should be appointed.

(f) A fire evacuation drill should be established and regularly practised.

3.6 Stress

FAST FORWARD

Excessive **stress** (caused by work overload/underload, insecurity, conflict and other factors) may have a detrimental effect on health and work performance.

Key term

Stress is a term which is often loosely used to describe feelings of tension of exhaustion – usually associated with too much, or overly-demanding, work. In fact, stress is the product of demands made on an individual's physical and mental energies: monotony and feelings of failure or insecurity are sources of stress, as much as the conventionally considered factors of pressure, overwork and so on.

It is worth remembering that demands on an individual's energies may be stimulating as well as harmful: many people, especially those suited to managerial jobs, work well under pressure, and even require some form of stress to bring out their best performance.

3.6.1 Symptoms of stress

Harmful stress, or strain, can be identified by its effects on the individual and his performance.

(a) **Nervous tension**. This may manifest itself in various ways: irritability and increased sensitivity, preoccupation with details, a polarised perspective on the issues at hand, or sleeplessness. Various physical symptoms – such as skin and digestive disorders – are also believed to be stress-related.

(b) **Withdrawal**. This is essentially a defence mechanism which may manifest itself as unusual quietness and reluctance to communicate, or as physical withdrawal in the form of absenteeism, poor time-keeping, or even leaving the organisation.

(c) **Low morale**: low confidence, dissatisfaction, expression of frustration or hopelessness.

(d) **Repression**: signs that the individual is trying to deny the problem. Forced cheerfulness, boisterous playfulness or excessive drinking may indicate this.

Some of these symptoms – say, absenteeism – may or may not be correctly identified with stress. There are many other possible causes of such problems, both at work (lack of motivation) and outside (personal problems). The same is true of physical symptoms such as headaches and stomach pains: these are not invariably correlated with personal stress.

All these things can adversely affect performance, however, which is why **stress management** has become a major workplace issue. Considerable research effort has been directed to:

- Investigating the causes of stress
- Increasing awareness of stress in organisations
- Designing techniques and programmes for stress control

3.6.2 Causes of stress

Causes or aggravators of stress include the following factors.

Cause	Comment
Personality	Competitive, sensitive and insecure people feel stress more acutely.
Ambiguity or conflict in the roles required of an individual	If a person is unsure what is expected of him at work, or finds conflict between two incompatible roles (employee and mother of small children, say), role stress may be a problem.
Insecurity, risk and change	A manager with a high sense of responsibility who has to initiate a risky change, and most people facing career change, end or uncertainty, will feel this kind of stress.
Management style	Particular management traits have been associated with stress and related health problems. • Unpredictability – constant threat of an outburst • Destruction of workers' self esteem – making them feel helpless and insecure • Setting up win/lose situations – turning work relationships into a battle for control • Providing too much – or too little – stimulation

Health and safety would make a good scenario question, drawing in elements from training (eg the need to make new recruits aware of safety policy), communication (eg alerting staff to hazards) and human resource management (eg attitudes to staff welfare management). Stress would also suit an essay question.

Question

Stress

What sources of stress are there in your own lifestyle? Are you aware of the symptoms of stress in yourself? What do you do (if anything) to control your stress?

3.6.3 Management stress

Greater awareness of the nature and control of stress is a feature of the modern work environment. **Stress management techniques** are increasingly taught and encouraged by organisations, and include the following.

- Counselling
- Time off or regular rest breaks
- Relaxation techniques (breathing exercises, meditation)
- Physical exercise and self-expression as a safety valve for tension
- Delegation and planning (to avoid work-load related stress)
- Assertiveness (to control stress related to insecurity in personal relations)

4 Summary

The main components of a systematic approach to health and safety may be illustrated as follows.

Systematic approach to health and safety

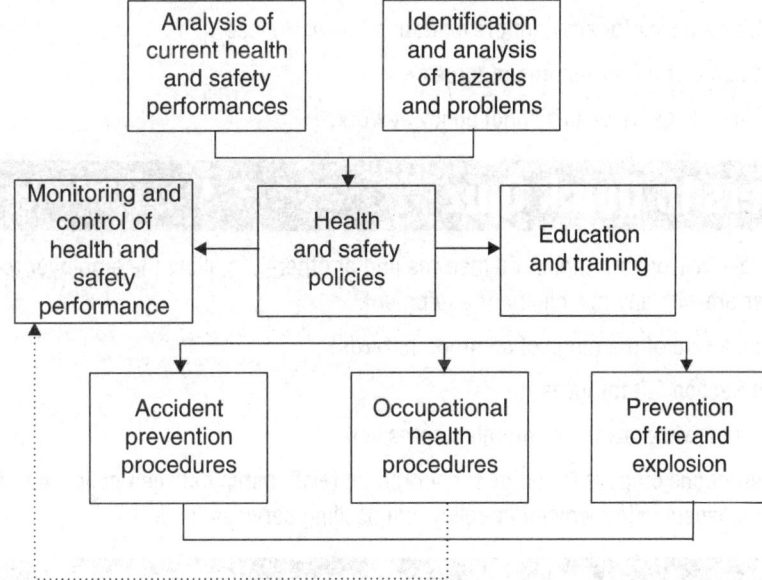

Chapter Roundup

- **Health and safety** are important for both ethical and business reasons.

- **Legislation** is not designed to represent best practice but offers a floor below which standards of conduct cannot drop, for the protection of employees.

- **Health and safety legislation** requires that the systems, environment, equipment and conduct of organisations be such as to minimise the risk to the health and safety of employees and visitors alike.

- Employees **share responsibility** for health and safety with employers, although the latter take responsibility for the environment, systems, equipment and training.

- Apart from obviously dangerous equipment in offices, there are many **hazards** to be found in the modern working environment.

- The **prevention of accidents** requires efforts on the part of employees and management.

- **Safety inspections** should be carried out to locate and define faults in the system that allow accidents to occur.

- **Fire** represents a further area for preventive action. The main causes of fire in industry and commerce tend to be associated with electrical appliances and installations, and smoking is a major source of fires in business premises.

- Excessive **stress** (caused by work overload/underload, insecurity, conflict and other factors) may have a detrimental effect on health and work performance.

Quick Quiz

1   What are employees' legal duties in respect of health and safety?

2   Which of the following is a health hazard in the workplace?

    A   Uncollected waste paper
    B   Heavy objects
    C   Frayed carpet
    D   All of the above

3   Outline a policy for accident prevention in the workplace.

4   List some of the symptoms of stress.

5   List the elements of an alcohol policy at work.

Answers to Quick Quiz

1   To take reasonable care of themselves and of others. To allow the employer to discharge his duties. Not to interfere with any machinery or equipment.

2   D: be aware of the range of common hazards!

3   See Section 3.3 for ideas.

4   Tension, withdrawal, low morale, repression

5   Restrictions on possession or consumption; relationship between policy and disciplinary procedures; role of managers in implementing policy; counselling services.

Now try the question below from the Exam Question Bank

Number	Level	Marks	Time
Q12	Tutorial	5	9 mins

Part D
Motivation and leadership

Motivation at work

Topic list	Syllabus reference
1 Overview of motivation	4 (a)
2 Content theories of motivation	4 (a)
3 Process theories of motivation	4 (a)
4 Choosing a motivational approach	4 (a)
5 Rewards and incentives	4 (a)
6 Pay as a motivator	4 (a)

Introduction

Human behaviour is a complex phenomenon. Managers need to understand something of what makes their team members 'tick' – particularly when it comes to the key question: how do you get them to perform well, or better?

That is what **motivation** is about.

Having explored motivation, and its impact on performance, in **Section 1**, we go on to look at a range of key **motivational theories** in **Sections 2-4.** There are some famous theoretical models here, and while it is definitely worth learning them, be careful how you *use* them in the exam: make sure they are relevant and that you identify them correctly!

In **Sections 5-6**, we look at a range of **financial and non-financial rewards** that may be used to motivate people. Take note, as you proceed through the chapter, that money is by no means the only (or necessarily the most effective) incentive to higher levels of performance…

The ability to 'motivate' people is also a key skill of leadership, as we will go on to see in Chapter 14.

Study guide

Section 2 – The role of management

- List the systems of performance reward for individual and group contribution

Section 5 – Team management

- Examine ways of rewarding a team

Section 8 – Standard setting and performance management

- Explain the term performance related pay

Section 23 – Motivation concepts, models and practices

See the introductory pages of this Study Text for full details of this session.

Exam guide

Motivation is likely to appear regularly in the exam, since it is an essential aspect of managerial responsibility. Since there is a large body of academic work, you must be prepared to outline theories and quote authorities. Motivation may be examined in the context of a scenario, as in December 2003, when the effect of bureaucratic culture on supervisors' motivation and morale was considered.

1 Overview of motivation

1.1 What is motivation?

FAST FORWARD

> **Motivation** is 'a decision-making process through which the individual chooses desired outcomes and sets in motion the behaviour appropriate to acquiring them'. (*Huczynski and Buchanan*).

Key term

> **Motivation** is 'a decision-making process through which the individual chooses desired outcomes and sets in motion the behaviour appropriate to acquiring them'. (*Huczynski and Buchanan*).

In practice the words **motives** and **motivation** are commonly used in different contexts to mean the following.

(a) **Goals or outcomes** that have become desirable for a particular individual. We say that money, power or friendship are motives for doing something.

(b) The **mental process of choosing desired outcomes**, deciding how to go about them (and whether the likelihood of success warrants the amount of effort that will be necessary) and setting in motion the required behaviours.

(c) The **social process** by which other people motivate us to behave in the ways they wish. Motivation in this sense usually applies to the attempts of organisations to get workers to put in more effort.

1.2 Needs and goals

People have certain **innate needs** (**Maslow**: physiological, security, love/social, esteem, self-actualisation). People also have **goals**, through which they expect their needs to be satisfied.

Individual behaviour is partly influenced by human biology, which requires certain basics for life. When the body is deprived of these essentials, biological forces called **needs** or **drives** are activated (eg hunger), and dictate the behaviour required to end the deprivation: eat, drink, flee and so on. However, we retain freedom of choice about *how* we satisfy our drives: they do not dictate specific or highly predictable behaviour. (Say you are hungry: how many specific ways of satisfying your hunger can you think of?)

Each individual also has a set of **goals**. The relative importance of those goals to the individual may vary with time, circumstances and other factors.

Influence	Comment
Childhood environment and education	Aspiration levels, family and career models and so on are formed at early stages of development
Experience	This teaches us what to expect from life: we will either strive to repeat positive experiences, or to avoid or make up for negative ones.
Age and position	There is usually a gradual process of goal shift with age. Relationships and exploration may preoccupy young employees. Career and family goals tend to compete in the 20-40 age group: career launch and take-off may have to yield to the priorities associated with forming permanent relationships and having children.
Culture	Collectivist cultures (see Chapter 3) show a greater concern for relationships at work, while individualist cultures emphasise power and autonomy.
Self-concept	All the above factors are bound up with the individual's own self-image. The individual's assessments of his own abilities and place in society will affect the relative strength and nature of his needs and goals.

The **basic assumptions of motivation** are that:

(a)   People behave in such a way as to **satisfy their needs** and fulfil their goals

(b)   An organisation is in a position to **offer some of the satisfactions** people might seek: relationships and belonging, challenge and achievement, progress on the way to self-actualisation, security and structure and so on

(c)   The organisation can therefore **influence** people to behave in ways it desires (to secure work performance) by offering them the means to satisfy their needs and fulfil their goals in return for that behaviour. (This process of influence is called motivation)

(d)   If people's needs are being met, and goals being fulfilled, at work, they are more likely to have a **positive attitude** to their work and to the organisation, and to experience **job satisfaction**

1.3 How useful is 'motivation' as a concept?

Motivation is a **useful concept**, despite the fact that the impact of motivation, job satisfaction and morale on performance are difficult to measure.

The **impact** of motivation and job satisfaction on **performance** is difficult to measure accurately.

(a) Motivation is about getting *extra* levels of commitment and performance from employees, over and above mere compliance with rules and procedures. If individuals can be motivated, by one means or another, they might work more efficiently (and productivity will rise) or they will produce a better quality of work.

(b) The case for job satisfaction as a factor in improved performance is not proven.

(c) The key is to work 'smarter' – not necessarily 'harder'.

Key term

> **Morale** is a term drawn primarily from a military context, to denote the state of mind or spirit of a group (esprit de corps), particularly regarding **discipline** and **confidence**. It can be related to satisfaction, since low morale implies a state of dissatisfaction.

The signs by which low **morale or dissatisfaction** are gauged are also **ambiguous**.

(a) **Low productivity** is not invariably a sign of low morale. There may be more concrete problems (eg with work organisation or technology).

(b) **High labour turnover** is not a reliable indicator of low morale: the age structure of the workforce and other factors in natural wastage will need to be taken into account. Low turnover, likewise, is no evidence of high morale: people may be staying because of lack of other opportunities in the local job market, for example.

However, there is some evidence that satisfaction correlates with mental health, so symptoms of **stress** or psychological dysfunction may be a signal that all is not well. (Again, a range of non-work factors may be contributing.)

Attitude surveys may also be used to indicate workers' perception of their job satisfaction, by way of interview or questionnaire.

Question

Personal motivation

What factors in yourself or your organisation motivate you to:

(a) Turn up to work at all?
(b) Do an average day's work?
(c) 'Bust a gut' on a task or for a boss?

Go on – be honest!

1.4 Theories of motivation

Many **theories** try to explain motivation and why and how people can be motivated.

One classification is between content and process theories.

(a) **Content theories** ask the question: '**What** are the things that motivate people?'

They assume that human beings have a *set* of needs or desired outcomes. Maslow's hierarchy of needs and Herzberg's two-factor theory, both discussed shortly, are two of the most important approaches of this type.

(b) **Process theories** ask the question: '**How** can people be motivated?'

They explore the process through which outcomes *become* desirable and are pursued by individuals. This approach assumes that people are able to select their goals and choose the paths towards them, by a conscious or unconscious process of calculation. Expectancy theory and Handy's 'motivation calculus', discussed later, are theories of this type.

Exam focus point

The distinction between process and content theories is a basic point – and a common pitfall for students: 5 marks were available just for explaining 'content theory' in the December 2003 exam. Make sure you can define each type of theory clearly and cite relevant examples. Note, as you read on, that despite the popularity of Maslow and Herzberg, they have their limitations – and they are not the *only* theories of motivation.

2 Content theories of motivation   12/01, 12/03

FAST FORWARD

Content theories of motivation suggest that the best way to motivate an employee is to find out what his/her needs are and offer him/her rewards that will satisfy those needs.

2.1 Maslow's hierarchy of needs   12/01

FAST FORWARD

Maslow identified a hierarchy of needs which an individual will be motivated to satisfy, progressing towards higher order satisfactions, such as self-actualisation.

Abraham Maslow described five innate human needs, and put forward certain propositions about the motivating power of each need.

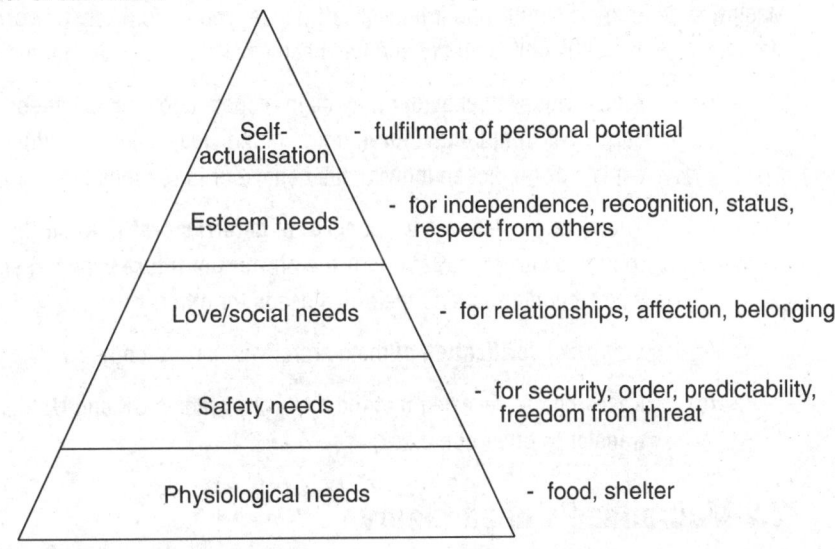

(a) An individual's needs can be arranged in a **'hierarchy** of relative pre-potency' (as shown). Each level of need is **dominant until satisfied**; only then does the next level of need become a motivating factor. A need which has been satisfied no longer motivates an individual's behaviour.

(b) The need for self-actualisation can rarely be satisfied.

(c) In addition, Maslow described:

(i) Freedom of enquiry and expression needs (for social conditions permitting free speech, and encouraging justice, fairness and honesty)

(ii) Knowledge and understanding needs (to gain knowledge of the environment, to explore, learn)

Question

Decide which of Maslow's categories the following fit into.

(a)   Receiving praise from your manager   (e)   A pay increase
(b)   A family party   (f)   Joining a local drama group
(c)   An artist forgetting to eat   (g)   Being awarded the OBE
(d)   A man washed up on a desert island   (h)   Buying a house

Answer

Maslow's categories for the listed circumstances are as follows.

(a)   Esteem needs
(b)   Social needs
(c)   Self-actualisation needs overriding lower-level needs!
(d)   Physiological needs
(e)   Safety needs initially; esteem needs above in a certain income level
(f)   Social needs or self-actualisation needs
(g)   Esteem needs
(h)   Safety needs or esteem needs

2.1.1 Evaluating Maslow's theory

Maslow's hierarchy is simple and intuitively attractive: you are unlikely to worry about respect if you are starving! However, it is only a theory and has been shown to have several major limitations.

(a)   An individual's behaviour may be in response to **several needs**, and the same need may cause **different behaviour** in different individuals, so it is difficult to use the model to explain or predict an individual's behaviour in response to rewards.

(b)   The hierarchy ignores the concept of **deferred gratification** (by which people are prepared to ignore current suffering for the promise of future benefits) and **altruistic behaviour** (by which people sacrifice their own needs for others).

(c)   **Empirical verification** of the hierarchy is hard to come by.

(d)   Research has revealed that the hierarchy reflects UK and US **cultural values**, which may not transfer to other contexts.

2.2 McClelland's need theory

David **McClelland** identified three types of motivating need, which can be identified using various psychometric tests.

(a)   **The need for power**. People with a high need for power usually seek positions in which they can influence and control others.

(b)   **The need for affiliation**. People who need a sense of belonging and membership of a social group tend to be concerned with maintaining good personal relationships.

(c)   **The need for achievement**. People who need to achieve have a strong desire for success and a strong fear of failure.

2.3 Herzberg's two-factor theory

FAST FORWARD

Herzberg identified two basic need systems: the need to avoid unpleasantness and the need for personal growth. He suggested factors which could be offered by organisations to satisfy both types of need: hygiene and motivator factors respectively.

Herzberg's two-factor theory is based on two needs: the need to avoid unpleasantness, and the need for personal growth.

(a) The need to avoid unpleasantness is satisfied through **hygiene factors**. Hygiene factors are to do with the environment and conditions of work, including:

Company policy and administration	Interpersonal relations
Salary	Working conditions
The quality of supervision	Job security

If inadequate, hygiene factors cause **dissatisfaction** with work (which is why they are also called 'dissatisfiers'). They work like sanitation, which minimises threats to health rather than actively promoting 'good health'.

(b) The need for personal growth is satisfied by **motivator factors**.

These actively create job satisfaction (they are also called 'satisfiers') and are effective in motivating an individual to superior performance and effort. These factors are connected to the work itself, including:

- Status (although this may be a hygiene factor too)
- Advancement (or opportunities for it)
- Recognition by colleagues and management
- Responsibility
- Challenging work
- A sense of achievement
- Growth in the job

A lack of motivator factors will encourage employees to concentrate on the hygiene factors, which will eventually dissatisfy.

Herzberg suggested that where there is evidence of poor motivation, such as low productivity, poor quality and strikes, management should not pay too much attention to hygiene factors such as pay and conditions. Despite the fact that these are the traditional target for the aspirations of organised labour, their potential for bringing improvements to work attitudes is limited. Instead, Herzberg suggested three types of **job design** which would offer job satisfaction through enhanced motivator factors.

- Job enlargement
- Job rotation   } discussed in Section 3 below.
- Job enrichment

2.4 Evaluating Herzberg's theory

Herzberg's original study was concerned with 203 Pittsburgh engineers and accountants. His theory has therefore been criticised as being based on:

(a) An inadequately small sample size
(b) A limited cultural context (Western professionals).

The impact of job satisfaction (from motivator factors) on work performance has proved difficult to verify and measure.

In December 2003, you were specifically asked to use Herzberg's theory to explain low morale among supervisors in the case study. (Clue: job dissatisfaction is caused by inadequate hygiene factors or lack of motivator factors.) The examiner was irritated by the fact that some candidates ignored Herzberg and wrote about Maslow instead: you must be aware that you only get marks for answering the question set! In addition, note that this question closely followed an article by the examiner in *Student Accountant* (October 2003): take the hint!

3 Process theories of motivation 5/02

FAST FORWARD

Process theories of motivation help managers to understand the dynamics of employees' decisions about what rewards are worth going for.

3.1 Vroom's expectancy theory

FAST FORWARD

Expectancy theory basically states that the strength of an individual's motivation to do something will depend on the extent to which he expects the results of his efforts to contribute to his personal needs or goals.

Victor **Vroom** stated a formula by which human motivation could be assessed and measured. He suggested that the strength of an individual's motivation is the product of two factors.

(a) The strength of his preference for a certain outcome. Vroom called this **valence**: it can be represented as a positive or negative number, or zero – since outcomes may be desired, avoided or regarded with indifference.

(b) His expectation that the outcome will in fact result from a certain behaviour. Vroom called this 'subjective probability' or **expectancy.** As a probability, it may be represented by any number between 0 (no chance) and 1 (certainty).

In its simplest form, the expectancy equation may be stated as:

$F = V \times E$

where:

F = the force or strength of the individual's motivation to behave in a particular way
V = valence: the strength of the individual preference for a given outcome or reward and
E = expectancy: the individual's perception that the behaviour will result in the outcome/ reward.

In this equation, the lower the values of valence or expectancy, the less the motivation. An employee may have a high expectation that increased productivity will result in promotion (because of managerial promises, say), but if he is indifferent or negative towards the idea of promotion (because he dislikes responsibility), he will not be motivated to increase his productivity. Likewise, if promotion was very important to him – but he did not believe higher productivity would get him promoted (because he has been passed over before, perhaps), his motivation would be low.

3.2 Equity theory 5/02

FAST FORWARD

Equity theory focuses on people's sense of whether they have been fairly treated in comparison with the way others have been treated.

Equity theory (usually associated with the work of JS Adams) is based on exchange theory, which suggests that people expect certain outcomes (or rewards) in exchange for their inputs (or contributions).

If they perceive that the **ratio of their outcomes to inputs** is unequal to that of other people, they experience a sense of **inequity** – whether positive (they feel they have been treated 'unfairly' well) or negative (they feel they have been treated 'unfairly' badly). If someone feels they are not getting paid enough for their work, compared to others, for example, they will have a sense of negative inequity.

A sense of inequity causes unpleasant tension, or **dissonance**, which motivates people to attempt to remove or reduce the perceived inequity by a variety of strategies. In the case of the person who feels (s)he is being under-paid, for example, dissonance may be reduced by:

- Changing the inputs (eg reducing hours or quality of work)
- Changing the outcomes (eg demanding better pay)
- Cognitive distortion (eg believing (s)he isn't really working as hard as (s)he is)
- Withdrawal (eg absenteeism or resignation)
- Influencing others to do any of the above (eg getting co-workers to put in extra hours, so the differential in pay appears fairer)
- Changing the comparison (eg comparing him/herself with a less well paid set of people)

Exam focus point

Equity theory featured as a ten-mark question part in the December 2002 exam, together with 'process theories' in general.

3.3 Handy's motivation calculus

Charles **Handy**'s motivation calculus is another expectancy approach. Individuals decide how much effort to invest towards a given goal by doing a calculation, weighing up:

(a) The strength or 'salience' of a need
(b) The expectancy that effort will lead to a particular result, and
(c) The likely effectiveness of the result in satisfying the need

The most appealing aspect of Handy's model is his identification of 'E' factors: a range of factors which an individual invests in action when motivated to do so. We have so far used the term 'effort', but this is only one 'E' factor: others include energy, excitement, expenditure, endeavour, excellence – and so on.

3.4 Managerial implications of process theories

Process theory suggests that:

(a) **Intended results should be made clear**, so that the individual can complete the motivation calculation by knowing what is expected, the reward, and how much effort it will take.

(b) Individuals are more committed to **specific goals** which they **have helped to set themselves**, taking their needs and expectations into account.

(c) Immediate and on-going **feedback** should be given. Without knowledge of actual results, there is no check that 'E' expenditure was justified (or will be justified in future).

(d) If an individual is **rewarded** according to performance tied to standards (management by objectives), however, he or she may well set lower standards: the expectancy part of the calculation (likelihood of success and reward) is greater if the standard is lower, so less expense of 'E' is indicated.

4 Choosing a motivational approach

12/03

Two influential writers of the neo-human relations school argue that a manager's approach to motivating people depends on the **assumptions** (s)he makes about 'what makes them tick'.

4.1 McGregor: Theory X and Theory Y

McGregor suggested that a manager's approach is based on attitudes somewhere on a scale between two extreme sets of assumptions: Theory X (workers have to be coerced) and Theory Y (workers want to be empowered).

Douglas **McGregor** *(The Human Side of Enterprise)* suggested that managers (in the USA) tended to behave as though they subscribed to one of two sets of assumptions about people at work: Theory X and Theory Y.

(a) **Theory X** suggests that most people dislike work and responsibility and will avoid both if possible. Because of this, most people must be coerced, controlled, directed and/or threatened with punishment to get them to make an adequate effort. Managers who operate according to these assumptions will tend to supervise closely, apply detailed rules and controls, and use 'carrot and stick' motivators.

(b) **Theory Y** suggests that physical and mental effort in work is as natural as play or rest. The ordinary person does not inherently dislike work: according to the conditions it may be a source of satisfaction or dissatisfaction. The potentialities of the average person are rarely fully used at work. People can be motivated to seek challenge and responsibility in the job, if their goals can be integrated with those of the organisation. A manager with this sort of attitude to his staff is likely to be a consultative, facilitating leader, using positive feedback, challenge and responsibility as motivators.

Both are intended to be extreme sets of assumptions – not actual types of people. However, they also tend to be self-fulfilling prophecies. Employees treated as if 'Theory X' were true will begin to behave accordingly. Employees treated as if 'Theory Y' were true – being challenged to take on more responsibility – will rise to the challenge and behave accordingly.

Theory X and Theory Y can be used to heighten managers' awareness of the assumptions underlying their motivational style.

Exam focus point

McGregor's Theory X and Theory Y are relevant to the 'role of management' topic as well as motivation: you might like to bear it in mind as you study leadership styles, too, in Chapter 14. 10 marks were available in the December 2003 exam for explaining McGregor's model.

4.2 Schein: four models of man

Schein suggested four managerial models of the worker: rational-economic, social, self-actualising and complex 'man'.

Edgar **Schein** *(Organisational Psychology)* proposed a set of four sets of managerial assumptions about worker motivation.

(a) **Rational-economic man** is primarily motivated by economic incentives. Like Theory X, this assumes that people are mainly passive and must be manipulated and controlled by the organisation, using incentive payments and rewards.

(b) **Social man** looks for fulfilment in social relationships, and is primarily motivated by opportunities to belong to the team.

(c)   **Self-actualising man** is primarily motivated by the need to grow and realise his full potential. Like Theory Y, this assumes that people are capable of maturity and will (given the chance) voluntarily integrate their personal goals with those of the organisation.

(d)   **Complex man** (Schein's own view) is variable and driven by many different motives. His needs and priorities change over time. People will not respond to any single managerial strategy, but will consider its appropriateness to their current needs and circumstances.

(You may notice that Schein's model reflects the assumptions of the scientific management, human relations, neo-human relations and contingency schools of thought, respectively.)

5 Rewards and incentives

FAST FORWARD

> Not all the **incentives** that an organisation can offer its employees are directly related to **monetary** rewards. The satisfaction of *any* of the employee's wants or needs may be seen as a reward for past performance, or an incentive for future performance.

Key terms

> A **reward** is a token (monetary or otherwise) given to an individual or team in recognition of some contribution or success.
>
> An **incentive** is the offer or promise of a reward for contribution or success, designed to motivate the individual or team to behave in such a way as to earn it. (In other words, the 'carrot' dangled in front of the donkey!)

Different individuals have different goals, and get different things out of their working life: in other words, they have different **orientations** to work. Why might a person work, or be motivated to work well?

(a)   The **human relations** school of management theorists regarded **work relationships** as the main source of satisfaction and reward offered to the worker.

(b)   Later writers suggested a range of 'higher-order' motivations, notably:

- **Job satisfaction**, interest and challenge in the job itself – rewarding work
- **Participation** in decision-making – responsibility and involvement

(c)   **Pay** has always occupied a rather ambiguous position, but since people need money to live, it will certainly be part of the reward package.

5.1 Intrinsic and extrinsic factors

FAST FORWARD

> **Rewards** may be **extrinsic** (external to the work and individual) or **intrinsic** (arising from performance of the work itself).

Rewards offered to the individual at work may be of two basic types.

(a)   **Extrinsic rewards** are separate from (or external to) the job itself, and dependent on the decisions of others (that is, also external to the control of the workers themselves). Pay, benefits, non-cash incentives and working conditions (Herzberg's hygiene factors) are examples.

(b)   **Intrinsic rewards** are those which arise from the performance of the work itself (Herzberg's motivator factors). They are therefore psychological rather than material and relate to the concept of job satisfaction. Intrinsic rewards include the satisfaction that comes from completing a piece of work, the status that certain jobs convey, and the feeling of achievement that comes from doing a difficult job well.

5.2 A reward system

Child has outlined management criteria for a reward system. Such a system should do six things.

(a) Encourage people to **fill job vacancies** and not leave.

(b) Increase the **predictability of employees' behaviour**, so that employees can be depended on to carry out their duties consistently and to a reasonable standard.

(c) Increase **willingness to accept change** and flexibility. (Changes in work practices are often 'bought' from trade unions with higher pay.)

(d) Foster and **encourage innovative behaviour**.

(e) **Reflect the nature of jobs** in the organisation and the skills or experience required. The reward system should therefore be consistent with seniority of position in the organisation structure, and should be thought fair by all employees.

(f) **Motivate**: that is, increase commitment and effort.

5.3 Job design as a motivator   12/04

FAST FORWARD

> The **job** itself can be used as a motivator, or it can be a cause of dissatisfaction. Job design refers to how tasks are organised to create 'jobs' for individuals.

5.3.1 Micro-design

One of the consequences of mass production and scientific management (see Chapter 2) was what might be called a **micro-division** of labour, or **job simplification**. Micro-designed jobs have the following **advantages**.

(a) **Little training**. A job is divided up into the smallest number of sequential tasks possible. Each task is so simple and straightforward that it can be learned with very little training.

(b) **Replacement**. If labour turnover is high, this does not matter because unskilled replacements can be found and trained to do the work in a very short time.

(c) **Flexibility**. Since the skill required is low, workers can be shifted from one task to another very easily.

(d) **Control**. If tasks are closely defined and standard times set for their completion, production is easier to predict and control.

(e) **Quality**. Standardisation of work into simple tasks means that quality is easier to predict.

Disadvantages of micro-designed jobs, however, include the following.

(a) The work is **monotonous** and makes employees tired, bored and dissatisfied. The consequences will be high labour turnover, absenteeism, spoilage, unrest. People work better when their work is variable, unlike machines.

(b) An individual doing a simple task feels like a small cog in a large machine, and has no **sense of contributing** to the organisation's end product or service.

(c) Excessive specialisation **isolates** the individual in his or her work and inhibits not only social contacts with 'work mates', but knowledge generation.

(d) In practice, excessive job simplification leads to **lower quality,** through inattention and loss of morale.

5.3.2 Job enrichment

FAST FORWARD

Frederick **Herzberg** suggest three ways of **improving job design**, to make jobs more interesting to the employee, and hopefully to improve performance: job enrichment, job enlargement and job rotation.

Key term

> **Job enrichment** is planned, deliberate action to build greater responsibility, breadth and challenge of work into a job. Job enrichment is similar to **empowerment**.

Job enrichment represents a 'vertical' extension of the job into greater levels of responsibility, challenge and autonomy. A job may be enriched by:

- Giving the job holder **decision-making tasks** of a higher order
- Giving the employee greater **freedom** to decide how the job should be done
- Encouraging employees to **participate** in the planning decisions of their superiors
- Giving the employee regular **feedback**

Job enrichment alone will not automatically make employees more productive. 'Even those who want their jobs enriched will expect to be rewarded with more than job satisfaction. Job enrichment is not a cheaper way to greater productivity. Its pay-off will come in the less visible costs of morale, climate and working relationships' *(Handy)*.

5.3.3 Job enlargement

Key term

> **Job enlargement** is the attempt to widen jobs by increasing the number of operations in which a job holder is involved.

Job enlargement is a 'horizontal' extension of the job by increasing task variety and reducing task repetition.

(a) Tasks which span a larger part of the total production work should reduce boredom and add to task meaning, significance and variety.

(b) Enlarged jobs might be regarded as having higher status within the department, perhaps as stepping stones towards promotion.

Job enlargement is, however, limited in its intrinsic rewards, as asking a worker to complete three separate tedious, unchallenging tasks is unlikely to be more motivating than asking him to perform just one tedious, unchallenging task!

5.3.4 Job rotation

Key term

> **Job rotation** is the planned transfer of staff from one job to another to increase task variety.

Job rotation is a 'sequential' extension of the job. Herzberg cites a warehouse gang of four workers, where the worst job was seen as tying the necks of the sacks at the base of the hopper, and the best job as being the fork lift truck driving: job rotation would ensure that individuals spent equal time on all jobs. Job rotation is also sometimes seen as a form of training, where individuals gain wider experience by rotating as trainees in different positions.

It is generally admitted that the developmental value of job rotation is limited – but it can reduce the monotony of repetitive work.

Exam focus point

Distinguishing clearly (and correctly) between related terms is a common focus of this exam. 15 marks were available in the Pilot Paper for differentiating between intrinsic and extrinsic rewards. In December 2004, it was job enrichment, enlargement and rotation. Make sure you get your 'related label's' straight!

5.3.5 Job optimisation

A well designed job should therefore provide the individual with five **core dimensions** which contribute to job satisfaction.

(a) **Skill variety**: the opportunity to exercise different skills and perform different operations

(b) **Task identity**: the integration of operations into a 'whole' tasks (or meaningful segments of the task)

(c) **Task significance**: the task is perceived to have a role, purpose, meaning and value

(d) **Autonomy**: the opportunity to exercise discretion or self-management (eg in areas such as target-setting and work methods)

(e) **Feedback**: the availability of performance feedback enabling the individual to assess his progress and the opportunity to give feedback, be heard and influence results

5.4 Feedback as a motivator

FAST FORWARD

Constructive performance **feedback** is important in job satisfaction and motivation.

There are two main types of feedback, both of which are valuable in enhancing performance and development.

(a) **Motivational feedback** is used to reward and reinforce positive behaviour and performance by praising and encouraging the individual. Its purpose is to increase **confidence**. By focusing on what is being done right (instead of on problems and shortcomings) the manager can energise employees to be more committed to overcoming their problems and shortcomings (Blanchard and Bowles).

(b) **Development feedback** is given when a particular area of performance needs to be improved, helping the individual to identify what needs to be changed and how this might be done. Its purpose is to increase **competence**. Note that this is still a 'positive' process: it should not be associated with 'negative' comments or criticism.

Constructive feedback is designed to widen options and encourage development. This does not mean giving only positive, motivational or 'encouraging' feedback about what a person has done: feedback about areas for improvement, given skilfully and sensitively, is in many ways more useful. It needs to be:

- Balanced with positives
- Specific
- Focused on behaviours/results – *not* personalities
- Objectives
- Supportive/co-operative, emphasising the resources available to help the person improve
- Selective (not tackling all shortcomings at once)
- Encouraging

5.5 Participation as a motivator

FAST FORWARD

Participation in decision making (if genuine) can make people more committed to the task.

People want more interesting work and to have a say in decision-making. These expectations are a basic part of the movement towards greater **participation** at work.

The methods of achieving increased involvement have largely crystallised into two main streams.

(a) **Immediate participation** is the term used to refer to the involvement of employees in the day-to-day decisions of their work group, eg through empowered or self-managed team working.

(b) **Distant participation** refers to the process of including company employees in the decision-making machinery of the organisation at a senior level, dealing with long-term policy issues including investment and employment. (This is a contentious area of European industrial policy, also called 'industrial democracy'.)

Participation can involve employees and make them feel committed to their task, given the following conditions (5 Cs).

- **Certainty**: participation should be genuine.
- **Consistency**: efforts to establish participation should be made consistently over a long period.
- **Clarity**: the purpose of participation is made quite clear.
- **Capacity**: the individual has the ability and information to participate effectively.
- **Commitment**: the manager believes in and genuinely supports participation.

6 Pay as a motivator

FAST FORWARD

Pay is the most important of the hygiene factors, but it is ambiguous in its effect on motivation.

Pay is important because:

- It is a major cost for the organisation
- People feel strongly about it: it 'stands in' for a number of human needs and goals
- It is a legal issue (minimum wage, equal pay legislation)

6.1 How is pay determined?

There are a number of ways by which organisations determine pay.

(a) **Job evaluation** is a systematic process for establishing the relative worth of jobs within an organisation. We have already encountered it in the context of performance appraisal in Chapter 11. Its main purpose is to provide a rational basis for the design and maintenance of an equitable (and legally defensible) pay structure.

(b) The salary structure is based on **job content**, and not on the personal merit of the job-holder. (The individual job-holder can be paid extra personal bonuses in reward for performance.)

(c) **Fairness.** Pay must be **perceived** and felt to match the level of work, and the capacity of the individual to do it.

(d) **Negotiated pay scales**. Pay scales, differentials and minimum rates may have been negotiated at plant, local or national level, according to factors such as legislation,

government policy, the economy, the power of trade unions, the state of the labour market for relevant skills, productivity agreements and so on.

(e)   **Market rates.** Market rates of pay will have most influence on pay structures where there is a standard pattern of supply and demand in the open labour market. If an organisation's rates fall below the benchmark rates in the local or national labour market from which it recruits, it will have trouble attracting and holding employees.

(f)   **Individual performance in the job**, resulting in merit pay awards, or performance-related bonuses.

6.2 What do people want from pay?

Pay has a central – but ambiguous – role in motivation theory. It is not mentioned explicitly in any need list, but it offers the satisfaction of many of the various needs.

Individuals may also have needs unrelated to money, however, which money cannot satisfy, or which the pay system of the organisation actively denies. So to what extent is pay an inducement to better performance: a motivator or incentive?

Although the size of their income will affect their standard of living, most people tend not to be concerned to **maximise** their earnings. They may like to earn more but are probably more concerned to **earn enough** and to know that **their pay is fair** in comparison with the pay of others both inside and outside the organisation.

Pay is a 'hygiene' factor: it gets taken for granted, and so is more usually a source of dissatisfaction than satisfaction. However, pay is the most important of the hygiene factors, according to Herzberg. It is valuable not only in its power to be converted into a wide range of other satisfactions, but also as a consistent measure of worth or value, allowing employees to compare themselves and be compared with other individuals or occupational groups inside and outside the organisation.

Research has also illustrated that workers may have an **instrumental orientation** to work: the attitude that work is not an end in itself but a means to other ends, through earning money.

 Case Study

In what became known as the 'Affluent Worker' research, **Goldthorpe, Lockwood *et al*** found that highly-paid Luton car assembly workers experienced their work as routine and dead-end. The researchers concluded that they had made a rational decision to enter employment offering high monetary reward rather than intrinsic interest: they were getting out of their jobs what they most wanted from them.

The Luton researchers did not claim that all workers have an instrumental orientation to work, however, but suggested that a person will seek a suitable balance of:

* The rewards which are important to him
* The deprivations he feels able to put up with

Even those with an instrumental orientation to work have limits to their purely financial aspirations, and will cease to be motivated by money if the deprivations – in terms of long working hours, poor conditions, social isolation or whatever – become too great.

High taxation rates may also weigh the deprivation side of the calculation: workers may perceive that a great deal of extra effort will in fact earn them little extra reward.

Pay is only one of several intrinsic and extrinsic rewards offered by work. If pay is used to motivate, it can only do so in a wider context of the job and the other rewards. Thanks, praise and recognition, for example, are alternative forms of positive reinforcement.

Question

Hertzberg says that money is a **hygiene** factor in the motivation process. If this is true, it means that lack of money can demotivate, but the presence of money will not in itself be a motivator.

How far do you agree with this proposition? Can individual be motivated by a pay rise?

6.3 Performance related pay (PRP)

FAST FORWARD

Performance related pay (PRP) is a form of incentive system, awarding extra pay for extra output or performance.

Key term

Performance related pay (PRP) is related to output (in terms of the number of items produced or time taken to produce a unit of work), or results achieved (performance to defined standards in key tasks, according to plan).

The most common individual PRP scheme for wage earners is straight **piecework**: payment of a fixed amount per unit produced, or operation completed.

For managerial and other salaried jobs, however, a form of **management by objectives** will probably be applied. PRP is often awarded at the discretion of the line manager, although guidelines may suggest, for example, that those rated exceptional get a bonus of 10% whereas those who have performed less well only get, say, 3%.

(a)   Key results can be identified and specified, for which merit awards will be paid.

(b)   There will be a clear model for evaluating performance and knowing when, or if, targets have been reached and payments earned.

(c)   The exact conditions and amounts of awards can be made clear to the employee, to avoid uncertainty and later resentment.

For service and other departments, a PRP scheme may involve **bonuses** for achievement of key results, or **points schemes**, where points are awarded for performance of various criteria (efficiency, cost savings, quality of service and so on). Certain points totals (or the highest points total in the unit, if a competitive system is used) then win cash or other awards.

6.3.1 Evaluating PRP

Benefits of PRP include:

(a)   Improves commitment and capability
(b)   Complements other HR initiatives
(c)   Improves focus on the business's performance objectives
(d)   Encourages two-way communication
(e)   Greater supervisory responsibility
(f)   It recognises achievement when other means are not available

Potential problems include:

(a)   Subjectivity of awards for less measurable criteria (eg 'teamwork')
(b)   Encouraging short-term focus and target-hitting (rather than improvements)
(c)   Divisive/against team working (if awards are individual)
(d)   Difficulties gaining union acceptance (if perceived to erode basic pay)

Question	PRP as a motivator

Why might PRP fail to motivate?

Answer

(a) The rewards from PRP are often too small to motivate effectively. Anyhow, some employees may not expect to receive the rewards and hence will not put in the extra effort.

(b) It is often unfair, especially in jobs where success is determined by uncontrollable factors.

(c) If people are rewarded individually, they may be less willing to work as a team.

(d) People may concentrate on short-term performance indicators rather than on longer-term goals such as innovation or quality. In other words, people put all their energy into hitting the target rather than doing their job better.

(e) PRP schemes have to be well designed to ensure performance is measured properly, people consider them to be fair and there is consent to the scheme.

6.4 Rewarding the team

FAST FORWARD

Various forms of **group rewards** can be used as an incentive to co-operative performance and mutual accountability.

6.4.1 Group bonus schemes

Group incentive schemes typically offer a bonus for a team which achieves or exceeds specified targets. Offering bonuses to a whole team may be appropriate for tasks where individual contributions cannot be isolated, workers have little control over their individual output because tasks depend on each other, or where team-building is particularly required. It may enhance team-spirit and co-operation as well as provide performance incentives, but it may also create pressures within the group if some individuals are seen not to be pulling their weight.

6.4.2 Profit-sharing schemes

Profit-sharing schemes offer employees (or selected groups) bonuses, directly related to profits or value added. Profit sharing is based on the belief that all employees can contribute to profitability, and that that contribution should be recognised. The effects may include profit-consciousness and motivation in employees, commitment to the future prosperity of the organisation and so on.

The actual incentive value and effect on productivity may be wasted, however, if the scheme is badly designed.

(a) The sum should be **significant**.

(b) There should be a **clear and timely link** between effort or performance and reward. Profit shares should be distributed as frequently as possible, consistent with the need for reliable information on profit forecasts, targets etc and the need to amass significant amounts for distribution.

(c) The scheme should only be introduced if profit forecasts indicate a **reasonable chance of achieving** the above: profit sharing is welcome when profits are high, but the potential for disappointment is great.

(d) The greatest effect on productivity arising from the scheme may in fact arise from its use as a focal point for **discussion** with employees, about the relationship between their performance and results, areas and targets for improvement etc. Management must be seen to be committed to the principle.

Chapter Roundup

- **Motivation** is 'a decision-making process through which the individual chooses desired outcomes and sets in motion the behaviour appropriate to acquiring them'. (*Huczynski and Buchanan*).

- People have certain **innate needs** (**Maslow**: physiological, security, love/social, esteem, self-actualisation). People also have **goals**, through which they expect their needs to be satisfied.

- **Motivation** is a **useful concept**, despite the fact that the impact of motivation, job satisfaction and morale on performance are difficult to measure.

- Many **theories** try to explain motivation and why and how people can be motivated.

- **Content theories** of motivation suggest that the best way to motivate an employee is to find out what his/her needs are and offer him/her rewards that will satisfy those needs.

- **Maslow** identified a hierarchy of needs which an individual will be motivated to satisfy, progressing towards higher order satisfactions, such as self-actualisation.

- **Herzberg** identified two basic need systems: the need to avoid unpleasantness and the need for personal growth. He suggested factors which could be offered by organisations to satisfy both types of need: hygiene and motivator factors respectively.

- **Process theories** of motivation help managers to understand the dynamics of employees' decisions about what rewards are worth going for.

- **Expectancy theory** basically states that the strength of an individual's motivation to do something will depend on the extent to which he expects the results of his efforts to contribute to his personal needs or goals.

- **Equity theory** focuses on people's sense of whether they have been fairly treated in comparison with the way others have been treated.

- **McGregor** suggested that a manager's approach is based on attitudes somewhere on a scale between two extreme sets of assumptions: Theory X (workers have to be coerced) and Theory Y (workers want to be empowered).

- **Schein** suggested four managerial models of the worker: rational-economic, social, self-actualising and complex 'man'.

- Not all the **incentives** that an organisation can offer its employees are directly related to **monetary** rewards. The satisfaction of *any* of the employee's wants or needs may be seen as a reward for past performance, or an incentive for future performance.

- **Rewards** may be **extrinsic** (external to the work and individual) or **intrinsic** (arising from performance of the work itself).

- The **job** itself can be used as a motivator, or it can be a cause of dissatisfaction. Job design refers to how tasks are organised to create 'jobs' for individuals.

- Frederick **Herzberg** suggest three ways of **improving job design**, to make jobs more interesting to the employee, and hopefully to improve performance: job enrichment, job enlargement and job rotation.

- Constructive performance **feedback** is important in job satisfaction and motivation.

- **Participation** in decision making (if genuine) can make people more committed to the task.

- **Pay** is the most important of the hygiene factors, but it is ambiguous in its effect on motivation.

- **Performance related pay (PRP)** is a form of incentive system, awarding extra pay for extra output or performance.

- Various forms of **group rewards** can be used as an incentive to co-operative performance and mutual accountability.

Quick Quiz

1   What is (a) 'positive reinforcement' and (b) self actualisation?

2   List the five categories in Maslow's Hierarchy of Needs.

3   How do an individual's goals change with age?

4   List some ways in which an organisation can offer motivational satisfaction.

5   What is the difference between a reward and an incentive?

6   According to Herzberg, leadership style is a motivator factor. *True or false?*

7   Explain the formula 'F = V × E'.

8   'People will work harder and harder to earn more and more pay.' Do you agree? Why (or why not)?

9   A 'horizontal' extension of the job to increase task variety is called:

    A   Job evaluation
    B   Job enrichment
    C   Job enlargement
    D   Job rotation

Answer to Quick Quiz

1   (a)   Encouraging a certain type of behaviour by rewarding it.
    (b)   Personal growth and fulfilment of potential

2   Physiological, safety, love/social, esteem, self-actualisation.

3   Increasingly they include forming relationships, having children, power and autonomy.

4   Relationships, belonging, challenge, achievement, progress, security, money.

5   A reward is given for some contribution or success. An incentive is an offer of reward.

6   False: it is a hygiene factor.

7   Force of motivation = Valence × Expectation

8   See Section 6.2.

9   C. Make sure you can define all the other terms as well.

Number	Level	Marks	Time
Q13	Examination	15	27 mins

Now try the question below from the Exam Question Bank

14

Effective leadership

Topic list	Syllabus reference
1 What is leadership?	4 (b)
2 Trait theories of leadership	4 (b)
3 Style theories of leadership	4 (b)
4 Contingency approaches to leadership	4 (b)

Introduction

We covered the role of the manager in Chapter 2.

Not all writers agree that 'leadership' can usefully be distinguished from 'management', but a number of attempts have been made to suggest what is different about '**leaders**' and why this might be important. We look at these issues in **Section 1** of this chapter, together with core **leadership skills**.

In **Sections 2-4**, we work through some of the major **leadership theories**, which are examinable in detail.

Perhaps the key challenge of this topic is to grasp the difference between **trait theories** (leaders simply have certain characteristics), **style theories** (leaders have different approaches, some of which are more effective than others) and **contingency approaches** (leaders can adopt specific behaviours to suit the specific situation).

This is also a good topic on which to practise your skills at *evaluating* theories: each has its strengths and weaknesses…

Study guide

Section 24 – Effective leadership

* See the introduction of this Study Text for full contents of this session of the Study Guide

Exam guide

This topic is likely to appear in Section B. Areas such as the difference between management and leadership, or an explanation of specific leadership style models, lend themselves to essay questions.

1 What is leadership?

Key term

> **Leadership** has been defined as:
>
> 'The activity of influencing people to strive willingly for group objectives' (*Terry*)
>
> 'Interpersonal influence exercised in a situation and directed, through the communication process, toward the attainment of a specialised goal or goals' (*Tannenbaum et al*)

1.1 Management and leadership

FAST FORWARD

> There are many different definitions of **leadership**. Key themes (which are also used to distinguish leadership from management) include: interpersonal influence; securing willing commitment to shared goals; creating direction and energy; and an orientation to change.

The terms 'management' and 'leadership' are often used interchangeably. In some cases, management skills and theories have simply been relabelled to reflect the more fashionable term. However, there have been many attempts to distinguish meaningfully between them.

(a) **Kotter** (2001) argues that leadership and management involve two distinct sets of action. Management is about coping with **complexity**: its functions are to do with logical, structure, analysis and control, and are aimed at producing order, consistency and predictability. Leadership, by contrast, is about coping with **change**: its activities include creating a sense of direction, communicating strategy, and energising, inspiring and motivating others to translate the vision into action.

(b) **Yukl** (1998) suggests that while management is defined by a prescribed role and position in the structure of the organisation, leaders are given their roles by the perception of others, through election, choice or influence. Leadership is an interpersonal process. In other words, managers have **subordinates**, but leaders have **followers**.

(c) **Zaleznik** (1992) suggests that managers are mainly concerned with order and **maintaining the status quo**, exercising their skills in diplomacy and focusing on decision-making processes within the organisation. Leaders, in contrast, direct their energies towards introducing **new approaches and ideas**. They create excitement and vision in order to arouse motivation, and focus with empathy on the meanings of events and actions for people. Leaders search out opportunities for change.

(d) **Katz and Kahn** (1974) point out that while management aims to secure compliance with stated organisational objectives, leadership aims to secure willingness, enthusiasm and commitment. Leadership is the **influential increment** over and above mechanical compliance with the routine directives of the organisation.

Management can be exercised over resources, activities, projects and other essential non-personal things. Leadership can only be exercised over **people**.

Although leadership has not come up often in exams under this syllabus so far, the difference between management and leadership would lend itself to a 'discussion'-style essay question. Make sure you are familiar with the debate, and some of the key leadership writers (identified in Section 1.1 above). It is difficult to come up with any one definition of leadership: formulate your own, as a useful exercise.

Some of the values used to distinguish between managers and leaders have also been identified as different styles of leadership (*Burns*).

(a) **Transactional leaders** see the relationship with their followers in terms of a trade: they give followers the rewards they want in exchange for service, loyalty and compliance.

(b) **Transformational leaders** see their role as inspiring and motivating others to work at levels beyond mere compliance. Only transformational leadership is said to be able to change team/organisation cultures and create a new direction.

1.2 Key leadership skills   6/04

FAST FORWARD

Key leadership skills may be identified in a range of interpersonal and business areas.

Transformational leadership is achieved through what Bass and Avolio call the 'Four Is'. These represent a useful description of key leadership skills.

(a) **Idealised influence**: identified with 'charisma'. The leader acts as a role model: putting the needs of others before personal interests; taking risks; demonstrating high standards of ethical conduct – and attracting the admiration, respect, trust and imitation of followers.

(b) **Inspirational motivation**: also identified with 'charisma'. The leader articulates the challenge, significance and meaning in work; arouses team spirit; shows enthusiasm and confidence; communicates high expectations and demonstrates commitment.

(c) **Intellectual stimulation**. The leader encourages free thinking and emphasises rational problem-solving, by: questioning assumptions; reinterpreting problems and issues in new ways; encouraging innovation and creativity; and avoiding punishing or publicly criticising mistakes.

(d) **Individualised consideration**. The leader treats followers on their own merits and seeks to develop them: accepting individual differences; attending to individuals' higher-level needs for growth and challenge; acting as coach/mentor; creating learning opportunities through delegation; and avoiding close monitoring of performance.

In addition, you might identify a range of business and managerial skills as important to a good leader, including:

(a) **Entrepreneurship**: the ability to spot business opportunities and mobilise resources to capitalise on them

(b) **Interpersonal skills**, such as networking, rapport-building, influencing, negotiating, conflict resolution, listening, counselling, coaching and communicating assertively

(c) **Decision-making and problem-solving** skills, including seeing the big picture (sometimes called 'helicopter ability')

(d) **Time-management and personal organisation**

(e) **Self-development** skills: the ability to learn continuously from experience, to grow in self-awareness and to exploit learning opportunities.

Remember, when thinking about leadership skills that *skills* are learned abilities to do things effectively: they are *not* the same as personality traits or characteristics, such as 'integrity' or 'vision'. If you get a question on this area in the exam, state your assumptions and define your terms clearly.

1.3 Why develop managers as 'leaders'?

FAST FORWARD

Leadership offers key **benefits** in a competitive, turbulent environment: activating commitment, setting direction, developing people and energising and supporting change.

Whether or not we make the distinction between management and leadership, attempts to define what makes leadership 'special' (such as those outlined above) have suggested some key points about the benefits effective leadership can bring and why it is valuable.

(a) Leaders energise and support **change**, which is essential for survival in highly competitive and fast-changing business environments. By setting visionary goals, and encouraging contribution from teams, leaders create environments that:

- Seek out new information and ideas
- Allow challenges to existing procedures and ways of thinking
- Invite innovation and creativity in finding better ways to achieve goals
- Support and empower people to cope with the turbulence.

(b) Leaders secure **commitment**, mobilising the ideas, experience and motivation of employees – which contributes to innovation and improved quality and customer service. This is all the more essential in a competitive, customer-focused, knowledge-based business environment.

(c) Leaders set **direction**, helping teams and organisations to understand their purpose, goals and value to the organisation. This facilitates team-working and empowerment (allowing discretion and creativity about how to achieve the desired outcomes) without loss of co-ordination or direction.

(d) Leaders support, challenge and develop **people**, maximising their contribution to the organisation. Leaders use an influence-based, facilitate-empower style rather than a command-control style, and this is better suited to the expectations of empowered teams and the need for information-sharing in modern business environments.

 Question

Leadership

Reflect on your own experience of working under the direction of others. Identify the 'best' leader you have ever 'followed'. (You may need to think about non-work leaders such as a sports coach or school teacher.) Think about how this person behaved and interacted with you and others.

What qualities makes you identify this person as a 'great leader', from your point of view as a follower?

1.4 Theories of leadership

FAST FORWARD

There are three basic **schools of leadership theory**: trait theories, style theories and contingency theories.

There are three basic 'schools' of leadership theory.

School	Comment
Trait theories	Based on analysing the personality characteristics or preferences of successful leaders.
Style theories	Based on the view that leadership is an interpersonal process whereby different leader behaviours influence people in different ways. More or less effective patterns of behaviour (or 'styles') can therefore be adopted.
Contingency theories	Based on the belief that there is no 'one best way' of leading, but that effective leaders adapt their behaviour to the specific and changing variables in the leadership context: the nature of the task, the personalities of team members, the organisation culture and so on.

We will look at each of these in turn.

2 Trait theories of leadership

FAST FORWARD

Early theories suggested that there are certain personality characteristics common to 'great men' or successful leaders. In other words, **'leaders are born, not made'**.

Various studies have attempted to determine exactly *which* traits are essential in a leader. One American study (cited by Rosemary Stewart) cites the following fifteen traits.

Judgement	Initiative	Integrity	Foresight	Energy
Drive	Human relations skill	Decisiveness	Dependability	Emotional stability
Fairness	Ambition	Dedication	Objectivity	Co-operation

Trait theory has been more or less discredited.

(a) The premise that certain traits are absolutely necessary for effective leadership has never been substantiated.

(b) The lists of traits proposed for leaders have been vast, varied and contradictory.

(c) 'A person does not become a leader by virtue of the possession of some combination of traits, but the pattern of personal characteristics must bear some relevant relationship to the characteristics, activities and goals of the followers' (Stodgill).

3 Style theories of leadership

FAST FORWARD

Leadership styles are clusters of leadership behaviour that are used in different ways in different situations. While there are many different classifications of style, they mainly relate to the extent to which the leader is focused primarily on task/performance (directive behaviour) or relationships/people (supportive behaviour). Key style models include:

- The **Ashridge Model**: tells, sells, consults, joins
- **Likert**: exploitative authoritative, benevolent authoritative, consultative, participative
- **Lewin**, Lippitt and White: autocratic, democratic, laissez-faire
- **Blake and Mouton**'s Managerial Grid: concern for task, concern for people

There are various classifications of leadership style. Although the labels and definitions of styles vary, style models are often talking (broadly) about the same thing: a continuum of behaviours from:

(a) Wholly task-focused, directive leadership behaviours (representing high leader control) at one extreme, and

(b) Wholly people-focused, supportive/relational leadership behaviours (representing high subordinate discretion) at the other.

3.1 A continuum of leadership styles

Tannenbaum and Schmidt proposed a continuum of behaviours (and associated styles) which reflected the balance of control exercised in a situation by the leader and the team.

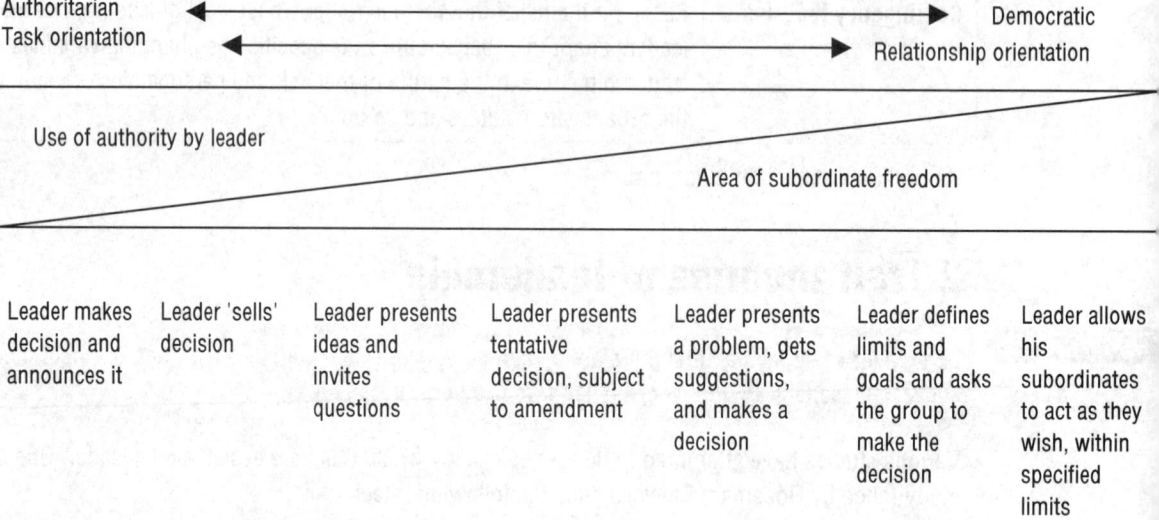

| Leader makes decision and announces it | Leader 'sells' decision | Leader presents ideas and invites questions | Leader presents tentative decision, subject to amendment | Leader presents a problem, gets suggestions, and makes a decision | Leader defines limits and goals and asks the group to make the decision | Leader allows his subordinates to act as they wish, within specified limits |

3.2 The Ashridge Management College model

The Research Unit at Ashridge Management College distinguished four different management styles. (These are outlined, with their strengths and weaknesses, in the following full-page table.) The researchers labelled their styles:

- Tells
- Sells
- Consults
- Joins

Other style models label similar styles as:

- Telling, Selling, Participating and Delegating (*Hersey and Blanchard*)
- Telling, Selling, Consulting and Coaching (*Tannenbaum and Schmidt; Gillen*)

The Ashridge studies found that:

(a) In an ideal world, subordinates preferred the 'consults' style of leadership.

(b) People led by a 'consults' manager had the most favourable attitude to their work.

(c) Most subordinates feel they are being led by a 'tells' or 'sells' manager.

(d) In practice, **consistency** was far more important to subordinates than any particular style. The least favourable attitudes were found amongst subordinates who were unable to perceive any consistent style of leadership in their superiors.

Style	Characteristics	Strengths	Weaknesses
Tells (autocratic)	The manager makes all the decisions, and issues instructions which must be obeyed without question.	(1) Quick decisions can be made when speed is required. (2) It is the most efficient type of leadership for highly-programmed routine work.	(1) It does not encourage subordinates to give their opinions when these might be useful. (2) Communication between manager and subordinates will be one-way and the manager will not know until afterwards whether the orders have been properly understood. (3) It does not encourage initiative and commitment from subordinates.
Sells (persuasive)	The manager still makes all the decisions, but believes that subordinates have to be motivated to accept them and carry them out properly.	(1) Employees are made aware of the reasons for decisions. (2) Selling decisions to staff might make them more committed. (3) Staff will have a better idea of what to do when unforeseen events arise in their work because the manager will have explained his intentions.	(1) Communications are still largely one-way. Subordinates might not accept the decisions. (2) It does not encourage initiative and commitment from subordinates.
Consults	The manager confers with subordinates and takes their views into account, but he has the final say.	(1) Employees are involved in decisions before they are made. This encourages motivation through greater interest and involvement. (2) An agreed consensus of opinion can be reached and, for some decisions, consensus can be an advantage rather than a weak compromise. (3) Employees can contribute their knowledge and experience to help solve more complex problems.	(1) It might take much longer to reach decisions. (2) Subordinates might be too inexperienced to formulate mature opinions and give practical advice. (3) Consultation can too easily turn into a facade concealing, a 'sells' style.
Joins (democratic)	Leader and followers make the decision on the basis of consensus.	(1) It can provide high motivation and commitment from employees. (2) It shares the other advantages of the consultative style (especially where subordinates have expert power).	(1) The authority of the manager might be undermined. (2) Decision making might become a very long process, and clear decisions might become difficult to reach. (3) Subordinates might lack experience.

Question

Suggest an appropriate style of management for each of the following situations. Think about your reasons for choosing each style in terms of the results you are trying to achieve, the need to secure commitment from others, and potential difficulties with both.

(a) Due to outside factors, the personnel budget has been reduced for your department and one-quarter of your staff must be made redundant. Records of each employee's performance are available.

(b) There is a recurring administrative problem which is minor, but irritating to every one in your department. Several solutions have been tried in the past, but without success. You think you have a remedy which will work, but unknown problems may arise, depending on the decisions made.

Answer

Styles of management suggested in the situations described, using the tells-sells-consults-joins model.

(a) You may have to 'tell' here: nobody is gong to like the idea and, since each person will have his or her own interests at heart, you are unlikely to reach consensus. You could attempt to 'sell', if you can see a positive side to the change in particular cases: opportunities for retraining, say.

(b) You could 'consult' here: explain your remedy to staff and see whether they can suggest potential problems. They may be in a position to offer solutions – and since the problem effects them too, they should be committed to solving it.

3.3 Rensis Likert

Likert (*New patterns of Management)* also described a range of four management styles or 'systems':

(a) System 1: **Exploitative authoritative**. The leader has no confidence or trust in his subordinates, imposes decisions, never delegates, motivates by threat, has little communication with subordinates and does not encourage teamwork.

(b) System 2: **Benevolent authoritative.** The leader has only superficial trust in subordinates, imposes decisions, never delegates, motivates by reward and, though sometimes involving others in problem-solving, is basically paternalistic.

(c) System 3: **Participative**. The leader has some confidence in subordinates, listens to them but controls decision making, motivates by reward and a level of involvement, and will use the ideas and suggestions of subordinates constructively.

(d) System 4: **Democratic**. The leader has complete confidence in subordinates who are allowed to make decisions for themselves. Motivation is by reward for achieving goals set by participation, and there is a substantial amount of sharing of ideas, opinions and co-operation.

Likert's research suggested that effective managers naturally use a System 3 or System 4 style. Both are seen as viable approaches, balancing the needs of the organisation and the individual.

3.4 Lewin, Lippitt and White

In an early study using boys' clubs, **Lewin, Lippitt and White** identified three styles of leadership.

(a) **Autocratic**: giving orders, overseeing work activities and giving out criticism and praise on a whim.

(b) **Democratic**: showing concern for team member welfare, participating in group activities, making suggestions as to what should be done but allowing team members to make decisions.

(c) **Laissez-faire**: tending to be 'stand-offish', not getting involved in team activities or welfare, and effectively letting the group run itself.

In subsequent research, Lippitt and White investigated the effect of leadership on productivity in different groups. They proposed the following conclusions.

(a) **Work-oriented conversation** was greatest in a democratic group, less in an autocratic group and least in a laissez-faire group.

(b) The amount of **work actually done** was greatest in an autocratic group and least in a laissez-faire group.

(c) **Motivation** was strongest in a democratic group, where members often carried on working even when the leader was absent. Even so, motivation was not sufficient to increase output above the level of the autocratic group.

(d) **Hostility and discontent** were greatest in an autocratic group: some members even left the group. In contrast, originality, group-mindedness and friendly playfulness were greatest in a democratic group.

Question	Participative leadership

In your career so far, you might have worked for a number of managers. Jot down the following features of each situation on a scale of 1-5 for comparative purposes.

(a) The degree to which you had autonomy over your own work

(b) The degree to which you were consulted on decisions which affected you

(c) The degree to which your advice was sought about decisions affecting your section

If you worked for managers who had different approaches to these issues, do you think these approaches influenced **your** effectiveness? What score to questions (a), (b) and (c) would you give your **ideal boss**? and your **current boss**?

3.5 Blake and Mouton's Managerial Grid   12/01

Robert Blake and **Jane Mouton** carried out research (The Ohio State Leadership Studies) into managerial behaviour and observed two basic dimensions of leadership: **concern for production** (or task performance) and **concern for people.**

Along each of these two dimensions, managers could be located at any point on a continuum from very low to very high concern. Blake and Mouton observed that the two concerns did not seem to correlate, positively or negatively: a high concern in one dimension, for example, did not seem to imply a high or low concern in the other dimension. Individual managers could therefore reflect various permutations of task/people concern.

Blake and Mouton modelled these permutations as a grid. One axis represented concern for people, and the other concern for production. Blake and Mouton allotted nine points on each axis, from 1 (low) to 9 (high).

A questionnaire was designed to enable users to analyse and plot the positions of individual respondents on the grid. This was to be used as a means of analysing individuals' **managerial styles** and areas of weakness or 'unbalance', for the purposes of management development.

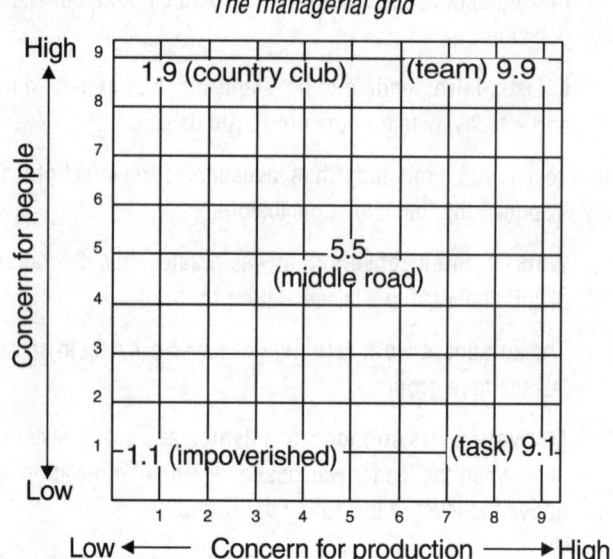

The managerial grid

The extreme cases shown on the grid are:

(a)   1.1 **impoverished:** the manager is lazy, showing little interest in either staff or work.

(b)   1.9 **country club:** the manager is attentive to staff needs and has developed satisfying relationships. However, there is little attention paid to achieving results.

(c)   9.1 **task management:** almost total concentration on achieving results. People's needs are virtually ignored.

(d)   5.5 **middle of the road** or the **dampened pendulum:** adequate performance through balancing the necessity to get out work while maintaining morale of people at a satisfactory level.

(e)   9.9 **team:** high work accomplishment through 'leading' committed people who identify themselves with the organisational aims.

The managerial grid was intended as an appraisal and management development tool. It recognises that a balance is required between concern for task and concern for people, and that a high degree of both is possible (and highly effective) at the same time.

3.5.1 Evaluating the managerial grid

The grid thus offers a number of useful insights for the identification of management **training and development** needs. It shows in an easily assimilated form where the behaviour and assumptions of a manager may exhibit a lack of balance between the dimensions and/or a low degree of concern in either dimension or both. It may also be used in team member selection, so that a 1.9 team leader is balance by a 9.1 co-leader, for example.

However, the grid is a simplified model, and as such has practical limitations.

(a)   It assumes that 9.9 is the desirable model for effective leadership. In some managerial contexts, this may not be so. Concern for people, for example, would not be necessary in a context of comprehensive automation: compliance is all that would be required.

(b)   It is open to oversimplification. Scores can appear polarised, with judgements attached about individual managers' suitability or performance. The Grid is intended as a simplified 'snapshot' of a manager's preferred style, not a comprehensive description of his or her performance.

(c)   Organisational context and culture, technology and other 'givens' (Handy) influence the manager's style of leadership, not just the two dimensions described by the Grid.

(d)   Any managerial theory is only useful in so far as it is useable in practice by managers: if the grid is used only to inform managers that they 'must acquire greater concern for people', it may result in stress, uncertainty and inconsistent behaviour.

Exam focus point

The *usefulness* of Blake and Mouton's grid was examined in December 2001. It is always worth recognising the limitations as well as advantages or key points of any given theory in the exam. Sometimes you are *asked* to do this, but the examiner appreciates evidence of critical thought.

Question   The managerial grid

Here are some statements about a manager's approach to meetings. Which position on Blake's Grid do you think each might represent?

(a)   I attend because it is expected. I either go along with the majority position or avoid expressing my views.

(b)   I try to come up with good ideas and push for a decision as soon as I can get a majority behind me. I don't mind stepping on people if it helps a sound decision.

(c)   I like to be able to support what my boss wants and to recognise the merits of individual effort. When conflict rises, I do a good job of restoring harmony.

Answer

Blake's Grid positioning of the given managerial approaches are:

(a)   1.1: low task, low people
(b)   9.1: High task, low people
(c)   1.9: high people, low task

3.6 Limitations of style approaches

Perhaps the most important criticism of the style approach is that it does not consider all the variables that contribute to the operation of effective leadership.

(a)   The manager's personality (or 'acting' ability) may simply not be flexible enough to utilise different styles effectively.

(b)   The demands of the task, technology, organisation culture and other managers constrain the leader in the range of styles effectively open to him. (If his own boss practices an authoritarian style, and the team are incompetent and require close supervision, no amount of theorising on the desirability of participative management will make it possible...)

(c)   Consistency is important to subordinates. If a manager adapts his style to changing situations, they may simply perceive him to be fickle, or may suffer insecurity and stress.

Huczynski and Buchanan note that 'There is therefore no simple recipe which the individual manager can use to decide which style to adopt to be most effective.'

It is the consideration of this wide set of variables that has led to the development of the contingency approach to leadership.

4 Contingency approaches to leadership

In essence, contingency theory sees effective leadership as being dependent on a number of variable or contingent factors. There is no one right way to lead that will fit all situations. Gillen *(Leadership Skills)* suggests that: 'Using only one leadership style is a bit like a stopped clock: it will be right twice a day but, the rest of the time, it will be inaccurate to varying degrees. Leaders need to interact with their team in different ways in different situations. This is what we mean by "leadership style".'

FAST FORWARD

> Leaders need to adapt their style to the needs of the team and situation. This is the basis of **contingency approaches** such as:
>
> - **Fiedler**'s 'psychologically close' and 'psychologically distant' styles
> - **Hersey and Blanchard**'s 'situational leadership' model
> - **John Adair**'s 'action-centred' leadership model
> - **Handy**'s 'best fit' model

4.1 F E Fiedler

Perhaps the leading advocate of contingency theory is Fiedler. He studied the relationship between style of leadership and the effectiveness of the work group and identified two types of leader.

(a) **Psychologically distant managers** (PDMs) maintain distance from their subordinates.

   (i) They formalise the roles and relationships between themselves and their superiors and subordinates.

   (ii) They choose to be withdrawn and reserved in their inter-personal relationships within the organisation (despite having good inter-personal skills).

   (iii) They prefer formal consultation methods rather than seeking the opinions of their staff informally.

   PDMs judge subordinates on the basis of performance, and are primarily task-oriented: Fiedler found that leaders of the most effective work groups tend to be PDMs.

(b) **Psychologically close managers** (PCMs) are closer to their subordinates.

   (i) They do not seek to formalise roles and relationships with superiors and subordinates.

   (ii) They are more concerned to maintain good human relationships at work than to ensure that tasks are carried out efficiently.

   (iii) They prefer informal contacts to regular formal staff meetings

Fiedler suggested that the effectiveness of a work group depended on the situation, made up of three key variables.

- The relationship **between the leader and the group** (trust, respect and so on)
- The extent to which the **task** is defined and structured
- The **power** of the leader in relation to the group (authority, and power to reward and punish)

A situation is **favourable** to the leader when:

- The leader is liked and trusted by the group
- The tasks of the group are clearly defined
- The power of the leader to reward and punish with organisation backing is high

Fiedler suggested that:

(a) A structured (or psychologically distant) style works best when the situation is either very favourable, or very unfavourable to the leader

(b) A supportive (or psychologically close) style works best when the situation is moderately favourable to the leader.

(c) 'Group performance will be contingent upon the appropriate **matching of leadership styles** and the **degree of favourableness** of the group situation for the leader.' (*Fiedler*)

4.2 Charles Handy

Handy argued that the ability of a manager to lead and to influence the work group will vary according to three factors.

(a) The **leader**: his personality and preferred style of operating

(b) The **subordinates**: their individual and collective personalities, and their preference for a particular style of leadership

(c) The **task**: its structure, complexity and variety

In addition, there is the wider leadership 'context', including:

(a) The position of **power** held by the leader within the organisation and the group. A leader with power is better able to manage the other variables.

(b) The norms, structure and technology of the **organisation** as a whole. No manager can act contrary to organisational constraints.

Each of the key variables can be plotted on a spectrum from 'tight' to 'flexible'. Handy suggests that the most effective managerial approach in any situation is one that brings all three variables as close as possible to a 'best fit', where they all align on the same level in the spectrum. While there may be long-term benefits to be achieved from re-defining the task (eg job enlargement) or from developing the subordinates, in the short term the most easily changed variable is often the leader's style.

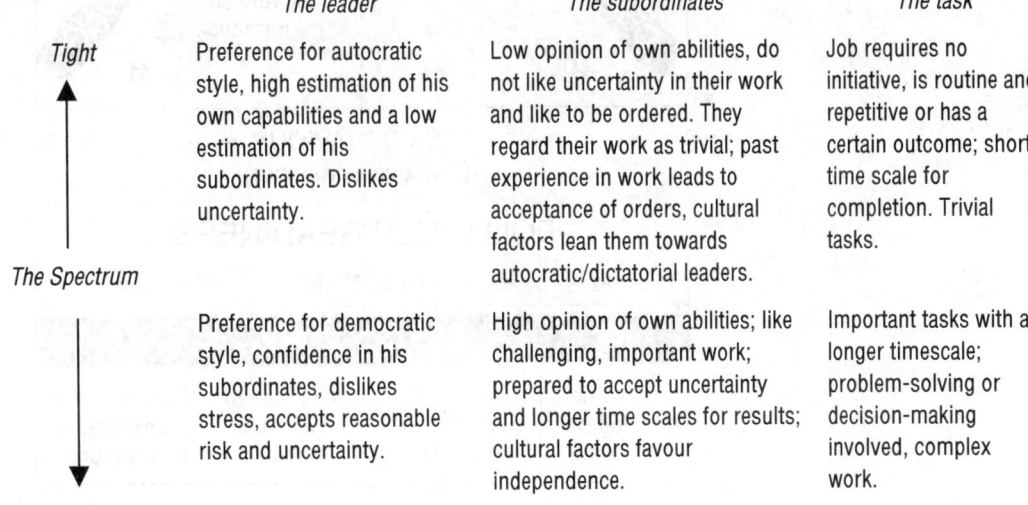

	The leader	The subordinates	The task
Tight	Preference for autocratic style, high estimation of his own capabilities and a low estimation of his subordinates. Dislikes uncertainty.	Low opinion of own abilities, do not like uncertainty in their work and like to be ordered. They regard their work as trivial; past experience in work leads to acceptance of orders, cultural factors lean them towards autocratic/dictatorial leaders.	Job requires no initiative, is routine and repetitive or has a certain outcome; short time scale for completion. Trivial tasks.
The Spectrum	Preference for democratic style, confidence in his subordinates, dislikes stress, accepts reasonable risk and uncertainty.	High opinion of own abilities; like challenging, important work; prepared to accept uncertainty and longer time scales for results; cultural factors favour independence.	Important tasks with a longer timescale; problem-solving or decision-making involved, complex work.
Flexible			

4.3 Hersey and Blanchard: situational leadership

In their influential **Situational Leadership** model, Hersey and Blanchard focus on the **readiness of the team members** to perform a given task, in terms of their *task ability* (experience, knowledge and skills) and *willingness* (whether they have the confidence, commitment and motivation) to complete the task successfully.

(a) *High-readiness* (R4) teams are able and willing. They do not need directive or supportive leadership: the most appropriate leadership style may be a joins or 'delegating' (S4) style.

(b) *High-moderate readiness* (R3) teams are able, but unwilling or insecure. They are competent, but require supportive behaviour to build morale: the most appropriate leadership style may be a consults or 'participating' (S3) style.

(c) *Low-moderate readiness* (R2) teams are willing and confident, but lacking ability. They require both directive and supportive behaviour to improve their task performance without damaging morale: the most appropriate leadership style may be a 'selling' (S2) style.

(d) *Low-readiness* (R1) teams are lacking ability and motivation/confidence. They require more directive behaviours in order to secure an adequate level of task performance: the most appropriate leadership style may be a 'telling' (S1) style.

This can be summed up as follows (drawn from *Hersey & Blanchard*, 1988).

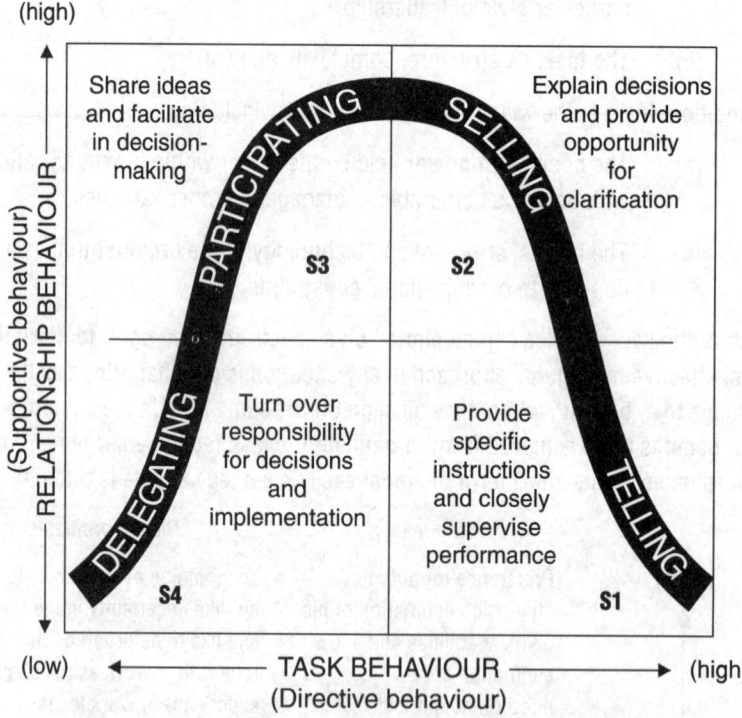

	FOLLOWER READINESS		
high	moderate		low
R4	**R3**	**R2**	**R1**
Able and willing or confident	Able but unwilling or insecure	Unable but willing or confident	Unable and unwilling or insecure

Question

Diagnose the 'readiness' of a work or study group of which you are a member. What sort of leadership is likely to be most effective, according to Hersey and Blanchard's model? What sort of leadership does your team leader actually exercise?

4.4 John Adair: action-centred leadership   6/04

John Adair's model (variously called 'action-centred', 'situational' or 'functional') is part of the contingency school of thought, because it sees the leadership process in a context made up of three interrelated variables: task needs, the individual needs of group members and the needs of the group as a whole. These needs must be examined in the light of the whole situation, which dictates the relative priority that must be given to each of the three sets of needs. Effective leadership is a process of identifying and acting on that priority, exercising a relevant cluster of roles to meet the various needs.

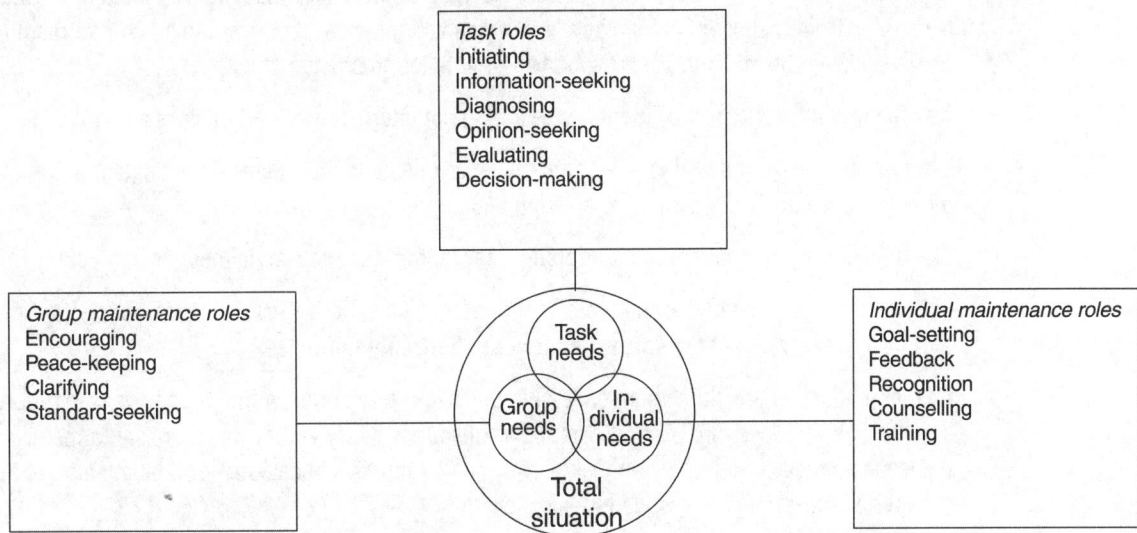

(Adair)

Adair argued that the common perception of leadership as 'decision making' was inadequate to describe the range of action required by this complex situation. He developed a scheme of leadership training based on precept and practice in each of eight leadership 'activities' which are applied to task, team and individual: hence, the **action-centred leadership** model.

- Defining the task
- Planning
- Briefing
- Controlling
- Evaluating
- Motivating
- Organising
- Setting an example

Exam focus point

9 Marks are available for explaining action centred leadership in the June 2004 exam. Most of these depended on your grasping the three key variables: task, group and individual needs.

4.5 An appraisal of contingency theory

Contingency theory usefully makes people aware of the factors affecting the choice of leadership style. However, **Schein** has pointed out that:

(a) Key variables such as task structure, power and relationships are difficult to measure in practice

(b) Contingency theories do not always take into account the need for the leader to have technical competence relevant to the task

Perhaps the major difficulty for any leader seeking to apply contingency theory, however, is actually to modify his or her behaviour as the situation changes.

Chapter Roundup

- There are many different definitions of **leadership**. Key themes (which are also used to distinguish leadership from management) include: interpersonal influence; securing willing commitment to shared goals; creating direction and energy; and an orientation to change.

- **Key leadership skills** may be identified in a range of interpersonal and business areas.

- Leadership offers key **benefits** in a competitive, turbulent environment: activating commitment, setting direction, developing people and energising and supporting change.

- There are three basic **schools of leadership theory**: trait theories, style theories and contingency theories.

- Early theories suggested that there are certain personality characteristics common to 'great men' or successful leaders. In other words, **'leaders are born, not made'**.

- **Leadership styles** are clusters of leadership behaviour that are used in different ways in different situations. While there are many different classifications of style, they mainly relate to the extent to which the leader is focused primarily on task/performance (directive behaviour) or relationships/people (supportive behaviour). Key style models include:

    - The **Ashridge Model**: tells, sells, consults, joins
    - **Likert**: exploitative authoritative, benevolent authoritative, consultative, participative
    - **Lewin**, Lippitt and White: autocratic, democratic, laissez-faire
    - **Blake and Mouton**'s Managerial Grid: concern for task, concern for people

- Leaders need to adapt their style to the needs of the team and situation. This is the basis of **contingency approaches** such as:

    - **Fiedler**'s 'psychologically close' and 'psychologically distant' styles
    - **Hersey and Blanchard**'s 'situational leadership' model
    - **John Adair**'s 'action-centred' leadership model
    - **Handy**'s 'best fit' model

Quick Quiz

1   What is the difference between a manager and a leader?

2   A 'manager' might also be identified as a transformational leader. *True or false*?

3   If a manager confers with subordinates, takes their views and feelings into account, but retains the right to make a final decision, this is a:

   A   Tells style
   B   Sells style
   C   Consults style
   D   Joins style

4   What is the most effective style suggested by Blake and Mouton's Managerial Grid? Why is it so effective in theory, and why might it not be effective in practice?

5   John Adair formulated the:

   A   Best fit model of leadership
   B   Action-centred model of leadership
   C   Follower-readiness model of leadership
   D   Trait theory of leadership

Answers to Quick Quiz

1   See Section 1.1 for a full range of points.

2   False. Management is identified with 'transactional' leadership.

3   C. Make sure you can define the other styles as well.

4   9.9. It is effective if there is sufficient time and resources to attend fully to people's needs, if the manager is good at dealing with people and if the people respond. It is ineffective when a task has to be completed in a certain way or by a certain deadline, whether or not people like it.

5   B. (You should be able to identify A as the work of Handy, and C as the work of Hersey and Blanchard)

Now try the question below from the Exam Question Bank			
Number	**Level**	**Marks**	**Time**
Q14	Examination	15	27 mins

Part E
Effective communication practices

Interpersonal and communication skills

Topic list	Syllabus reference
1 Interpersonal skills and working relationships	5 (a)
2 Assertiveness	5 (a), 5 (b)
3 Communication in the organisation	5 (b)
4 Face-to-face and oral communication	5 (b)
5 Textual communication	5 (b)
6 Counselling	5 (c)

Introduction

Interpersonal skills are essential for managers, because (as we have seen throughout this Study Text) they can only achieve their aims with and through other people!

This is not a 'soft' area of the syllabus: there are plenty of theoretical and procedural matters to get to grips with.

In **Section 1**, we look at **interpersonal skills** and their uses, and in **Section 2**, we focus on the particular skill of **assertive communication** (clearly distinguishing it from aggressive and passive responses).

In **Sections 3-5,** we look at the crucial area of **communication** and its organisational implications, and at particular communication **media** and **skills**. Bear in mind what you learned in Chapter 3.

In **Section 6**, we look at a particular context of communication: **counselling**.

Perhaps the key challenge of this topic is to appreciate the potential barriers to interpersonal *and* organisational communication, and how they can be overcome.

It may also be helpful to refer back to Chapter 3, and be aware of how culture (both organisational and national) impacts on our communication styles and assumptions…

Study guide

Section 25 – Working with people – interpersonal skills

Section 26 – Communication

Section 27 – The role of counselling

The detailed contents of these sections can be found in the introductory pages of this Study Text.

Exam guide

This is a topic that could appear in either section A or section B and as a stand-alone question, or as an aspect of a wider question. Many sub-topics – such as barriers to communication, qualities of effective communication, assertiveness, counselling and so on – may be set as individual questions. Beware basing answers on 'common sense' and personal experience alone: this may look like a 'soft' area of the syllabus, but the examiner expects to see evidence of reading and theoretical knowledge.

1 Interpersonal skills and working relationships 6/02

1.1 What is interpersonal behaviour?

FAST FORWARD

Interpersonal behaviour is behaviour between one or more individuals and the behaviour of one individual in relation to others.

Key term

Interpersonal behaviour is behaviour between people. It includes:

(a) Interaction between people: a two way process such as communication, delegating, negotiating, resolving conflict, persuading, selling, or influencing.

(b) An individual's behaviour in relationship to other people.

The way you behave in response to other people includes:

- How you **perceive** other people
- **Listening to** and **understanding** other people
- **Behaving** in a way which builds on this understanding
- Being **sensitive** to the impression you give, in the light of the roles you are expected to play.

Interpersonal skills are, therefore, skills in dealing with other people. It is possible to see them as two 'tiers' of skill: the basic elements of interpersonal skill (first-order skills) and the skills which apply them in specific interaction styles and contexts (second-order skills).

Second order skills

- Persuading/influencing
- Assertiveness
- Negotiation
- Team working

- Leadership
- Managing conflict
- Counselling
- Coaching

First order skills

- Giving and receiving feedback
- Listening and observing
- Questioning
- Communicating clearly
- Understanding and using body language

1.2 Why are interpersonal skills important?

FAST FORWARD

Interpersonal skills are vital to effective motivation, team working, negotiation and other management roles.

Interpersonal skills are needed by an individual in order to:

(a) Understand and manage the roles, relationships, attitudes and perceptions operating in any situation in which two or more people are involved

(b) Communicate clearly and effectively

(c) Achieve his or her aims from an interpersonal encounter (ideally, allowing the other parties to emerge satisfied too)

Good interpersonal skills assist in the following areas of the manager's task.

Area	Comment
Motivation	Work can satisfy people's social needs, according to Maslow, through positive relationships.
Communication	Bad interpersonal relationships can form a barrier to communicating effectively.
Teamworking and team building	Team working requires a climate in which people can communicate openly and honestly. It also depends on conflict management.
Negotiation	Negotiation and influencing are key interpersonal skills.
Customer care	Good interpersonal skills are recognised as being increasingly important when dealing with customers.
Career development	Good interpersonal skills are increasingly sought-after by employers.

Area	Comment
Managerial roles	Chapter 3 listed some management roles. Many of these -such as the liaison role – require interpersonal skills. The manager's HR functions – appraisal, interviewing etc – also require interpersonal competence.
Power	Interpersonal skills can be a source of personal power in an organisation. A manager may not be in a position to command information or co-operation: assertiveness, persuasion and other skills may be required.

Exam focus point

The importance of interpersonal skills and communication is a key area for examination questions. In an article in *Student Accountant* (23 April 2003), the examiner pointed out that 'if there is one prerequisite that sets accountancy apart from other professions, it is the need to communicate clearly and concisely both internally and externally. Communication is the core of the accountancy profession, transmitting information from one person to another, from one organisation to another – or a combination of both – and to the shareholders and other stakeholders of the organisation.' The article goes on to discuss various barriers to communication and how they can be overcome. Revise this topic carefully! (Note also that the 40-mark question in the June 2003 exam – following the article – was on this topic. Take the hint!)

2 Assertiveness   6/02

FAST FORWARD

Assertiveness is one interpersonal skill which is highly valued (in Western cultural contexts). It consists of clear, honest and direct communication.

Key term

Assertiveness may be defined as: 'behaviour based on valuing yourself enough to insist on getting what you want and need by using reasonable and fair means'. (*Guirdham*)

2.1 Assertive communication

FAST FORWARD

Assertive communication must be distinguished clearly from aggressive (fight) and passive (flight) behaviours.

Human beings have certain psychological and physical mechanisms which prepare them to 'fight' or 'flee' in response to interpersonal threats or conflicts: by instinct, we fight back (aggression) or give in (passivity). However, we also have a third option: to use rational thinking and language to work our way through a problem in more constructive ways. This is the assertive approach.

According to **Back & Back** (*Assertiveness at Work)* the differences between assertive, aggressive and passive behaviour can be seen as follows.

	Aggressive behaviour	Passive behaviour	Assertive behaviour
Origins	'Fight' reaction to frustration, conflict or threat	'Flight' reaction to frustration, conflict or threat	'Flow' (rational) response to frustration, conflict or threat
Assumptions	I am more important than others	I am less important than others	I am important, but so are others
Main aim	To 'win' or dominate, if necessary at the expense of others	To please, to be liked and accepted, to avoid conflict	To communicate, maintain relationship and get the needs of both parties met
Typical behaviours	• Standing up for your rights in such a way that you violate the rights of others • Ignoring or dismissing the needs, wants, feelings or viewpoints of others • Expressing your own needs, wants and opinions in inappropriate ways	• Failing to stand up for your rights, or doing so in such a way that others can easily disregard them • Expressing your needs, wants, opinions, feelings and beliefs in apologetic, diffident or self-effacing ways • Failing to express honestly you needs, wants, opinions, feelings and beliefs	• Standing up for your own rights in such a way that you do not violate another person's rights • Expressing your needs, wants, opinions, feelings and beliefs in direct, honest and appropriate ways

This is a very important set of distinctions, as being assertive is often misunderstood as being 'aggressive', whereas in fact the two behaviours (and the assumptions underpinning them) are quite different.

As an example, imagine it is Thursday morning and your manager asks you to drop what you are doing and work on an urgent job that needs to be done by the following day.

(a) An **aggressive** response might be to stand up, point your pen at the manager, and shout: 'You're not doing this to me again! I'm in the middle of something. Get someone else to do it!'

(b) A **passive** (or **non-assertive**) response might be to avoid the manager's eye and slump tiredly in your chair, while murmuring: 'Oh... well... I suppose I could work late, or come in early tomorrow... again... Don't worry, I'm sure I could manage somehow...'

(c) An **assertive** response might be to meet the manager's eye and calmly state: 'I understand that you'd like this job done today. However, I'd really prefer to finish the project I'm currently working on. I could start your job first thing tomorrow morning. Would that work for you?'

Note that aggressive, passive and assertive behaviours are both **verbal** (what you say) *and* **non-verbal** (what you do: your body language).

2.2 Guidelines for assertive behaviour

FAST FORWARD

Techniques of assertive communication can be used in situations such as: asking for what you want; saying no; and giving and receiving feedback.

Assertiveness is a skill that must be learned and practised over time. Some of the key principles of assertive behaviour are as follows.

Assertive behaviours	Comment
Respect your feelings, but manage them	• If you are angry or anxious, breathe slowly, control your body language and speak calmly. • Don't use exaggerated language to label your feelings (eg 'angry' when you are only 'mildly annoyed'). • Keep your messages clear: if you've said 'yes' when you wanted to say 'no', don't start giving 'no' signals (eg sulking).
Say what you want, feel or think: directly, honestly and without games	• Don't assume that others will know, or work out from vague hints, what it is that you really want. • Don't feel the need to justify or apologise: be simple and direct. • Don't be pushed into a decision: if you are hesitant about whether to say 'yes' or 'no', say so.
Be persistent	If you don't get a proper response, repeat your statement or request, without raising your voice (the 'broken record' technique). You have the right to be heard – but you must also respect the other person's response.
Focus on the problem, not the person	• Use 'I' statements expressing how *you* perceive and feel about the other person's behaviour, and focus on specifics (not exaggerated generalities). You are focusing on the problem and its impact on you – not attacking the other person. • It would be aggressive to say: 'You're always so inconsiderate: you make me angry!' It would be assertive to say: 'When you're late, I feel annoyed because it suggests that you don't care about my time.' This is particularly important in **giving criticism** constructively: describe the undesirable behaviour specifically and objectively; specify the change you want; and end on a positive note.
Acknowledge and encourage other points of view	• Use 'I' statements to distinguish opinions from facts: 'As I see it…' • Show that you understand the other person's point of view, by summarising their argument. • Tackle parts of a view that you specifically disagree with, rather than globally rejecting it: 'I agree that it's a problem, but I don't think it's that damaging'. This is particularly important in **receiving criticism** constructively. The assertive response is to encourage specific, objective feedback: 'Can you give me an example? How do you think I could do that better?'
Express willingness to look for joint solutions	Expressions such as 'How can we make this work?' focus attention on **shared goals** (if only the desire to preserve a co-operative working relationship).

Rewards of assertiveness

What can you see as the (a) immediate or apparent benefits ('payoffs') and (b) the actual longer term results of:

- Behaving passively or non-assertively?
- Behaving aggressively?
- Behaving assertively?

Answer

You may have come up with some of the following points. Note that assertiveness is an effective strategy for interpersonal relations!

Passive behaviour

Apparent/immediate payoffs: you avoid conflict and unpleasantness; you get to feel good for sacrificing your needs to others; people may like you.

Longer-term results: you do not get your needs met; you may feel angry and resentful later; others may lose respect for you; dominant people may feel they can exploit you whenever they wish.

Aggressive behaviour

Apparent/immediate payoffs: you get your way; you may enjoy dominating people; you can let off some steam or anger; you may be respected for your 'forthrightness'.

Longer-term results: others may resent or fear you; others may withdraw from relationship with you; if others are equally dominant, conflict may escalate; you may feel guilty later.

Assertive behaviour

Apparent/immediate payoffs: you get your needs met; you have the satisfaction of expressing your feelings; you don't need to feel guilty or resentful later; interpersonal relationships are maintained or improved; new solutions to problems can be reached.

Longer-term results: as apparent/immediate payoffs, precisely because assertive behaviour takes this into consideration in deliberately managing communication for long term benefits.

2.3 Assertiveness and the role of women at work

Assertiveness training is popularly seen as a prime means of remedying underachievement in women, or of helping women to avoid exploitation at work. It is likely to be a part of a 'Women Into Management' or similar training and education programme. The techniques and insights involved are likely to be of benefit to men as well, but it has been recognised that it is primarily women who are disadvantaged in western society by the failure to distinguish between assertion and aggression, submission and conflict-avoidance.

Exam focus point

> A detailed question on interpersonal skills – specifically including assertive/aggressive/passive behaviour – was set as the Case Study in Section A. Don't neglect areas such as the importance of interpersonal skills just because this seems like a 'soft' topic!

3 Communication in the organisation

6/05

In any organisation, the communication of information is necessary for:

(a) **Management decision-making**

(b) **Interdepartmental co-ordination**. All the interdependent systems for purchasing, production, marketing and administration can be synchronised to perform the right actions at the right times to co-operate in accomplishing the organisation's aims.

(c) **Individual motivation and effectiveness,** so people know what they have to do and why.

3.1 The communication process

FAST FORWARD

> Communication can be depicted as a **'radio signal'** model. The sender codes the message and transmits it through a medium to the receiver who decodes it into information.

The process of communication can be shown as follows.

The communication process

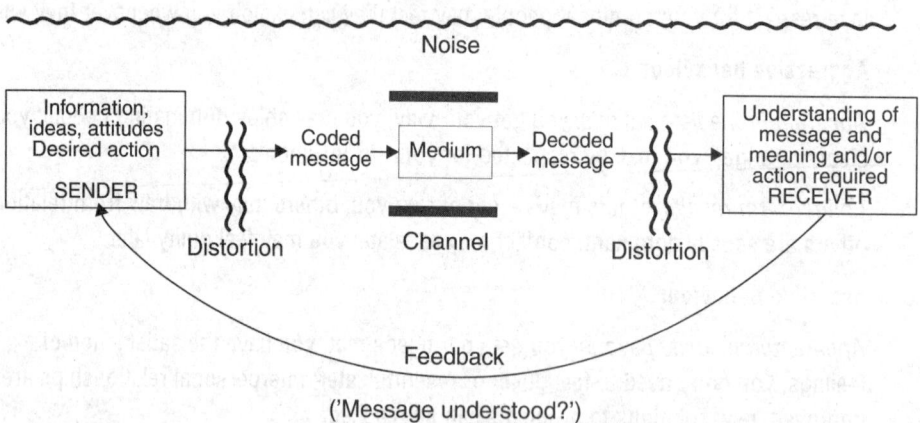

('Message understood?')

Element	Comments
Coding and decoding	The code or 'language' of a message may be verbal (spoken or written) or non-verbal (pictures, diagrams, numbers or body language). The needs and abilities of the target recipient of the message must be taken into account: not all codes (eg technical jargon or unlabelled diagrams) will be accessible to others.
Media and channels	The choice of medium (letter, memo, e-mail, report, presentation, telephone call) and channel of delivery (telecom system, notice board, postal system, World Wide Web) depends on a number of factors. • Urgency: the speed of transmission (eg phone or e-mail as opposed to post) • Permanency: the need for a written record for legal evidence, confirmation of a transaction or future reference • Complexity: eg the need for graphic illustration to explain concepts • Sensitivity/confidentiality (eg a private letter) • Ease of dissemination: wide audience (eg a notice board) • Cost effectiveness (taking into account all the above)

Element	Comments
Feedback	The process by which the sender checks – and recipient signals – that the message has been received and understood. This is vital, as it makes communication a two-way – and much more reliable – process. Feedback may include: • Verbal messages ('I'd like to clarify…', 'What does that mean?') • Non-verbal cues (eg nodding and making encouraging noises, or looking perplexed) • Appropriate action (eg doing as requested by the message)
Distortion	A process through which the meaning of a message is lost in the coding or decoding stages. Misunderstandings may arise from technical or ambiguous language, misinterpretation of symbols or tones of voice and so on.
Noise	Interference in the environment of communication which prevents the message getting through clearly. This may be: • Physical noise (eg passing traffic) • Technical noise (eg a bad Internet connection) • Social noise (eg differences in the personalities, status or education of the parties) • Psychological noise (eg anger or prejudice distorting what is heard)

3.2 Direction of communication flows   12/03

FAST FORWARD

Communication in an organisation **flows** downwards, upwards, sideways and diagonally.

Formal channels of communication in an organisation may run in three main directions.

(a) **Vertical**: ie up and down the scalar chain.

    (i) **Downward** communication is very common, and takes the form of instructions, briefings, rules and policies, announcement of plans and so on, from superior to subordinate.

    (ii) **Upward** communication is rarer – but very important for the organisation. It takes the form of reporting back, feedback, suggestions and so on. Managers need to encourage upward communication to take advantage of employees' experience and know-how, and to be able to understand their problems and needs in order to manage better.

(b) **Horizontal or lateral:** between people of the same rank, in the same section or department, or in different sections or departments. Horizontal communication between 'peer groups' is usually easier and more direct then vertical communication, being less inhibited by considerations of rank.

    (i) **Formally:** to co-ordinate the work of several people, and perhaps departments, who have to co-operate to carry out a certain operation

    (ii) **Informally:** to furnish emotional and social support to an individual

(c) **Diagonal**. This is interdepartmental communication by people of different ranks. Departments in the technostructure which serve the organisation in general, such as Human Resources or Information Systems, have no clear 'line authority' linking them to managers in other departments who need their involvement. Diagonal communication aids co-

ordination, and also innovation and problem-solving, since it puts together the ideas and information of people in different functions and levels. It also helps to by-pass longer, less direct channels, avoiding blockages and speeding up decision-making.

3.3 Effective communication   12/02, 6/03

> **FAST FORWARD** ▶▶
>
> **Effective communication** basically means that the right person receives the right information in the right way at the right time.

What does 'good communication' look like? It is perhaps easiest to identify *poor* or ineffective communication, where information is not given; is given too late to be used; is too much to take in; is inaccurate or incomplete; is hard to understand.

It must be:

(a)   **Directed to appropriate people**. This may be defined by the reporting structure of the organisation, but it may also be a matter of discretion, trust and so on.

(b)   **Relevant to their needs**: not excessive in volume (causing overload); focused on relevant topics; communicated in a format, style and language that they will be able to understand and use.

(c)   **Accurate and compete** (within the recipient's needs). Information should be 'accurate' in the sense of 'factually correct', but need not be minutely detailed: in business contexts, summaries and approximations are often used.

(d)   **Timely:** information must be made available within the time period when it will be relevant (as input to a decision, say).

(e)   **Flexible**: suited in style and structure to the needs of the parties and situation. Assertive, persuasive, supportive and informative communication styles have different applications.

(f)   **Effective in conveying meaning**. Style, format, language and media all contribute to the other person's understanding or lack of understanding. If the other person doesn't understand the message, or misinterprets it, communication has not been effective.

(g)   **Cost-effective**. In business organisations, all the above must be achieved, as far as possible, at reasonable cost.

3.4 Barriers to effective communication   6/05

> **FAST FORWARD** ▶▶
>
> **Barriers to communication** include 'noise' (from the environment), poorly constructed or coded/decoded messages (distortion) and failures in understanding caused by the relative positions of senders and receivers.

General problems which can occur in the communication process include:

- **Distortion** and **noise** (described earlier)
- **Misunderstanding** due to lack of clarity or technical jargon
- **Non-verbal signs** (gesture, facial expression) contradicting the verbal message
- Failure to give or to seek **feedback**
- **'Overload'** – a person being given too much information to digest in the time available
- **Perceptual selection:** people hearing only what they want to hear in a message
- **Differences** in social, racial or educational background
- **Poor communication skills** on the part of sender or recipient

Additional difficulties may arise from the **work context**, including:

(a) **Status** (of the sender and receiver of information)

    (i) A senior manager's words are listened to closely and a colleague's perhaps discounted.

    (ii) A subordinate might mistrust his or her superior's intentions and might look for 'hidden meanings' in a message.

(b) **Jargon.** People from different job or specialist backgrounds (eg accountants, HR managers, IT experts) can have difficulty in talking on a non-specialist's wavelength.

(c) **Priorities.** People or departments have different priorities or perspectives so that one person places more or less emphasis on a situation than another.

(d) **Selective reporting.** Subordinates giving superiors incorrect or incomplete information (eg to protect a colleague, to avoid 'bothering' the superior). A senior manager may only be able to handle edited information because he does not have time to sift through details.

(e) **Use.** Managers who are prepared to make decisions on a 'hunch' without proper regard to the communications they may or may not have received.

(f) **Timing.** Information which has no immediate use tending to be forgotten.

(g) **Opportunity.** Mechanisms, formal or informal, for people to say what they think may be lacking, especially for upward communication.

(h) **Conflict**. Where there is conflict between individuals or departments, communications will be withdrawn and information withheld.

(i) **Cultural values** about communication. For example:

    (i) **Secrecy.** Information might be given on a need-to-know basis, rather than be considered as a potential resource for everyone to use.

    (ii) **Can't handle bad news.** The culture of some organisations may prevent the communication of certain messages. Organisations with a 'can-do' philosophy may not want to hear that certain tasks are impossible.

3.5 Improving the communications system

Depending on the problem, measures to improve communication may be as follows.

(a) **Encourage, facilitate and reward** communication. Status and functional barriers (particularly to upward and inter-functional communication) can be minimised by improving opportunities for formal and informal networking and feedback.

(b) **Give training and guidance** in communication skills, including consideration of recipients, listening, giving feedback and so on.

(c) **Minimise the potential for misunderstanding**. Make people aware of the difficulties arising from differences in culture and perception, and teach them to consider others' viewpoints.

(d) **Adapt technology, systems and procedures** to facilitate communication: making it more effective (clear mobile phone reception), faster (laptops for e-mailing instructions), more consistent (regularly reporting routines) and more efficient (reporting by exception).

(e) **Manage conflict and politics** in the organisation, so that no basic unwillingness exists between units.

(f)   **Establish communication channels and mechanisms** in all directions: regular staff or briefing meetings, house journal or Intranet, quality circles and so on. Upward communication should particularly be encouraged, using mechanisms such as inter-unit meetings, suggestion schemes, 'open door' access to managers and regular performance management feedback sessions.

Exam focus point

The nature and direction of organisational communication, the need for good communication, the qualities of good communication, barriers to communication and ways to improve it are all key examinable topics, because of their importance to the accountant's role. In fact, many of these aspects were applied to a single case study question in the June 2003 exam. The December 2003 exam also contained a question on the direction of communication. These are topics to watch!

Communication between superiors and subordinates will be improved when **interpersonal trust** exists. Exactly how this is achieved will depend on the management style of the manager, the attitudes and personality of the individuals involved, and other environmental variables. **Peters and Waterman** advocate 'management by walking around' (MBWA), and **informality in superior/subordinate relationships** as a means of establishing closer links.

3.6 The importance of consultation

FAST FORWARD

Consultation is particularly important, as a mechanism for upward communication.

Consultation is, basically, a process of gathering information and views from another party before making a decision.

(a)   **Formal consultation** is required in some business contexts. Employers must consult with elected employee representatives on issues of concern to them and their work, including re-structuring and proposed redundancies.

(b)   **Informal consultation** is a managerial style (see Chapter 14), in which the manager invites team members to contribute their views and input to decisions.

Consultation encourages **upward communication**. It may be important in:

(a)   Improving the **quality of decision**, by taking account of information from those closest to customers and processes

(b)   Improving the **acceptance and ownership** of decisions by staff, since they have had a chance to contribute to them

(c)   Improving **trust** between managers and staff, which in turn may harness more positive upward communication: suggestions for improvements and innovations and so on

(d)   Facilitating **change management**, by reducing insecurity, uncertainty and resistance

(e)   Improving **employee relations**, by showing managerial willingness to listen to staff concerns and inputs.

4 Face-to-face and oral communication

FAST FORWARD

Face-to-face communication (eg meetings and interviews) and **oral communication** (eg phone calls) bring a range of listening and non-verbal skills into play.

4.1 Face-to-face communication

Face-to-face communication plays an important part in the life of any organisation, whether it is required by government legislation or the Articles of a company, or is held informally for information exchange, problem-solving and decision-making.

Face-to-face communication is good for:

- Generating new ideas
- 'On the spot' feedback, constructive criticism and exchange of views
- Co-operation and sensitivity to personal factors
- Spreading information quickly through a group of people

However, such communication can be non- or counter-productive unless:

(a) People **know the reason** for the group discussion.

(b) Participants are **willing and effective communicators** and are concise and clear in what they have to say.

(c) There is sufficient **guidance** or leadership to control proceedings.

(d) People maintain standards of **courtesy**.

4.2 Listening

Listening is about decoding and receiving information and carries much of the burden of communication. Listening is more than just a natural instinct, and listening skills can be taught and developed. **Effective listening** helps:

- Both parties to gather more (and better quality) information
- Reduce the effect of 'noise'
- Resolve problems by encouraging understanding from someone else's viewpoint

The following are some basic guidelines on being a good listener.

(a) **Be prepared to listen**. Put yourself in the right frame of mind (ie a readiness to maintain attention). In meetings, be prepared to grasp the main concepts.

(b) **Try to be interested.** Make an effort to analyse the message for its relevance.

(c) **Keep an open mind.** Your own beliefs and prejudices can get in the way of what the other person is actually saying.

(d) **Keep an ear open for the main ideas.** Learn to distinguish between the 'gist' of the argument and supporting evidence.

(e) **Listen critically.** Assess what the other person is saying by identifying any assumptions, omissions and biases.

(f) **Avoid distraction.** People have a natural attention curve, high at the beginning and end of an oral message, but sloping off in the middle.

(g) **Take notes,** although note taking can be distracting at times.

(h) **Wait** before contributing: don't interrupt.

(i)   Use **active listening** techniques: give encouraging feedback, summarise and check understanding ('You said that … Is that right?'), ask questions.

4.3 Non-verbal communication

FAST FORWARD

Non-verbal communication (including tone of voice and body language) can support or undermine verbal messages: it needs to be carefully interpreted and managed.

Non-verbal communication (often called **body language**) consists of facial expression, posture, proximity, gestures and non-verbal noises (grunts, yawns etc).

(a)   Consciously or unconsciously, we send messages through body language during every face to face encounter.

(b)   We can use it deliberately to confirm our verbal message – for example, by nodding and smiling as we tell someone we are happy to help them – or to contradict it, if we want to be sarcastic (saying 'How interesting!' with a yawn, for example).

(c)   More often, however, our body language *contradicts* our verbal message without our being aware of it, giving a 'mixed message' like your saying you understand an instruction while looking extremely perplexed.

(d)   Body language can also 'give away' messages that we would – for social or business reasons – rather not send, such as lack of interest, hostility or whatever.

Control and use of body language is needed to:

(a)   Provide appropriate 'physical' feedback to the sender of a message (eg a nod of understanding)

(b)   Create a desired impression (eg a confident posture)

(c)   Establish a desired atmosphere or conditions (eg a friendly smile)

(d)   Reinforce spoken messages with appropriate indications (eg nodding 'yes')

Reading other people's body language helps you to:

-     Receive feedback from a listener and modify the message accordingly.
-     Recognise people's real feelings when their words are constrained by formalities.
-     Recognise existing or potential personal problems.
-     'Read' situations in order to modify our own communication and response strategy.

4.3.1 Improving your non-verbal skills

You can improve your skills as a non-verbal communicator in the following ways.

(a)   Become more **aware** of what your body language is 'saying' to people.

(b)   **Control your body language**. If you are bored or irritated when talking to a customer, in particular, suppress the signals. On the other hand, you can use positive body language to reinforce the message you want to give – of professionalism, confidence etc.

(c)   **Seek feedback** when communicating: you will then discover when a recipient is getting a 'mixed message' from you.

(d)   Ask colleagues and friends to be honest with you about when your body language is confusing or off-putting, to help you become more aware.

4.4 Committees

FAST FORWARD

> A **committee** is a group of people who meet for a particular purpose, often on a permanent basis. It is a useful mechanism for cross-functional communication.

Committees can be used for:

(a) **Making decisions**

(b) **Delaying** decisions (for more information)

(c) The **relaying of decisions** and instructions (eg briefings)

(d) The **dissemination of information** and the collection of feedback

(e) **Problem solving**, by consultation with people in different departments or fields (eg a task force or working party)

(f) **Brainstorming**: free exchanges with a view to generating new approaches and ideas

(g) **Co-ordination** of the efforts of a large number of people representing department or interest groups

(h) Formal **recommendations** that others follow a course of action

(i) **Representation** of a number of people from different disciplines

4.4.1 Limitations of committees

Committees have certain limitations and disadvantages.

(a) **Size.** They are apt to be too large for constructive action, since the time taken by a committee to resolve a problem tends to be in direct proportion to its size.

(b) **Time-consuming and expensive.** In addition to the cost of highly paid executives' time, secretarial costs will be incurred in the preparation of agendas, recording of proceedings and the production and distribution of minutes.

(c) **Delays** may occur in the production cycle if matters of a routine nature are entrusted to committees.

(d) **Distraction.** Operations of the enterprise may be jeopardised by the frequent attendance of executives at meetings, and by distracting them from their real duties.

(e) **Superficiality.** Incorrect or ineffective decisions may be made, owing to the fact that members of a committee are unfamiliar with the deeper aspects of issues under discussion.

(f) **Weakened individual responsibility** throughout the organisation.

(g) **Dominance.** Proceedings may be dominated by outspoken or aggressive members, thus unduly influencing decisions and subsequent action, perhaps adversely; there may be 'tyranny' by a minority.

4.4.2 Using committees successfully

Here are some guidelines on using committees successfully.

(a) **Well defined areas** of authority, time scales of operations and purpose must be specified in writing. (Similarly clear agendas should be provided for all committee meetings.)

(b) The **chairman must have the qualities** of leadership to co-ordinate and motivate the other committee members and to lead meetings: keeping to the agenda and schedule, ensuring balanced contribution from all members and so on.

(c)   **Size.** The committee should not be so large as to be unmanageable.

(d)   **Membership.** The members of the committee must have the necessary skills and experience to do the committee's work. Where the committee is expected to liaise with functional departments, the members must also have sufficient status and influence with those departments.

(e)   **Minutes.** Minutes of the meetings should be taken and circulated, with any action points arising out of the meetings notified to the members responsible for doing the work.

Exam focus point

> 10 marks were available in the June 2003 case study question for outlining the usefulness and shortcomings of committees. Be aware that the examiner is interested in this level of detailed preparation!

4.5 Other group communication methods

Brainstorming sessions are problem-solving conferences of six to twelve people who produce spontaneous 'free-wheeling' ideas to solve a particular problem. Ideas are produced but not evaluated at these meetings, so that originality is not stifled in fear of criticism. Brainstorming sessions rely on the ability of conference members to feed off each other's ideas. They have been used in many organisations and might typically occur, for example, in advertising agencies to produce ideas for a forthcoming campaign.

Quality circles emerged first in the United States, but it was in Japan that they were adopted most enthusiastically. They are still used, but some commentators suggest they are outmoded and are being superseded by other team-based working methods.

Key term

> A **quality circle** consists of a group of employees which meets regularly to discuss problems of quality and quality control in their area of work, and perhaps to suggest ways of improving quality. The quality circle has a leader or supervisor who directs discussions and possibly also helps to train other members of the circle.

A **team briefing** is a means of communicating at team level, not at the more impersonal or abstract level of the house journal or noticeboard. It is given by a **team leader**, who should have been thoroughly trained and briefed, or, occasionally, a more senior member of management.

Key term

> **Team briefings** are a form of face-to-face communication mechanism which are designed to increase the commitment and understanding of the workforce.

The **purpose of a team briefing** is to communicate and explain management decisions in the hope of reducing disruption, dispelling rumours, and enhancing employees' commitment. Subjects include:

- Policies (new or changed, and why)
- Plans
- Progress
- Personnel issues

4.6 Interviews

The interview, informal or otherwise, is an excellent internal system for handling the problems or queries of individuals, allowing confidentiality and flexible response to personal factors. Interviews are, however, costly in terms of managerial time. Some interviews are built into the formal communication system.

(a)   **Grievance** interviews are where employees can have their complaints heard.

(b)   **Disciplinary** interviews are where managers address unacceptable performance or conduct of staff.

(c) **Appraisal** interviews are used to discuss the employee's performance, progress and possible need for improvement.

(d) **Counselling** interviews are used to help individuals identify and solve personal or performance problems.

4.7 Telephone calls (and visual equivalents)

The **telephone** provides all the interactive and feedback advantages of face to face communication, while saving the travel time. It is, however, more 'distant' and impersonal than an interview for the discussion of sensitive personal matters, and it does not by itself provide the concreteness of written media.

Video conferencing and **webcasts** allow 'virtual' meetings between participants in remote locations, using broadcast images of the other participants.

5 Textual communication

FAST FORWARD

A range of **written communication media** is used in business contexts, for one-to-one or one-to-group communication. Each has its own applications and conventions of format and style.

5.1 Forms

Routine information flow is largely achieved through the use of forms. A well designed form can be filled quickly and easily with brief, relevant and specifically identified details of a request or instruction. Forms are simple to file, and information is quickly retrieved and confirmed. Examples include: expense forms, timesheets, insurance forms, stock request forms etc. A variety of forms can now be filled (and filed) electronically or online.

5.2 Notice board

A notice board is a channel through which various written media can be cheaply transmitted to a large number of people. It allows the organisation to present a variety of information to any or all employees: items may have a limited time span of relevance but will at least be available for verification and recollection for a while. The drawbacks to notice boards are that:

(a) They can easily fall into neglect, and become untidy or irrelevant (or be sabotaged by graffiti).

(b) They are wholly dependent on the intended recipient's curiosity or desire to receive information.

5.3 House journal

Larger companies frequently run an internal magazine or newspaper to inform employees about:

- Staff appointments and retirements
- Meetings, sports and social events
- Results and successes; customer feedback
- New products or machinery
- Motivating competitions eg for suggestions, office maintenance, safety

This function may also be fulfilled by a staff web page or intranet, with e-mail newsletters or e-zines to staff members.

5.4 Organisation manual or handbook

An organisation (or office) manual is useful for drawing together and keeping up to date all relevant information for the guidance of individuals and groups as to:

- The structure of the organisation
- Background: the organisation's history and geography
- The organisation's products, services and customers
- Rules and regulations
- Conditions of employment: pay structure, hours, holidays, notice etc
- Standards and procedures for health and safety
- Procedures for grievance, discipline, salary review
- Policy on trade union membership
- Facilities for employees

Again, this information may also be published in the staff area of the corporate intranet or website.

5.5 Letters and faxes

The letter is flexible in a wide variety of situations, and useful in providing a written record and confirmation of the matters discussed.

(a)   It is widely used for external communication, via the external mailing system (Post Office) or courier.

(b)   A personal letter may be used internally in certain situations where a confidential written record is necessary or personal handling required.

Fax achieves the same object as a letter, but is 'delivered' electronically – with significant time and cost savings especially in overseas communication.

5.6 Memoranda

A memorandum is the equivalent of the letter in internal communication. It is sent via the internal mail system of an organisation. Memoranda are useful for exchanging many sorts of message and particularly for confirming telephone conversations: sometimes, however, they are used instead of telephone conversations, where the call would have been quicker, cheaper and just as effective. Many memoranda are unnecessarily typed where a short hand-written note would be adequate.

5.7 E-mail

As an alternative to paper-based media such as letters and memos, people are increasingly using e-mail, especially in firms with a high penetration of networked PCs.

E-mail is extremely versatile, fast and cost-effective. However, there are also problems.

(a)   **Information overload**: it is easier to send an e-mail than to distribute a memo, so people perhaps send unnecessary messages.

(b)   E-mails are **not private**, and can be cited in legal actions for libel or harassment if improperly used.

(c)   E-mail is **impersonal**, and it can be difficult to convey complex messages (especially 'tone of voice' and humour) without seeming abrupt.

(d)   E-mail transmits **instantly**: it is important to check messages carefully for content and tone of voice before pressing the 'send' button.

5.8 Report writing

A formal report enables a number of people to review the complex facts and arguments relating to an issue on which they have to base a plan or make a decision. This is primarily an internal medium used by management, but can be used externally for the information of shareholders, the general public, government agencies etc (eg the company's Annual Report).

The written report does not allow for effective discussion or immediate feedback, as does a meeting, and can be a time-consuming and expensive document to produce. However, as a medium for putting across a body of ideas to a group of people, it has several **advantages.**

(a) People can study the material in their own time, rather than arranging to be present at one place and time

(b) No time need be wasted on irrelevancies and the formulation of arguments, such as may occur in meetings

(c) The report should be presented objectively and impartially, in a formal and impersonal style: emotional reactions or conflicts will be avoided.

5.8.1 Report style

Stylistic requirements in the writing of reports are as follows.

(a) A report must first **identify** the recipient, the preparer, the date and subject matter.

(b) Reports are generally written in an **impersonal** style. Bias and emotive language can undermine the credibility of the report and its recommendations.

(c) Reports are generally written in relatively **formal** style. Avoid colloquialisms and abbreviated forms.

(d) **Ease of understanding** is the key to effective reports.

    (i) Write for the **user:** jargon is suitable for some readers, but intimidating to others.

    (ii) **Organise** material logically, especially if it is leading up to a conclusion or recommendation.

    (iii) **Signal** relevant themes by appropriate headings or highlighting.

    (iv) The **layout** of the report should display data clearly and attractively. Figures and diagrams should be used with discretion, and it might be helpful to highlight key figures which appear within large tables of numbers.

(e) Certain **section headings** are conventional in reports, as shown below.

REPORT

To: [Name(s)/position(s) of recipient(s)]
From: [Sender]
Date:
Subject: [Title of report, such as *Communication Media in A Ltd*]

Contents:

1   Terms of reference (or Introduction, or Background)

2   Executive summary

3   Analysis (or Findings, or appropriate topic headings)

4   Conclusion (or Recommendations, or whatever was asked for)

1   **Terms of reference** (or **Introduction**, or **Background**)

[Here is laid out the scope and purpose of the report: what is to be investigated, what information is required, whether recommendations should be made; background to the problem etc]

2   **Executive summary** [Many reports have a brief description of their key points at the top.]

3   Analysis (or Findings etc)

3.1 [Reports could use numbered paragraphs like this. This makes it easier for the user to refer to them.]

3.2 [The content in this and the following sections should be complete but concise and clearly structured in chronological order, order of importance or any other logical relationship.]

4   **Conclusion** (or **recommendations**)

[This section allows for a summary of main findings and their implications. Recommendations could come here, referenced, if necessary, to the findings of the earlier section. The recommendations will allow the recipient to make a decision if necessary.]

Question

Media

Indicate the most effective way in which the following situations should be communicated.

(a)   Spare parts needed urgently

(b)   A message from the managing director to all staff

(c)   Fred has been absent five times in the past month and his manager intends to take action

(d)   You need information quickly from another department

(e)   You have to explain a complicated operation to a group

Answer

Communicating the situations given might best be done as follows.

(a)   Telephone, confirmed in writing (order form, letter)

(b)   Noticeboard, general meeting or email

(c)   Face-to-face conversation. It would be a good idea to confirm the outcome of the meeting in writing so that records can be maintained.

(d)   Telephone, face to face or e-mail.

(e)   Team briefing

6 Counselling

Counselling is an interpersonal interview, the aim of which is to facilitate another person in identifying and working through a problem.

Key term

'**Counselling** can be defined as 'a purposeful relationship in which one person helps another to help himself. It is a way of relating and responding to another person so that that person is helped to explore his thoughts, feelings and behaviour with the aim of reaching a clearer understanding. The clearer understanding may be of himself or of a problem, or of the one in relation to the other.' (*Rees*)

6.1 When is counselling required?

The need for workplace counselling can arise in many different situations.

- During appraisal, to solve work or performance problems
- In grievance or disciplinary situations
- Following change, such as promotion or relocation
- On redundancy or dismissal
- As a result of domestic or personal difficulties
- In cases of sexual, racial or religious harassment or bullying at work (to support the victim and educate the perpetrator)

6.2 Benefits of counselling

Effective counselling is not merely a matter of pastoral care for individuals, but is very much in the organisation's interests. Counselling can:

(a)   **Prevent underperformance**, reduce labour turnover and absenteeism and increase commitment from employees

(b)   Demonstrate an organisation's **commitment** to and concern for its employees

(c)   Give employees the confidence and encouragement necessary to take responsibility for self and career development

(d)   Recognise that the organisation may be contributing to the **employees' problems** and therefore it provides an opportunity to reassess organisational policy and practice

(e)   Support the organisation in **complying with its obligations** (eg in regard to managing harassment in the workplace).

6.3 The counselling process

FAST FORWARD

Counselling is facilitating others through the **process** of defining and exploring their own problems: it is primarily a non-directive role.

Managers may be called on to use their expertise to help others make informed decisions or solve problems by:

(a)   **Advising:** offering information and recommendations on the best course of action. This is a relatively *directive* role, and may be called for in areas where you can make a key contribution to the *quality* of the decision: advising an employee about the best available training methods, say, or about behaviours which are considered inappropriate in the workplace.

(b)   **Counselling:** facilitating others through the process of defining and exploring their own problems and coming up with their own solutions. This is a relatively *non-directive* role, and may be called for in areas where you can make a key contribution to the *ownership* of the decision: helping employees to formulate learning goals, for example, or to cope with work (and sometimes non-work) problems.

The counselling process has three broad stages (*Egan*).

Step 1   **Reviewing the current scenario**: helping people to identify, explore and clarify their problem situations and unused opportunities. This is done mostly by listening, encouraging them to tell their 'story', and questioning/probing to help them to see things more clearly.

Step 2   **Developing a preferred scenario:** helping people to identify what they want, in terms of clear goals and objectives. This is done mostly by encouraging them to envisage their desired outcome, and what it will mean for them (in order to motivate them to make the necessary changes).

Step 3   **Determining how to get there:** helping people to develop action strategies for accomplishing goals, for getting what they want. This is done mostly by encouraging them to explore options and available resources, select the best option and plan their next steps.

| Question | Counselling skills |

Before you read on, which of the interpersonal skills covered in this chapter would you consider particularly helpful for a manager in the role of counsellor?

6.4 Counselling skills

FAST FORWARD

Counselling skills include *orientations* (such as interest, sensitivity, empathy and non-judgement); *communication skills* (such as active listening, questioning and use of body language); and *problem-solving skills* (in order to explore goals and alternative options for pursuing them).

The aim of counselling is to help the other person to help himself. Counsellors need to have the **belief** that individuals have the resources to solve their own problems, albeit with facilitation and help.

Counsellors need to be **observant** and **knowledgeable** enough about people to notice and interpret behaviours which may indicate a problem: the other person may not have clearly identified or expressed what the problem is.

They need to be **sensitive** to beliefs and values which may be different from their own: for example, religious beliefs. They need to be **empathetic** (attempting to see the problem from the other person's point of view, and reflecting their understanding back to the other person so that they feel heard) – and yet also **impartial** (refraining from judging or giving advice unnecessarily).

They also need a range of first-order interpersonal skills:

(a)   **Active listening:** to encourage the other person to talk (eg by **attentive** behaviour and giving supportive **feedback**); and to ensure (and demonstrate) that they are genuinely trying to understand the other person's viewpoint (eg by **reflecting back** what they think they are hearing).

(b)   Using different **questioning styles:** to encourage the other person to speak; to think more deeply or clearly (probing and challenging); to check their own understanding.

Using **body language** (to convey attentiveness, interest, support) and interpreting the other person's body language carefully (in order to explore the feelings underlying the other person's verbal messages).

6.5 Confidentiality

There will be situations when an employee cannot be completely open unless he is sure that his comments will be treated confidentially. However, certain information, once obtained by the organisation (for example about fraud or sexual harassment) calls for action. In spite of the drawbacks, therefore, the CIPD Statement on counselling in the workplace is clear that employees must be made aware when their comments will be passed on to the relevant authority, and when they will be treated completely confidentially.

Case Study

'The findings of more than 80 studies on workplace counselling show that 90% of employees are highly satisfied with the process and outcome. Evidence suggests that counselling helps to relieve work-related stress and reduces sickness absence rates by up to half. That view is borne out by Mike Doig, medical director at Chevron Europe: "For every $1 spent on workplace counselling, $6–$10 was saved for our company, with the workforce receiving the direct benefit," he says. (*People Management*, May 2003)

Exam focus point

A 15-mark question was set specifically on counselling in the June 2003 exam, covering the definition of counselling in the workplace, skills of a counsellor and advantages of counselling for the organisation.

Chapter Roundup

- **Interpersonal behaviour** is behaviour between one or more individuals and the behaviour of one individual in relation to others.

- **Interpersonal skills** are vital to effective motivation, team working, negotiation and other management roles.

- **Assertiveness** is one interpersonal skill which is highly valued (in Western cultural contexts). It consists of clear, honest and direct communication.

- **Assertive communication** must be distinguished clearly from aggressive (fight) and passive (flight) behaviours.

- **Techniques of assertive communication** can be used in situations such as: asking for what you want; saying no; and giving and receiving feedback.

- **Communication** is a two-way process involving the transmission or exchange of information, and the provision of feedback.

- Communication can be depicted as a '**radio signal**' model. The sender codes the message and transmits it through a medium to the receiver who decodes it into information.

- **Communication** in an organisation **flows** downwards, upwards, sideways and diagonally.

- **Effective communication** basically means that the right person receives the right information in the right way at the right time.

- **Barriers to communication** include 'noise' (from the environment), poorly constructed or coded/decoded messages (distortion) and failures in understanding caused by the relative positions of senders and receivers.

- **Consultation** is particularly important, as a mechanism for upward communication.

- **Face-to-face communication** (eg meetings and interviews) and **oral communication** (eg phone calls) bring a range of listening and non-verbal skills into play.

- **Non-verbal communication** (including tone of voice and body language) can support or undermine verbal messages: it needs to be carefully interpreted and managed.

- A **committee** is a group of people who meet for a particular purpose, often on a permanent basis. It is a useful mechanism for cross-functional communication.

- A range of **written communication media** is used in business contexts, for one-to-one or one-to-group communication. Each has its own applications and conventions of format and style.

- **Counselling** is an interpersonal interview, the aim of which is to facilitate another person in identifying and working through a problem.

- **Counselling** is facilitating others through the **process** of defining and exploring their own problems: it is primarily a non-directive role.

- **Counselling skills** include *orientations* (such as interest, sensitivity, empathy and non-judgement); *communication skills* (such as active listening, questioning and use of body language); and *problem-solving skills* (in order to explore goals and alternative options for pursuing them).

Quick Quiz

1   Draw a simple diagram of the communication process using dotted or broken lines where 'distortion' may be a problem.

2   Give five examples of non-verbal communication, and suggest what they might be used to indicate.

3   What is the difference between aggression and assertiveness?

4   Communication between two members of a project team from different functions, but the same level of authority, is:

  (A)   Upward
  (B)   Downward
  (C)   Lateral
  (D)   Diagonal

5   What are the advantages and disadvantages of giving orders or briefings by telephone?

6   What might be covered in regular 'team briefings'?

7   What are the main purposes of upward communication in organisations?

8   What are the stages of the counselling process?

9   A group of employees which meets regularly to discuss quality issues is called a brainstorming circle. *True or false?*

Answers to Quick Quiz

1   Refer to Section 3.1. The dotted lines would run alongside all the arrows.

2   A nod of agreement; a smile to encourage; a frown to disapprove; a yawn to show boredom; turning away to discourage.

3   Aggressive behaviour is competitive; assertion means that every individual has certain rights, and is entitled to stand by them.

4   C

5   Advantages: it cuts down on time and physical movement. Disadvantages: only one person is reached at a time, there are no non-verbal signals and it is more difficult to persuade and to respond to physical factors.

6   Organisational policy and changes, plans, progress, results.

7   To give feedback, to inform and to make suggestions.

8   Recognition and understanding; empowerment; resourcing.

9   False: it is called a 'quality circle' (although brainstorming may occasionally be used to generate ideas.)

Now try the question below from the Exam Question Bank

Number	Level	Marks	Time
Q15	Examination	15	27 mins

Conflict, grievance and discipline

Topic list	Syllabus reference
1 Conflict in organisations	5 (d)
2 Causes and symptoms of conflict	5 (d)
3 Managing conflict	5 (d)
4 Discipline	5 (d)
5 Grievance	5 (d)

Introduction

Conflict of various kinds is almost inevitable in organisations, where there are individuals and groups with different interests, and not always enough power and resources to go round...

In this chapter, we examine the role of **conflict** in organisations. Perhaps the key point is that it is not necessarily negative or destructive, but can be managed for the organisation's benefit.

In **Section 2**, we look at the **causes** and **symptoms** of conflict, and in **Section 3** we look at various ways in which it can be dealt with (or *not* dealt with...)

Sections 4 and 5 cover two major formal mechanisms for managing conflict. **Discipline** is initiated by management to deal with an employees' failure to perform or behave to the standards set by the organisation. **Grievance** is initiated by an employee to deal with his or her own perception that (s)he has been wrongly or unfairly treated.

These are key areas in which a systematic and 'correct' procedure is essential to manage issues fairly: get to grips with the procedural requirements.

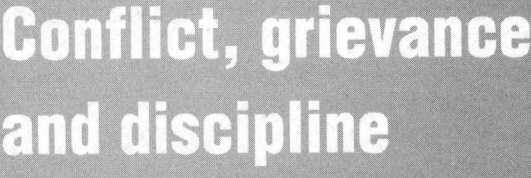

Study guide

Section 28 – Controlling conflict, grievance and discipline

See the Introductory pages of this Study Text for details of this session.

Exam guide

Conflict is a major topic in organisational studies and could form the basis for a question in either Section A or Section B. Grievance and discipline are rather more specialised aspects of human resource management, and are perhaps most likely to appear as Section B questions: discipline has come up *twice* in 2004, so attention may turn to grievance soon ….

1 Conflict in organisations

Conflict in organisations can be viewed as inevitable (due to competition for scarce power and resources) or unnatural (caused by poor management).

1.1 The happy family view: conflict is unnatural

The happy family view presents organisations as:

(a) **Co-operative structures**, designed to achieve agreed common objectives, with no systematic conflict of interest.

(b) **Harmonious environments**, where conflicts are exceptional and arise from:

- Misunderstandings
- Personality factors
- The expectations of inflexible employees
- Factors outside the organisation and its control

Conflict is thus blamed on bad management, lack of leadership, poor communication, or 'bloody-mindedness' on the part of individuals or interest groups that impinge on the organisation. The theory is that a strong culture, good two-way communication, co-operation and motivational leadership will eliminate conflict.

Question

Happy family?

How accurate is the happy family perspective when applied to your own organisation, or to any organisation with which you are sufficiently familiar?

To what extent would you subscribe to the claim that the 'happy family' view is publicised by managers within their own organisations, not so much as an accurate description of reality, but rather because adoption of the 'happy family' perspective itself helps to reduce the level of articulated conflict?

Answer

The happy family perspective rarely fits most organisations, even those pursuing a common ideological goal, like a political party. Cynics argue that managers promote the 'happy family' view to suppress conflict.

1.2 The conflict view

In contrast, some see organisations as **natural arenas** for conflict on individual and group levels.

(a) Members compete for limited resources, status, rewards and professional values.

(b) **Organisational politics** involve constant struggles for control, and choices of structure, technology and organisational goals are part of this process. Individual and organisational interests will not always coincide.

1.3 The evolutionary view

This view regards conflict as a means of maintaining the status quo, as a useful basis for evolutionary change.

(a) Conflict keeps the organisation **sensitive to the need to change**, while reinforcing its essential framework of control.

(b) The **legitimate pursuit of competing interests** can balance and preserve social and organisational arrangements.

This **constructive conflict** view may perhaps be the most useful for managers and administrators of organisations, for two reasons.

(a) It does not attempt to dodge the issues of conflict, which is an observable fact of life in most organisations.

(b) Neither does it seek to pull down existing organisational structures altogether.

1.4 Conflict: good or bad?

FAST FORWARD

> Conflict can be **constructive**, if it introduces new information, encourages ideas testing and creativity and 'clears the air'. It can be **destructive** if it distracts attention from the task or inhibits communication.

Conflict can be highly desirable. Conflict is **constructive**, when its effect is to:

- Introduce different solutions to problems
- Define power relationships more clearly
- Encourage creativity and the testing of ideas (avoiding 'groupthink')
- Focus attention on individual contributions
- Bring emotions out into the open
- Release hostile feelings that have been, or may be, repressed otherwise

Conflict can also be **destructive**. It may:

- Distract attention from the task
- Polarise views and 'dislocate' the group
- Subvert objectives in favour of secondary goals
- Encourage defensive or 'spoiling' behaviour
- Force the group to disintegrate
- Stimulate emotional, win-lose conflicts, ie hostility

Case Study

Tjosvold and Deerner researched conflict in different contexts. They allocated to 66 student volunteers the roles of foremen and workers at an assembly plant, with a scenario of conflict over job rotation schemes. Foremen were against, workers for.

One group was told that the organisational norm was to 'avoid controversy'; another was told that the norm was 'co-operative controversy', *trying* to agree; a third was told that groups were out to win any arguments that arose, 'competitive controversy'. The students were offered rewards for complying with their given norms. Their decisions, and attitudes to the discussions, were then monitored.

(a)   Where controversy was avoided, the foremen's views dominated.

(b)   Competitive controversy brought no agreement – but brought out feelings of hostility and suspicion.

(c)   Co-operative controversy brought out differences in an atmosphere of curiosity, trust and openness: the decisions reached seemed to integrate the views of both parties.

But can real managers and workers be motivated to comply with useful organisational norms in this way?

1.5 Conflict between groups

Conflicts of interest may exist throughout the organisation – or even for a single individual. There may be conflicts of interest between:

(a)   Local management of a branch or subsidiary and the organisation as a whole

(b)   Sales and production departments in a manufacturing firm (over scheduling, product variation)

(c)   Trade unions and management

Interest groups such as trade unions tend to wield greater power in conflict situations than their members as individuals. Trade Unions are organisations whose purpose it is to promote their members' interests.

Question   Conflict of interest

What other examples of 'conflicts of interest' can you identify within an organisation? Having selected some instances, can you detect any common patterns in such conflicts?

Answer

Conflicts occur anywhere in an organisation. Individuals, groups, departments or subsidiaries compete for scarce (financial/human/physical) resources.

Conflict can also operate *within* groups.

Case Study

In an experiment reported by *Deutsch* (1949), psychology students were given puzzles and human relation problems to work at in discussion groups. Some groups ('co-operative' ones) were told that the grade each individual got at the end of the course would depend on the performance of his group. Other groups ('competitive' ones) were told that each student would receive a grade according to his own contributions.

No significant differences were found between the two kinds of group in the amount of interest and involvement in the tasks, or in the amount of learning. But the co-operative groups, compared with the competitive ones, had greater productivity per unit time, better quality of product and discussion, greater co-ordination of effort and sub-division of activity, more diversity in amount of contribution per member, more attentiveness to fellow members and more friendliness during discussion.

2 Causes and symptoms of conflict

2.1 Causes of conflict

> **FAST FORWARD**
>
> **Conflicts** are typically **caused by**: different objectives; competition for power or resources; ambiguities and frustrations; and personal differences.

The following may be identified as typical causes of conflict in organisations.

(a) **Differences in the objectives** of different groups or individuals.

(b) **Scarcity of resources**, information and power, for which individuals and groups must compete.

(c) **Interdependence of two departments** which have to work together: this may cause frustration because of different cultures, time scales, ways of working or levels of effectiveness.

(d) **Disputes about the boundaries of authority**

    (i) The technostructure may attempt to encroach on the roles or territory of line managers and usurp some of their authority.

    (ii) One department might start 'empire building' and try to take over the work previously done by another department.

(e) **Personal differences**, as regards goals, attitudes and feelings, are also bound to crop up. This is especially true in diverse organisations.

2.2 Symptoms of conflict

> **FAST FORWARD**
>
> **Conflict** may **manifest** itself in: poor communication; friction between individuals and groups; widespread use of arbitration and other conflict mechanisms; and various political games.

Conflict – or differences and competition, if poorly managed – may result in:

- Poor communications, in all directions
- Interpersonal friction
- Inter-group rivalry and jealousy
- Low morale and frustration
- Widespread use of arbitration, appeals to higher authority, and inflexible attitudes

The tactics of conflict include:

(a)   **Withholding information** from others who need it

(b)   **Distorting information**. This will enable the group or manager presenting the information to get their own way more easily.

(c)   **Empire building**. A group (especially a specialist group such as accounting) which considers its influence to be neglected might seek to impose rules, procedures, restrictions or official requirements on other groups, in order to bolster their own importance.

(d)   **Office politics**. A manager might seek to by-pass formal channels of communication and decision-making by establishing informal contacts and friendships with people in a position of importance.

(e)   **Fault-finding** in the work of other departments.

3 Managing conflict

3.1 A range of managerial responses

FAST FORWARD

Strategies for managing conflict range from denial or suppression though various resolution approaches (dominance or compromise), to more collaborative ways of working.

A range of managerial responses to conflict (not all of which are effective) may be summarised as follows, according to John **Hunt**.

Response	Comment
Denial/withdrawal	'Sweeping it under the carpet'. If the conflict is very trivial, it may indeed blow over without an issue being made of it, but if the causes are not identified, the conflict may grow to unmanageable proportions.
Suppression	'Smoothing over', to preserve working relationships despite minor conflicts. As Hunt remarks, however: 'Some cracks cannot be papered over'.
Dominance	The application of power or influence to settle the conflict. The disadvantage of this is that it creates all the lingering resentment and hostility of 'win-lose' situations.
Compromise	Bargaining, negotiating, conciliating. To some extent, this will be inevitable in any organisation made up of different individuals. However, individuals tend to exaggerate their positions to allow for compromise, and compromise itself is seen to weaken the value of the decision, perhaps reducing commitment. Negotiation is: 'a process of interaction by which two or more parties who consider they need to be jointly involved in an outcome, but who initially have different objectives seek by the use of argument and persuasion to resolve their differences in order to achieve a mutually acceptable solution'.
Integration/ collaboration	Emphasis must be put on the task, individuals must accept the need to modify their views for its sake, and group effort must be seen to be superior to individual effort.
Encourage co-operative behaviour	Joint problem-solving team, goals set for all teams/departments to follow.

Question
Conflict scenarios

In the light of the above consider how conflict could arise, what form it would take and how it might be resolved in the following situations.

(a)   Two managers who share a secretary have documents to be typed.

(b)   One worker finds out that another worker who does the same job as he does is paid a higher wage.

(c)   A company's electricians find out that a group of engineers have been receiving training in electrical work.

(d)   Department A stops for lunch at 12.30 while Department B stops at 1 o'clock. Occasionally the canteen runs out of puddings for Department B workers.

(e)   The Northern Region and Southern Region sales teams are continually trying to better each others' results, and the capacity of production to cope with the increase in sales is becoming overstretched.

Answer

(a)   Both might need work done at the same time. Compromise and co-ordinated planning can help them manage their secretary's time.

(b)   Differential pay might result in conflict with management – even an accusation of discrimination. There may be good reasons for the difference (eg length of service). To prevent conflict such information should be kept confidential. Where it is public, it should be seen to be not arbitrary.

(c)   The electricians are worried about their jobs, and may take industrial action. Yet if the engineers' training is unrelated to the electricians' work, management can allay fears by giving information. The electricians cannot be given a veto over management decisions: a 'win-lose' situation is inevitable, but both sides can negotiate.

(d)   The kitchen should plan its meals better – or people from both departments can be asked in advance whether they want puddings.

(e)   Competition between sales regions is healthy as it increases sales. The real conflict lies between sales regions and the production department. In the long-term, an increase in production capacity is the only solution. Meanwhile, proper co-ordination methods should be instituted.

3.2 The win-win model

FAST FORWARD

One constructive response to conflict is the **'win-win' model**, in which both parties explore options for mutual satisfaction.

One useful model of conflict resolution is the win-win model (*Cornelius & Faire*). This states that there are three basic ways in which a conflict or disagreement can be worked out.

Method	Frequency	Explanation
Win-lose	This is quite common.	One party gets what (s)he wants at the expense of the other party: for example, Department A gets the new photocopier, while Department B keeps the old one (since there were insufficient resources to buy two new ones). However well-justified such a solution is (Department A needed the facilities on the new photocopier more than Department B), there is often lingering resentment on the part of the 'losing' party, which may begin to damage work relations.
Lose-lose	This sounds like a senseless outcome, but actually compromise comes into this category. It is thus very common.	Neither party gets what (s)he really wanted: for example, since Department A and B cannot both have a new photocopier, it is decided that neither department should have one. However 'logical' such a solution is, there is often resentment and dissatisfaction on both sides. (Personal arguments where neither party gives ground and both end up storming off or not talking are also lose-lose: the parties may not have lost the argument, but they lose the relationship …) Even positive compromises only result in half-satisfied needs.
Win-win	This may not be common, but working towards it often brings out the best solution.	Both parties get as close as possible to what they really want. How can this be achieved?

It is critical to the win-win approach to discover **what both parties really want** – as opposed to:

- What they think they want (because they have not considered any other options)
- What they think they can get away with
- What they think they need in order to avoid an outcome they fear

For example, Department B may want the new photocopier because they have never found out how to use all the features (which do the same things) on the old photocopier; because they just want to have the same equipment as Department A; or because they fear that if they do not have the new photocopier, their work will be slower and less professionally presented, and they may be reprimanded (or worse) by management.

The important questions in working towards win-win are:

- What do you want this for?
- What do you think will happen if you don't get it?

These questions get to the heart of what people really need and want.

In our photocopier example, Department A says it needs the new photocopier to make colour copies (which the old copier does not do), while Department B says it needs the new copier to make clearer copies (because the copies on the old machine are a bit blurred). Now there are **options to explore**. It may be that the old copier just needs fixing, in order for Department B to get what it really wants. Department A will still end up getting the new copier – but Department B has in the process been consulted and had its needs met.

3.2.1 Win-win: the classic example

In the classic example used by win-win proponents, two men are fighting over an orange. There is only one orange, and both men want it.

(a)   If one man gets the orange and the other does not, this is a win-lose solution.

(b)   If they cut the orange in half and share it (or agree that neither will have the orange), this is a lose-lose solution – despite the compromise.

(c)   If they talk about what they each need the orange for, and one says 'I want to make orange juice' and the other says 'I want the skin of the orange to make candied peel', there are further options to explore (like peeling the orange) and the potential for both men to get exactly what they wanted. This is a win-win approach.

Win-win is not always possible. It is working towards it that counts. The result can be mutual respect and co-operation, enhanced communication, more creative problem-solving and – at best – satisfied needs all round.

Question   Win-win

Suggest a (a) win-lose, (b) compromise and (c) win-win solution in the following scenario.

Two of your team members are arguing over who gets the desk by the window: they both want it.

Answer

(a)   **Win-lose**: one team member gets the window desk, and the other does not. (Result: broken relationships within the team.)

(b)   **Compromise**: the team members get the window desk on alternate days or weeks. (Result: half satisfied needs.)

(c)   **Win-win**: what do they want the window desk for? One may want the view, the other better lighting conditions. This offers options to be explored: how else could the lighting be improved, so that both team members get what they really want? (Result: at least, the positive intention to respect everyone's wishes equally, with benefits for team communication and creative problem-solving.)

Exam focus point

A detailed question on the definition, causes and characteristics of conflict was set in the June 2002 paper. Make sure you read the instruction key words to such questions carefully and distinguish between **causes** and **effects**, for example.

4 Discipline   12/01, 6/04, 12/04

Key term

Discipline can be considered as: 'a condition in an enterprise in which there is orderliness, in which the members of the enterprise behave sensibly and conduct themselves according to the standards of acceptable behaviour as related to the goals of the organisation'.

4.1 Positive and negative discipline

FAST FORWARD

Discipline has the same end as **motivation**: to secure a range of desired behaviour from members of the organisation.

Another definition of 'positive' and 'negative' discipline makes the distinction between methods of maintaining sensible conduct and orderliness which are technically co-operative, and those based on warnings, threats and punishments.

(a) **Positive (or constructive)** discipline relates to procedures, systems and equipment in the work place which have been designed specifically so that the employee has no option but to act in the desired manner to complete a task safely and successfully. A machine may, for example, shut off automatically if its safety guard is not in place.

(b) **Negative discipline** is the promise of sanctions designed to make people choose to behave in a desirable way. Disciplinary action may be punitive (punishing an offence), deterrent (warning people not to behave in that way) or reformative (calling attention to the nature of the offence, so that it will not happen again).

The best discipline is **self discipline**. Even before they start to work, most mature people accept the idea that following instructions and fair rules of conduct are normal responsibilities that are part of any job. Most team members can therefore be counted on to exercise self discipline.

Exam focus point

Do not confuse 'discipline' with 'punishment'. There is more to it than simply punishing people for 'doing things wrong'. Positive and negative discipline were the subject of a question part in the June 2004 exam. More generally, be aware of the importance of encouraging discipline, and using fair and systematic disciplinary procedures, so that discipline is as 'positive' as possible.

4.2 Types of disciplinary situations   6/04

There are many types of disciplinary situation which require attention by the manager. Internally, the most frequently occurring are these.

- Excessive absenteeism
- Poor timekeeping
- Defective and/or inadequate work performance
- Poor attitudes which influence the work of others or reflect on the image of the firm
- Improper personal appearance or conduct (eg offensive humour or aggression)
- Breaking safety rules
- Other violations of rules, regulations and procedures
- Open insubordination, such as the refusal to carry out a work assignment.

Managers might also be confronted with disciplinary problems stemming from employee behaviour off the job, such as alcohol or drug abuse. In such circumstances, whenever an employee's off-the-job conduct has an impact upon performance on the job, the manager must be prepared to deal with such a problem within the scope of the disciplinary process.

The purpose of discipline is not punishment or retribution. Disciplinary action must have as its goal the improvement of the future behaviour of the employee and other members of the organisation.

4.3 The Advisory, Conciliation and Arbitration Service (ACAS)

ACAS has published a **Code of Practice** for grievance and disciplinary procedures, as well as having a role in helping resolve industrial disputes.

ACAS was formed under the Employment Protection Act 1975 to 'promote the improvement of industrial relations'. In individual or collective disputes, its role is (as its name implies):

(a)   **Conciliation**: getting conflicting parties together for informal discussion to resolve a dispute

(b)   **Mediation**: providing a mediator or mediation board which hears arguments and makes proposals and recommendations as a basis for settlement

(c)   **Arbitration**: assisting in the appointment of independent arbitrators who make a binding ruling.

The Employment Act 2002 put forward proposals to encourage internal resolution of workplace disputes, by introducing **minimum internal disciplinary and grievance procedures**, and encouraging employees to raise grievances with their employer before applying to an industrial tribunal. These provisions are currently being implemented: watch for developments!

Meanwhile, the framework for disciplinary action in the UK is primarily the 2000 ACAS Code of Practice on disciplinary and grievance procedures (also currently being reviewed).

4.4 Disciplinary procedures

The ACAS Code of Practice recommends the following criteria for an effective disciplinary procedure.

Good disciplinary procedures should:

- Be in writing

- Specify to whom they apply

- Be non-discriminatory

- Provide for matters to be dealt with without undue delay

- Provide for proceedings, witness statements and records to be kept confidential

- Indicate the disciplinary actions which may be taken

- Specify the levels of management which have the authority to take the various forms of disciplinary action

- Provide for workers to be informed of the complaints against them and where possible all relevant evidence before any hearing

- Provide workers with an opportunity to state their case before decisions are reached

- Provide workers with the right to be accompanied

- Ensure that, except for gross misconduct, no worker is dismissed for a first breach of discipline

- Ensure that disciplinary action is not taken until the case has been carefully investigated

- Ensure that workers are given an explanation for any penalty imposed

- Provide a right of appeal – normally to a more senior manager – and specify the procedure to be followed

4.5 Progressive discipline

FAST FORWARD

Progressive discipline includes the following stages.

- Informal talk
- Oral warning
- Written/official warning
- Lay-off or suspension
- Demotion
- Dismissal

Many minor cases of poor performance or misconduct are best dealt with by **informal advice, coaching or counselling**. An *informal oral warning* may be issued. None of this forms part of the formal disciplinary procedure, but workers should be informed clearly what is expected and what action will be taken if they fail to improve.

When the facts of the case have been established, it may be decided that *formal disciplinary* action is needed. The Code of Practice divides this into three stages. These are usually thought of as consecutive, reflecting a *progressive response*. However, it may be appropriate to miss out one of the earlier stages when there have been serious infringements.

4.5.1 Warnings

A *first formal warning* could be either oral or written depending on the seriousness of the case.

(a)   An **oral warning** should include the reason for issuing it, notice that it constitutes the first step of the disciplinary procedure and details of the right of appeal. A note of the warning should be kept on file but disregarded after a specified period, such as 6 months.

(b)   A **first written warning** is appropriate in more serious cases. It should inform the worker of the improvement required and state that a final written warning may be considered if there is no satisfactory improvement. A copy of the first written warning should be kept on file but disregarded after a specified period, such as 12 months.

If an earlier warning is still current and there is no satisfactory improvement, a *final written warning* may be appropriate.

4.5.2 Disciplinary sanctions

The final stage in the disciplinary process is the imposition of sanctions.

(a)   **Suspension without pay**

This course of action would be next in order if the employee has committed repeated offences and previous steps were of no avail. Disciplinary lay-offs usually extend over several days or weeks. Some employees may not be very impressed with oral or written warnings, but they will find a disciplinary lay-off without pay a rude awakening. This penalty is only available if it is provided for in the contract of employment.

(b)   **Demotion**

The employee is set back to a lower position and salary. This is not regarded as an effective solution, as it affects the employee's morale and motivation.

(c)   **Dismissal**

Dismissal is a drastic form of disciplinary action, and should be reserved for the most serious offences. For the organisation, it involves waste of a labour resource, the expense of training a new employee, and disruption caused by changing the make-up of the work team. There also may be damage to the morale of the group.

Exam focus point

Think of the disciplinary procedure as a progressive, six stage process:

1   Informal talk (not included in a formal ACAS procedure)
2   Oral warning
3   Written warning
4   Suspension
5   Demotion
5   Dismissal

This was examined in December 2004 and June 2005.

Question   Disciplinary policy

How (a) accessible and (b) clear are the rules and policies of your organisation/office: do people really know what they are and are not supposed to do? Have a look at the rule book or procedures manual in your office. How easy is it to see – or did you get referred elsewhere? is the rule book well-indexed and cross-referenced, and in language that all employees will understand?

How (a) accessible and (b) clear are the disciplinary procedures in your office? Are the employees' rights of investigation and appeal clearly set out, with ACAS guidelines? Who is responsible for discipline?

4.6 Relationship management in disciplinary situations

Even if the manager uses sensitivity and judgement, imposing disciplinary action tends to generate **resentment**. The challenge is to apply the necessary disciplinary action as constructively as possible.

(a)   **Immediacy**

Immediacy means that after noticing the offence, the manager proceeds to take disciplinary action as *speedily* as possible, subject to investigations, while at the same time avoiding haste and on-the-spot emotions which might lead to unwarranted actions.

(b)   **Advance warning**

Employees should know in advance (eg in a Staff Handbook) what is expected of them and what the rules and regulations are.

(c)   **Consistency**

Consistency of discipline means that each time an infraction occurs appropriate disciplinary action is taken. Inconsistency in application of discipline lowers the morale of employees and diminishes their respect for the manager.

(d)   **Impersonality**

Penalties should be connected with the act and not based upon the personality involved, and once disciplinary action has been taken, no grudges should be borne.

(e)   **Privacy**

As a general rule (unless the manager's authority is challenged directly and in public) disciplinary action should be taken in private, to avoid the spread of conflict and the humiliation or martyrdom of the employee concerned.

4.7 Disciplinary interviews

FAST FORWARD

Disciplinary interviews should be systematic, in order to ensure fairness and as positive a resolution as possible (as well as compliance with employment protection requirements, in the event of dismissal).

4.7.1 Preparation

Preparation for the disciplinary interview may include the following steps.

(a) **Gathering the facts** about the alleged infringement

(b) **Determination of the organisation's position:** How valuable is the employee, potentially? How serious are his offences/lack of progress? How far is the organisation prepared to go to help him improve or discipline him further?

(c) **Identification of the aims of the interview**: punishment? deterrent to others? improvement? Specific standards of future behaviour/performance required need to be determined.

(d) Ensure that the organisation's **disciplinary procedures** have been followed

   (i) Informal oral warnings (at least) have been given.

   (ii) The employee has been given adequate notice of the interview for his own preparation.

   (iii) The employee has been informed of the complaint, his right to be accompanied by a colleague or representative and so on.

4.7.2 The interview process

The disciplinary interview will then proceed as follows.

Step 1 The manager will explain the purpose of the interview.

Step 2 The charges against the employee will be delivered, clearly, unambiguously and without personal emotion.

Step 3 The organisation's expectations with regard to future behaviour/performance should be made clear.

Step 4 The employee should be given the opportunity to comment, explain, justify or deny. If he is to approach the following stage of the interview in a positive way, he must not be made to feel 'hounded' or hard done by.

Step 5 Specific, measurable, performance-related and realistic improvement targets should be jointly agreed.

Step 6 Measures to help the employee (such as training, mentoring or counselling) should be agreed, where necessary.

Step 7 The manager should explain the reasons behind any penalties imposed on the employee. There should be a clear warning of the consequences of failure to meet improvement targets.

Step 8 The manager should explain the organisation's appeals procedures: if the employee feels he has been unfairly treated, there should be a right of appeal to a higher manager.

Step 9 Once it has been established that the employee understands all the above, the manager should summarise the proceedings briefly.

Step 10 Records of the interview will be kept for the employee's personnel file, and for the formal follow-up review and any further action necessary.

Formal disciplinary procedure

Outline the steps involved in a formal disciplinary procedure and show how the procedure would operate in a case of:

(a)   Persistent absenteeism

(b)   Theft of envelopes from the organisation's offices

Answer

Apart from the outline of the steps involved – which can be drawn from the chapter, this question raises an interesting point about the nature of different offences, and the flexibility required in the handling of complex disciplinary matters.

There is clearly a difference in kind and scale between:

- Unsatisfactory conduct (eg absenteeism)
- Misconduct (eg insulting behaviour, persistent absenteeism, insubordination), and
- 'Gross misconduct' (eg theft or assault)

The attitude of the organisation towards the purpose of disciplinary action will to a large extent dictate the severity of the punishment.

- If it is punitive, it will 'fit the crime'.
- If it is reformative, it may be a warning only, and less severe than the offence warrants.
- If it is deterrent, it may be more severe than is warranted (ie to 'make an example').

The absenteeism question assumes that counselling etc. has failed, and that some sanction has to be applied, to preserve credibility. The theft technically deserves summary dismissal (as gross misconduct), but it depends on the scale and value of the theft, the attitude of the organisation to use of stationery for personal purposes (is it theft?) etc.

5 Grievance   6/05

Key term

> A **grievance** occurs when an individual feels that (s)he is being wrongly or unfairly treated by a colleague or supervisor and wishes to assert his or her rights.

5.1 Purposes of formal grievance procedure

FAST FORWARD

> **Grievance procedures** embody the employee's right to appeal against unfair or otherwise prejudicial conduct or conditions that affect him and his work.

When an individual has a grievance, (s)he should be able to pursue it and ask to have the problem resolved. Some grievances may be capable of solution informally by the individual's manager. However, if an informal solution is not possible, there should be a formal grievance procedure:

(a)   To allow **objective grievance handling** – including 'cooling off' periods and independent case investigation and arbitration

(b)   To **protect employees** from victimisation – particularly where a grievance involves their immediate superiors

(c) To provide **legal protection** for both parties, in the event of a dispute resulting in claims before an Employment Tribunal

(d) To **encourage grievance airing** – which is an important source of feedback to management on employee problems and dissatisfactions

(e) To **require full and fair investigation** of grievances, enabling the employer-employee relationship to be respected and preserved, despite problems

5.2 Elements of formal grievance procedures   6/05

FAST FORWARD

Grievance procedures are generally based on **appeals** to progressively higher levels of authority, if necessary.

A **formal grievance procedures** should do the following.

(a) State the **rights** of the employee for each type of grievance. For example, an employee who is overlooked for promotion might be entitled to a review of his annual appraisal report, or to attend a special appeals promotion/ selection board if he has been in his current grade for at least a certain number of years.

(b) State what the **procedures** for pursuing a grievance should be.

   (i) The individual should **discuss the grievance** with a staff/union representative (or a colleague). If his case seems a good one, he should take the grievance to his immediate boss. The grievance should ideally, be stated in writing.

   (ii) The **first interview** will be between the immediate manager (unless he is the subject of the complaint, in which case it will be the next level up) and the employee, who has the right to be accompanied by a colleague or representative.

   (iii) If the immediate manager cannot resolve the matter, or the employee is otherwise dissatisfied with the first interview, the case should be referred to his superior (and if necessary in some cases, to an even higher authority).

   (iv) Cases referred to a **higher manager** should also be reported to the personnel department. Line management might decide at some stage to ask for the assistance/advice of a personnel manager in resolving the problem.

(c) Allow for the involvement of an individual's or group's **trade union or staff association representative**. Indeed, many individuals and groups might prefer to initiate some grievance procedures through their union or association rather than through official grievance procedures.

(d) State **time limits** for initiating certain grievance procedures and subsequent stages of them (such as appeals). There should also be timescales for management to determine and communicate the outcome of the complaint to the employee.

(e) Require **written records** of all meetings concerned with the case to be made and distributed to all the participants.

5.3 Grievance interviews

Grievance interviews follow: exploration, consideration, reply.

The dynamics of a grievance interview are broadly similar to a disciplinary interview, except that it is the subordinate who primarily wants change to result from it. Prior to the interview, the manager should have some idea of the complaint and its possible source. The meeting itself can then proceed through three phases.

Step 1 **Exploration**. What is the problem: the background, the facts, the causes (manifest and hidden)? At this stage, the manager should simply try to gather as much information as possible, without attempting to suggest solutions or interpretations: the situation must be seen to be open.

Step 2 **Consideration**. The manager should:

(a) Check the facts

(b) Analyse the causes – the problem of which the complaint may be only a symptom

(c) Evaluate options for responding to the complaint, and the implication of any response made

It may be that information can be given to clear up a misunderstanding, or the employee will – having 'got it off his chest' – withdraw his complaint. However, the meeting may have to be adjourned (say, for 48 hours) while the manager gets extra information and considers extra options.

Step 3 **Reply**. The manager, having reached and reviewed his conclusions, reconvenes the meeting to convey (and justify, if required) his decision, hear counter-arguments and appeals. The outcome (agreed or disagreed) should be recorded in writing.

5.4 Taking grievance seriously

Grievance procedures should be seen as an employee's right. To this end, managers should be given formal training in the grievance procedures of their organisation, and the reasons for having them. Management should be persuaded that the grievance procedures are beneficial for the organisation and are not a threat to themselves (since many grievances arise out of disputes between subordinates and their boss).

Exam focus point

Make sure you can distinguish clearly between discipline (when an employee 'does wrong') and grievance (when an employee 'feels wronged'). This is a surprisingly common exam pitfall. Grievance procedures have not come up in this exam for a while, but they lend themselves well to an essay question: revise the topic carefully.

Question

Grievance procedure

Find your organisation's grievance procedures in the office manual, or ask your union or staff association representative. Study the procedures carefully. Think of a complaint or grievance you have (or have had) at work. Have you taken it to grievance procedures? If so, what happened: were you satisfied with the process and outcome? If not, why not?

Chapter Roundup

- **Conflict** in organisations can be viewed as inevitable (due to competition for scarce power and resources) or unnatural (caused by poor management).

- Conflict can be **constructive**, if it introduces new information, encourages ideas testing and creativity and 'clears the air'. It can be **destructive** if it distracts attention from the task or inhibits communication.

- **Conflicts** are typically **caused by**: different objectives; competition for power or resources; ambiguities and frustrations; and personal differences.

- **Conflict** may **manifest** itself in: poor communication; friction between individuals and groups; widespread use of arbitration and other conflict mechanisms; and various political games.

- **Strategies for managing conflict** range from denial or suppression though various resolution approaches (dominance or compromise), to more collaborative ways of working.

- One constructive response to conflict is the **'win-win' model**, in which both parties explore options for mutual satisfaction.

- **Discipline** has the same end as **motivation**: to secure a range of desired behaviour from members of the organisation.

- **ACAS** has published a **Code of Practice** for grievance and disciplinary procedures, as well as having a role in helping resolve industrial disputes.

- **Progressive discipline** includes the following stages.
  - Informal talk
  - Oral warning
  - Written/official warning
  - Lay-off or suspension
  - Demotion
  - Dismissal

- **Disciplinary interviews** should be systematic, in order to ensure fairness and as positive a resolution as possible (as well as compliance with employment protection requirements, in the event of dismissal).

- **Grievance procedures** embody the employee's right to appeal against unfair or otherwise prejudicial conduct or conditions that affect him and his work.

- Grievance procedures are generally based on **appeals** to progressively higher levels of authority, if necessary.

- **Grievance interviews** follow: exploration, consideration, reply.

Quick Quiz

1   What are the features of the 'happy family view' of the organisation?

2   Give an alternative to the happy family view.

3   When can conflict be constructive?

4   What happens when two groups are put in competition with each other?

5   Compromise is an example of a:

    A   Win-win result
    B   Win-lose result
    C   Lose-win result
    D   Lose-lose result

6   What causes conflict?

7   A grievance occurs when an employee infringes organisational rules or expectations. *True or false*?

8   What is progressive discipline?

9   What factors should a manager bear in mind in trying to control the disciplinary situation?

10   Outline typical grievance procedures, or the grievance procedures of your own firm.

Answers to Quick Quiz

1   Organisations are co-operative and harmonious. Conflict arises when something goes wrong.

2   Conflict is inevitable, being in the very nature of the organisation. Conflict can be constructive.

3   It can introduce solutions, define power relations, bring emotions, hostile or otherwise, out into the open.

4   They become more cohesive internally and more achievement-orientated.

5   D

6   Different objectives, scarcity of responses, personal differences, interdependence of departments.

7   False: this is a disciplinary action. (Try and define 'grievance' yourself.)

8   A system whereby the disciplinary action gets more severe with repeated 'offence'.

9   Immediacy, advance warning, consistency, impersonality, privacy.

10   Grievance procedures should state employees' rights, the procedures distinguish between individual and collective grievances state time limits. The interview should explore the facts, consider the issues and provide a resolution.

Now try the question below from the Exam Question Bank

Number	Level	Marks	Time
Q16	Examination	15	27mins

Exam question bank

1 Mechanistic and organic approaches

27 mins

Contrast the **mechanistic** and **organic** approaches to management.

(15 marks)

2 Proposals

18 mins

Contrast the proposals of **two** of the following writers regarding the role/functions of the manager.

(5 marks each)

(a)   Fayol
(b)   Drucker
(c)   Handy
(d)   Mintzberg

(10 marks)

3 Organisational culture

27 mins

(a)   Define organisational culture and describe the most important factors in its development.(5 marks)

(b)   Explain the meaning of **two** of role culture, task culture, power culture and person culture. Illustrate your choices with examples.   (10 marks)

(15 marks)

4 Team success (pilot paper)

27 mins

A team differs from an informal work group.

Required

(a)   Explain the way in which a team differs from an informal work group.   (5 marks)
(b)   Describe any five factors required to ensure team success.   (10 marks)

(15 marks)

5 Delegation

27 mins

Professional accountants often need to delegate duties to others in the organisation.

Required

(a)   Explain what is meant by delegation   (5 marks)
(b)   Explain how effective delegation might be achieved   (10 marks)

(15 marks)

6 Good business sense

18 mins

Explain the arguments for and against the claim that the exercise of social responsibility makes good business sense.   **(10 marks)**

7 Job analysis (pilot paper)   27 mins

The manager of the finance department has asked you to carry out a job analysis of the other employees in your department.

Required

(a)   Briefly explain what is meant by the term 'job analysis'.   (3 marks)

(b)   Briefly explain the four stages involved in carrying out a job analysis.   (4 marks)

(c)   Identify and briefly explain the information you would expect to collect during the job analysis
        investigation.   (8 marks)

(15 marks)

8 Selection interviews   27 mins

'The one-to-one selection interview is irredeemably flawed because it offers too much scope for the exercise of prejudice and favouritism.'

(a)   To what extent do you agree with this statement?   (8 marks)

(b)   Discuss alternatives to the one-to-one selection process.   (7 marks)

(15 marks)

9 Equal opportunity   27 mins

A recent report from the International Labour Organisation, collating research from around the world, shows that women continue to be excluded from senior executive positions and are clustered in occupations that are segregated by gender, such as cleaning, catering and the health service. Worldwide, the average female participation in management jobs is just 20 per cent.

(a)   What are the causes of this state of affairs?   (8 marks)

(b)   Why should it be a cause for concern?   (7 marks)

(15 marks)

10 Learning style (pilot paper)   27 mins

Different learning styles and approaches suit different individuals.

(a)   Identify and explain Honey & Mumford's theory on learning styles.   (10 marks)

(b)   Explain the experiential learning cycle.   (5 marks)

(15 marks)

11 Performance management   27 mins

(a)   What in practice are the differences between 'performance appraisal' and 'performance
        management'?   (10 marks)

(b)   Why has there been a shift towards 'performance management' and away from 'performance
        appraisal'?   (5 marks)

(15 marks)

12 Office risks

9 mins

List the likely risks of personal injury and ill-health **in the office.**

(5 marks)

13 Rewards (pilot paper)

27 mins

Financial rewards are not appropriate in all circumstances.

Required

(a) Briefly explain what is meant by intrinsic rewards.   (3 marks)
(b) Briefly explain what is meant by extrinsic rewards.   (3 marks)
(c) List any six types of extrinsic reward.   (9 marks)

(15 marks)

14 Leadership styles

27 mins

'Choosing a leadership style which is entirely appropriate to any given situation is one of the most important skills that an effective manager can possess.'

Describe the range of leadership styles which it is possible for managers to display.   **(15 marks)**

15 Communication (pilot paper)

27 mins

Much of the work of professional accountants involves communicating information for others to use.

Required

(a) Explain the importance of clear communication.   (5 marks)
(b) Explain two main communication methods.   (5 marks)
(c) Describe two barriers to communication.   (5 marks)

(15 marks)

16 Discipline mistakes

27 mins

(a) What are the common mistakes made by managers when conducting disciplinary interviews?

(7 marks)

(b) What are the fundamental criteria which should be met by an organisation's disciplinary procedure?   (8 marks)

(15 marks)

17 Scenario: accounts clerk (pilot paper)

72 mins

Deborah Williams, the Finance Director of SMG Ltd, thinks that the staff in the accounts department are overworked and has asked the Human Resource Department for an additional accounts clerk, preferably two.

SMG has no formal procedures or processes to ensure that appropriate and qualified staff are appointed. In the past SMG Ltd has relied on agencies and informal contacts to recruit new employees.

SMG Ltd has recently appointed you as assistant Human Resource Manager. You have been asked to take charge of the situation, to see if Ms Williams has a case and then to manage the new appointments process if the vacancy is approved.

Required

(a) Explain how you would establish whether Deborah Williams has a legitimate case for a new member of staff. (8 marks)

(b) Given that the vacancy is approved, discuss the procedure you would take to appoint a qualified accounts clerk. (7 marks)

(c) Describe the contents of a job description and person specification for the new accounts clerk. (10 marks)

(d) Explain how you would carry out the recruitment and selection of the new clerk. (10 marks)

(e) What might be the benefits of ongoing training and development to the clerk and the business? (5 marks)

(40 marks)

Exam answer bank

1 Mechanistic and organic approaches

> **Tutorial note.** This is useful practice of your exam technique, because it is an unstructured question. You need to plan your essay, in order to determine – and then follow – a structure of your own. The instruction keyword is 'contrast', which indicates that you need to focus on drawing out the differences between the two organisation types. The underlying structure may therefore be *either* discussing each feature of organisation in turn (indicating how mechanistic and organic forms 'do' them differently) *or* discussing mechanistic and organic forms in turn: we have chosen this latter option, as it gives a better overview of the topic for revision purposes.

Contrast between mechanistic and organic approaches

The distinction between mechanistic and organic organisations was highlighted by Burns and Stalker, who coined the terms.

Characteristics of a mechanistic organisation

(a) **Hierarchy**: each lower office is under the control and supervision of a higher one.

(b) **Specialisation and training**: there is a high degree of specialisation of labour. Employment is based on ability, not personal loyalty.

(c) **Impersonal nature**: employees work full time within the impersonal rules and regulations and act according to formal, impersonal procedures.

(d) **Professional nature of employment**: an organisation exists before it is filled with people. Officials are full-time employees, promotion is according to seniority and achievement; pay scales are prescribed according to the position or office held in the organisation structure.

(e) **Rationality**: the 'jurisdictional areas' of the organisation are determined rationally. The hierarchy of authority and office structure is clearly defined. Duties are established and measures of performance set.

(f) **Uniformity:** in the performance of tasks is expected, regardless of whoever is engaged in carrying them out.

(g) **Technical competence** in officials is rarely questioned within the area of their expertise.

(h) **Stability**.

Mechanistic systems are **unsuitable in conditions of change** because they tend to deal with change by cumbersome methods.

Organic structures

(a) There is a **contributive nature** where specialised knowledge and experience are contributed to the common task of the organisation.

(b) Each individual has a realistic task which can be understood **in terms of the common task of the organisation.**

(c) **Flexible job descriptions**. There is a continual re-definition of an individual's task, through interaction between the individual and others.

(d) There is a spread of **commitment** to the concern and its tasks.

(e) There is a **network** structure of authority and communication.

(f) Communication tends to be *lateral* rather than vertical (ie gangplanks, rather than up and down the scalar chain).

(g) Communication takes the form of **information and advice** rather than instructions and decisions.

In contrast to mechanistic structures, Burns and Stalker identified the organic structure. Organic structures are better suited to conditions of change than mechanistic structures. The organic structure has the following characteristics.

2 Proposals

> **Tutorial note.** You are asked to discuss *two* of the writers named in the question. We have covered all four, for completeness. The instruction keyword 'contrast' indicates that your answer needs to draw out the differences between the two theories you discuss: we have made more general comments (drawing out contrasts in all four approaches) than you might have done.

(a) **Fayol**

Henri Fayol, an early management theorist working in nineteenth century France, proposed that certain functions were common to the management of all types of organisations.

(i) **Planning**. This is selecting objectives, and the strategies, policies, programmes and procedures for achieving the objectives either for the organisation as a whole or for a part of it.

(ii) **Organising**. This is the establishment of a structure of tasks that support the organisation's goals; grouping these tasks into individual jobs; creating groups of jobs within sections and departments; delegating authority to carry out the jobs; and providing systems of information and communication.

(iii) **Commanding**. This is giving instructions to subordinates to carry out tasks over which the manager has authority for decisions and responsibility for performance.

(iv) **Co-ordinating**. This is the task of harmonising individual activities and reconciling differences in approach, effort, interest and timing. This is best achieved by showing how individual efforts contribute to the overall goals of the organisation.

(v) **Controlling**. This is the task of measuring and correcting the activities of individuals and groups, to ensure that their performance is in accordance with plans.

Fayol was writing at a time when large organisations were fairly uncommon and tended to be concerned with fairly stable activities, such as the operation of railways. There is a link between his ideas and scientific management in that both were concerned with efficiency of operation. Fayol was aware of the importance of the human factor, but the functions outlined above do not include any specifically concerned with the human resource, such as training or leadership.

(b) **Drucker**

Drucker grouped the operations of management into five categories.

(i) **Setting objectives for the organisation**. Managers decide what the objectives of the organisation should be and quantify the targets of achievement for each objective. They must then communicate these targets to other people in the organisation.

(ii) **Organising the work**. The work to be done must be divided into manageable activities and manageable jobs. The jobs must be integrated into a formal organisation structure, and people must be selected to do the jobs.

(iii) **Motivation**. Managers must motivate employees and communicate information to them to enable them to do their work.

(iv) **The job of measurement**. Management must establish yardsticks of performance, measure actual performance, appraise it against the yardsticks, and communicate the findings both to subordinate employees and to superiors.

(v) **Developing people**. The manager 'brings out what is in them or he stifles them. He strengthens their integrity or he corrupts them'.

It is clear from this analysis that Drucker was much more concerned than Fayol with the human resource aspects of management. He also differed from Fayol in suggesting that management of commercial enterprises was fundamentally different from managing other types of organisation. Management can only justify its existence and authority by the economic results it produces. He suggested there were three aspects.

- **Managing a business**. This revolves around marketing and innovation.

- **Managing managers**. Drucker was the first to use the phrase 'management by objectives'.

- **Managing worker and work**

(c) **Handy**

Charles Handy suggested that a definition of a manager or a manager's role is likely to be so broad as to be fairly meaningless. His own analysis of being a manager was divided into three aspects.

The manager as a general practitioner. Managers are the first recipients of the organisation's problems. They must identify the symptoms (such as falling sales); diagnose the cause of the trouble (such as increased competition); decide how it might be dealt with (for instance by increasing promotional spending); and start the treatment. Handy suggested that typical strategies for health would involve changing **people**, either literally or figuratively, restructuring **work** or making changes to **systems and procedures**.

The managerial dilemmas. Managers are regularly faced with dilemmas which have to be resolved.

(i) **The dilemma of the cultures**. Management must guide the development of an appropriate culture. As managers rise in seniority, they will find it necessary to behave in a **culturally diverse** manner to satisfy the requirements of both work and the expectations of employees.

(ii) **The dilemma of time horizons**. The manager must reconcile the frequent conflict between short and long term priorities.

(iii) **The trust-control dilemma**. Management must delegate, but this inevitably reduces immediacy of control.

(iv) **The commando leader's dilemma**. Junior managers often prefer working in project teams, to working within the bureaucratic structure of a large organisation. Unfortunately, having too many ad hoc groups leads to confusion.

The manager as a person. Management is increasingly seen as a profession and managers accorded appropriate status. However, at the same time the manager is coming under more pressure from customers to deliver and from employees and society to exercise social responsibility.

Handy's analysis contrasts with both Fayol's and Drucker's in its lack of prescription. Instead of specifying a list of functions, Handy discusses some of the types of problems the manager may have to solve.

(d) **Mintzberg**

Handy's rather vague approach is much improved upon by Henry Mintzberg's empirical research into how managers in fact do their work. He contends: 'The classical view says that the manager organises, co-ordinates, plans and controls; the facts suggest otherwise.'

Mintzberg instead identifies three types of role which a manager must play.

(i) **Interpersonal roles**. Senior manager spend much of their time in figurehead or ceremonial roles. The leader role involves hiring, firing and training staff, motivating employees and reconciling individual needs with the requirements of the organisation. The liaison role is performed when managers make contacts outside the vertical chain of command.

(ii) **Informational roles**. As a leader, a manager has access to every member of staff, and is likely to have more external contacts than any of them. Managers are a channels of information from inside the department to outside and vice versa. The manager monitors the environment, and receives information from subordinates or peers, much of it informally. The manager disseminates information both formally and informally to subordinates. As a spokesman the manager provides information to interested parties.

(iii) **Decisional roles**. The manager takes decisions of several types relating to the work of the department. A manager acts as a sort of **entrepreneur** by initiating projects to improve the department or to help it react to a changed environment. A manager responds to pressures and is therefore a disturbance handler taking decisions in unusual situations which are impossible to predict. A manager takes decisions relating to the allocation of **scarce resources**. **Negotiation** inside and outside the organisation is a vital component of managerial work.

Mintzberg drew a number of conclusions about managerial work which contrast strongly with Fayol's prescriptions and even Drucker's more pragmatic approach.

(i) Managerial work is disjointed and planning is conducted on a day to day basis, in between more urgent tasks.

(ii) Managers perform a number of routine duties, particularly of a ceremonial nature, such as receiving important guests.

(iii) Managers prefer *verbal* communication. Information conveyed in an informal way is likely to be more current and concrete than that produced by a formal management information system.

(iv) General management is, in practice, a matter of judgement and intuition, gained from experience in particular situations rather than from abstract principles. 'The manager is . . . forced to do many tasks superficially. Brevity, fragmentation and verbal communication characterise his work.'

3 Organisational culture

Tutorial note. Check that you have read the question carefully and addressed its particular requirements. Part (a) asks for a definition *and* a description of the factors in the development of culture. You will need to distinguish clearly between these factors and – for example – elements of cultures, or manifestations of culture, which are *not* relevant to the question as set. Note also that you are asked for only *two* of the cultures specified in part (b): we have covered all four only for your revision. This is a crucial point: surprising numbers of exam candidates waste precious time and therefore lose marks by answering more questions than they need to!

(a) **Culture** is the pattern of beliefs, attitudes and behaviour which distinguishes a society. **Organisation culture is the particular type of culture which prevails within a given organisation.** Not all organisations have the same culture. There are a number of influences on the development of an organisation's culture.

   (i) The **wider cultural background of society** influences basic assumptions and sets limits upon what is appropriate within the culture of the organisation.

   (ii) Within that setting, the **industry itself may have strong cultural norms**, as for instance in mining or the film industry.

   (iii) A major **influence** can be exerted by the organisation's **founder**, in both commercial and not-for-profit organisations. This is particularly apparent when charismatic individuals establish new methods and approaches.

   (iv) The organisation's history and the way the organisation has developed. Many business organisations originate with successful sole traders or partnerships but grow, sometimes rapidly, to many times their original size. **Success reinforces the methods and attitudes** prevailing in such organisations and increasing size brings its own imperatives.

   (v) **Management style** both reflects organisation culture and helps to form it. An organisation with a strong culture, of whatever type, will tend to recruit managers who will conform to its norms. A more anonymous organisation may find recruits shaping its culture in their own image.

(b) Harrison's analysis of organisational culture into four types called role, task, power and person was popularised by Charles Handy in his book *The Gods of Management*.

   (i) The **role culture** is typical of the large organisation operating in a stable environment. Generally, this cultural type will have the following characteristics.

      (1) Its structure is likely to be formal and static, with functional departmentation and clear lines of authority and responsibility.

      (2) It will be process oriented, with considerable prescriptiveness about communication, procedure and behaviour. Individuals will be appointed to discharge defined responsibilities in accordance with the rules. Initiative may not be welcomed. Efficient discharge of duty is the priority.

      (3) The culture is not entrepreneurial and will be slow to change. It takes its environment for granted but is very effective when not faced with sudden change.

   This type of culture is found in military services, central and local government, nationalised monopolies and conservative businesses such as banks and insurance companies.

(ii) The **task culture** is more dynamic and responsive. It is based on a team work approach to changing circumstances. An organisation with this culture will have the following characteristics.

   (1) Structure will be flexible and fluid, with project teams formed and adjusted as required. There will be little hierarchy or formal leadership responsibility since members will tend to be specialists and experts in their own fields.

   (2) The main concern will be results rather than procedures and expertise will be employed wherever it can be found.

   (3) There will be an expectation of high personal satisfaction. Technical challenge and an opportunity to make a contribution will be valued highly.

   This type of culture is common in some professional practices, such as architects and engineers, in advertising agencies and in creative work such as film and television production.

(iii) The **power culture** is found in highly centralised organisations, typically those run by an entrepreneurial owner-manager.

   (1) All decisions are taken at the centre and all the strings are in the owner's hands. Like the task culture, this culture enhances the ability to respond to a rapidly changing environment, but authority is exercised much more clearly.

   (2) Subordinates will have little freedom to manoeuvre or develop. They must accept their role as supporting the leader.

   Successful start-up businesses often develop this culture; it is also seen in smaller military units and voluntary bodies which employ talented individuals to administer them.

(iv) The **person culture** grows up where the organisation exists to serve its members.

   (1) An **example** is a barristers' chambers, where professionals come together to share expenses and employ staff collectively to organise the facilities they need.

   (2) Power is shared among the principal members and the managers may be of lower status, often no more than administrators.

   (3) The members of such an organisation value independence and achievement and may work more or less in isolation from their colleagues.

4 Team success

Tutorial note. This is a typical essay question for this paper. The introductory stem focuses your attention on key topic terms. The question is clearly structured, and you need to pay attention to the mark allocation to know how much time to devote to each question part. Part (b) specifically asks for five factors – and note that these are factors required fro team success, not 'attributes of successful teams'.

(a) While different from one another, informal work groups and teams are both **groups** and have shared attributes.

   • Purpose and leadership
   • A sense of identity
   • Loyalty to the group

   The differences between teams and informal work groups lie within these shared attributes and exist primarily because of the sharp distinction in **reason for existence**.

(i)   **Teams** are established by an organisation to perform organisational tasks, often with an official leader.

(ii) **Informal groups** come into existence in response to the social and personal needs of the members. This difference is reflected in the nature of the leadership exercised within the two types of group.

In an informal group, leadership is likely to be exercised in a more **fluid** way, possibly with several members sharing the leadership role. Satisfaction of group and individual needs will depend on individual initiatives by the more perceptive and influential members of the group. Loyalty and identification with the group may be very strong, but this is likely to result from commonality of personal interest rather than effective leadership.

(b) **A variety of factors will contribute to team success**

(i)   **Leadership** is probably the most important single factor and the one most often lacking. Good leadership will promote co-operation between team members, motivate the individuals towards the task and ensure that work is properly organised.

A team is likely to have a **leader** appointed by the organisation and it is one of the tasks of leadership to promote the coherence of the group. This will include motivating, organising and controlling the efforts of individuals in pursuit of the team's work objectives; these are what *Adair* calls **task needs**.

Adair suggests that the leader should also pursue **individual needs** and **group needs.** The process of motivation is also an individual need, as are the requirements for recognition and counselling. Group needs include peacekeeping and standard setting. Successful leadership is likely to produce a sense of identity and loyalty to the team almost as by-products of the satisfaction of other group and individual needs.

(ii) The **task** or **role** of the team must be defined. This can be seen in terms of the objectives set for the leader, since the leader must take responsibility for the team's work.

(iii) The members of the team must possess the **skills** required for them to perform their roles. To some extent, these can be learned on the job, under the supervision of the leader.

(iv) A proper level of **resources** must be provided, though motivation can overcome many resource deficiencies.

(v)   The efforts of the team must be **co-ordinated** with those of the rest of the organisation. To some extent this is a task for the leader, but there must be mechanisms in place to allow sideways communication between team members and other parts of the organisation and to permit proper response to changed circumstances.

5 Delegation

Tutorial note. This should be a straightforward question. It is possible to tackle part (b) in two ways: *either* outline a process for effective delegation (the five steps of 'how to delegate' for two marks each) *or* explain the factors or conditions that make delegation *effective*. For revision purposes, our answer illustrates this slightly less structured approach.

(a) **Delegation** occurs in an organisation when a superior grants to a subordinate the **authority to take decisions within specified terms of reference**. The authority granted must lie within the superior's own area of responsibility. The subordinate becomes responsible to the superior for the proper use of the authority granted, but the superior remains responsible to the next higher echelon for the overall performance level achieved.

Delegation enables formal organisations to **make use of the efforts and abilities of large** numbers of people while retaining direction and control.

(b) **A number of features contribute to effective delegation**.

The **subordinate must possess the personal qualities, ability, training and experience** required to discharge the allotted duties.

The **superior must maintain a proper degree of supervision**. This will vary from case to case and there is a difficult balance to strike between control and interference. Management by objectives (MBO) can be used at more senior levels, where proper use of discretion may be relied upon. The essence of MBO is that the subordinate's tasks or targets are agreed in discussion with the superior and objective performance measures are established.

Authority and responsibility must be commensurate. Authority without responsibility leads to arbitrary decisions and careless behaviour, while responsibility without authority leads to stagnation and stress for the subordinate. The allocation of a proper level of resources is an important aspect of this balance.

The subordinate's responsibility and authority must be **clearly specified and understood by all those affected**. This ensures that the subordinate can exercise authority and obtain the co-operation required from other managers. MBO can form a basis for the establishment and promulgation of written authority, though a less detailed specification is probably more appropriate. With more senior managers a brief statement of overall responsibility is probably most appropriate, so that initiative is encouraged.

6 Good business sense

> **Tutorial note.** This is not a full exam question, although it might be a 10-mark *part* of a question on organisational objectives say. It is at least of *exam standard*, since it asks you to make a critical appraisal of an important concept. Exam questions may ask for such a balanced essay form in various ways: 'critically discuss', 'evaluate' or 'describe the advantages and disadvantages ...' say.

Economists such as Milton Friedman suggest that so long as a company obeys the law, it discharges any **social responsibility** it may have by **maximising its profits**. This is because the profits depend on economic efficiency and effectiveness and the company that makes high profits is by definition making the best use of its resources. It is providing customer satisfaction, paying its work force, paying taxes and paying its providers of capital. The last category are increasingly pension funds whose incomes benefit large sections of society.

An alternative view is that business and society are **interdependent** and if business ignores society's concerns, society will find a way to punish it. This is almost a marketing approach, emphasising the wholeness of a business's relationship with society. It can be seen cynically as emphasising the PR aspect of business and the importance of image.

A synthesis of these two views is possible.

(a) Most companies behave to some extent as though ordinary business motivations like profitability and market share are their main concerns, but with social responsibility as a subsidiary concern.

(b) This means that socially responsible actions are evaluated in terms of costs and benefits to the company before they are undertaken.

Examples include:

- Sponsorship of the arts, which can raise publicity among key audiences

- Secondments of management and staff can be good for motivation and morale

- Charitable giving, which can also be publicised

- Companies with high standards can shape the political debate more easily than those seen dragging their feet, and may also enjoy a competitive advantage if others have to catch up with them

7 Job analysis

Tutorial note. This is a helpfully structured question: make sure you keep an eye on the mark allocations for each part to ensure that you do enough in the time available to earn the marks – without spending too long on any one section. Key instruction words include: 'term' (part(a)), indicating that a definition is required; 'stages' (part (b)), focusing on the process of analysing jobs; and 'information' (part (c)), focusing on the content of the analysis (ie not techniques or other aspects). Make sure you have accurately distinguished 'job analysis' from similar terms such as 'job evaluation' or 'performance appraisal'.

(a) **Job analysis** is the process of examining a job to determine its essential characteristics, including its component tasks and the circumstances and constraints under which it is performed. It provides the basis for the preparation of a job description and may also contribute to a scheme of **job evaluation**.

(b) There are four main sources of information about a job. It would be sensible to approach them in the order given below.

  (i) There may be **documentation** such as written procedures, organisation charts, quality manuals and even earlier job descriptions. These can be consulted at leisure.

  (ii) An early approach to the relevant **supervisor** is advisable. This person is likely to have clear ideas about what the job includes and may be able to resolve subsequent queries.

  (iii) The **job holder** should be consulted. What the person concerned thinks the job consists of is likely to differ noticeably both from what the supervisor thinks is done and from what the documentation says should be done.

  (iv) A possible final stage is **observation** of what the job-holder **actually does**. Once again, this may differ from what the job-holder has described.

  (v) A full picture of the job will emerge from these four sources. An important task for the analyst is to establish what adjustments need to be made to the documentation and whether extra activities that have developed should be done elsewhere.

(c) **Job analysis should produce information that relates to both the job and, in general terms, to the person doing it.**

  Job-related information should start with the overall **purpose and scope** of the job. This sets the job in its organisational context and should be stated briefly. For example, the scope of an accounts clerk's job might be to maintain ledgers on a computerised system. Direct accountability may be included at this stage by stating the supervisor to whom the job-holder reports

  It will then be appropriate to list the specific **duties and responsibilities** of the job, setting them out in logical groups. For instance, it would be sensible to list all the duties relating to the purchase ledger separately from those relating to the sales ledger. **Performance** criteria should be included.

Duties and **responsibilities** may be discussed together or separately, depending on the nature of the job. However, it is important to include information on the levels of responsibility held for staff, money, equipment and other resources.

The **environment** and **conditions** of the job should be investigated. This includes such factors such as pay and benefits, shift work and holidays. Particular attention should be paid to the physical environment and to potential hazards.

The **social factors** relating to the job should be stated. This will include whether it is done in isolation or as part of a team; the level in the organisation at which the job-holder interacts; and whether there is external contact, as with customers, for instance.

8 Selection interviews

Tutorial note. Part (a) of this question is interesting because it asks for your opinion or response. This does not mean, however, that you can simply state a view: in such circumstances, you are expected to put forward a balanced argument (for and against) before reaching a conclusion. Part (b) is asking for alternatives to 'one-to-one' interviewing: this may be interpreted as referring to panel interviews (not 'one-to-one') or to testing and other methods (not interviews). We have covered both possibilities.

(a) **Flaws in the one-to-one selection interview?**

While not 'irredeemably' flawed (as will be suggested below), the one-to-one selection interview undoubtedly has limitations. It is barely better than pure chance at predicting a candidate's success in the job.

The statement attributes this to the scope given to prejudice and favouritism. This is supported by the following observations.

(i) **Candidates can disguise their lack of knowledge**, in areas of which the interviewer also knows little and is therefore unable to challenge the candidate. Conversely, a candidate's knowledge may go untested or unrecognised by an interviewer who does not ask the right questions or appreciate the answers.

(ii) The **interviewer's perception may be selective or distorted**, due to stereotyping, personal prejudice or inadequate information, and this lack of objectivity may go unchallenged, since (s)he is the sole arbiter.

(iii) The **greater opportunity to establish personal rapport** with the candidate may cause a **weakening of the interviewer's objective judgement**: (s)he may favour someone (s)he 'got on with', over someone who was better-qualified, but perceived as unresponsive. Again, there will be no counter- balancing view.

However, this is also an opportunity to observe and experience the candidate's **personality, rapport-building, image-projecting, influencing and communication skills** and self-concept and expression in action. The flaws of prejudice and favouritism are arguably in some interviewers – not in the interpersonal dynamic of the one-to-one interview itself, which can be an advantage.

(b) **Alternatives to the one-to-one selection process**

Panel and selection-board interviews are designed to overcome the dangers of bias by providing a **multiple (and therefore balanced) assessment**. They have the additional advantage of allowing information gathering and provision by different stakeholders in the selection decision, at the same time. On the other hand, they are **more daunting for the candidate than a one-to-one interview**, offering less opportunity to assess the candidate's rapport- building skills, and potentially some performance distortion from nervous tension. The situation is **more formal and artificial**, and therefore potentially less relevant to job performance. The pressures favour individuals who are confident and extraverted – which may not be relevant to all positions for which they are being assessed.

Group selections, using role-play exercises, case studies and simulations, can offer more **extensive, 'live' opportunities to observe candidates' interpersonal skills** (and their reception by others in a team situation), problem-solving abilities and leadership potential, as well as their demonstrated knowledge/expertise and expressed attitudes. They may therefore be more relevant to the competency requirements of the job, as well as offering direct comparability between candidates. As a specialist tool, they are more frequently supported by trained assessors and prepared criteria and standards of assessment than one-to-one interviewing.

Testing of various kinds (psychometric, cognitive, aptitude, proficiency) are also alternatives to the one-to-one approach, and score relatively highly (.40 and above) on the predictive validity scale.

9 Equal opportunity

Tutorial note. This is a useful question, because it reminds you to revise not just lists of factors, legislative provisions or procedures, but the underlying themes and issues of a topic. Part (b) is asking why equal opportunity is important: an opportunity for you to demonstrate a real-world, business-focused awareness – *not* just philosophical/political correctness!

(a)   **Causes of exclusion/segregation of women in employment**

(ii)   There are **continuing social pressures on women to bear and rear children**, and on the man to be the 'breadwinner'. Employers have assumed that women's paid work would be short-term or interrupted, and that training and development was not sound investment. In practice, child-bearing and family responsibilities do interrupt women's career progressions, or limit them to part-time employment which may restrict prospects for promotion.

(ii)   The 'heavy' nature of earlier industrial work placed legal restrictions on women's employment in areas such as mining, nightwork in factories and so on. This also contributed to the lack of organisation and trade union influence of women (except in segregated industries like textiles) up until the 1970s and 1980s.

(iii)   Segregation, once established, tends to be self-perpetuating. Once an occupation becomes dominated by one sex, those of the opposite sex will tend to depart.

(iv)   Segregation is reinforced by stereotypical modelling of gender roles at home and in the education system. For example, lack of encouragement to girls to study maths and sciences has been evident even in the West, and in more traditional cultures, access to educational opportunities and career aspirations for women are severely restricted.

(v)   Career ladders (including, for example, apprenticeships) often fail to fast-track women.

(b)   **Reasons for concern**

Quite apart from any philosophical or humanitarian concerns about the stereotyping of gender roles and inequality of access to educational and career opportunities, there are 'business' reasons to address employment discrimination.

(i)   Stereotypical and discriminatory assumptions may lead organisations into illegal practices through indirect discrimination (as defined by the Sex Discrimination Acts) in which a policy or practice appears fair in form but is discriminatory in operation. This in turn has negative consequences in terms of legal costs and damaged reputation, possibly with knock-on problems in attracting skilled female staff.

(ii)   Women make up a high proportion of the consumer base. In societies where equal opportunity has a high profile, women may exercise protest influence by choosing to purchase from less discriminatory competitors.

(iii)   Women make up a significant proportion of the workforce, if not in managerial grades: by perceived discriminatory policies and practices, the organisation may reduce its ability to attract and retain skilled female employees in the support, HR and other areas in which it relies on their contribution. In other words, it may damage its 'employer brand'.

(iv)   In times of persistent skill and local labour shortages – despite overall decline in the demand for labour – organisations can ill afford to overlook or alienate a significant source of ability and experience, particularly where there is potential for enriching business practice with additional or alternative viewpoints and strengths. A recent report in *Personnel Management*, for example, suggested that women had been instrumental in increasing 'emotional intelligence' in business.

10 Learning style

> **Tutorial note.** This should be straightforward, as long as you accurately identified the two theories. Exam questions frequently ask you to explain specific models: make sure you associate the right authors and terminology with a given model!

(a)   **Honey and Mumford**

The way in which people learn best will differ according to personal preferences in regard to information gathering, information processing and interpersonal styles. These preferences were classified by Peter Honey and Alan Mumford as four distinct learning styles.

(i)   **Theorists** seek to understand basic principles and to take an intellectual, 'hands-off' approach based on logical argument. They prefer training to be:

- Programmed and structured
- Designed to allow time for analysis
- Provided by teachers who share his/her preference for concepts and analysis

(ii)   **Reflectors**

- Observe phenomena, think about them and then choose how to act
- Need to work at their own pace
- Find learning difficult if forced into a hurried programme
- Produce carefully thought-out conclusions after research and reflection
- Tend to be fairly slow, non-participative (unless to ask questions) and cautious

(iii)   **Activists**

- Deal with practical, active problems and do not have patience with theory
- Require training based on hands-on experience
- Are excited by participation and pressure, such as new projects
- Flexible and optimistic, but tend to rush at something without due preparation

(iv)   **Pragmatists**

- Only like to study if they can see its direct link to practical problems
- Good at learning new techniques in on-the-job training
- Aim is to implement action plans and/or do the task better
- May discard good ideas which only require some development

Training programmes should ideally be designed to accommodate the preferences of all four styles, or the needs of the individual trainee where feasible.

(b)   **Kolb** suggests that effective learning takes place in a cycle of four phases.

(i)   The first stage is to be involved in a new experience.

(ii)   The second stage is to review and reflect upon the experience.

(iii)   The third stage is to use concepts and theories to integrate the experience and the reflection, deriving generalisations, principles and hypotheses.

(iv)   The final stage is one of application: to test out the principles/hypotheses in new situations.

Kolb felt that some people have a preference for a particular phase and so do not complete the cycle. They thus do not learn as effectively as they might. The learning cycle is extensively used for managerial self-development, as it enables everyday work experiences to be turned into learning opportunities.

11 Performance management

Tutorial note. 'Performance management' is sometimes used as a general term to cover a range of techniques including disciplinary and grievance handling. In this context, however, it should be clear that it is used as a technical term: it may be worth starting your answer with concise definitions, as we do.

(a)   **The difference between a 'performance appraisal' and a 'performance management approach**

Performance appraisal is traditionally a process whereby the performance of employees, over the past year, is assessed according to various criteria (from personality factors to more effective key results indicators), for a variety of purposes, including reward-setting, identification of training needs and standard- setting.

Performance management is a process of continuous collaborative planning and control, whereby managers and individuals or teams jointly set key accountabilities, objectives, measures and priorities for performance and performance improvement, and review and adjust performance on an on-going basis.

Key differences in these approaches

(i)   The emphasis of appraisal was primarily retrospective. Performance management focuses on the following review period, and on progress towards continuous improvement goals, and is therefore more forward-looking, pro-active and stimulating in its orientation.

(ii)   Appraisals have traditionally been held annually, especially where they are tied in to pay awards. Performance management is an on-going control system, with in-built feedback and review timescales.

(iii)   Appraisal, at its most positive and solution-focused, can concentrate exclusively on the (personal) development and reward aspirations of the employee, at the expense of the need to add value to the business.

(iv)   Performance management is more thoroughly focused on performance, through the integration of employee improvement and reward goals with the strategic objectives of the business.

(b)   **Reasons for the shift towards 'performance management'**

(i)   Competitive pressures make continuous improvement a condition of survival.

(ii)   It is now realised that strategic objectives can be more effectively implemented by linking them to individual objectives.

(iii)   The new focus on quality has necessitated the feeding through of new quality standards to performance management processes.

(iv)   Performance-related pay is being used more widely, necessitating clear objectives, measures and time scales.

Increased employee expectations and increased competitive pressures have led to a recognition that business success requires both attention to employee development and satisfaction and the requirement that employees 'add value' to the business. Performance management focuses on both, by dovetailing employee objectives, problem- solving and developmental goals with the strategic objectives of the organisation.

12 Office risks

Tutorial note. This is obviously not a full exam question although it might be an exam standard question part in an essay or case study, for example. The point of the question is to alert you to the hazards of office environments: a basic point, if you are to take responsibility for your own safety at work, as required by law. Your answer (for five marks) may not have listed as many hazards as we have done, for revision purposes.

Risk in the workplace is often associated with building sites or factories with heavy machinery or coal mines, but administrative working environments also contain many potential **sources of injury** or **ill-health.**

- Slippery or uneven floors
- Frayed carpets
- Trailing electric leads, telephone cables and other wires
- Obstacles (boxes, files, books, open drawers) in gangways
- Standing on chairs (particularly swivel chairs) to each high shelving
- Blocked staircases, for example where they are used for extra storage space
- Lifting of heavy items without bending properly
- Removal of the safety guard on a machine to free a blockage or to make it run faster
- Use of chemicals without protective clothing or adequate ventilation
- Inadequate work breaks, allowing excessive exposure or strain

Sometimes none of these things are needed to cause an accident: it is very easy to do it without props. Carelessness or foolishness are major causes of accidents. Practical jokes and cutting corners in work practices can have unforeseen consequences.

13 Rewards

(a) **Intrinsic rewards** are those which arise from the performance of the work itself. They are therefore psychological rather than material and relate to the concept of job satisfaction. Intrinsic rewards include the satisfaction that comes from completing a piece of work, the status that certain jobs convey, the feeling of achievement that comes from doing a difficult job well. Intrinsic rewards tend to be associated with autonomy in the planning and execution of work.

(b) **Extrinsic rewards** are separate from the job itself and dependent on the decisions of others. Pay, benefits and working conditions are all examples of extrinsic rewards.

(c) **Rewards**

- Pay
- Bonuses
- Car
- Medical insurance
- Pension scheme
- Subsidised canteen facilities
- Working clothing such as uniform, but not safety equipment
- Share option schemes
- Subsidised loans and mortgages
- Subsidised transport to and from work
- Assistance with child care
- Holiday entitlement

14 Leadership styles

The 'range' of leadership styles a manager may display may be discussed across the body of leadership style theories, taking in, for example, the following different classifications.

(a) Huneryager and Heckman: dictatorial, autocratic, democratic, laissez-faire

(b) The Ashridge Studies: tells, sells, consults, joins

(c) Douglas McGregor: Theory X and Y

(d) Tannenbaum and Schmidt: a continuum between autocratic and democratic

(e) Rensis Likert: exploitative-authoritative, benevolent-authoritative, consultative-authoritative and participative

(f) FE Fiedler: psychologically distant or close

Broadly, the classifications are based on continuums from authoritarian to democratic (or 'tight' to 'loose' control) and from wholly task-focused to wholly people-focused.

We will describe the range of style across one such continuum.

The research unit at Ashridge Management College carried out studies in UK industry in the 1960s and identified four styles.

(a)   **Autocratic or 'tells' style**. This is characterised by one-way communication between the manager and subordinate, with the manager telling the subordinate what to do. The leader makes all decisions and issues instructions, without consultation, and expecting compliance.

(b)   **Persuasive or 'sells' style**. The manager still makes all the decisions, but believes that subordinates need to be motivated to accept them before complying. (S)he therefore tries to explain instructions and decisions in an effort to get subordinates' agreement and co-operation.

(c)   **'Consults' style**. This involves discussion between the leader and the subordinates who will be involved in carrying out a decision, while the leader retains authority to make the decision. By consulting before making the decision, the leader takes account of subordinates' attitudes and feedback. Consultation is a form of limited participation in decision making for team members – but it is easily 'faked', if the leader has already made up his or her mind before 'asking' the group: a facade for a 'sells' style'.

(d)   **Democratic or 'joins' style**. This is an approach whereby the leader empowers the team to make a decision on the basis of consensus or agreement. It is the most democratic style of leadership identified by the study. Subordinates with the greatest understanding of the problem will have most influence over the decision. The joins style is therefore most effective where all members of a team are able to contribute.

15 Communication

> **Tutorial note.** This is a typical essay question on communication, and a useful revision overview of key topic areas. Make sure you address the topic key words for each part: 'importance' and 'clear' (part (a)); 'methods' (part (b)); and 'barriers' (part (c)). Note also that you are only required to discuss *two* barriers in part (c) : in order to give you a better revision overview, we have discussed two broad 'sources' of barriers. You may have chosen to discuss factors such as 'noise' and 'distortion' (or two other specific barriers) in more detail.

(a)   Communication is the process of transferring information from one person to another. In an organisational context, communication may be internal, as when colleagues discuss a problem, or it may be that the participants are representatives of their organisations, as when a credit control manager writes to a named manager in an overdue debtor organisation.

Organisations exist to achieve goals which individuals could not achieve independently. Communication is therefore fundamental to their operations. The classic managerial functions of planning, organising, directing and controlling depend on the manager's ability to communicate requirements and information and to obtain reports. Other management responsibilities such as motivating, training and counselling depend equally upon clear communication.

It is in the general area of human behaviour and relations that manner, tone and body language become important supplements to the written or spoken word. This applies equally to managers and to members of work groups who must communicate with one another.

If communication is not **clear**, there will be bias, omission and distortion. Confusion, conflict and stress arise as a result.

(b)   The two main methods of communication are **speech** and **writing**. Both may be used between individuals, as in the interview or personal letter, or by an individual to more than one person, as in the lecture or circulated memo.

The two basic methods vary in their effect and usefulness in different situations. Speech is immediate and tone, manner and body language can be used to enhance its impact. Feedback can be instant and a disciplined discussion can cover a lot of ground rapidly. The written word is easier to use with precision, though this takes time, practise and ability. It is inherently capable of repeated reference using the simplest technology; speech requires electronic equipment such as a video system if its full impact is to be recorded.

A wide range of media may be used for both spoken and written communications. Some are listed below.

Speech may be used face-to-face, on the telephone, on video (including video conferencing) on public address and loudspeaker systems and on radio broadcast.

Writing is used in paper communications of all kinds, including letters, memos, procedure manuals, forms and books. It is also used in e-mail, fax and telex systems and in pager systems.

(c)   Good communication is essential to getting any job done: co-operation is impossible without it. Difficulties occur because of **general faults** in the communication process.

(i)   Distortion or omission of information by the sender

(ii)   Misunderstanding due to lack of clarity or technical jargon

(iii)   Non-verbal signs (gesture, posture, facial expression) contradicting the verbal message, so that its meaning is in doubt

(iv)   'Overload' – a person being given too much information to digest in the time available

(v)   Differences in social, racial or educational background, compounded by age and personality differences, creating barriers to understanding and co-operation

(vi)   People hearing only what they want to hear in a message

         There may also be **particular difficulties** in a work situation.

(vii)   A general tendency to distrust a message in its re-telling from one person to another, (eg a subordinate mistrusting his superior and looking for 'hidden meanings' in a message)

(viii) The relative status in the hierarchy of the sender and receiver of information (a senior manager's words are listened to more closely and a colleague's perhaps discounted)

(ix)   People from different job or specialist backgrounds (accountants, personnel managers, DP experts) having difficulty in talking on a non-specialist's wavelength

(x)   People or departments having different priorities or perspectives so that one person places more or less emphasis on a situation than another

(xi)   Conflict in the organisation. Where there is conflict between individuals or departments, communications will be withdrawn and information withheld

16 Discipline mistakes

> **Tutorial note.** This is an unusual and challenging question. You may have needed to think through model disciplinary procedures in order to come up with potential pitfalls for part (a). We have interpreted part (b) in the sense of general qualities: it would be equally valid to discuss more procedural matters such as progressive discipline, representation, right of appeal and other recommendations of the ACAS Code of Practice.

(a) **Common mistakes**

    (i)   Not following the right procedure. Most firms have a disciplinary procedure, commencing with verbal warnings, followed by more formal written warnings if the 'offence' is repeated. Failure to follow this procedure can invalidate the process.

    (ii)   Failure to investigate the problem properly and prejudging the issue. As it is a serious matter, the 'offence' should be properly investigated. Facts are often in dispute. This is especially a problem in the existence of a personality clash between manager and subordinate.

    (iii)   Confusing disciplinary with appraisal interviews. An appraisal is an ongoing process to review past performance with a view to improving it, even though, if performance is not up to scratch, this can also result in dismissal. A disciplinary interview is generally the result of a specific issue.

    (iv)   Failure to keep records and to follow-up. To be successful the disciplinary interview must have a result, even if this is only a mild rebuke or an acceptance that there has been a problem disciplinary interview.

(b) **Fundamental criteria of a disciplinary procedure**

    (i)   **Immediacy**. Disciplinary action needs to be speedy, so that the action and the 'offence' are related to each other. A time lapse can make it harder to take action. However, investigation can take time and in some cases a person might be suspended on full pay pending the results of the enquiry.

    (ii)   **Advance warning**. Employees should know what the rules are and managers should make clear that everybody knows what is expected from them. Also, the details of the procedure should be laid down in the staff handbook.

    (iii)   **Consistency**. Each time an infraction occurs, disciplinary action should result. Inconsistency leads to charges of favouritism and even discrimination. Also standards will fall to that of the lowest common denominator.

    (iv)   **Impersonality**. The disciplinary action should be directed at the offence not the person. Penalties should be based on the offence. However, the offence will remain on file, and any repetition will lead to more serious consequences.

    (v)   **Privacy**. As far as possible, discipline should be private affair to avoid excess humiliation and the resentment it causes and the creation of a 'martyr'.

17 Scenario: accounts clerk

Tutorial note. Parts (b) and (d) of this question appear to be asking for the same thing. One possible approach – which we have used in our answer – is to view part (b) as the *resourcing* process, looking at all options, and part (d) as the *recruitment/selection* process, after the decision has been taken to fill the vacancy in this way. Case study questions are highly structured: make sure you accurately address the *topic* and *instruction* key words of each part and plan your time according to the mark allocations.

(a) **Deborah's case for a new staff member**

Staff are a major element of **cost** and headcount should be subject to careful control. In a large, mature organisation with established procedures and methods, the **human resource plan** or establishment document would lay down the staff requirements for the accounts department.

Permission to recruit would depend on either a member of staff having left (staff **turnover**), or the **expansion of the department's task**. The latter might result from organisational growth or, particularly in the case of an accounts department, from the increasing burden of government-imposed work, as with the maintenance of working time records, for instance. Where the task had expanded, the human resource plan would have to be amended.

However, SMG Limited 'has no formal procedures or processes' for recruitment and, therefore, reference to an agreed establishment is not possible. It will be for Deborah Williams to demonstrate just why she thinks that the accounts staff are overworked before recruitment is authorised.

Another way would be to look to see if the accounts department can be run more efficiently. An examination of its procedures would be extremely time consuming and probably beyond the capacity of a human resources specialist. However, it may be possible to carry out a job analysis in broad terms if the department is not too large. This would attempt to measure the volume and nature of the work flowing through the office by collecting information from four sources:

- Documentation, such as forms and instructions
- Interviews with managers and supervisors
- Interviews with job holders
- Observation

If it is found that this is not possible, the fall-back position would be for Deborah Williams to justify the recruitment in concrete terms. However, because Deborah Williams is a director of the company, a recently appointed assistant manager in HR would find it difficult to demand such a justification. A suitable procedure would probably have to be established by agreement among the directors: perhaps Deborah has the authority anyway.

(b) **Procedures to appoint a qualified accounts clerk**

Step 1 Obtain agreement that there is a vacancy – already presupposed from the question.

Step 2 Clearly detail the total mix of tasks to be carried out in the department, including work that is not being done owing to lack of resources.

Step 3 Assess whether current employees have the competences currently to carry out all the tasks, or whether these can be developed.

Step 4 Assess whether the current allocation of work amongst employees genuinely reflects their competences. Could there be greater job specialisation?

Step 5 Assess the future needs of the department in terms of the quality and nature of competences required.

Step 6 Identify the mix of training and resourcing needs necessary to carry out the department's task.

Step 7 Develop or revise job descriptions based on the roles currently performed in the department. Existing members of staff will welcome clear descriptions of what is expected of them if roles are to change.

Step 8 Develop person specification as the basis of the recruitment and selection process, based on the job descriptions and required competences which are going to be met by recruitment.

Step 9 Develop plan for recruitment and selection of new staff, if this is the preferred way of matching the resource and competences of the department with the work expected of it.

Step 10 Implement the plan (see part (d) of this answer).

The process involves **two types of company policy**:

(i) The procedures manual, which deals with the steps gone through, any legal requirements (guaranteeing conformance with equal opportunities legislation)

(ii) The human resources plan, which details the overall requirements for employees, investment in training and so on.

(c) **Job description and person specification**

A **job description** is a statement of the tasks, responsibilities and working relationships making up a job. At lower levels it will concentrate on the specification of duties, but at managerial levels it is likely to be written in broader terms dealing with scope and responsibilities. It forms an important part of the documentation needed by a complex organisation, since, in combination with other job descriptions, it defines how work is done.

A **person specification** details the personal qualities, abilities, qualifications and experience required of the holder of a job. A job description is useful in several human resource management contexts, including recruitment, appraisal and career development. A person specification, on the other hand, is rarely useful for anything other than recruitment.

Since it is rare to find a perfect fit between any job and its holder, the task of recruitment is eased if the job description is divided into core and peripheral elements. This allows the features of the person specification to be divided into those that are essential and those that are merely desirable. This split makes it easier to select the best person for the job when no ideal candidate applies.

(d) **Recruitment and selection of the clerk**

The recruitment and selection process is based on the needs of the department, and the state of the labour market. There are a number of different steps. Once it has been decided that recruiting a new member of staff (rather than redeploying current members) is the right course then the following steps should be taken.

Step 1 Obtain job description, which details job content, responsibilities, and the job's relation to other positions in the department, authorisation limits. It might be phrased in more general terms as an accountability profile.

Step 2 If a person specification has not yet been drawn up, identify the type of candidate suitable for the job, noting essential attributes (eg for an accounts clerk post, the firm may require a candidate with the ACCA's Certified Accounting Technician qualification), desirable attributes (eg experience in a similar **company**) and contra-indications (ie matters that would rule out the candidate, for example no work experience at all).

Step 3 Identify appropriate media for recruitment. To reach the right people, the firm has to find the right medium.

The firm could use a **recruitment agency** to suggest suitable candidates already on their books, to do some preliminary screening and to suggest a shortlist.

The firm may choose to **advertise**. The job advertisement will cover details of the role and the company and should be targeted at the target candidates, with an attractive, but realistic, description of the company and role; salary details may also be included. Most importantly, contact details and the desired manner of application (eg letter and cv, or application form) must be made clear.

Step 4 Place the advertisement in suitable **publications** (such as newspapers, professional journals). The firm might also use **government employment offices** (job centres, in the UK). Moreover, firms are increasingly advertising on the **Internet**, either on their own websites or via recruitment services (often owned or run by newspaper groups) such as workthing.com.

Step 5 Review application forms/CVs received. As a matter of courtesy all applicants should receive a reply; some may be rejected out of hand; others may be told that their application has been received and is being reviewed. Application forms are a standard way of gathering data, for comparison, and also to require candidates to answer specific questions, to collect data about qualifications and experience and to allow the candidate to write about themselves and why the want the position.

Step 6 Shortlist desirable candidates and contact them to arrange interviews. Write to unsuccessful candidates

Step 7 Most firms use the **interview** as the heart of their recruitment procedures even though it is not reliable as a predictor of job performance. It does enable a firm to assess some of the candidate's interpersonal skills. A mixture of open and closed questions should be used. The interview is also an opportunity for the candidate to talk about the role

Step 8 A variety of **tests** can be employed, often relating to the task to be done. This may be of limited relevance to an accounts position where work experience can be validated. However, it should be possible to assess basic numeracy. A person with a technician or professional qualification may have a training record which can be used as evidence of competence. More complicated tests (psychometric etc) are not appropriate for this position.

Step 9 **Make offer, subject to references**. References are of limited value, but they can be used to check the candidate's basic honesty (eg in seeing that the candidate's past employment history is truthful, that the candidate worked in a the positions and over the timescales mentioned).

The offer of employment may contain contractual details.

Step 10 **Induction**. When the new employee starts, he/she needs to become familiar with the firm.

(e)   **Training** is the process by which workpeople are taught job-related skills.

Development is a more general process by which people are prepared for wider future responsibilities.

Both training and development are likely to offer benefits to the individual and to the organisation.

(i)   Increased job competence makes the organisation more efficient. It also reduces stress on the individual and is a source of pride and competence and hence of motivation. The achievement of a specific qualification or level of competence may entitle the individual to a pay rise.

(ii)   Organisational flexibility is enhanced when staff are well trained, since they can deputise for absent colleagues and adapt rapidly to new procedures and other changing circumstances.

(iii)   A programme of personal development contributes to succession and promotion planning.

(iv)   It helps with the identification of people with the potential for promotion.

(v)   It provides promotees with at least some of the knowledge and skills they will need, so that they can tackle their new responsibilities with confidence. The efficiency of the organisation is thus enhanced, and the individuals concerned are advanced in their careers. Even if they are not promoted, they are likely to be more employable. This improves their job security within the organisation and their prospects elsewhere if they wish to move.

Index

Review Form & Free Prize Draw – Paper 1.3 Managing People (6/05)

All original review forms from the entire BPP range, completed with genuine comments, will be entered into one of two draws on 31 January 2006 and 31 July 2006. The names on the first four forms picked out on each occasion will be sent a cheque for £50.

Name: _____   Address: _____

_____

_____

How have you used this Interactive Text?
(Tick one box only)

☐ Home study (book only)

☐ On a course: college _____

☐ With 'correspondence' package

☐ Other _____

Why did you decide to purchase this Interactive Text? *(Tick one box only)*

☐ Have used BPP Texts in the past

☐ Recommendation by friend/colleague

☐ Recommendation by a lecturer at college

☐ Saw advertising

☐ Saw information on BPP website

☐ Other _____

During the past six months do you recall seeing/receiving any of the following?
(Tick as many boxes as are relevant)

☐ Our advertisement in *ACCA Student Accountant*

☐ Our advertisement in *Pass*

☐ Our advertisement in *PQ*

☐ Our brochure with a letter through the post

☐ Our website www.bpp.com

Which (if any) aspects of our advertising do you find useful?
(Tick as many boxes as are relevant)

☐ Prices and publication dates of new editions

☐ Information on Text content

☐ Facility to order books off-the-page

☐ None of the above

Which BPP products have you used?

Text	☑	Success CD	☐	Learn Online	☐
Kit	☐	i-Learn	☐	Home Study Package	☐
Passcard	☐	i-Pass	☐	Home Study PLUS	☐

Your ratings, comments and suggestions would be appreciated on the following areas.

	Very useful	Useful	Not useful
Introductory section (Key study steps, personal study)	☐	☐	☐
Chapter introductions	☐	☐	☐
Key terms	☐	☐	☐
Quality of explanations	☐	☐	☐
Case studies and other examples	☐	☐	☐
Exam focus points	☐	☐	☐
Questions and answers in each chapter	☐	☐	☐
Fast forwards and chapter roundups	☐	☐	☐
Quick quizzes	☐	☐	☐
Question Bank	☐	☐	☐
Answer Bank	☐	☐	☐
Index	☐	☐	☐
Icons	☐	☐	☐

Overall opinion of this Study Text   Excellent ☐   Good ☐   Adequate ☐   Poor ☐

Do you intend to continue using BPP products?   Yes ☐   No ☐

On the reverse of this page are noted particular areas of the text about which we would welcome your feedback. The BPP author of this edition can be e-mailed at: edmundhewson@bpp.com

Please return this form to: Nick Weller, ACCA Publishing Manager, BPP Professional Education, FREEPOST, London, W12 8BR

Review Form & Free Prize Draw (continued)

Please note any further comments and suggestions/errors below

Free Prize Draw Rules

1   Closing date for 31 January 2006 draw is 31 December 2005. Closing date for 31 July 2006 draw is 30 June 2006.

2   Restricted to entries with UK and Eire addresses only. BPP employees, their families and business associates are excluded.

3   No purchase necessary. Entry forms are available upon request from BPP Professional Education. No more than one entry per title, per person. Draw restricted to persons aged 16 and over.

4   Winners will be notified by post and receive their cheques not later than 6 weeks after the relevant draw date.

5   The decision of the promoter in all matters is final and binding. No correspondence will be entered into.

ACCA Order

To BPP Professional Education, Aldine Place, London W12 8AW

Tel: 020 8740 2211
email: publishing@bpp.com
Order online www.bpp.com/mybpp
Fax: 020 8740 1184
website: www.bpp.com

Mr/Mrs/Ms (Full name) _____

Daytime delivery address _____

Postcode _____

Daytime Tel _____

Date of exam (month/year) _____ Scots law variant Y / N

Occasionally we may wish to email you relevant offers and information about courses and products. Please tick to opt into this service. [ ]

	6/05 Texts	1/05 Kits	1/05 Passcards	Success CDs	7/05 i-Learn	7/05 i-Pass	Learn Online
PART 1							
1.1 Preparing Financial Statements (UK)	£26.00	£12.95	£9.95	£14.95	£40.00	£30.00	£100
1.2 Financial Information for Management	£26.00	£12.95	£9.95	£14.95	£40.00	£30.00	£100
1.3 Managing People	£26.00	£12.95	£9.95	£14.95	£40.00	£30.00	£100
PART 2							
2.1 Information Systems	£26.00	£12.95	£9.95	£14.95	£40.00	£30.00	£100
2.2 Corporate and Business Law (UK)**	£26.00	£12.95	£9.95	£14.95	£40.00	£30.00	£100
2.3 Business Taxation FA2004 (12/05 exams)	£24.95 (8/04)†	£12.95	£9.95	£14.95	£34.95 (8/04)	£24.95 (8/04)	£100
2.3 Business Taxation FA2005	£26.00 (9/05)	£12.95	£9.95	£14.95	£40.00 (9/05)	£30.00 (9/05)	£100
2.4 Financial Management and Control	£26.00	£12.95	£9.95	£14.95	£40.00	£30.00	£100
2.5 Financial Reporting (UK)	£26.00 (7/05)	£12.95	£9.95	£14.95	£40.00	£30.00	£100
2.6 Audit and Internal Review (UK)	£26.00	£12.95	£9.95	£14.95	£40.00	£30.00	£100
PART 3 (i-Pass: 8/04)							
3.1 Audit and Assurance Services (UK)	£26.00	£12.95	£9.95	£14.95		£30.00 (4/05)	£60
3.2 Advanced Taxation FA2004 (12/05 exams)	£24.95 †	£12.95	£9.95	£14.95		£24.95	£60
3.2 Advanced Taxation FA2005	£26.00	£12.95	£9.95	£14.95		£30.00 (9/05)	£60
3.3 Performance Management	£26.00	£12.95	£9.95	£14.95		£24.95	£60
3.4 Business Information Management	£26.00	£12.95	£9.95	£14.95		£24.95	£60
3.5 Strategic Business Planning and Devt	£26.00	£12.95	£9.95	£14.95		£24.95	£60
3.6 Advanced Corporate Reporting (UK)	£26.00 (7/05)	£12.95	£9.95	£14.95		£24.95	£60
3.7 Strategic Financial Management	£26.00	£12.95	£9.95	£14.95		£24.95	£60
INTERNATIONAL STREAM (7/05)							
1.1 Preparing Financial Statements (Int'l)	£26.00	£12.95	£9.95		£40.00	£30.00	£100
2.2 Corporate and Business Law (Global)	£26.00	£12.95	£9.95				
2.5 Financial Reporting (Int'l)	£26.00	£12.95	£9.95		£40.00	£30.00	£100
2.6 Audit and Internal Review (Int'l)	£26.00	£12.95	£9.95		£40.00	£30.00	£100
3.1 Audit and Assurance Services (Int'l)	£26.00	£12.95	£9.95		£40.00	£30.00	£60
3.6 Advanced Corporate Reporting (Int'l)	£26.00	£12.95	£9.95		£40.00 (12/05)	£30.00	£60
Success in Your Research and Analysis							
Project - Tutorial Text (10/05)	£26.00						
Learning to Learn Accountancy (7/02)	£9.95						
Business Maths and English (6/04)	£9.95						

SUBTOTAL £ [ ]

POSTAGE & PACKING

Study Texts/Kits

	First	Each extra	Online
UK	£5.00	£2.00	£2.00
EU*	£6.00	£4.00	£4.00
Non EU	£20.00	£10.00	£10.00

Passcards/Success CDs/i-Learn/i-Pass

	First	Each extra	Online
UK	£2.00	£1.00	£1.00
EU*	£3.00	£2.00	£2.00
Non EU	£8.00	£8.00	£8.00

Learning to Learn Accountancy/Business Maths and English

	Each	Online
UK	£3.00	£2.00
EU*	£6.00	£4.00
Non EU	£20.00	£10.00

Grand Total (incl. Postage) £ [ ]

I enclose a cheque for [ ] (Cheques to *BPP Professional Education*)

Or charge to Visa/Mastercard/Switch

Card Number [ ]

Expiry date [ ]   Start Date [ ]

Issue Number (Switch Only) [ ]

Signature _____

We aim to deliver to all UK addresses inside 5 working days; a signature will be required. Orders to all EU addresses should be delivered within 6 working days. All other orders to overseas addresses should be delivered within 8 working days. *EU includes the Republic of Ireland and the Channel Islands. **For Scots law variant students, a free **Scots Law Supplement** is available with the 2.2 Text. Please indicate in the name and address section if this applies to you.

† **8/05** for 6/06 & 12/06 exams. New edition Kit, Passcard, i-Learn and i-Pass available in 2006)

ACCA Order

To BPP Professional Education, Aldine Place, London W12 8AW

Tel: 020 8740 2211
Fax: 020 8740 1184

email: publishing@bpp.com
website: www.bpp.com

Order online www.bpp.com/mybpp

Mr/Mrs/Ms (Full name)

Daytime delivery address

Postcode

Date of exam (month/year)

Scots law variant Y / N

Daytime Tel

	Home Study Package*	Home Study PLUS*	Success CDs	7/05 i-Learn	Learn Online
PART 1					
1.1 Preparing Financial Statements UK	£115.00	£180.00	£14.95	£40.00	£100.00
1.2 Financial Information for Management	£115.00	£180.00	£14.95	£40.00	£100.00
1.3 Managing People	£115.00	£180.00	£14.95	£40.00	£100.00
PART 2					
2.1 Information Systems	£115.00	£180.00	£14.95	£40.00	£100.00
2.2 Corporate and Business Law UK***	£115.00	£180.00	£14.95	£40.00	£100.00
2.3 Business Taxation FA2004 (12/05 exams)	£115.00	£180.00	£14.95	£34.95 (8/04)	£100.00
2.3 Business Taxation FA2005 (2006 exams)	£115.00	£180.00	£14.95	£40.00 (9/05)	£100.00
2.4 Financial Management and Control	£115.00	£180.00	£14.95	£40.00	£100.00
2.5 Financial Reporting UK	£115.00	£180.00	£14.95	£40.00	£100.00
2.6 Audit and Internal Review UK	£115.00	£180.00	£14.95	£40.00	£100.00
PART 3					
3.1 Audit and Assurance Services UK	£115.00	£150.00	£14.95		£60.00
3.2 Advanced Taxation FA2004 (12/05 exams)	£115.00	£150.00	£14.95		£60.00
3.2 Advanced Taxation FA2005 (2006 exams)	£115.00	£150.00	£14.95		£60.00
3.3 Performance Management	£115.00	£150.00	£14.95		£60.00
3.4 Business Information Management	£115.00	£150.00	£14.95		£60.00
3.5 Strategic Business Planning and Development	£115.00	£150.00	£14.95		£60.00
3.6 Advanced Corporate Reporting UK	£115.00	£150.00	£14.95		£60.00
3.7 Strategic Financial Management	£115.00	£150.00	£14.95		£60.00
INTERNATIONAL STREAM					
1.1 Preparing Financial Statements (Int'l)	£115.00	£180.00		£40.00	£100.00
2.2 Corporate and Business Law (Global)	£115.00				
2.5 Financial Reporting (Int'l)	£115.00	£180.00		£40.00	£100.00
2.6 Audit and Internal Review (Int'l)	£115.00	£180.00		£40.00	£100.00
3.1 Audit and Assurance Services (Int'l)	£115.00	£150.00			£60.00
3.6 Advanced Corporate Reporting (Int'l)	£115.00	£150.00		£40.00 (12/05)	£60.00
Success in Your Research and Analysis					
Project - Tutorial Text (10/05)	£26.00				
Learning to Learn Accountancy (7/02)	Free/£9.95				
Business Maths and English (6/04)	Free/£9.95				

SUBTOTAL £

Occasionally we may wish to email you relevant offers and information about courses and products. Please tick to opt into this service. ☐

POSTAGE & PACKING

Home Study Packages

	First	Each extra	Each
UK**	£6.00	£6.00	-
EU**	-	-	£15.00 £
Non EU	-	-	£50.00 £

Success CDs/i-Learn

	First	Each extra	Online
UK	£2.00	£1.00	£1.00 £
EU**	£3.00	£2.00	£2.00 £
Non EU	£8.00	£8.00	£8.00 £

Learning to Learn Accountancy/Business Maths and English/Success in Your Research and Analysis Project

	Each	Online
UK	£3.00†	£2.00 £
(†£5.00 Success in Your Research and Analysis Project)		
EU**	£6.00	£4.00 £
Non EU	£20.00	£10.00 £

Postage and packing not charged on free copy ordered with Home Study Course.

Grand Total (incl. Postage) £

I enclose a cheque for
(Cheques to *BPP Professional Education*)

Or charge to Visa/Mastercard/Switch

Card Number

Expiry date   Start Date

Issue Number (Switch Only)

Signature